From the Stage to the Stars

Robert Loraine

Actor and Pioneer Aviator

Oliver Clutton-Brock

First published 2025 by Aviation Books Ltd., Merthyr Tydfil, CF47 8RY, United Kingdom.

Copyright © 2025 Oliver Clutton-Brock

The right of Oliver Clutton-Brock to be identified as Author of this work is asserted by him in accordance with the Copyright, Designs and Patents Act 1988.

All rights reserved. No part of this publication may be reproduced, stored in a retrieval system, transmitted in any form or by any means, electronic, mechanical or photocopied, recorded or otherwise, without the written permission of the copyright owners.

The information in this book has been researched, compiled and written by its author, who has made every effort to ensure the accuracy of the information contained in it. The author will not be liable for any damages caused, or alleged to be caused, by any information contained in this book. E. and O.E.

A CIP catalogue reference for this book is available from the British Library.

ISBN 9781915335456

Front cover: *Robert Bilcliffe Loraine*. Photo by Bassano Ltd, 29 October 1919. © National Portrait Gallery, London.

Contents

Acknowledgements 4

Glossary 6

Preface 9

Introduction 11

Chapter One: Early Years 22

Chapter Two: Soldier 29

Chapter Three: Aviator 48

Chapter Four: Bournemouth International Aviation Meeting, 11-16 July 1910 67

Chapter Five: Isle of Wight Adventure, 16 July 1910 78

Chapter Six: Blackpool Flying Carnival, August 1910 104

Chapter Seven: 'One of the most sensational flights in history.' 128

Chapter Eight: Autumn Manoeuvres, Salisbury Plain, September 1910. 163

Chapter Nine: The First World War, 1914–1918 191

Chapter Ten: The Last Act 268

Appendix I: Some significant dates in the life of Robert Bilcliffe Loraine 300

Appendix II: Some Aviation Records, October 1890–September 1910 305

Appendix III: Aviation-related deaths 1908-1910 311

Appendix IV: Notes on Airmen 315

Appendix V: Major Eric Lewis Conran 401

Bibliography 410

Acknowledgements

This book could not have completed without the vast and valuable input of Richard Holleyman, a great admirer of Robert Loraine who gave me many pointers and made many corrections towards putting my knowledge to rights.

I am also very grateful to Lanayre Liggera ("Lannie"), in the USA, who likewise gave much help, and kindly gave me permission to quote from her book *The Life of Robert Loraine*. Many thanks, too, go to Rob Schmidt, Robert Loraine's grandson, for his help and hospitality.

It was Lannie who kindly put me on to David Railton, who did much research for her prior to the publication of her book. David has now generously passed-on to me a great deal of his research relating to Robert and his family, for which I am most appreciative.

I am also grateful to author Roy Sloan for making several pertinent suggestions as to this book's composition which, I trust, is all the better for it.

The following have also made valuable contributions: Peter Booton (for portrait of Lewis Tregonwell, "founder" of Bournemouth); Center for Research Libraries (for making copies of *The Aero* available); Veronika Chambers (for permission to quote from the *Lost Hospitals of London* website); W.R. "Bill" Chorley (author, for First World War details); Don Clark (Australia, 211 Squadron website owner); Perry Clifton (Archivist, Wight Aviation Museum); T.G.S. Crawford (Wiltshire military historian & author); William Cross, FSA *Scot.* (re Lady Tredegar); Mike Curtis (the Wirral History & Heritage Association, re Robert's birthplace); Andrew Dawrant (Trustee, RAeC Trust, for permission to use photographs etc.); Caroline Dudley (Freshwater & Totland Archive Group, Isle of Wight); Norman Gould (Melksham, for Isle of Wight postcards); David Gunby (New Zealand, for permission to quote from *Sweeping the Skies*); Reed Harmer (re Thorne Baker); Simon Hepworth (owner of Aviation Books Ltd); Wendy Holleyman (for her hospitality, much appreciated); John Howes (for his very generous research at TNA); Robert Jones (for his kindnesses re the Blackpool meetings); Joël Lacey (editor *Dorset Life*); Terry Mace (for permission to use a photograph); Denise Martin (Colourpoint Creative Ltd, for help contacting author Guy Warner); Steve Mills (for permission to quote from his book); Bob Montgomery (for permission to use a photograph); Thomas Moore (Secretary, Freshwater Bay Golf Club, Isle of Wight); Roger Moss (for permission to use information from his website re Bournemouth aviators); Hartley Moyes (re the Hon. C.S. Rolls, and Rolls-Royce); Peter Reese (for permission to quote from *The Flying Cowboy*); Andrew Renwick (Senior Curator, photographs, RAF Museum, Hendon); the Rolls Royce Heritage Trust (re the Hon. C.S. Rolls); Lucia Wallbank (Assistant Curator, RAF Museum, Hendon); Guy Warner (for permission to quote from *Pioneers, Showmen and the RFC*); Corranne Wheeler (Archives Assistant, Cambridgeshire and Huntingdonshire Archives, for her great and kindly help re affairs at Portholme island, regrettably a subject now omitted).

Other indispensable resources were the three contemporary aviation magazines: *Flight*; *The Aero*; and *The Aeroplane*. *Flight* proudly announced in its header that it was the 'First Aero Weekly in the World' and the 'Official Organ of the Royal Aero Club of the United Kingdom'. Its founder, and editor, Stanley Spooner, first published *Flight* on Saturday, 2 January 1909. It was also, it declared: 'A Journal Devoted to the Interests, Practice, and Progress of Aerial Locomotion and Transport.'

The Aero, incorporating "Flying" (established 1902) and "The Airship", initially edited by Charles Grey Grey, was first published from an office at 20 Tudor Street, London, E.C., on Tuesday, 25 May 1909 (later published on Wednesdays, and then, from April 1911, monthly on the first of the month or as near to that as was possible). Its last monthly issue was in May 1913, when it was announced that, henceforth, it would be published annually, or bi-annually 'should it be found necessary.' Issue No.1, Vol.1, announced: '*The Aero* is produced with the intention of giving to the people of the British Empire an impartial, disinterested, and comprehensive review of the science and sport of flying. It is a matter of principle that *The Aero* shall not favour any particular type of machine, any particular flying association, or any particular aviator unduly, but that everyone shall be given his just due.'

Grey then became the founder and editor of the aviation magazine *The Aeroplane*, No. 1, Volume 1 of which, published on Thursday, 8 June 1911, came with the following explanation: 'To use a well-worn phrase, *The Aeroplane* has been started "to fill a long-felt want," but this time the phrase has rather more than usual significance. There really is room to-day for a thoroughly independent weekly paper dealing with aviation in all its phases, a paper which is unconnected with any club or society, and so can give vent freely to criticism of the doings of anybody and everybody, and a paper the proprietors and conductors of which are devoted solely to the interests of aviation, and are, therefore, untrammelled by the influence of other sports or trades.'

Other indispensable resources are *The London Gazette*, which publishes all official pronouncements, including officers' commissions, promotions, appointments, and awards, and the Government Census records every ten years from 1841 to 1911.

Glossary

AA	Anti-aircraft – *see* "Archie" "Archibald"
A&SD	Administrative and Special Duties
A/Cdre	Air Commodore
ACF	Aéro-Club de France
AFC	Air Force Cross; Australian Flying Corps
"Archie" "Archibald"	RFC nickname for German anti-aircraft gunfire – see *page 201*.
BBC, The	British Broadcasting Corporation, The
B.E.	<u>B</u>lériot <u>E</u>xperimental aircraft designation, as in aeroplane type B.E.2c
CB	Companion of the Order of the Bath
CBE	Commander of the Most Excellent Order of the British Empire
CMG	Companion of the Most Distinguished Order of Saint Michael and Saint George
CO	Commanding Officer
Col	Colonel
DFC	Distinguished Flying Cross
DSO	Companion of the Distinguished Service Order
E.A.	Enemy aeroplane
F.E.	<u>F</u>arman <u>E</u>xperimental aircraft designation, as in F.E.2b, F.E.8.
FF	French *franc*. At the time, 25 French *francs* = £1 = $5 US, approximately
GRT; g.r.t.	Gross Registered Tonnes
GS	General Service
GSO1	General Staff Officer (Grade 1), Lt-Col or Col in charge of the General saff Branch
GSOII	General Staff Officer (Grade 2), usually in rank of Major, deputy to
H.A.	Hostile Aeroplane
HMATS	His Majesty's Australian Troop Ship
hp, h.p.	horse power
HS	Home Service
Jasta	An abbreviation of the German *Jagdstaffel*, fighter squadron
KIA	Killed in action
Kms	Kilometres
L.D.	Light Duty (-ies)
Lt-Col	Lieutenant-Colonel
MC	Military Cross

MGC	Machine Gun Corps
MiD	Mention(ed) in Despatches
m.p.h.	miles per hour
MRAF	Marshal of the Royal Air Force
MT	Motor Transport
NZEF	New Zealand Expeditionary Force
OM	Order of Merit
OTC	Officer Training Corps
PBI	"Poor Bloody Infantry"
PC; P.C.	Privy Counsellor; Police Constable
POB	Person(s) on board
POW	Prisoner of War
Pusher biplane	Aeroplane with propeller *behind* the pilot – see *Tractor biplane*
RA	Royal Artillery
RAeC	Royal Aero(nautical) Club
RAE	Royal Aircraft Establishment, from 1 April 1918
RAF	Royal Aircraft Factory up to 31 March 1918 (See RAE); Royal Air Force from 1 April 1918 (on formation)
RAS	Reserve Aeroplane Squadron
RE	Royal Engineers
R.E.	Reconnaissance Experimental aircraft designation, as in R.E.8
RFA	Royal Field Artillery
RFC	Royal Flying Corps
RGA	Royal Garrison Artillery
RHA	Royal Horse Artillery
RMA	Royal Marine Artillery
RMC	Royal Military College
RMLI	Royal Marine Light Infantry
RMS	Royal Mail Ship
RNAS	Royal Naval Air Service
RNVR	Royal Naval Volunteer Reserve
RS	Reserve Squadron
S.E.	Initially Santos Experimental, but later Scouting Experimental aircraft designation, as in S.E.5
SOC	Struck Off Charge (of squadron)
Spec. Res.	Special Reserve [of Royal Flying Corps]
SS	Steam Ship
Strafe	Borrowed from the German word *strafe*, to punish or punishment

(T); TF	(Territorial); Territorial Force
(T) Squadron	(Training) Squadron
(temp.)	Temporary
TNA	The National Archives, Kew, London
Tractor biplane	Aeroplane with propeller in *front* of the pilot – see *Pusher biplane*.
TSS	Twin Screw Steamer
U	*Untersee*, as in U-35 – U-boat, submarine
u/t	under training
VC	Victoria Cross
vol plané	flying (gliding) with engine switched-off
WAAF	Women's Auxiliary Air Force

Preface

The idea for this book began several years ago with the purchase of eight high-quality postcards showing 'the Farman Biplane of Robt. Loraine Esq' on the Isle of Wight in July 1910. The unknown photographer/publisher[1] very helpfully provided the time and date on which the photographs were taken, together with their particular location on the isle and their technical details. All eight postcards are reproduced herein.

At the time of their purchase, I was researching the history of 148 (Special Duties) Squadron, RAF, which had formed as the 148th Squadron, Royal Flying Corps, at Andover, Hampshire, on 10 February 1918. The squadron was attached to the 36th Training Wing commanded by a certain Lieutenant-Colonel Robert B. Loraine DSO, MC. It came as no surprise to learn that the 1910 Robert Loraine and the 1918 Lieutenant-Colonel Loraine were the one and the same. It then emerged that, in 1900, he had served in the ranks during the Second Boer War (1899-1902) and, having learnt to fly in 1910, thus making him a true pioneer aviator, had valiantly served King and Country during the First World War. Commissioned as second lieutenant in 1914 he ended the war as a lieutenant-colonel, having been seriously wounded twice and, not for nothing, having been awarded two gallantry medals.

There are also two biographies of Robert. The first, *Robert Loraine. Actor, Soldier, Airman*, was published by his widow, Winifred Loraine (1898–1986), in 1938. She used much of Robert's keenly collected material as a basis for it. Unfortunately, Robert, an actor through and through, was an embellisher of the truth, and several of his claims and stories should, perhaps, be treated with caution. Most of his acts and actions are, however, beyond dispute.

The second biography, *The Life of Robert Loraine. The Stage, the Sky, and George Bernard Shaw*, by Lanayre D. Liggera, was published in the USA in 2013. It is a comprehensive account of Robert's life concentrating, as the title suggests, on Robert's stage career, but detailing much of the rest of his life, too, including his soldiering and flying experiences.

Robert's surname has been mis-spelt frequently, not least by several authors who should have known better. Robert himself commented on these mis-spellings in *Off-Stage Views of Stage People* [circa 1925]: 'A newspaper friend of mine once told me an axiom of his profession. It was this: "Misquote a man if you must, but don't misspell his name."

'Probably nobody on two continents can appreciate that quite as much as I. All my life I have had what amounts to insurmountable difficulty in getting my name spelled correctly.

---

[1] He was possibly Lindsay McLennan of School Green, Freshwater, Isle of Wight, born in Edinburgh on 3 Mar 1882. Another photographer to take photos of Robert's Farman on the Isle was Mr Gallop of Freshwater – see, for example, his credited photo on p.69, *The Aero*, 27 Jul 1910.

The Loraines from whom I am descended have always used a single "r" in the middle of the names, whereas most others with the name use the letter twice. People evidently have not wanted me to go through life cheated, so they have bestowed that second "r" upon me. No matter how many times I have explained I have no title to it and do not want it.

'Perhaps it seems an unimportant thing about which to struggle but, after all, a name is a name, and why not have your own instead of somebody else's? Since I began here in *The Man With a Load of Mischief* I guess my name has been misspelled fifty times. Frankly, it bothers me so much I am seriously considering changing it to Jones or Smith.

'P.S. I wonder if I'll get two "r"s in this article, when the printer finishes with it.'

Robert Bilcliffe Loraine 1876 - 1935

Introduction

'Early aeroplaning was most agreeable, apart from the machines. Everyone was a bit "crackers." No really self-respecting person would have anything to do with it.'

'I go back to those early days when… all who tried to solve the problems of flight were just amiable lunatics.'

Lord Brabazon of Tara, PC, MC.[2]
(Holder of the first flying certificate ever issued by the Royal Aeronautical Club)

♦ ♦ ♦

Robert Bilcliffe Loraine was born in 1876 to parents both of whom were travelling actors. Robert followed in their footsteps and, by the turn of the century and up to the start of the First World War, had become a renowned actor in his own right in London's West End theatres.

He was only twenty-one years old when, in 1897, he married American actress Julie Opp. The marriage, destined to be short, ended in late 1900 when, on his return from fighting in the Second Boer War as a mounted trooper, his wife presented him with divorce papers on the grounds of his desertion.

A civilian once more, and single, his acting career flourished on both sides of the Atlantic. He was to become great friends with the philosopher, playwright and theatre critic George Bernard Shaw and his wife Charlotte (née Payne-Townshend), their paths having crossed before Robert went to fight in South Africa. 'From 1905 through 1907, Robert immersed himself in both a professional and personal relationship with Shaw… [who] not only helped revitalize Robert's acting credentials but also introduced him to the thrill of flight by taking him for a ride in a hot-air balloon'[3] (see page 50 below).

♦ ♦ ♦

The Birth of Powered Flight. Having been born in an age when the only things that usually flew were birds, kites and balloons, Robert was almost twenty-eight years of age when the first successful, sustained flight in a heavier-than-air flying machine powered by an engine was made on 17 December 1903 at Kill Devil Hills, North Carolina, USA. The effect of the achievement of Wilbur Wright, assisted by his brother Orville, caused not a

---

[2] First quote – *The Royal Aero Club Gazette,* Special Golden Jubilee Number, 1901 – 1951, p.37; second – *Pigs Might Fly,* p.6 Forty Years On 1909 – 1949, Handley Page Ltd., (London, Radlett and Reading, 1949).
[3] *The Life of Robert Loraine*, p.63.

few ripples among Very Important Persons, leading to a resolution being passed by the Olympic Congress in Brussels, on 10 June 1905, calling for the creation of an association 'to regulate the sport of flying... the various aviation meetings and advance the science and sport of Aeronautics.' As a result of that resolution a conference was held in Paris from 12–14 October 1905, on the last day of which the *Fédération Aéronautique Internationale* ("FAI") was created as the world's governing body for air sports and aeronautics.

The conference was attended by representatives of the leading aero clubs of eight countries: France (*Aéro-Club*, founded 1898);[4] Switzerland (*Aero-Club der Schweiz*, 1900); Belgium (*Aero Club Royal de Belgique*, 1901); Great Britain (*Aeronautical Club of the United Kingdom*, 1901); Germany (*Deutscher Aero Club e.V*); Italy (*Aero Club d'Italia*, 1904); Spain (*Real Aero Club de España*, 1905); and the United States (Aero Club of America, 1905).

The Aeronautical Club of the United Kingdom was formed by 'three wealthy motorists, Frank Hedges Butler, his daughter Vera and the Hon Charles Rolls',[5] and from 1905, before the advent of the aeroplane, the club issued Aeronauts' Certificates for balloonists. On 15 February 1910, the club was permitted to call itself the Royal Aeronautical Club ("RAeC"),

Sergeants Frank James (left) and Alfred Robert May, RFC Service nos. 152 and 167 respectively

---

[4] The *Aéro-Club* was founded on 20 Oct 1898, 'to encourage aerial locomotion'. Its name was changed on 20 Apr 1909 to Aéro-Club de France.
[5] *www.royalaeroclub.co.uk*. Frank Butler (17 Dec 1855–27 Nov 1928) was a wealthy wine merchant, and owner of one of the first motor cars in Britain.

and thereafter it was the RAeC that issued Aviators' Certificates, internationally recognised under the rules of the FAI, to aircraft pilots who had passed a stipulated test in Britain.

RAeC certificates nos. 1 and 2 were awarded on 8 March 1910 to J.T.C. Moore-Brabazon and to the Hon. C.S. Rolls respectively. The actual date of the award of certificates numbers 1–452 was that on which the RAeC committee sat to approve them, even though the aviator might have flown his test a week or two earlier. The date for certificates 453 onwards was backdated to the date of the flying test. By the start of the First World War on 4 August 1914 the RAeC had awarded 864 certificates. No. 864 actually went to Sergeant F. James on 28 July 1914 though, for some reason, no. 863 was not awarded to Sergeant A.R. May until 4 August.[6]

Being the United Kingdom representative on the FAI, the RAeC 'was responsible for control in the UK of all private and sporting flying, as well as records and competitions... It borrowed heavily from existing sports such as horse racing for its early regulations, the first air racing rules, for example, containing the injunction that "No rider shall interfere with another rider on the course".'[7]

With effect from 1 March 1910, it was decreed that the rules governing the authorisation of aviators' certificates awarded in another country were as follows: '... Foreigners belonging to a country represented on the F.A.I. can only receive a certificate from the Royal Aero Club of the United Kingdom after having obtained the consent from the national sporting authority approved by the F.A.I. But a certificate may also be granted to a foreigner whose country is not represented on the F.A.I., without further application.'

It was thus a requirement that anyone wishing to fly in a competition held under FAI rules had to have been issued with a flying certificate from a body registered with the FAI, for example the ACF or RAeC.

◆ ◆ ◆

It would seem that the Wright brothers' momentous flight made less of an impact on Robert than that of Louis Blériot in July 1909, who staggered the world by flying across the English Channel. Given the unreliability of aero-engines at the time, this was considered to have been an outstanding achievement and one of great bravery.

Already enthralled by flying and determined to enjoy the new sport, Robert went to France to witness Blériot's departure, and so enthusiastic did he become after this epic flight that he determined to learn the new art for himself. Flying at this time was available only to men and women with deep pockets, but Robert was sufficiently wealthy to be able to afford

---

[6] Both these men would survive the First World War, and both would serve in the Second. May, born 24 Nov 1891, died in hospital on 12 Sep 1964, and James, born 19 Feb 1888, in (probably) Dec 1974.
[7] *www.royalaeroclub.co.uk/.*

to go to the Farman School at Mourmelon-le-Grand, France, in early 1910 to learn to fly. He was awarded flying certificate no. 126 by the *Aéro-Club de France* (ACF) on 21 June 1910, by which date the RAeC had issued only thirteen such certificates. He was able, too, to buy an expensive aeroplane, a Farman racing biplane, at a time when demand for these fragile machines exceeded supply.

Such would be the pleasure that he got from flying that he was apparently credited by *The Oxford English Dictionary* at the time as having coined in his diary the new word "joystick", for the lever that the pilot used to operate the elevator and aileron controls of an aeroplane.

Though he was not a naturally-gifted "driver", as pioneer pilots were known, he was regarded as being "plucky", and only fourteen months after Blériot's cross-Channel adventure, he would fly over twice the distance that Blériot had covered when, in an attempt to fly from Anglesey, Wales, to Phoenix Park, Dublin, Ireland, he was forced down into the waters of the Bay of Dublin, only yards from the Irish coast. It was considered to have been a very brave effort, plucky, and one rightly deemed by the prestigious Royal Aeronautical Club to have been worthy of a special medal.

Robert saw flying as a challenge and would, nevertheless, be remembered for several flying records. While enjoying the fame that his flying achievements brought, he gained a strong and well-deserved reputation accordingly. Long before the days of the cinema, radio and television, his feats would be publicised in newspaper articles (cuttings of which he was a prodigious collector) and in photographs (usually as postcards). He also enjoyed being seen flying at aviation shows, such events being a wonder to behold, when folk flocked in their thousands to gaze in ignorant awe at the plucky aviators risking life and limb in their dangerous aeroplanes. The public always needs its heroes and, for a few years, the pioneer aviators were the "stars" of their day.

Ever the showman, Robert Loraine wanted his part in it. His flying career was, however, to be short, lasting in the main for only the second half of 1910 and up to mid-1911, during which time he was kept in the air by a cantankerous but devoted French mechanic. Given the ability of flying machines in those days to easily come to grief, it was essential for all aeroplane owners to have a mechanic on more or less permanent call. Well aware of this, Robert engaged Jules Védrines, an employee of the Farman school, as his mechanic. Védrines would play a vital part in Robert's short flying career.

♦ ♦ ♦

Jules Charles Toussaint Védrines was born on 29 December 1881 in the industrial Paris suburb of St. Denis. He was described by one author as a 'man of tempestuous temperament and great physical endurance... He was the short, swarthy son of a Paris working-class family, and an avowed socialist.'[8]

After an apprenticeship at the Gnôme engine manufacturing company, he was employed by the Farman School at Mourmelon-le-Grand. It was there that he went for his first flight and where his ambition to become a qualified pilot was nurtured. When Robert therefore offered him a ridiculously high salary, enough money to pay for his flying tuition, he grabbed the opportunity with both hands.

For the next three months or so he would be put to the test on many an occasion as Robert frequently crashed his flimsy aeroplane. Each time, grumbling and moaning and cursing everything English, Jules would make good Robert's precious Farman and would be with Robert at several major events during the summer of 1910: the Bournemouth International

Jules Védrines at the Blériot School, Pau, after he had left Robert's services to become a first-class aviator in his own right. He sent this postcard to Robert at 51A Conduit Street, London, probably in 1912 (via Richard Holleyman).

---

[8] *Contact! The Story of the Early Birds*, p.128.

Aviation Meeting in July; the Blackpool Aviation Meeting in August; and the sensational flights to North Wales and to Ireland in August and September.

After the Ireland flight Jules had saved sufficient funds to become an aviator and left Robert's employ, notwithstanding Robert's plea to renew their contract: 'Moi aussi, je veux être aviateur', Jules recalled ('I, too, want to be an aviator.') Returning to France, Jules went to Louis Blériot's school at Pau where he gained ACF pilot's licence no. 312 on 7 December 1910.

No longer *mécanicien* to the great Loraine, he rapidly rose to fame as an aviator in his own right. In 1911 he won the Paris to Madrid air race in May with a Morane-Borel monoplane and, in the same year, came second in the Circuit of Britain race and third in the Circuit of Europe race.

Left: Jules Védrines's overturned Blériot at the start of the Paris-Madrid race, 21 May 1911; right: his aeroplane at Lark Hill during the Circuit of Britain. His racing no. 9 is visible under the wings.

In 1912, in a Deperdussin Racing monoplane he was the first person to fly an aircraft at more than 100 m.p.h. (160 km/h), and won the Gordon Bennett Trophy race. In 1913 he flew to Cairo in a Blériot (controversially flying over Germany, which the Germans said was illegal). When war came in 1914 he joined the French air force and, during the conflict, mostly flew clandestine missions, or dropped or picked-up agents behind enemy lines.

He met his end on 21 April 1919 when one of the two engines failed on the converted Caudron C.23 bomber that he was flying from Villacoublay to Rome, Italy. Attempting a forced landing near St. Rambert d'Albon, Lyon, both he and his mechanic, Marcel Guillain, were killed.

The wreckage of Védrines's Caudron aeroplane, 21 April 1919

♦ ♦ ♦

Also helping Robert to achieve his success in 1910 was former Army officer and great friend George Smart. Essentially becoming Robert's "director of operations", he made arrangements for all Robert's aviation needs as and when they arose during the summer and autumn of 1910.

George Henry Smart, born in Bombay on 29 April 1883, was the only son of the late Major-General G.J. Smart, RA,[9] and of Mrs. E. Larminie, of Killiney, County Dublin, Ireland.[10] Educated at Dover College and at the Royal Military College, Sandhurst, he was commissioned into the West Yorkshire Regiment in 1901. Serving in the Second Boer War from November 1901 to May 1902, he was awarded the Queen's Medal with three clasps. He was promoted lieutenant in 1904, but retired from the Regular Army in 1909. The 1911 Census shows him resident at 29 Audley House, Margaret Street, London W. Under "Personal Occupation" he stated: 'Captain – Special Reserve – in receipt of retired pay in respect of 8 years service in Regular Army.'

---

[9] Major-General Smart had served in the Indian Mutiny, being twice mentioned in dispatches.
[10] Emily Larminie, born 19 Feb 1855, died 16 Aug 1945.

George Henry Smart

He gave up his career in the army to 'pursue a very different career as a novelist and playwright… His attempts to become a writer were mostly unsuccessful'.[11] It was through hoping to become a playwright that he met Robert Loraine. In 1909, he 'thrust a script into Robert's hands one night' as Robert was leaving His Majesty's Theatre, where he was starring in Sheridan's play *The School for Scandal*.[12] (In that play, which had opened on 8 April 1909, Robert was also re-introduced to a young actress, Marie Löhr, of whom more later). George asked him to look at the play he had written but Robert, to his subsequent regret, was not interested in it. Nevertheless, a strong friendship was to grow between them.

When he became in effect Robert's "road manager", George wrote a journal in which 'he recorded the incidents that took place, the people he encountered and his conversations with them.'[13] These jottings became the basis for his unpublished manuscript entitled *Flights and Fancies. The true story of an English summer and an Aeroplane*. Most of George's quotes hereafter are taken from this document.

George continued to see Robert after the Irish flight in September 1910, and occasionally flew with him, for example when Robert flew in the 1910 Army manoeuvres later in September.

Soon after the start of the war in 1914 George was attached from the 4th (Extra Reserve) Battalion, The Prince of Wales's Own (West Yorkshire Regiment), for active service with the 1st Battalion, Loyal North Lancashire Regiment. He was serving in the trenches when killed in action on 22 December 1914 at Le Touret, France, following a German counter-attack, as noted in the Regimental diary: 'Moved in buses to Vieille Chapelle (21st) then advance to Le Touret. Took part in attack to regain lost trenches near the orchard north-east of Festubert. Went forward 7.20 p.m. and objective gained within the hour. Casualties – Captains G.H. Smart (West Yorkshire attached) and G.M. Graham (Worcestershire attached) killed, 4 officers wounded, 408 other ranks killed, wounded or missing.'[14] George, with no known grave, is commemorated on the Le Touret Memorial, Pas-de-

---

[11] Holleyman and Sloan in their introduction to George Smart's unpublished *Flights and Fancies*.
[12] *The Life of Robert Loraine*, p.90.
[13] Ibid.
[14] Quoted in www.greatwarforum.org/.

Calais, France, as is Captain Alec George Malcolm Graham, 6th (Res.) Battalion, Worcestershire Regiment. Captain Graham was forty-three years of age.

Winifred Loraine, Robert's widow, paid a fine tribute to George who, she said, 'wrote most of his impressions in a daily journal in which, however, he failed to give himself credit for the part he played. Many of [Robert's] flights could never have taken place but for Smart. It was his unfailing industry and resource in the Loraine cause that made it possible for Robert to gain the Overseas Flying Records for 1910. For Robert could only snatch at aviation.'[15]

After George's death, Robert felt guilty that he had not done more for his friend, as Winifred movingly explained: 'Smart had meant much, done much for him, lovely had been their companionship. Lovely the years beyond recall! He wished he had produced a play by Smart. That was how they had first met: Smart had pressed a play into his hands just inside a stage-door. Robert had read and refused it, but Smart had come to his rooms subsequently to collect the script, and so had started their friendship. A friendship in which Smart had never failed to serve. He had continued to write plays down the years, and Robert had continued to refuse them ... in flowed waves of self-reproach, Robert could not help them. A production would have meant so much to the dear chap. Fulfilment and recognition was what he had lacked in life. Robert could have given them to him. Could have, but did not. He had hesitated, waiting for Smart to write a "winner." Yet Smart had never hesitated in his service to him. Now, there was nothing he could do for Smart, nothing.'[16]

After George's death, *Flights and Fancies* passed into Robert's hands, and when he died in 1935 Winifred used it when writing her biography of her late husband. It then passed to their daughter, Joan, who, years later, in turn allowed Richard Holleyman and Roy Sloan to have access to it. It is now with Rob Schmidt, Robert's grandson.

♦ ♦ ♦

Robert did a little more flying in early 1912 and in 1913 at Hendon, but no more until the First World War. Commissioned into the Special Reserve of the Royal Flying Corps on 12 August 1914[17] at the age of 38, he flew some thirty reconnaissance flights as an Observer before being seriously wounded in action in November 1914. Very fortunate to survive, he was seriously wounded in action again in July 1918, again being very fortunate to survive. For his courage, bravery and leadership he would be honoured by his King with two high awards for gallantry in the field.

---

[15] *Robert Loraine. Actor, Soldier, Airman*, p.99.
[16] Ibid., p.236.
[17] *The London Gazette*, 11 Aug 1914, no. 28667.

Physically, he was battered by nearly five years on active service, being forty-two years of age when it was all over in 1918. Towards the end he had had to resort to the use of pain-killing drugs, and had become somewhat addicted to the comfort of morphine in its several guises.

Nevertheless, though somewhat crippled from his second wound – shot in the knee-cap – he soldiered on, and tried to revive his very successful pre-war acting career. He found himself less favoured, however, and was occasionally out of work, which led to him having dark periods.

In 1920-21, he went on a trip around the world and, on the ship from India back to England, met Winifred Lydia Strangman, who was half his age. After a whirlwind romance, they married, and had three daughters in the 1920's. This marriage, too, was destined to not be the most successful until, with Robert spending more and more of his time in the USA looking for work, Winifred sought a divorce in 1935.

During this period in the USA, in which he made a handful of "movies", Robert had a final flying flurry gaining his US License in 1933, at the age of fifty-seven. He made his last flight in August 1935. Whether he knew it or not, he had not long to live, and returned to England shortly after that last flight. He secured a contract with the BBC to play the part of Scrooge in two readings of Charles Dickens' *A Christmas Carol*, to be broadcast on Boxing Day and on 27 December 1935, but just before Christmas, following an operation, he met his untimely death at the age of fifty-nine.

Robert Bilcliffe Loraine
[Photo by Bassano Ltd. © National Portrait Gallery, London]

'We live in deeds, not years; in thoughts, not breaths;
In feelings, not in figures on a dial.
We should count time by heart-throbs. He most lives
Who thinks most – feels the noblest – acts the best.'

Festus, P.J. Bailey (1816-1902)

Chapter One: Early Years

One of the first persons, if not *the* first, to witness the arrival on this earth on 14 January 1876 of Robert Bilcliffe Loraine, to be known variously throughout his life as Robbie, Bobbie, Bob, or Robert, was Caroline Davis, a 26-year-old "monthly nurse".[18] Paid to look after Robert's mother during her confinement, it was she who notified the authorities of Robert's birth, declaring that she was present at the happy event that took place at 5 Mersey Terrace, Liscard, in the sub-district of Wallasey, Cheshire (see the birth certificate below). Mersey Terrace is a row of five houses on Tollemache Street, New Brighton.

In his book *The Inviting Shore: A Social History of New Brighton* Anthony M. Miller explains that 'most of the major building development in this area [i.e. Liscard] occurred during the 1860s and 1870s, when the gaps between the early terraces and cottages were filled by a prolific period of building activity in the resort [of New Brighton].' He adds that

Copy of Robert's corrected birth certificate showing the clerical errors.

---

[18] A "monthly nurse" was so called as the period of a mother's "confinement" was reckoned to last four weeks.

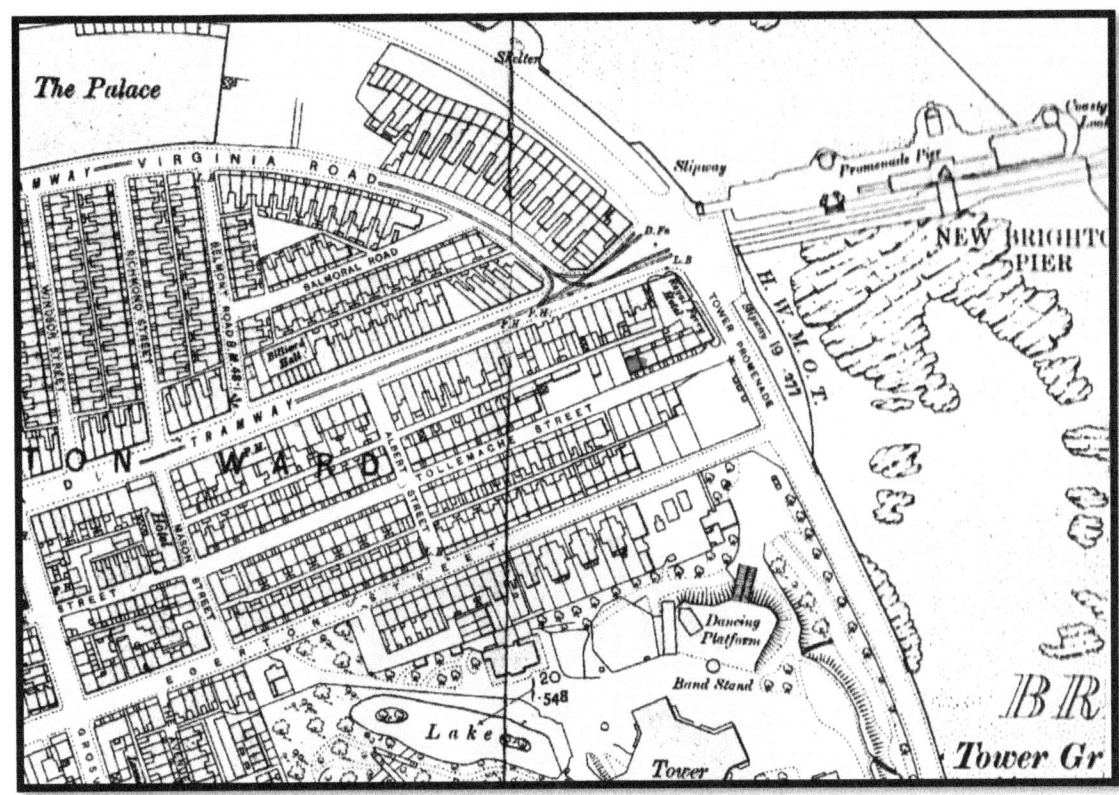

Map showing 5 Belmont Terrace (marked in red), Tollemache Street, New Brighton (from an OS map published in 1909). No. 5 Belmont Terrace is today re-numbered No. 57 Tollemache Street. [David Railton]

Mersey Terrace 'housed some specially fine examples.'[19] The same applied to a row of thirteen houses at the other end of, and on the south side of, Tollemache Street, namely Belmont Terrace, between Albert Street and Mason Street. It was at 5 Belmont Terrace that Robert's Aunt Bella lived.

When someone noticed that there was an error on Robbie's birth certificate – his middle name was Bilcliffe and not, as in columns two and four, "Witcliffe" – Robert's mother, Mary Ellen (just Ellen on her son's birth certificate), went to the Registrar on 6 April 1876 to have Witcliffe amended to Bilcliffe.

Robert's father was born Henry Bilcliffe on 17 November 1820. Rather than follow in his father's footsteps as a carpenter/builder, young Henry determined to become an actor. As this was not at all what Henry's father, Thomas, had in mind for his son he, Thomas, disinherited him, forbidding him to use the name Bilcliffe on the stage. Henry simply added Loraine.

---

[19] From information generously supplied by David Railton.

Henry's first wife was Mary Ann Mangan (though when they were married is not known), and they had four, possibly five, children: Eleanor Catherine Ada Bilcliffe Loraine, born in Clapham, London, on 18 May 1846;[20] Henry Bilcliffe Loraine, born at Bradford in 1849; George Bilcliffe Loraine, born in Birmingham on 16 February 1852, but he died sometime in the last quarter of 1853; and Thomas Edward Bilcliffe Loraine, born in April quarter 1856 and baptised in St. Xavier's Roman Catholic church, Liverpool, on 25 January 1857. He, too, is believed to have died very young. There may have been a fifth child, for a William Charles Bilcliffe Loraine, born sometime in 1847, was buried at Huddersfield on 25 March 1849, just nineteen months old.

In 1856 Henry, who by this time gave his occupation as "Comedian", went to try his luck in the United States. He was unsuccessful at first but by 1859 had gained a decent reputation. Sadly, it was in the USA that Mary Ann, who had gone with him, died.

Eleven years later Henry married 22-year-old Mary Ellen Baylis, known as Nell, at Wolstanton, Staffordshire, in January 1870, when both were travelling actors. Nell, whose residence on 17 February 1870 was noted as 10 Gloucester Street, Hanley, was born in Birkenhead around April 1848, the youngest of the six children of Robert and Isabella (née Stelling) Baylis: Martha (born 1835); Isabella ("Aunt Bella", 1838); Clara Lee (1840); Emily (1842); Charles (1846), and Mary Ellen ("Nell", 1848). The children's dates of birth are based on their ages given in the 1851 Census. Robert Baylis was aged 51, and Isabella, his wife, was 38 according to this Census.

By 1872 Nell was using the stage name Edith Kingsley,[21] and Henry, who by this time was calling himself a "Tragedian", was, for example, playing *Othello* at the Theatre Royal, Middlesbrough, on 1 March 1872.

Robert's childhood is sketchily documented, though his two major biographers have provided a number of undated and separate, but not conflicting, snippets of those early days. Putting them into chronological order, however, is not easy. For instance, it was said that, having no wish for young Robert to be brought up in their travelling life style, his parents put him into the care of Aunt Bella until the age of four.[22] Presumably this was until sometime in 1880, but no precise date is given.

Aunt Bella had married Walter Powell Sinnotte (1824–1879) on 17 August 1863. At the time of Walter's death, she was still living at 5 Belmont Terrace, and was receiving an income from "letting apartments". 'A sweet but firm woman was widowed, lace-capped Aunt Bella: the family were deeply religious.'[23]

---

[20] Eleanor, aged 19, married Abraham William Abbott in London in 1865.
[21] *The Life of Robert Loraine*, p.9.
[22] *Robert Loraine. Actor, Soldier, Airman*, p.25.
[23] *Robert Loraine. Actor, Soldier, Airman*, p.24. Emigrating to Australia, she died in Melbourne on 15 May 1905.

By 1880, Henry and Nell had given up the touring life and had returned to New Brighton, probably because young Robbie, still with Aunt Bella, had had a very severe brain illness – 'Nell had lost her first son, Arthur, who had died as a baby; she did not wish to lose her second and only one.'[24] Arthur Bilcliffe Loraine, born 4 May 1870 in Everton, Liverpool, died early in 1871.

Difficulties with dates at this period of Robbie's life persist but, by the end of 1880, his father, Henry, was in financial difficulties. Help was provided by 'an insolvency practitioner', who loaned them the funds on which to live. It may well be that Henry and Nell did, indeed, take Robbie with them on tour to earn the money to settle the debt, for the April 1881 Census finds them all lodging at 12 Skinner Street, Ruswarp, Whitby, Yorkshire. Henry was now calling himself a 'Dramatic Actor', and Nell an 'Actress', while young Robbie, aged 5, was not yet a scholar.

It is not known when the family returned to New Brighton, but Henry's debt was paid off by 1883, after he had been made a manager at Liverpool's Royal Court Theatre.[25]

Though, perhaps, destined to become an actor like his father, Robbie needed an education, and funds were found, mostly by his mother,[26] for him to go to New Brighton High School, 'the best private school in Cheshire.' There is some doubt as to precisely how long Robbie spent at the school, but his mother and father were, again, not doing well financially, and it is possible that he had to leave the school through non-payment of fees. There is a story, though, that he left one day in 1889 after a teacher, without looking at Robbie's geometry work, had told him to do it again. In a dramatic display of temper Robbie tore his exercise book in half, then 'snapped the master's cane in two… strode to the door and opened it, slammed it and locked it from the outside', tossing the key into the hall fire.[27] Only thirteen-years old, he never went back.

This may, or may not, be true, as may be the further story that, determined to seek his fortune in the USA, he got a job at the Liverpool docks with the intention of stowing away on a ship. As luck would have it, none was leaving for ten days and, so the story goes, lacking funds, he went to the sailors' dives that abounded in the dock area, and earned money by writing and acting in short plays to entertain the sailors.

Every large port had its "sailortown" area, which, in Liverpool, was 'clustered around the city centre, extending inland from Albert, Canning and Salthouse Docks.' The area included 'a Sailor's Home and Seamen's Mission to dance halls, bars, boarding houses and

---

[24] *Robert Loraine. Actor, Soldier, Airman*, p.38.
[25] The author here gratefully acknowledges Lannie Liggera's research in *The Life of Robert Loraine*, p.10.
[26] 'Nellie managed to put aside half the weekly takings for the next six weeks and bank them' – *Robert Loraine. Actor, Soldier, Airman*, p.41. Henry Loraine was not good with money, just as his son would prove to be in his later years.
[27] *Robert Loraine. Actor, Soldier, Airman*, p.42.

shops with most connected to the port.'²⁸ Young Robbie clearly became familiar with Liverpool's sailortown.

Then, one fine day in May 1889, so another story goes, strolling through Liverpool, he went into a theatre, and persuaded the manager to give him a part in a forthcoming production. So fine was his performance as an old man that the manager offered him further parts, as a younger person, at a fee of 30/- (£1.50) per week, which at least allowed Robbie to quit "sailortown".

He gave a glimpse of his early life in Liverpool in a 1932 interview for an American magazine: 'With hearty good humor he recalls those fledgling days, just as he recalls earlier tea and toast and twenty shillings for six plays a week, twice a day apiece, in a Liverpool sailor's dive with a three-penny tip. For these two pursuits – the theatre and flying – have dominated his life. He is admirably equipped for both.' (*The Sportsman*, March 1932).

The less romantic story is that the money earned by him at the Liverpool theatres helped to keep the family in funds and that he had never intended to go to the United States anyway.

Soon, though, he was seeking fame and fortune away from Liverpool. The 1891 Census recorded him as an actor, aged 15, resident at 17 Brook Street, Leek, Staffordshire, together with Esther E. Loraine, theatrical actress, aged 34. "Esther" was, apparently, his mother, who was a little older than her stated age! No. 17 Brook Street appears to have been a lodging house for persons with theatre-related jobs for, with Robbie and his mother, there were five other actors/actresses.

It was around this time that Robbie's parents finally gave up touring, and went to London. In April 1891, Henry was playing in Charles Reade's *It's Never Too Late To Mend* at the Theatre Royal, Drury Lane. Robbie, too, would go to London, making his stage debut in that city on 22 May 1894 in the play *Ne'er-do-well*.

By this time his mother, Nell, who had been paralyzed from a fall, became seriously ill, 'placed under the care of a specialist'²⁹ suffering from a spinal injury and stomach cancer.³⁰ Admitted to hospital in July 1895, she died two weeks later, on 1 August 1895. Robbie and his father were then living together. Though 'the shock of losing Nell had driven Henry into dementia,'³¹ he was well enough by December 1896 to appear in Shakespeare's *As You Like It* at St. James's Theatre. Also on the bill were Robbie and a certain Julie Florence Opp (born in New York City, USA, on 28 January 1871), whom Robbie had already met in *The Prisoner of Zenda* earlier in 1896.

---

²⁸ *Share your memories of Sailortown*, BBC, 23 Dec 2010.
²⁹ *Robert Loraine. Actor, Soldier, Airman*, p.42.
³⁰ *The Life of Robert Loraine*, p.12.
³¹ *The Life of Robert Loraine*, p.18.

Robbie as Rudolf Rassendyll in The Prisoner of Zenda; Julie Opp (via Lanayre Liggera).

(In the 1880 US Federal Census Julie's name is given as Julia and this is also the name she gave when applying for an American passport on 15 December 1894. She also declared on the application that she was 5 feet 9½ inches tall, had grey eyes, brown hair and a fair complexion.)

Having become romantically entangled Robbie and Julie, as she now was, were married at the St. Giles Registry Office, London, on 4 November 1897,[32] he, aged 22, of 15 Keppel Street, Russell Square, London, and she, apparently aged 23, of Albany Mansions, Albert Street [*sic* – Albert Bridge Road], Battersea, London SW. Yet, on 6 November 1897, Julie left her husband of two days and sailed from Southampton aboard the SS *St. Paul*, bound for New York, to pursue *her* acting career in the United States.

In anticipation of her return, Robbie bought a house at Staines, on the Thames, significantly a few miles west of the beating heart of London's theatreland. After Julie was back in England in January 1899, Robbie took her to the house, but she rejected it for being too far from the heart of London. Robbie angrily stormed out with never a backward glance,

---

[32] The two witnesses were Frances Foster and L. Shepherd.

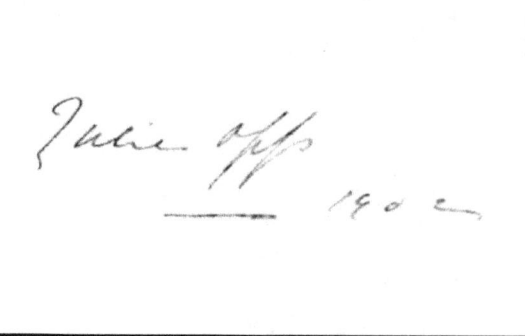

Signatures of Robert (1908) and Julie (1902) [author's collection]

the two never to be reconciled. For much of his life, though, it would seem that, a perfectionist, he had the knack of rubbing-up people the wrong way. This not to say, however, that he couldn't be caring but, on the whole, he was seen as his own man – with a short temper.

Julie did, though, live in the Staines house in the following summer, returning to theatreland for the winter, which at least gave Robbie the opportunity to sell the house and pay off his debts.

Adding to Robbie's marital woes was the death, on 10 July 1899, of his father, Henry. He was buried on 13 July.

A few months later, soon after the start of the Second Boer War, Robbie answered the call to the Colours, and in March 1900 went off to fight the Boer in South Africa.

Chapter Two: Soldier

Silver cap badge of the Montgomeryshire Imperial Yeomanry

On 11 October 1899, three months after Robbie's father's death, came the momentous, if not unexpected, news that the British Empire had declared war on the Boer states in South Africa. Robbie, keen to play his part in it, signed Army Form B.111, the Attestation form, on 20 December 1899 in London. Swearing under oath that he would serve for Short Service (one year with the Colours) as Trooper No. 8175 in the Montgomeryshire Imperial Yeomanry, he was notified that if 'the War in South Africa lasts longer than one year… you will be detained until the war is over.' He named Mrs. Robert Loraine (wife) of St. James' Theatre, London, as his next-of-kin.

◆ ◆ ◆

Background to the Second Boer War, South Africa. On 9 October 1899, having had enough of British interference in their affairs, the Transvaal government issued an ultimatum demanding that all points of difference between the South African Government and the Imperial Government should be referred to arbitration; that Imperial troops on the border be instantly withdrawn; that all troop reinforcements landed in South Africa be withdrawn; and that Her Majesty's troops now on the high seas should not be landed in any South African port. 'In the event of no satisfactory answer being received by 5 o'clock on October 11, or any further movement of troops taking place, the Transvaal Government would be compelled to regard the action of Her Majesty's Government as a declaration of war.'[33]

Following the British government's inevitable rejection of this impossible ultimatum, the second Boer war officially began at 5 p.m., Transvaal time, on 11 October 1899, and would continue until 31 May 1902.

◆ ◆ ◆

---

[33] *Whitaker's Almanack 1900*, p.596.

Paul Krüger (seated, right) and Transvaal Cabinet Ministers (date unknown).

Robert's second wife, Winifred, would write that he 'needed this War. He was sick of himself. He had to get away to something fresh.' The war was now 'his chance promising new life, adventure, glory, self-sacrifice'.[34]

With war inevitable, the British Army's Reserves were called out on 7 October 1899 and, on 13 December 1899, the War Office agreed that volunteer forces, based on the standing yeomanry regiments, could serve overseas. With the Royal Warrant of 24 December 1899, the new Imperial Yeomanry would be raised on a county basis: 'Commanding officers of Yeomanry regiments were authorized to enrol men into their units who had had previous service and who could ride and shoot efficiently. From the augmented regiments volunteer contingents were grouped to form a large body of mounted infantry called the Imperial

---

[34] Quotes from *Robert Loraine. Actor, Soldier, Airman*, pp.30, 54.

A mounted infantryman of the Boer War on the veldt [IWM]

Yeomanry. Each regimental contingent of 116 men constituted a company, and four companies were formed into a composite battalion. Altogether there were nineteen of these battalions…

'All mounted infantrymen had the same equipment. They had 150 rounds of ammunition carried in three leather bandoliers; one of which was worn round each shoulder and the third, which also supported a bayonet, round the waist. A water-bottle and haversack were carried on the man, and a rolled cavalry greatcoat, a canteen and nose-bags filled with corn on the saddle.'[35]

Robbie's chance to take part in the war came with the formation of the Montgomeryshire Imperial Yeomanry ["M.I.Y."]. Following the summoning of a public meeting of the County of Montgomery on 1 January 1900 by Sir Herbert Lloyd Watkin Williams-Wynn, Bart. (1860–1944), local landowner, and by the High Sheriff (Oliver Ormrod Openshaw, 1863–1908), such was the rush to join the M.I.Y. from all over Britain 'that two companies, as the squadrons were officially termed, were formed… The two companies, which were numbered the 31st and 49th, were mobilized at Welshpool on January 4th [1900].'

The 31st (Montgomeryshire) and 49th (Montgomeryshire) Companies, together with the 29th (Denbighshire) and 30th (Pembrokeshire) Companies, formed the new 9th Battalion, commanded by Lieutenant-Colonel H.R.L. Howard. 'Owing to the want of room at Welshpool the 31st was removed to Newtown.'[36] Here the men were 'billeted in the various public-houses and inns of the villages.'[37]

---

[35] *The Mounted Troops of the British Army*, p.228.
[36] *The Montgomeryshire Yeomanry*, p.59.
[37] *Half a Life*, p.65.

Broad Street, Welshpool, as Robbie would have known it (photo taken soon after the end of the Boer War)

Arriving at Welshpool for training on 16 January 1900, 8175 Trooper Robert Loraine, M.I.Y., was attached to the 49th Company's Gun Section. Formed shortly after mobilization, the Gun Section was supposedly something of a *corps d'élite*. 8201 Private Claude Scudamore Jarvis, writing of his Boer War experiences with the M.I.Y. in *Half a Life*, recalled that 'only the best men and best horsemen were to be selected for it. Names were called for, and the subaltern of our troop, a rather nervous young man, read them over on parade, commenting on their suitability or otherwise. After some time he came to Loraine.

'"Trooper Loraine," he said in a weak, nervous voice.

'"Er – a bad horseman, aren't you?"

'"No, sir," shouted Loraine, in the ringing voice of D'Artagnan in "The Three Musketeers"… "an extremely good one, sir."

'Actually this was a gross misstatement of fact…

'"Oh, I'm sorry," mumbled the subaltern bashfully.'[38]

---

[38] *Half a Life*, pp. 68-9.

And so, for the time being, Robbie was attached to the Gun Section. Word may already have reached the nervous officer that Robbie had earlier taken a tumble when 'a sergeant ordered Robert to mount a horse bareback. Men gathered to laugh, thinking he would be thrown right away. Instead, after a few dizzying turnabouts with Robert hanging onto the mane for dear life, the horse fell suddenly to its knees and rolled over and would not get up. The horse had been unhitched from a gun carriage, and the sergeant who oversaw this team came over and reprimanded the other sergeant roundly, telling him it was a trick horse that had been presented to them. Robert, for his part, took it all in [his] stride and remarked to a friend, "What luck and how odd!"' Odd, because in the play *The Great Ruby* the same thing had happened to him with a 'trick charger.'

His comrades were wary of Robert, or Bob as they called him. To them 'he was such a queer chap, so quick with his fists and easily offended, you never knew where you were with him. For all his good humour and camaraderie, he bristled with susceptibilities, and whatever his mood, you had to fall in with it. You were noisy, if he were gay; stopped horseplay, if he were serious. Even when he was reeling off poetry you listened.' Once a trooper came after Bob with a horse-whip. Though the man was bigger and heavier, Rob flung him down a flight of stairs, breaking his shoulder. 'After that, word went round his gun-section: "Let Loraine speak first, and take him as you find him."'[39]

Claude Jarvis was to get to know Robbie well. He remembered him as 'a strikingly handsome young man of fine physique', with 'a very striking personality', but found 'it difficult to describe him, for one cannot judge him from ordinary standards. He was, I suppose, conceited, but this, after all, is a very natural failing in a young man who has suddenly risen from obscurity to fame and popularity in a year or less. I should say also that he was selfish and self-opiniated... He was a man who... would compel instant dislike from possibly nine men out of ten and unbounded admiration from the tenth, who would detect the human and very likeable soul behind the veneer of pomposity and aggressiveness that he affected. He was improvident, and impulsive, and apparently very sure of himself...

Claude Jarvis, in later years (from the cover of his book Half a Life)

'From what I saw of him during the South African war and what I have read of him since, one has the feeling that he was a personality who missed being an outstanding one through some chink in his armour'.[40]

---

[39] *Robert Loraine, Actor, Soldier, Airman*, pp.14-15.
[40] *Half a Life*, pp. 93-4.

"Wynnstay", home of Sir H. L. W. Williams-Wynn, c. 1904

SS Montrose, showing her official troopship number, 93, near the bow.

Training of the M.I.Y. continued apace, often in heavy snow, until, on 'February 13th [1900] the two Montgomeryshire Companies were moved to Wynnstay in order that their training might proceed together.'[41]

At last, on 13 March, the two companies, 'each numbering 116 N.C.O.'s and men, Gun Section, and 120 horses', were entrained for Liverpool's Langton Dock, where they embarked on the steamship *Montrose*.[42] Also aboard were the 30th (Pembrokeshire) 'and a Company of the (46th) Irish Yeomanry, under Lord Longford, making up in all 516 officers and men, and 279 horses.' All were reinforcements summoned to the Cape Colony by the shocked British Army.

At around 9 p.m. on Tuesday, 13 March 1900, the *Montrose* began the first of her eight voyages as a Boer War troopship from Liverpool to Cape Town. As she pulled away from the dock 'the air was rent by piercing noise and shock that shook the *Montrose* from prow to stern. Sirens! Every tug, ferry and liner in the Mersey started blasting on her steam whistles as the *Montrose* swung into midstream. The hooting was taken up by factories along the river-bank, ships behind the *Montrose*, and ships out of sight at the river mouth. The noise was indescribable…'[43]

After a relatively smooth voyage the *Montrose* reached Las Palmas, Canary Islands, on 19 March 1900, anchoring off Gran Canaria. 'At Las Palmas, Messrs. Elder, Dempster and Co. entertained the officers on shore while the ship was coaling, and the thanks of all were warmly expressed to their Chairman, Sir Alfred Jones, for the many arrangements that had been made for the comfort of all on board, including the horses.'[44]

Life for the men and horses on board, however, was far from good. 8226 Trooper Sidney George Critten, 31st M.I.Y., sent several letters home describing the voyage aboard the *Montrose* (and subsequent events in South Africa).[45] On 20 March, he wrote that the ship 'sailed again at 6 p.m. just as the sun went down'.[46] Steaming south over the calm sea, the temperature rose, causing hardship to the men but worse to their horses. He wrote again, on 22 March, that one horse died during the night, and on 23 March: 'Very hot today. Horses very ill and some of them off their feed. The water they get is quite hot and ours is luke warm.' Two more horses died on 24 March, and were thrown overboard.

---

[41] *The Montgomeryshire Yeomanry*, p.61.
[42] Built at Middlesbrough for Elder, Dempster & Co, just over 443 feet long, and weighing 5,440 gross tons, she was launched on 17 Jun 1897.
[43] *Robert Loraine. Actor, Soldier, Airman*, pp.27-28.
[44] *The Montgomeryshire Yeomanry*, p.63.
[45] Critten was born at Southwold, Suffolk, at the end of 1877. A tall man at 6' 3½", he enlisted at Newtown on 6 Jan 1900, and was discharged at Gosport on 13 Jun 1901. He died in the Transvaal, South Africa, in 1962.
[46] www.samilitaryhistory.org.

The men were also suffering, usually for only a day or two, from their inoculations. The *Montrose* steamed on, "crossing the line" (the Equator) on 26 March. Though no men had died, by the end of 30 March the M.I.Y. had lost three horses, 'these dying of pneumonia', out of a total of nine horses that had perished.[47]

It is likely that conditions aboard the *Montrose* were no different to other ships. 7448 Trooper Harry William Blackburne, West Kent Imperial Yeomanry, was on the transport-ship *Cymric*: 'After the tropics were reached, the heat was terrific and it was then that the work with the horses became wellnigh unbearable. The stench was overwhelming, and all in charge of the horses were continually running to the ventilators for a breath of air.'[48]

Robbie was fortunate on the unpleasant voyage to have been recognised by the ship's Chief Engineer, a keen theatre-goer, who 'had seen him at Drury Lane and admired his father at Stoke-on-Trent long years before him. For this reason also he was to dine with the Chief every evening of the trip.'[49]

There was some excitement aboard *Montrose* when, after three weeks at sea, a damaged transport ship, the *Winkfield* (7,000 tons), was sighted. She was also making for Cape Town with forty-nine crew, 300 men and 300 horses aboard when, at 1.20 a.m. on the morning of 5 April 1900, some 80 miles north of Cape Town, she collided in fog with the RMS

Contemporary view of Cape Town from the pier, with the imposing mass of Table Mountain beyond.

---

[47] *The Montgomeryshire Yeomanry*, p.64.
[48] *Trooper to Dean*, p.7. The *Cymric*, 12,552 GRT, completed in 1898, was sunk on 8 May 1916 by the *U-20*.
[49] *Robert Loraine. Actor, Soldier, Airman*, p.55.

Mexican (4,668 gross tons) which was heading north and which had left Table Bay on 4 April with 102 passengers, 142 crew and mail. With attempts to plug the hole in the *Mexican*'s side proving futile, all, bar the captain and a skeleton crew, were transferred to the *Winkfield* as their ship continued to fill with water. The *Mexican* was abandoned later in the day, and sank soon afterwards. The *Winkfield*, though herself badly damaged, managed to limp into Table Bay, Cape Town (Kapstaad), early on the morning of 6 April,[50] the *Montrose* dropping anchor there on the same day.

As there were no vacant berths in the Cape Town docks, it was not until the morning of Sunday, 8 April 1900, that the *Montrose* was able to disembark the troops and their horses. Making their way to Maitland Camp, some five miles away, the men found conditions to be poor, as noted by Harry Blackburne: 'Twelve soldiers slept at night in each bell-tent, with saddles for pillows. There was no room to move…'. The long-suffering horses, however, 'very weak after the voyage, were well fed and gently exercised.'[51]

Claude Jarvis wrote that at Maitland the M.I.Y. 'were issued with the remainder of our horses. We had brought from England about half the mounts we required… the horses we received were lamentable.'[52] Lamentable, too, was the very bad treatment of horses throughout the early stages of this Boer war, especially so as the horse was such a vital part of the strategic fighting.[53]

A sight that would have been familiar to the M.I.Y. – 14th Hussars leaving Maitland Camp, 1900 (the right half of a stereoscopic pair by Underwood & Underwood, courtesy National Army Museum, Study Collection, NAM. 1998-01-135-65).

The Boer *commandos*, as their fighting units were called, also relied heavily on the horse, as it allowed them to execute surprise attacks on the British columns at a time and place of their own choosing. One way to counter these tactics was for the British to use their own cavalry against them but, as Claude Jarvis says, the mounted yeomanry had, at first, no idea how to operate their horses, burdening the poor creatures with so much baggage that they developed 'swollen and throbbing withers', which put them 'out

---

[50] The *Winkfield* would eventually be struck from *Lloyds Register* in 1912.
[51] *Trooper to Dean*, p.8.
[52] *Half a Life*, p.73.
[53] 'Ultimately £22 million was spent on horses for the British Army in South Africa, or about one-tenth of the cost of the war.' *The Mounted Troops of the British Army*, p.227.

of action for at least three months and probably for the rest of the war.'⁵⁴ The regular Cavalry regiments, too, proved to be just as inexperienced in the treatment of their horses.

It was possibly while at Maitland Camp that Robbie met his old friend Dr. James Purves-Stewart, the two having become close friends a couple of years earlier. Having left his practice at 133 Harley Street, London, Purves-Stewart was now physician to the Imperial Yeomanry Field Hospital in South Africa: 'One night Green and I rode across to Maitland camp, several miles on the other side of Capetown .... On our way back we happened to pass through the lines of the Montgomeryshire Yeomanry. I halted haphazard before a tent and called for information about trooper Loraine. By an extraordinary coincidence Robert Loraine emerged from that very tent and sprang to the salute. I secured permission from his commanding officer to take him out a few nights later, to spend a joyous evening in Capetown.'⁵⁵

During the voyage to South Africa, Robbie had formed a low opinion of the commanding officer of the Gun Section: 'This officer knew nothing whatever about machine guns which were a hobby with Trooper Loraine.'⁵⁶ By the time that the *Montrose* had reached Cape Town, Robbie had decided to transfer from the Gun Section to the 49th Company itself.

Robbie's opinion of this officer, Lieutenant E.E. Hutton, is unfortunate, for the poor man, certainly doing his best, fell victim to the deadly enteric (typhoid) fever, 'a systemic disease characterized by fever and abdominal pain', usually caused by contaminated water or fecal contamination. The 49th Company was not to escape it: 'On May 31st [1900] the 49th left Bloemfontein with its terrible enteric – 75 deaths in one day – and marched with the West Riding Regiment to Vet River. Lieutenant E.E. Hutton of the gun section, with two men of the 49th, were left in hospital, and Lieutenant G. Pritchard Rayner and six men sickened on the march. The former [Pritchard-Rayner] died on July 1st at the Volks Hospital, Bloemfontein, while Lieutenant Hutton and the others were invalided home.'⁵⁷

Claude Jarvis, adamant that their inoculations on board the *Montrose* had not been 'particularly efficacious', went on to say that 'when there was a suggestion, about a year later, that we should be inoculated a second time, there was a partial mutiny, and the greater part of the Squadron flatly refused to undergo the treatment.'⁵⁸

◆ ◆ ◆

---

⁵⁴ *Half a Life*, p.75.
⁵⁵ *The Life of Robert Loraine*, p.35. Sir James Purves-Stewart. KCMG, CB, MB, CM Edin (1894), MA, MD, FRCP (1906), 20 Nov 1869–14 Jun 1949.
⁵⁶ *Robert Loraine. Actor, Soldier, Airman*, p.58.
⁵⁷ *The Montgomeryshire Yeomanry*, p.64.
⁵⁸ *Half a Life*, p. 79.

The memorial clock tower, Llangefni.

George Pritchard-Rayner,[59] born on 23 June 1872, was commissioned second lieutenant in the Montgomeryshire Yeomanry Cavalry with effect from 8 May 1895, and lieutenant in June 1897. As he had lived at Trescawen, Llangwyllog, Anglesey, a clock-tower was erected in his memory in Bulkeley Square, Llangefni, two or three miles from Llangwyllog.

Ernest Edward Hutton, "Gentleman", was appointed second lieutenant in the Denbighshire (Hussars) Yeomanry Cavalry on 6 February 1900. On the same day he was appointed 'Machine Gun Commander, with the temporary rank of Lieutenant in the Army. Dated 7th February, 1900.' (*The London Gazette*, 6 Feb 1900). On 16 February 1900 he was 'seconded for service with the Imperial Yeomanry', and within a matter of days was in charge of the 49th's Gun Section. (In these circumstances, it is hardly surprising that Hutton 'knew nothing whatever about machine guns.')

Hutton survived his fever, and by early 1902 was a major (temporary) and second-in-command of the recently-raised Imperial Yeomanry's 36th Battalion (159th, 160th, 161st, 162nd Companies). He returned to South Africa early in 1902, before leaving the Army on

---

[59] George's hyphenated surname was the result of his father, on his marriage, adding his wife's name of Rayner.

3 February 1903: 'Temporary Major E. E. Hutton relinquishes his Commission and is granted the honorary rank of Major in the Army, with permission to wear the uniform of the Corps.' (*The London Gazette*, 10 March 1903).

Born in Haverfordwest, Pembrokeshire in 1878, Major Ernest Edward Hutton died on 28 February 1944 in West Summerland, British Columbia, Canada.

◆ ◆ ◆

After Hutton had fallen ill with enteric fever, the senior NCO of the Gun Section, Sergeant S.A. Stirton, requested Robbie's return. Samuel Alexander Stirton, an "old soldier" born in 1866, enlisted in the Royal Artillery aged 15 as a Trumpeter. Re-mustering as a Gunner in 1884, he served in India until January 1893, when he returned home. On 12 September 1901 he was court-martialled for 'Drunkenness and on duty' and suffered a 'Reduction in rank'.

A list compiled in 1901 (see the Roll below) shows that at some point the Gun Section comprised the following NCO's and Other Ranks (listed as privates, not troopers), and that Robbie had been made-up to lance-corporal:

8244 Sergeant S.A. Stirton; 8280 Sergeant C.F. Trippe; 9962 Lance-Corporal E.L.C. Blythe; 8175 Lance-Corporal R. Loraine; 8164 Private A.G. Bolingbroke; 8254 Private C. Bridges; 8197 Private T.E. Charlton; 8235 Private F. Featherstone; 9961 Private A.J. Harris; 15307 Private T. Hubbard; 8202 Private S.H. Lemon; 8178 Private H. Rait; 8179 Private W.H. Smith; 8246 Private C. Sullivan; 8180 Private J.M. Taylor; 8279 Private P. Thornton; 9963 Private J.O. Walcot.[60]

Two men not listed on the Roll below – Private J. Clarke and 8238 Private J.H. Gibb – also served with the machine guns.[61]

◆ ◆ ◆

---

[60] Walcot went to South Africa with the 49th Company on 17 March 1900, serving with them until 6 February 1901. Later Lance-Sergeant. On 7 February he transferred to the Army Service Corps, remaining with them until the cessation of hostilities. Commissioned 2nd Lt. TNA file WO 100/357.

[61] Regimental numbers of individuals (inc. Robbie's elevation to lance-corporal) are taken from the Roll dated 9 July 1901 of the men of the 31st Machine Gun Section, 9th Battalion, who were entitled to wear the Queen's South Africa Medal and Clasps [TNA file WO 100/124]. See also *The Montgomeryshire Yeomanry*, p.132.

Extract from the Roll of the men of the 31st Machine Gun Section, 9th Battalion, who were entitled to wear the South Africa Medal and Clasps, signed by Lt-Col. G. Wentworth Forbes aboard HMT Roslin Castle. Note that Robbie is the only one of this group entitled to the Wittebergen Clasp, that he was not entitled to the Orange Free State clasp and that he was 'Invalided Dec 1900'. [TNA file WO 100/124]

Left: The gas-operated, belt-fed, air-cooled Colt-Browning, here being demonstrated by Canadian soldiers who nicknamed it the "Potato Digger" because of dirt and debris it kicked-up as it fired; right: the Dundonald "galloping carriage", seen here with a Maxim machine-gun.

The M.I.Y.'s Gun Section possessed two Colt 'quick-firing guns on galloping Dundonald carriages with ammunition waggons.'[62] The Colt gun, properly the M1895 Colt-Browning machine gun, was capable of firing 400–450 rounds per minute using the standard British .303 ammunition. The "galloping carriage" on which the gun was mounted was developed in 1900 by Douglas Cochrane, 12th Earl of Dundonald, who, in November 1899, had been appointed Commander of the Mounted Brigade, part of the South Natal Field Force. These mobile, seated carriages were unofficially, and privately, purchased by the commanding officers of some Volunteer Battalions.[63]

♦ ♦ ♦

As there was little work for the guns, Robbie once again rejoined his squadron, where he asked for another transfer, 'into Robert's Horse, Kitchener's Horse, or the Kaffrarian Rifles.' It is probable that this transfer never happened. Robbie did, however, spend some of his time in a section of four, an optimum size for messing purposes as it would prove. Making-up the foursome were Claude Jarvis and, probably, 8193 Private Percy Trevelyan Lemon and 8176 Private Frank Harvey Murray.

In his book *Half a Life* Jarvis gives Percy Lemon the name Waller, describing him as 'a Canadian cowboy' who 'was to be exact a Canadian by choice, for he had been born in England and had gone to the Dominion as a very young man to farm'. Percy Lemon was born on 21 August 1872 at Sherborne, Dorset, England, but had emigrated to Brandon, Manitoba, Canada, where he became a farmer. Rallying to the call, he sailed on the SS

---

[62] *The Montgomeryshire Yeomanry*, p.60.
[63] www.reddit.com; www.heritage-images.com.

Germanic from New York to Liverpool in November 1899 and enlisted in the 31st Company in London on 28 December 1899. Passing his medical examination at Welshpool on 16 January 1900, he joined the 31st at Newtown. Robbie was a big man for those days, but Percy was more than his equal, at 5' 11½" tall and 180 lbs.[64] He was a sergeant when discharged on termination of service on 15 July 1901 with the Queen's South Africa medal and the three commonest clasps to his name – Transvaal; Orange Free State; Cape Colony. Returning to Canada, he died there on 14 April 1939.[65]

Claude Jarvis remembers Frank Murray as a 'bookmaker's clerk', who 'hailed from Brighton, ex London Town' and was 'a most versatile and amusing little cockney'. Born in Peckham, London, 22-year-old Frank Murray had been, prior to enlisting, a horse-dealer from Hove while his father, Edwin, had once been a Turf Accountant. Though barely 5' 7" tall, Frank weighed a hefty 161 lbs. when he arrived at Newtown on 3 January 1900. He was discharged at Wrexham on 15 July 1901, his duty done, also with the Queen's South Africa medal and the three commonest clasps to his name. Little is known of his subsequent life, or death, though a man of his name died in Brighton in early 1922.

As for 8201 Private Claude Scudamore Jarvis, author of *Half a Life*, he was born in Forest Gate, Essex on 20 July 1879. He stood 5' 6½" tall and weighed a trim 130 lbs. on enlistment on 1 January 1900. According to his Records, he saw action at Prinsloo's Surrender (30 July 1900), Hammond's Kraal (20 August 1900), and Warmbad (August/September 1900).[66]

Discharged at his own request on 5 July 1901 he returned to military service with a commission in the Dorsetshire Regiment in 1902, ending his career as Major C.S. Jarvis CMG, OBE and Governor of Sinai for thirteen years. He died in Ringwood, Hampshire, on 8 December 1953.

It is unclear for how long the four remained together. Records show that only Robbie and Claude were entitled to the Wittebergen Clasp to the Queen's South Africa Medal (see photo on page 46 below): 'A clasp inscribed "Wittebergen" will be granted to all troops who were inside a line drawn from Harrismith to Bethlehem, thence to Senekal and Clocolan, along the Basuto border, and back to Harrismith, between July 1st and 29th, 1900, both dates inclusive.' This operation in July 1900 was part of "the great De Wet hunt", an attempt by the British to capture the eminent Boer general Christian de Wet.

Earlier, the M.I.Y. had reached Bloemfontein on 28 May 1900, as Lord Roberts moved his troops forward in an attempt to reach the east coast and thereby cut-off sea-borne

---

[64] Robert stood 5' 10" tall and weighed 164 lbs. on enlistment.
[65] See *Half a Life*, pp.92, 96-7.
[66] Erskine Childers wrote in his diary: 'August 17. (2 p.m.) We are halted to feed... Later on we went into action but never fired... The Wilts and Montgomery Yeomanry are with us' – *In the Ranks of the C.I.V.*, pp.211-2.

supplies to the Boers. Unfortunately, under Piet de Wet, younger brother of Christian, the Boers attacked the British lines of supply, and in the process captured many hundreds of men of the 13th Yeomanry.

Now, though the M.I.Y. were raring to get into action, their commander, Lieutenant-Colonel H. B. Howard, 'twice disobeyed a direct order from his commanding officer, General George Pretyman.[67] Howard said he could not proceed until his battalion was complete. After the men under his command had sent a petition to Roberts, asking to be brought forward immediately, Howard was ordered once more to bring his troops up. This time he claimed his horses were unfit. The horses had actually been loaded onto the train when Howard ordered them taken off again. The Montgomeryshires were therefore struck off Lord Roberts's list of useful troops, a great disappointment to Howard's men.

Robbie's work for the time being involved, as he explained, 'riding with dispatches to the different camps. I am on duty twenty-four hours of the day.' Detached to serve as a "galloper" (dispatch rider or messenger) to the acting brigadier, Colonel Lloyd, 'a splendid fellow', he could be sent wherever needed. Conditions were harsh and, up at a place called Welgelegen, Robbie and others of his troop were 'on duty, scouting and patrolling for three days and two nights with about four hours' sleep all told… Then I took a turn in the trenches and lay for hours and hours in burning sun and soaking rain alternately… We stayed on patrolling the surrounding country for some weeks and then were ordered to rejoin the Squadron at Vet River.'[68]

Keeping healthy on active service in the *veldt* was to prove difficult, with some forty per cent of Robbie's squadron going down with enteric fever or dysentery: 'One officer and five men out of the Squadron have died. Although we have done little fighting, we have great hardships to endure: days and nights in the pouring rain with no tents, lying at night in the mud with a blanket round you which freezes stiff as soon as the rain ceases; or at sundown, on top of a blazing hot day, experiencing a sudden drop in temperature of 30 degrees. Short rations and bad water have also played havoc.'[69]

With the war rumbling on, the M.I.Y. 'were peremptorily summoned once more to join the Field Marshal's column.' After laagering on Pretoria's racecourse, the Regiment formed "flying squads" of mounted cavalry to assist the foot soldiers flogging their way further north into the Transvaal. It was arduous work, with 'ceaseless fighting and sniping in mountain fastnesses round Lyndenburg; in gruelling shell and rifle-fire at Warmbad…' Nor was twenty continuous hours in the saddle uncommon.

---

[67] Coincidentally, when serving on No. 3 Squadron in France in late 1914 during the First World War, Robert would fly as an observer with George Frederick Pretyman, son of Maj-Gen. Sir George Tindal Pretyman.
[68] *Robert Loraine. Actor, Soldier, Airman*, pp.61-2.
[69] *Robert Loraine. Actor, Soldier, Airman*, p.62.

Imperial Rest Camp, Durban.

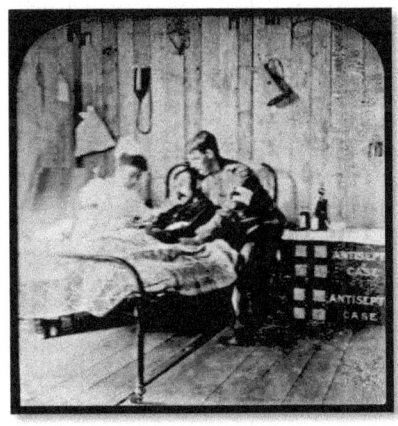

A poor-quality photograph, the right half of a stereo pair, whose caption reads: 'The last message home – a scene at the Orange River Hospital, South Africa'. If nothing else, it shows the basic, but caring, treatment available in 1900.

The Montgomeryshires were still in the thick of it when, one day in the autumn of 1900, Bob Loraine (not Robbie now) and another trooper, with three Boer prisoners in tow, came upon a farm flying a white flag, and stopped for a drink. Bob was handed some water by a Dutch girl: 'He was used to bad water, Heaven knows, but not to whatever it was the Dutch girl put into that drink.'[70] It was enough, though, to put Bob into the Imperial Branch Yeomanry Hospital at Eastwood, Arcadia, Pretoria.

When well enough, Bob was put aboard a hospital ship at Durban, his fighting done – for a few years at least – and sailed for England on 15 November 1900.

For his services, Robert was awarded the Queen's South Africa Medal, with three bars: Wittebergen, Transvaal, and Cape Colony.

---

[70] *Robert Loraine. Actor, Soldier, Airman*, p.68.

Queen's Medal, with three Bars: Wittebergen; Transvaal; Cape Colony. The medal shown here, for illustrative purposes, was awarded to 5421 Private J. Sissons, 2 East Yorks Regt. For photo of Robert's medal see page 267.

Bob had played a large part in silencing two Boer gun batteries in an action at Sand River in June 1900 and, on another occasion, carrying messages between Colonels Baden-Powell and Plumer, had ridden 'all night long across a shadowless plain under the moon.' He 'arrived at G.H.Q. at dawn with two bullet holes through his helmet, and a bullet and three sizzle tracks in the coat on the saddle strapped behind him.'[71]

He later told a reporter from *Era* that, after 'unjamming a machine-gun in action… and so repulsing an enemy attack', he 'was promoted to be a corporal…' Although his Army record shows no such promotion, the Roll of members of the 31st Machine Gun Section (see page 41) lists him as lance-corporal, presumably following an unofficial promotion in the field. Records, however, show that on 13 January 1901 he was 'Discharged at his own request from further services in connection with the war in S. Africa', and, on 30 July 1901, was paid a War Gratuity as a Private. He had officially served for one year and seventeen days – seventy-six days at Home (28 December 1899 to 13 March 1900), two hundred and forty-six in South Africa (including travel there), and sixty at Home (15 November 1900 to 13 January 1901, including time at sea on his return).

Listed on his M.I.Y. papers are the "campaigns" in which he participated: Slabbert's Nek; Retieff's Nek; Wonderboom; Pyramids; Uitspan; Waterval; Pienaar's River; Warm Baths [sic – Warmbad].

Long after Robert had left for home. the 31st and 49th Companies (and Gun Section) were withdrawn to Cape Town on 2 June and 23 May 1901 respectively. Both companies had reached Southampton, England, on 8 July 1901 and were back in Wales two days later. They were shortly afterwards disbanded at Ruabon.

---

[71] *Robert Loraine. Actor, Soldier, Airman*, p.57.

Casualties among the officers and men of the 31st Company were slight – thirty-seven sick, and five wounded. The 49th, on the other hand, suffered thirty-nine sick, sixteen wounded, and eight dead (killed or died of wounds or fever, details where known):[72]
Lieutenant G. Pritchard Rayner (see page 38); 8306 Lance Corpl. J.R. Pryse – died 19 August 1900, Onderste Spruit; 15309 Lance Corpl. Charles B. Sells – died 22 January 1901, Deelfontein; Private W. Wilkie – transferred to the Pretoria Police; 1258 Constable Wilkie (died 15 January 1901?); 8347 Private E.D. Ford – died 20 January 1901, Pretoria; 8399 Private G.D. Verrall – died 28 December 1900, Pretoria, having transferred to the Transvaal Constabulary as 1263 Constable Verrall; 15322 Private T. Riley – died 23 September 1900, Deelfontein; Private E.T. Campbell – not found.

Even though, overall, the men of the two companies had fought in over sixty actions and had trekked over 3,000 miles, awards to them were few. Two NCOs of the 31st were each awarded the DCM and were MiD. In the 49th, one NCO and one private were awarded the DCM (the latter also being MiD), another private was MiD, and Sergeant Trippe of the Gun Section was also MiD. Robbie's name was not among them.

---

[72] Names from *The Montgomeryshire Yeomanry*, p.70.

Chapter Three: Aviator

Back on "Civvy Street". Free of the Army, Robert was offered a two-season's theatre engagement in New York by the American entrepreneur Daniel Frohman. Sailing "Saloon" class for the USA on the SS *Oceanic* on 16 January 1901, he made his stage debut there on 4 March 1901 as Ralph Percy in *To Have and to Hold* at the Academy of Music, Baltimore. Returning from New York on the SS *St. Louis*, he was back in England on 22 May 1901, only to find that his wife, Julie, was suing him for divorce.

Divorce. In her Petition, filed on 26 July 1901, Julie stated that Robert had 'deserted her for two years and upwards without reasonable excuse.' She added, for good measure, that Robert had committed adultery, on or about 16 July 1901, 'with a woman whose name is unknown' at the Louis le Grand Hotel, Rue Louis le Grand, in the 2eme arrondissement, Paris. Whether or not he was indeed in Paris on this day was irrelevant, the legal niceties being duly observed anyway, and due process took its course – Setting Down Cause on 2 May 1902; Decree Nisi on 16 June 1902; and the Final Decree (Absolute) signed on 18 December 1902.

Left: '"Women were made to / love! Every one of us!" / "Pretty Peggy" / Robert Loraine / October 1904'.
Right; Signed promotional card for Man & Superman, Criterion Theatre.

Wasting no time, Julie married the British actor William Faversham on 29 December 1902, which came as no surprise to those in the know in "theatreland". Rumour had it that they were "an item" back in 1901, and Faversham's wife had procured her divorce in February 1902.[73]

Robert's acting career would flourish not only in England but also back in the USA where, in 1902-03, he played the part of David Garrick 'in *Pretty Peggy*, a play by Frances Aymar

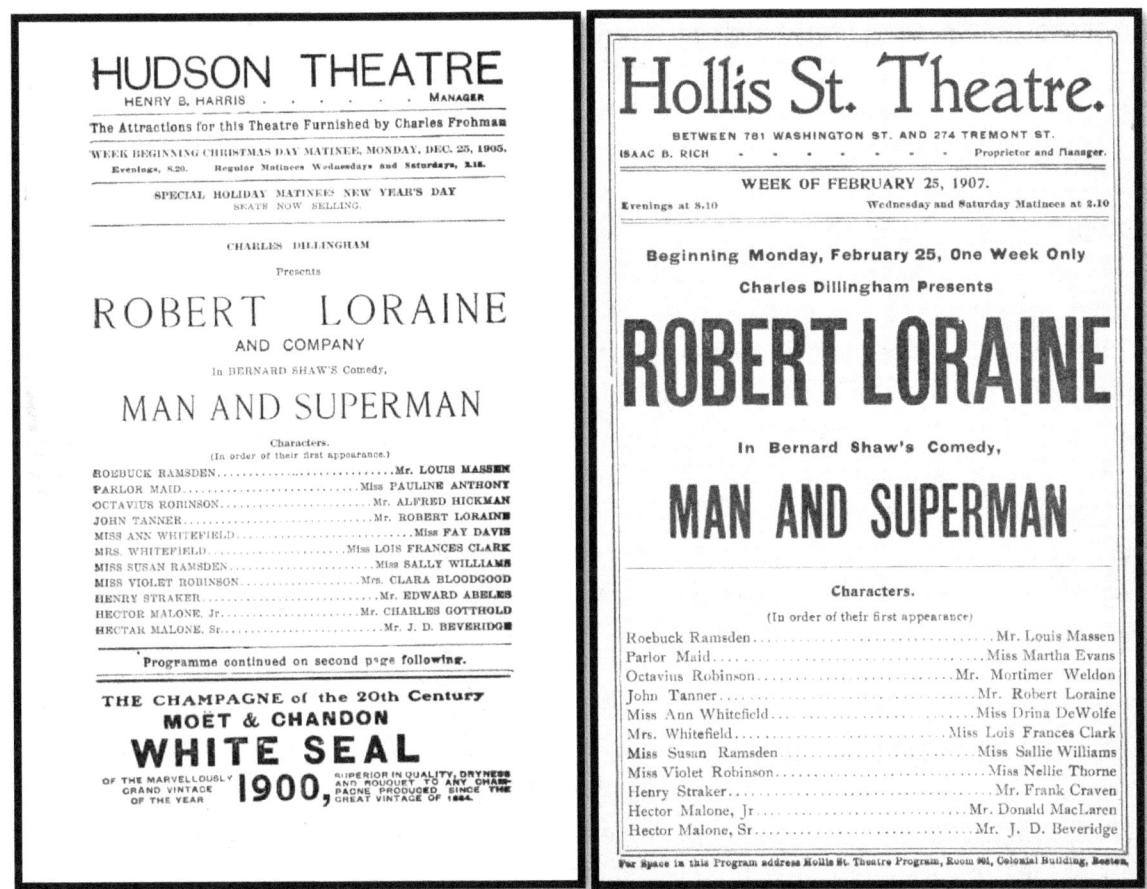

(Left) Hudson Theatre, New York programme December 1905; (Right) Hollis Street Theatre, Boston, programme, February 1907. In both there was this disclaimer: 'Mr. Loraine regrets that it is not in his power to present the entire play contained in Mr. Bernard Shaw's published volume, "Man and Superman". It has been found desirable to omit the purely episodical third act and the long retrospective passage in the first, neither of which affects the comedy. The reason for this curtailment is the great length of the published play which would occupy nearly seven hours in the performance...'

---

[73] *The Life of Robert Loraine*, p.51. Julie died aged 50 following a botched operation on 9 Apr 1921.

Matthews loosely based on the life of Peg Woffington and her romance with David Garrick.'[74]

Still not satisfied with his lot, though, he 'was desperately considering some other way of making a living when, on a train journey from Boston to New York', he read George Bernard Shaw's 1903 *Man and Superman*. So convinced was he of its merits, not least for its monetary value as a stage production, that he pressed hard for its production in the United States.

But it wasn't until he was once again back in England that his luck changed, and the Shaw play was produced in London. He returned to the USA, again on the *Oceanic*, arriving in New York on 29 June 1905. *Man and Superman* opened on 4 September 1905 at the Hudson Theatre, and was a huge success, breaking box-office records within a few weeks. It ran until February 1906, when 'Robert took the show on the road. First, they went to Washington, DC, then to Brooklyn, then back to the Hudson for a week, then on to Philadelphia, and then to Boston.'[75]

Robert found time to return to England on the *Baltic*, arriving at Liverpool on 14 June 1906. He went back to the USA on the SS *Rijndam*, arriving at New York on 20 August 1906. *Man and Superman* opened at Boston's Hollis Street Theatre in February 1907. Of the eleven members of the cast from the Hudson Theatre in December 1905, only Robert and four others "survived" to play in Boston fourteen months later.

Robert returned to London in May 1907, again to play John Tanner in *Man and Superman*, a part that would earn him the huge fortune of £40,000 (over £5½ million in today's money). [*£1 at this time would be worth around £145 today, 2023*].

Aviator. Robert's first close encounter with things aerial came in 1906, before the aeroplane had truly made its mark. His friend George Bernard Shaw, wishing to find out for himself what ballooning was all about, hired the balloon *Norfolk* from Percival Green Spencer (1864–1913), who would be its pilot, and invited Robert to join him on 3 July 1906 at the Wandsworth Gas Works, where the balloon was filled with the necessary lifting agent. With them were Mrs. Cholmondeley (Shaw's sister) and Harley Granville Barker (1877–1946), the eminent literary figure and actor. Shaw had decided not to tell his wife about the trip until afterwards, because he thought it would make her nervous! After their flight 'Robert was captivated'[76] and Percival Spencer issued a certificate to Shaw which confirmed that he had ascended in the *Norfolk* from Wandsworth and, having been in the

---

[74] *The Life of Robert Loraine*, p.54.
[75] *The Life of Robert Loraine*, p.72.
[76] *Wonder Aces of the Air*, p.22.

(Left) Robert Loraine (in car) and Fay Davis, 1905. (Right) poster of a 40hp Fiat used in the 1911 production of Man & Superman at the Criterion Theatre, London

Left: The balloon Norfolk being filled at Wandsworth, 3 July 1906; right: Robert (in white coat) and Mrs. Cholmondeley, in the foreground (photos courtesy the Loraine family, via Richard Holleyman).

The village of Llanbedr.

air for two and a half hours, at a maximum altitude of 9,000 feet, had landed at Chobham Place, Surrey.[77]

In July 1907 George Bernard Shaw and his wife Charlotte went to live near the sea at Hafod y Bryn, Llanbedr, between Harlech and Barmouth, North Wales.

Robert joined them, driving up from London 'in the Maxwell automobile he had bought in the United States.'[78] On 2 August the two men were out for a walk. As it was Shaw's wont to regularly bathe in Tremadog Bay, they decided to go for a swim even though, there having been a storm during the night, the sea was rough. Once in the water, they made their way past the first line of crashing waves, heading further out, without at first realising that the tide was dragging them further away from the shore. Now, appreciating the danger, they started to swim back, but so tired and helpless did Robert become that he was all for giving up. Suddenly, his foot touched a rock: 'Miraculously I found myself standing on solid ground... We had struck a sandbank or possibly an old causeway. I staggered ashore and flopped onto the sand gasping. Shaw came to land side by side with me.'[79]

'When we had enough breath to talk, Shaw said "That was a narrow shave," and I said "Yes." After another interval of deep breathing, we asked each other what our feelings were as we were in the throes of dissolution. For we had both been very close to death.

---

[77] Copy of said certificate supplied to author by Richard Holleyman, via research of Lannie Liggera.
[78] The Life of Robert Loraine, p.86.
[79] Robert Loraine. Actor, Soldier, Airman, p.94.

'We had felt all the pangs and sensations that we should if we had drowned, and our next stage would have been unconsciousness. To all intents and purposes, we had experienced death by drowning.'[80]

(Left) Henry Farman; (right) Could Robert be one of those cheering Henry Farman's arrival in his Voisin-Farman I aircraft at Issy-les-Moulineaux on 13 January 1908? Farman had just completed a circular, one kilometre, course in 1 minute 28 seconds to win the Grand Prix de l'Aviation, a prize of 50,000 FF, which had been offered by Henri Deutsch in 1904.

Later that year, wanting a rest from acting, Robert went to Paris, not only to learn French but to talk to Frenchmen about aviation, France at the time being the cradle of this new sport. In January 1908 he watched Henry Farman[81] fly a powered heavier-than-air machine, a Voisin aeroplane, at Issy-les-Moulineaux, near Paris. So excited was he that, there and then, he ordered an aeroplane the same as Farman's: 'It was to have been delivered in ten months' time, but had never arrived.'[82]

The year 1908 proved to be a busy one for Robert, several plays coming his way, among them *Bellamy the Magnificent*, which also featured Sir Charles Wyndham. At the end of the year, as if to confirm his position in society, Robert was initiated as a Freemason into the Green Room Lodge, No. 2957, on 4 December 1908.

Then, one day in early July 1909, Robert appeared, unannounced, at George Smart's lodgings in London, as George recalled: 'I had just eaten my breakfast roll and butter and had sat down to cudgel my brains preparatory to my morning's work, and I had better confess it here at the start of things, my work consists in the writing of fiction – fiction in all its forms, and I regret to say, at scarcely any remuneration. The abrupt entrance of

---

[80] From the article *On Facing Death*, written by Robert, date unknown, via Richard Holleyman.
[81] Henry Farman (26 May 1874–17 Jul 1958) was born in Paris to an English father and French mother.
[82] George Smart quoted in Robert Loraine. Actor, Soldier, Airman, p.101.

A scene from Bellamy the Magnificent, at the New Theatre: Charles Wyndham centre, Robert far right

Robert dragged my mind back from its desperate gropings. I rubbed my eyes. Robert Loraine stood before me – clothed, shaved and full of some suppressed excitement – and that at half past nine in the morning, an hour of the day with which he had scarcely a bowing acquaintance. Also, he was looking at me in an intense, queer way that made me draw my dressing gown more closely around me, to hide the fact that my pyjamas proclaimed the unmarketable quality of my fiction.

'Robert is successful and rich, which invariably makes me feel rather envious when I meet him. He strode across the room, fixing me firmly with his eyes and blurted it out.

'"I am going to fly", he snapped.

'I beg your pardon?

'I endeavoured surreptitiously to pinch myself into a state of wakefulness.

'"I have made up my mind to fly", he repeated.

'Quite so – quite so', I said soothingly.

'"But you don't understand", he said petulantly, "I am going to buy an aeroplane at once."'

(Robert had, of course, made a fortune from *Man and Superman*.)

'Then I grasped it and began immediately to speak words of admiration and encouragement.'

'This was the early summer of 1909, remember, and although a few people had flown a little, aviation was hardly regarded seriously, in England at any rate… Robert had, however, acquired the fever even in those early days and he proceeded to rap out his plans. He would go round the English firms of constructors. Not a long journey as there were only two of them, and then he would go to France. He would see everything, and finally he would buy the very best and latest thing in aeroplanes. The very best and latest is usually almost good enough for Robert.

'And what about your work?' I expostulated.

'"Oh, that's all right", he answered carelessly.'[83]

George tried to dissuade Robert from this venture, but Robert's enthusiasm took him to Sangatte, near Calais, France, to be with Louis Blériot and Hubert Latham, both of whom were hoping to be the first to fly across the English Channel. Robert was there when Latham in an Antoinette went first, on 19 July 1909. Unluckily, his engine failed and he came down into the English Channel, where he was picked-up by the French torpedo-boat destroyer *Harpon*.

Blériot, waiting for calmer weather to make his cross-Channel flight, suffered an accident on 23 July, which left him on crutches. Despite this handicap, he was determined to fly and, two days later, when the weather was suitably calm, Robert 'watched him disappear in the haze and then drove to the abandoned Channel Tunnel building at Sangatte, where a wireless receiver had been set up.' Then came the news that Blériot had made history: 'The crossing of the English Channel by M. Blériot on [Sunday] July 25th, 1909, marks an epoch in Aviation and in the history of the twentieth century. M. Blériot, who has achieved the marvellous feat of flying across the Channel, completing a distance of 31 miles in 43 minutes.'

Following his cross-Channel success, Louis Blériot opened a flying school in November 1909 at Pont-Long, eight kilometres or so from Pau in the south-west of France. Blériot himself suggested to Robert that he should go to Pont-Long to see what flying machines were on offer, and also to learn to fly.

Robert announced to George Smart that he was going to Pau. George appears to have been confused as to when, precisely, Robert told him this: 'It was towards the end of April [*sic* – Robert was in Pau by early March] that the day arrived when he could contain himself no longer. We were in Surrey on a certain golf course which is as precious for its beautiful surroundings as it is for the spitefulness of its hazards, and the day was just one

---

[83] From *Flights and Fancies*, via Richard Holleyman; by kind permission of the Loraine family.

Calais / Baraques. 'The Aero Club of France / has erected this monument / to commemorate / the first crossing of the Channel / in an aeroplane / by / Louis Blériot / on 25 July 1909 / Les Baraques – Dover'

of those where the golden sunshine of spring seemed to dance and effervesce and get into one's blood like champagne.'

'Robert always considers himself as about to drive on to the green, when he stands on the tee, quite regardless of the fact that the hole may be six hundred yards long. Mentally he tells himself firmly that it is not possible to do otherwise than drive on to the green. It is a principle with him and he can produce numberless excellent arguments in its favour. But on this occasion the method had worked singularly unsuccessfully. I knew that the only chance of a contest lay in the hope that he would lose his temper and thereby concentrate a little more on the business in hand, and after he had driven three balls in succession out of bounds, at the fifth hole my hopes rose high. But this was the moment he chose to turn on me with his eyes blazing.

'"Tomorrow I am going to Pau," he said.'

'"I am going to learn to fly – at the Blériot school – I ordered a machine last year – it is ready now – and I have contracted to be taught."

'I gasped. He gazed at the blue sky and the scudding cotton-wool clouds, and continued, half to himself. "Yes, by this time next week, I expect to be flying."'[84]

Robert managed to get to Pau during the first week of March 1910, though he had only a few days in which to learn before he was due back in London for *She Stoops to Conquer*.

Robert wrote that when he arrived at the school for training pilots near Pau, he 'found the procedure for the pupils somewhat leisurely' for his needs, as he had 'only six days to spare from the London theatre where I was acting but was resolved to accomplish a flight before I left.'

'The Blériot school was equipped with some half-dozen machines of similar type to the one in which he had flown the Channel, a small single-seater monoplane with an air cooled three-cylinder radial Anzani engine giving perhaps 25 h.p.'

Robert (left) and unknown golfing companion; date and place also unknown [photo courtesy Rob Schmidt]

---

[84] *Flights and Fancies*. By kind permission of Richard Holleyman.

The flying school at Pont-Long, c.1910.

Also present at Pau were fellow would-be aviators W.D. McArdle, Armstrong Drexel, Oscar Morison and Graham Gilmour: 'Morison was a fine sight, rushing his machine down the course with chin stuck out and pipe at an aggressive angle, eyes flashing, clearly feeling and angrily resenting at being confined to the to earth much longer than he thought necessary.

'But these men had more time to spend than I had.'

Robert also wrote about his experiences at Pau in a 1925 article headed *Flying for Fun / Thrills and Marvels of the Air*: 'When I learned to fly in 1910 at the Blériot School at Pau there was no dual control, no clear instruction, no reliable instructional machine. Very briefly and perfunctorily the pupil was shown the working of the controls and the use of the throttle and switch, and, having grasped this (or not as the case may be), he was given a push and turned loose with orders to drive about on his wheels till he could steer straight.

'In order that he should not blunder inadvertently into the air, the central lever, otherwise the cloche or "joy stick," was tied well forward. So he rushed around like a decapitated chicken until he flopped sideways – probably with one wing-tip broken. Soon, however, he would acquire the necessary trick to keep her straight, and then he steered her up and down the aerodrome, still on the ground, with her tail up, all ready to jump into the air but for the cloche being tied in the forward position. After several days or weeks of this practice the restraining cord was removed and the budding aviator made a hop; later he would fly round the aerodrome, and, if his engine lasted for three circuits (which was very unusual), he was given his brevet or ticket and was a pilot *aviateur*.

'After a few days of this ground steering, I felt that time was flying but I was not, so in the seclusion of a distant part of the aerodrome I stopped the machine and unknotted the cord that held the cloche forward – now I was free, or so I thought. I opened the throttle and raced along the ground, and when I judged my speed sufficient I pulled back on the cloche. She should have risen – but she did not. I was greatly puzzled. I now know that the old, worn-out engine on that particular machine would not give power enough to get a kite off the ground. And the tying forward of the cloche was as unnecessary a precaution as it would be to tie an ostrich's head back to keep it from flying. Next day I was at the school before dawn and bribed the mechanic in charge to let me have a newer machine. Again I untied the cloche and opened the throttle, and when I had full speed on I pulled back on the cloche with great determination and we leaped into the air. At last! I was flying! I, myself, alone; I was fulfilling an instinct so strong that it easily over-rides that other instinct of self-preservation which is said to be the foremost of all our guides.

'I looked at the ground and felt like a conqueror. I looked at the sky and wanted more. More of this exaltation. More altitude; in fact. more height. Nothing simpler. I pulled back on the cloche. The machine leaped higher, so did my heart. higher still – then – paff! -

'Mr. H. D. Cutler, who is now at Pau with Mr. Morrisson's [sic] and Mr. Graham Gilmour's Blériot machines, sends us this interesting photograph of one of the many smashes to which rash pupils are subject. Mr. Lorraine [sic], acting against Blériot's advice, attempted to leave the ground before getting used to the machine on the ground. Consequently he dived from a height of 30ft. and turned over. Mr. Cutler is on the extreme right of the picture, and Mr. Morrisson [sic] next. Mr. Lorraine, in bandages, is on the left.' (The Aero, 29 March 1910). Third and fourth from the left are Drexel and McArdle, who would soon inaugurate their own flying school at East Boldre, near Beaulieu. For more on Cutler, see Appendix IV.

Other accidents at Pau

– I came to earth, having stalled and crashed. As I picked myself out of the debris, somewhat dazed from a gash on my forehead, I realised that I must cultivate a lighter hand on the joystick. But all the same... I was very contented and very happy.'[85]

After his accident on 10 March, Robert noted: 'The Blériot school not unreasonably declined to provide me with another machine when I turned up the next day, anxious to fly again, and the day after that I left Pau and returned to London and my theatrical engagements.'

After his return to London from Pau, Robert appeared in *The Rivals*, which opened on 4 April 1910. Then, with a gap in his busy acting career, he went back to France to see Henry Farman at Mourmelon-le-Grand, twenty kilometres north of Châlons-sur-Marne (today Châlons-en-Champagne), to continue his flying lessons.

Robert was also keen to purchase a Farman Racer machine – it had shorter lower planes than the standard model – but Henry assured him that there wasn't one for sale, and that none would be ready within the next twelve months. Robert, though, had already spotted a

A postcard, sent from Mourmelon-le-Grand on 13 January 1909, of Henry Farman in his No.1 flying machine. It was from there that, on 30 October 1908, he made the first powered flight from one town to another, a distance of 27 kilometres (17 miles), in twenty minutes.

---

[85] The *Daily Mail*, 8 Sep 1925, via Richard Holleyman.

likely-looking machine in a shed, took Farman over to it, and told him that *that* was the one he wanted. Not put off by Farman's reply that *that* particular machine had already been sold and was simply waiting for its owner to come and collect it, Robert managed to persuade him to part with it for a lot more than the first buyer had proffered.[86] In her biography of Robert, Winifred Loraine says that he parted with a modest £7,000 for his aeroplane.[87]

And there and then, at Mourmelon, Robert continued his flying lessons and took his 'pilot's certificate without risking damage to my own beautiful new racer'.[88] To earn his "ticket", he was required to fly 'two figures-of-eight, three landings within twenty yards of a mark, an ascent to 400 feet followed by the cutting out of the engine at 100 and a volplané to earth with the same twenty-yard margin of error.'[89] Having achieved this, the Aéro-Club de France awarded him pilot's certificate no. 126 on 21 June 1910.[90]

It was essential for the owner of an aeroplane to employ a mechanic / carpenter and so, before returning to England, Robert hired Jules Védrines (see page 15), who wrote that Robert said to him: 'Come with me.'

'With you, Mr. Loraine? Where to?'

'To England. I want you to be my mechanic.'

'Impossible!'

'Why?'

'It would be very expensive for you.'

'I'll give you 500 francs a month.'

'Peuh!'

'800.'

'I want a thousand.'[91]

And so, Robert agreed and, giving Jules his address, departed for London, telling the Frenchman to come over to his house as soon as he got to England.

Once in London, Jules decided to walk to Robert's house, rather than pay for a taxi. Losing his way, he asked a policeman for directions, only to be met with a lot of arm waving, which Jules failed to comprehend. After the policeman had repeated his

---

[86] *The Life of Robert Loraine*, note 8, p.115.
[87] *Robert Loraine. Actor, Soldier, Airman*, p.106. This must be the cost at date of the publication of her book in 1938, for in 1910 new aeroplanes, with engine, could be had for £400 or £500, equivalent today to something like £60,000 (£1 in 1910 = £117 in 2023. A year later, A. V, Roe & Co., for example, were asking £600 for a '*Biplane, new, with 30 H.P. Green engine; for passenger and cross country.*')
[88] *Robert Loraine. Actor, Soldier, Airman*, p.106.
[89] *Wonder Aces of the Air*, p.25.
[90] Had Robert flown for his brevet in England, the RAeC would have issued him with a certificate in the 14–17 range, no. 13 having been issued on 14 June 1910.
[91] *La Vie d'un aviateur*, p.129.

gesticulations several more times, Jules lost his temper and, tapped on the shoulder by the guardian of the law's truncheon, was arrested!

All was well, however, and once Jules had announced that he was a friend of Robert Loraine and also an aviator like him ('Je suis un ami de master Robert Loraine, aviateur comme lui'), the policeman said that he would escort him to Robert's house. What more could he ask? ('Qu' est-ce que je pouvais demander de plus?').[92]

Over the ensuing months, Jules would be kept very busy as Robert's mechanic and carpenter. Nevertheless, he had a high opinion of his employer: 'Loraine was very brave, very courageous, with a remarkable mind, but he had the soul of a poet and we all know that poetry and piloting are two things altogether incompatible, especially for a pupil aviator.'[93]

Now a certificated aviator, Robert was keen to make his first public appearance as a pilot, and the opportunity presented itself at the Bournemouth International Aviation Meeting, due to begin on 11 July 1910 at Southbourne, to the east of Bournemouth. He entered using the pseudonym "Jones". He was asked why Jones? 'It happened this way. When I went to Bournemouth I thought I would make a name from my initials, "R L", turning it into "Airelle", but when I saw it painted on my things I didn't like it. It seemed too foppish, so I had it painted out. I didn't know what else to adopt, so on the spur of the moment thought that the distinguished name of Jones would do as well.'[94]

Jules is tending to the Farman's engine while Robert watches on. (Flight, 23 September 1911).

Jules Védrines was sent to McArdle and Drexel's aerodrome, on Lord Montagu's estate, at Beaulieu, near Southampton, where he would find Robert's Farman biplane: 'Vous mettrez tout au point et vous m'attendrez!'[95] Essentially, just go straight there, and wait for me!

Robert was soon there, too, and made two flights, each of which ended in breakages on landing, which, of course, Védrines repaired in the shed that had been erected for the Farman's

---

[92] *La Vie d'un aviateur*, p.131.
[93] *La Vie d'un aviateur*, p.128.
[94] From an unknown source in a scrapbook of cuttings in possession of the Loraine family, via Richard Holleyman.
[95] *La Vie d'un aviateur*, p.132.

assembly. Then Robert announced that he was going to fly to Southbourne and back to Beaulieu, and shrugged away Védrines' advice that there was insufficient fuel in the tank. Needless to say, Robert was forced to land in a cornfield about ten miles away, where Védrines found him calmly smoking a cigarette. Robert said that he had only broken one wheel, which the Frenchman thought was progress! The Farman went back to Beaulieu, and Robert went back to London.

On his Sundays off from the theatre, Robert would fly, and break, his Farman, and Jules Védrines would repair it. Having decided that he would fly the aeroplane directly from Beaulieu to Southbourne, Robert managed to crash twice. With the Bournemouth Aviation Meeting only two days away, the Farman was in bits, and Védrines told his boss that he didn't have enough time in which to get it repaired. It was, he said, impossible. 'Impossible?' said Robert. 'Nothing is impossible!' And so, the bits were put into six boxes, and carted the rest of the way to their appointed hangar at Southbourne.

Robert also wired George Smart to come to Bournemouth: 'If going to Bournemouth be there on Saturday. Have arranged rooms Hotel Burlington.'

George, as ever, obliged: 'Upon arrival at Bournemouth, I drove straight to the hotel, deposited my luggage and proceeded by tram to the aerodrome. I had never been to a flying meeting before, and as I entered the Bournemouth aerodrome 1 was chiefly impressed by the extraordinary expense of it all... There were acres of enclosures, huge grandstands and miles of wooden palisading along the edge of the course. At one end some dozen hangars had been erected of wood and canvas. Each of these bore the name of the aviator concerned and the flag of his country above it... I found Robert's hangar, but it was empty and there were no signs of life about it. A number of aeroplanes had arrived, and the place was alive with machines, newspaper reporters, and official persons with colourful bands round their arms.

'I wandered about for a time, gazing ignorantly at the various types of aeroplanes which were being unpacked, and then I returned to Robert's hangar.'

He sat down on the grass in front of the large canvas curtain which covered the hangar's opening: 'I remained thus dutifully on guard, with my hat in my hand, prepared to cheer at the slightest encouragement, until it was too dark to see. But nothing happened.'

George returned to the Burlington by tram and, as there was no sign of Robert, dined alone. Afterwards, he 'sat in the lounge watching the front door and consuming innumerable pipes. I don't know what I expected to happen, something rousing at any rate. I don't think I should have been vastly surprised if Robert had suddenly flown into the crowded lounge through a window and upset the coffee and liqueurs of the beautifully dressed gathering.

'At half past eleven he arrived in a motor car, very dirty and unshaved and dressed in a thick knickerbocker suit. He was looking very grim and determined, so I immediately

The large, 200-bed Hotel Burlington at Boscombe, between Bournemouth and the Southbourne airfield

understood that something had gone wrong. He was also very hungry and demanded food. Whilst he ate, I gathered more or less what had happened. Of course, he had intended to fly to Bournemouth. The other aviators were quite content to bring their machines along in an ordinary way, neatly packed up in wooden cases.

'Not so Robert. He must demonstrate the practicality of aeroplanes, and his own pre-eminence as an aviator at one and the same time, and that time must be a day before the real Flying Week commenced. Unfortunately, something had gone wrong. He had smashed badly, and it was highly probable that it would be impossible to repair the damage in time to fly at the meeting at all. Robert, however, when everything is going wrong, is at his finest. He clenches his teeth and refuses to see the apparently obvious.

'We sat up late into the night talking of reliefs of men, acetylene night flares, transport from the New Forest, and generally arranging to turn night into day until the repairs should be completed. Next morning we awoke to discover that a hated rival had not only stolen Robert's beautiful idea but had succeeded in carrying it out and had, in fact, arrived in the early hours at the aerodrome, having flown half-way across Hampshire under his own power and with a Gladstone bag containing a suit of pyjamas and a toothbrush. We were very silent at breakfast and very gloomy but most emphatically resolute. Robert, I began to discover, cannot endure to be cast for any role other than that of the leading star.'[96] The "hated rival", William McArdle, was not, in the event, an official competitor, but see page 70.

---

[96] *Flights and Fancies.*

Chapter Four: Bournemouth International Aviation Meeting, 11-16 July 1910

Captain Tregonwell, c. 1810

Advert in The Aero, 28 June 1910

The decision to hold an aviation meeting was made at a public meeting at Bournemouth's *Theatre Royal* in January 1910, with Lord Montagu of Beaulieu in the chair. It was agreed by the members of the Bournemouth Centenary Fêtes Committee that, the roots of Bournemouth having been planted in July 1810 by Captain Lewis Dymoke Grosvenor Tregonwell, they should mark the town's 100th anniversary with a series of memorable events, beginning on 6 July 1910.[97]

The Committee's suggestion that there should be an international flying meeting to mark the occasion was agreed, to be held over the six days from Monday, 11 July to Saturday, 16 July 1910, on land at Southbourne, to the east of the town. The meeting would fall 'under the Rules of the Fédération Aéronautique Internationale, represented by the Royal Aero Club of the United Kingdom, with the collaboration of "l'Auto" of Paris.'[98] Entries would close on 23 June.

---

[97] It was not until 23 July 1890 that Bournemouth became a municipal borough, the date on which its Charter was sealed.
[98] From the *Official Programme* (price 6d).

The programme's colourful front cover

As no aerodrome then existed at Southbourne, a space was cleared 'on a mile of grassland between Tuckton and Double Dykes near Hengistbury Head.'[99] Hedges were ripped out, ditches filled in, and over forty allotments removed for the flying circuit, aeroplane hangars, and spectator areas.

In the hope of increasing their revenue from the visiting public, a number of enterprising local businesses placed adverts in flying magazines, for example: 'Blenheim Tower, Boscombe – Aviation Weeks – En pension from 15/0 per day; garden; 15 minutes tram from aerodrome.' Or 'Attractive board-residence, five minutes from Aerodrome; booking now. – Miss Myers, The Haven, Beaufort Road, West Southbourne.'

Flight magazine ran an extensive column in its edition of 9 July 1910: 'All who are interested in aviation in Great Britain will turn their thoughts to Bournemouth during next week, where the first international flying meeting of the year on British soil opens there on Monday.'

The timing of the Bournemouth meeting was unfortunate in that it was due to begin just one day after the big aviation meeting at Reims, France, was due to end on 10 July 1910. Reims had attracted almost eighty aviators, the great majority of whom were French. As *Flight* said, it would have been difficult for many of the Reims participants to have got to Southbourne in time. This undoubtedly accounted for the presence there of only nineteen aviators (see list below), fourteen of whom were British (including S.F. Cody, who had become a naturalised Briton on 21 October 1909). Each of the nineteen competitors was given a competition number as per the left-hand column below, with their make of aeroplane and aero-engine listed on the right. Note that m=monoplane; b=bi-plane; and make of engine with number of cylinders and horsepower:

---

[99] www.dorsetlife.co.uk/2008/07/bournemouths-flying-circuses/. The *Double Dykes*, across the neck of land, were an Iron Age fortification protecting the port at Hengistbury Head.

Though a handful of the Southbourne competitors held certificates from both the ACF and the RAeC, few had had any competitive flying experience, hardly surprising given that the first competition, however small, had only been held at Juvisy, France, in May 1909. Others followed in France, Italy, Belgium, Germany, the USA, Egypt, Spain, Luxembourg and Hungary, with the first in Britain being held in October 1909 at both Doncaster and at Blackpool. The Midlands Aviation Meeting at Wolverhampton followed in June/July 1910 and then the Bournemouth International Aviation Meeting.

No.	Name	Aeroplane
1	Audemars, Edmond (Swiss)	Bayard-Clément (m); Bayard-Clément, 4 cyl, 35 hp
2	Barnes, George Arthur	Humber-Blériot (m); Humber, 3 cyl, 30 hp
3	Boyle, Hon. Alan Reginald	Avis (m); E.N.V., 8 cyl, 40 hp
4	Christiaens, Josef (Belgian)	Farman (b); E.N.V., 8 cyl, 65 hp
5	Cody, Samuel Franklin	Cody (b); Green, 4 cyl, 50 hp
6	Colmore, George Cyril	Short (b); Green, 4 cyl, 50 hp
7	Dickson, Captain Bertram	Farman (b); Gnôme, 7 cyl, 60 hp
8	Drexel, John Armstrong (USA)	Blériot (m); Gnôme, 7 cyl, 60 hp
9	Gibbs, Louis Dwarris Launcelot	Sommer/Farman (b); Gnôme, 7 cyl, 60 hp
10	Grace, Cecil Stanley	Short (b); E.N.V., 8 cyl, 65 hp
11	Grahame-White, Claude	(1) Farman (b); Gnôme, 7 cyl, 60 hp;
		(2) Blériot (m); Gnôme, 7 cyl, 60 hp
12	Loraine, Robert Bilcliffe ('Jones')	Farman (b); Gnôme, 7 cyl, 60 hp
13	Moore-Brabazon, John Theodore Cuthbert	(1) Short (b); E.N.V., 8 cyl, 65 hp;
		(2) Voisin (b); Green, 4 cyl, 60 hp
14	Morane, Florentin Léon (French)	Blériot (m); Gnôme, 7 cyl, 60 hp
15	Ogilvie, Alexander ("Alec")	Short Wright (b); Wright-Bollée, 4 cyl, 35 hp
16	Radley, James	Blériot (m); Anzani, 3 cyl, 25 hp/J.A.P., 8 cyl, 35 hp
17	Rawlinson, Alfred	Farman (b); E.N.V., 8 cyl, 65 hp
18	Rolls, Hon. Charles Stewart	(1) Short Wright (b); Wright Bros, 4 cyl, 30 hp;
		(2) Farman (b); Gnôme, 7 cyl, 60 hp
19	Wagner, Louis (French)	Auguste Hanriot (m); Clerget, 4 cyl, 40 hp.

Early 1900s photograph looking east from Southbourne towards Hengistbury Head (top right). The south-eastern end of the aviation circuit lay in the middle of the picture, beyond the large house in the foreground.

Confidence in it was high, as C.G. Grey noted: 'Before the meeting began at all, its success, bar bad weather, was a foregone conclusion. All "Aerodom" seemed to be collected at Bournemouth, and, on the days preceding the opening, practically everyone connected with the sport began to make their way thither… At the Burlington [Hotel], which had been taken over as the headquarters of the Royal Aero Club, were located practically all those who govern the sport and most of those who practise it.'

'No preliminary flying was done till the day before the opening, for all the competitors were still busy getting their machines together. However, in the morning of that day considerable excitement was caused by the arrival of Armstrong Drexel's machine by air from his aerodrome at Beaulieu, some fifteen miles away.[100] The machine was driven over by McArdle, the other partner in the Beaulieu Aerodrome, and, like a wise man, instead of flying direct over the New Forest, where there is nothing but pine trees and fern scrub to land on, he flew out to Lymington and along the sea to Christchurch. On the way he reached a height of 2.000ft., and lost his way in the clouds. Descending a few hundred feet he found

---

[100] The McArdle/Drexel aerodrome was at East Boldre, in the New Forest, near Brockenhurst Station.

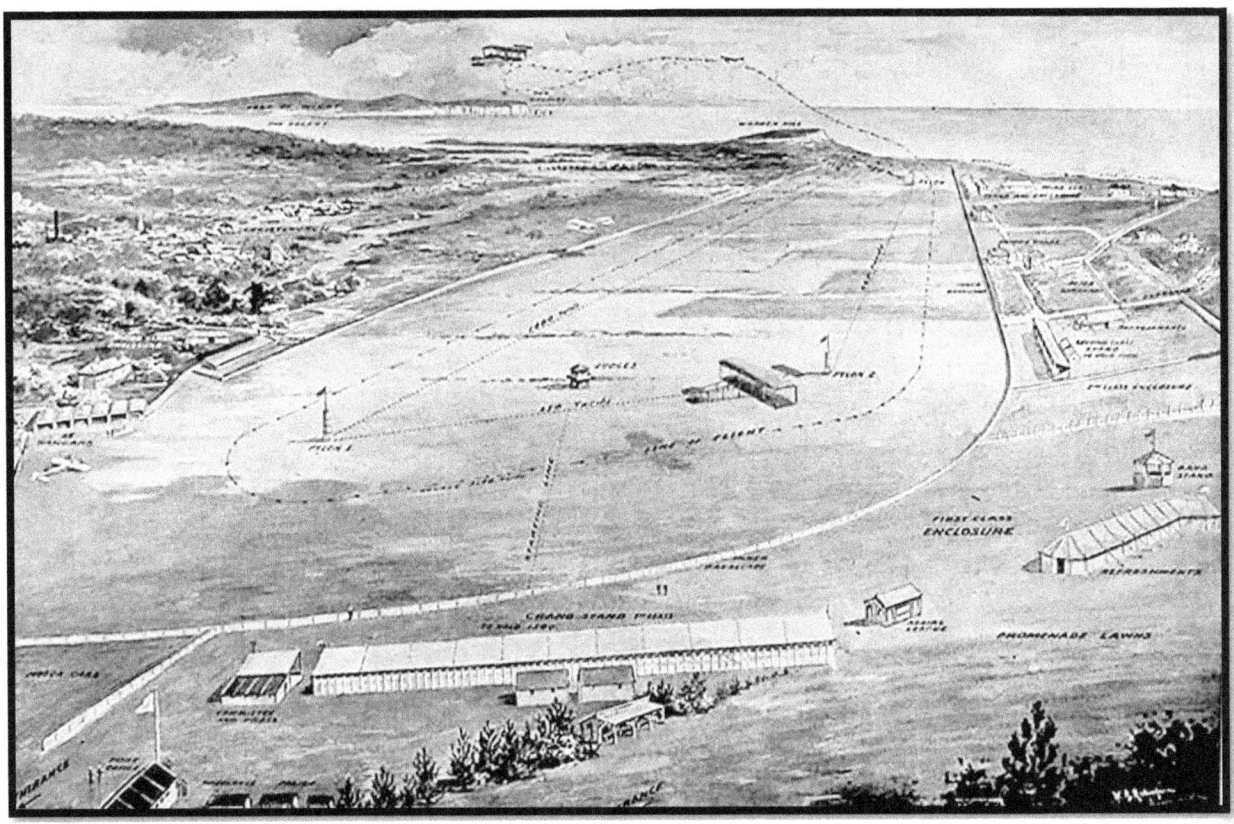
An artist's impression of Southbourne aerodrome, looking towards Hengistbury Head and The Needles, Isle of Wight, in the far distance. [The Illustrated London News, 9 July 1910]

himself over the Needles, and so headed north-west for the aerodrome. Altogether a very fine performance, and one which shows that it is well for some of the other competitors that McArdle does not approve of competition flying.

'During the evening Captain Dickson did a couple of pretty flights, one with a passenger. Christiaens (the only foreign competitor ready), Radley, and Grahame-White also made trial trips.' (*The Aero*, 20 July 1910).

Launcelot Gibbs went out later, but his propeller flew to pieces, causing damage to the wings.[101]

As most of the aviators (and officials) were staying at the Hotel Burlington, it was agreed that the first pilot to wake up after 4.30 a.m. on Monday, 11 July, 'would wake all the others, so that they could make some tests before the official flights started.'

'Some of them did get up early, with the result that Cecil Grace started a trial flight at 6 a.m., and was brought down through his engine stopping suddenly, with disastrous results'.

---

[101] It was a feature of solid, wooden propellers that they would suddenly "burst". This led to them being made of laminated wood, thereby making them much stronger.

The Hon. C.S. Rolls' wrecked aeroplane. There's nothing to be done.

He had run 'into a sunken road which crosses the aerodrome, at a point where it has not been filled up, absolutely wrecking his machine past all repair. He had hopes, however, of getting a fresh machine during the day, and took his loss most philosophically.' (*The Aero*, 20 July 1910).

Robert and his Farman had yet to arrive!

The meeting began on schedule, and not a little flying was seen throughout the Monday. Tuesday, 12 July, however, was to prove an awful day. Charlie Rolls went up in a stiff breeze in the competition to land as close as possible to the centre of a white circle "bull's-eye," twelve feet in diameter, itself in another white circle some fifty yards in diameter.

'His preliminary short lap of the course called for a fair amount of skill merely to maintain a straightforward flight. Having reached the fourth mark tower, he turned out towards the grandstands and flew above them, so that he could approach the circle in the teeth of the wind. Evidently it was his intention to make a trial descent, for he executed a sharp dive towards the ring. His angle of descent was extremely steep, and necessarily so, for the circle had been drawn only about 50 yards from the barrier, and it must have seemed to him, at that altitude, immediately beneath him almost as soon as he had cleared the grandstands. Realising that his angle of descent was too exaggerated for safety, or possibly because he was struck by a wind-gust, he suddenly put the elevator up to the end of its range in an attempt to bring the machine into a more reasonable attitude. But, just as he had apparently succeeded, something happened, and it fell vertically head-first to the ground…

'In natural sympathy with the disaster flying was at once stopped for the day.' (*Flight*).

Robert's Farman was still under repair on Wednesday, 13 July, with Jules Védrines and others working feverishly to get it ready, as George Smart recorded: 'Robert's machine had been fetched from the New Forest in small, broken pieces. The whole week [*sic*] our hangar had known neither night or day, only ceaseless work, with relays of English workmen, each of whom had departed dragging tired legs and with heads buzzing with echoes of strange, fierce French exhortations. Védrines had worked with feverish energy and vitality that was positively amazing. Robert had stood most of the time, glowering Napoleonically in a corner, and I, at intervals, had endeavoured to translate French to the bewildered working men. It had been a crowded week and even now I can shut my eyes and hear: "*Meester Smart. Voulez-vous expliquer à ces gens la?*" ("Mr Smart. Can you explain it to these men?") and then a gabble of incomprehensible technicalities.' Not for nothing was Robert's hangar known as "Hammer Hangar"!

At last, on Thursday, 14 July, Robert 'brought out his new type Farman, which he smashed up at Beaulieu a week before, and practically rebuilt in his hangar with the assistance of some workmen from Southampton. He flies well and steadily, but his machine is a slow one, and after flying a couple of laps he came down at the second pylon and stayed there most of the evening. The rebuilding was a fine piece of work, for he and his men were at it for three nights without stopping.' (*The Aero*, 20 July 1910).

There was no flying on the morning of Friday, 15 July, but in the afternoon Léon Morane went for the sea flight prize to The Needles, off the Isle of Wight, and back, followed by Armstrong Drexel. Morane reached The Needles and returned in a fraction over twenty-five minutes, having flown 21 miles, 18 of which were over water, at an average speed of 50 miles an hour. It was a remarkable achievement, given that there was a fair wind blowing during his flight.

Drexel appeared to be blown too much to the west, and took ten minutes longer than Morane. Both flights were deemed to have been 'splendid achievements.'

On Saturday, 16 July there 'was a little flying in the morning, the first man out being Loraine, who flew for 16m. 17$\frac{1}{5}$ s. in a wind estimated at 14 m.p.h., but actually being nearer 25 in the gusts. His fastest lap was 3m. 13$\frac{2}{5}$ s.' (*The Aero*, 25 July 1910). *Flight* reported: 'A fair breeze and a cold morning had the exhilarating effect of producing a fine flight by "Jones" on his racing Farman, but the wind was too much to permit of the plucky aviator putting up a good record for the speed prize. Indeed, it was often as much as the pilot could do to keep the course at all, and he said afterwards that the control frequently called for the exercise of considerable muscular effort.' (*Flight*, 23 July 1910).

'Bournemouth Aviation Week. / Mr Jones (R. Loraine) the plucky actor aviator.' He is seen here testing the engine.

Two views of Robert talking to Bertram Dickson. Jules Védrines can be seen on his haunches by the wheels. It would be tempting to believe that this is the moment shortly before Robert took off for his epic flight to The Needles on 16 July, but his flying attire suggests that the photos were probably taken two days earlier, on Thursday, 14 July.

'Morane getting into his monoplane about to start for the Needles Rocks...', 15 July 1910

Notwithstanding the inclement weather, Robert was determined to try for the Needles prize, and said to George Smart: '"I am going to start now" . . . He waited for me to urge him to do no such thing but I had observed that his chin was sticking out even more than usual. Therefore I refrained. When Robert's chin does that there is only one hope of persuading him to do the wise thing, and that is to agree with him and produce arguments in favour of the foolish one.

'It is a quarter to three,' I said, looking at my watch. 'If you don't go now, you will not have time to get back, change the tanks and go for the long distance before closing time.' But it was no good.'

'"Sortez Védrines" ("We're going, Védrines"), he commanded. Védrines… was running round and round the Farman biplane apparently just stroking the wires. He stopped abruptly – struck an attitude and observed: "Il-y-a du vent!" ("It's too windy!"). Robert shrugged his shoulders, picked up a cork lifebelt from the biplane's skid and strode away from the hangar.'

George Smart went 'to the Stewards' Office to give warning that Loraine was about to enter for the flight across the Channel to the Isle of Wight and back… My warning caused a sensation in the Stewards' Office, where lunch was going on peacefully.'

'Accompanied by a couple of stewards, flushed with a combination of lunch and anxiety, I made my way across to Robert. He had already climbed into the aeroplane's seat and was testing the working of the steering lever.'

Flight reported: 'All the morning the weather was cold and grey, so that no one was surprised when a shower of rain immediately followed the luncheon interval. At three o'clock there was a slight improvement, and "Jones" – who is well known in another sphere of life as the actor, Robert Loraine – decided to fly for the sea prize, and promptly made a start under weather conditions that would have deterred, we should have thought, a far more experienced pilot from making the attempt. However, the competition was open, and it was no business of the officials to interfere with the start of a competitor who had decided to take the risks, for, as we have already said, sound judgment is one of the most valuable assets of a pilot, and the man who thinks he can succeed where others feel sure they would fail is the man who is going to do most for the progress of aviation – if he succeeds ...' (*Flight*, 23 July 1910).

Without further ado, Robert flew the required lap of the Southbourne circuit before heading out to sea. A disconsolate George Smart returned to Robert's empty hangar, as the rain fell in sheets: 'And then a man ran at me and began to gesticulate like a windmill as he talked in a voice of rising crescendo. It was Védrines, and his face was wild and white. I was vaguely conscious that he was blaming me. "Why had I permitted Mr Loraine to depart across the sea? Could I not observe the coming storm? No, it was impossible that any machine built by mortal man could live in such a tempest. Without doubt Mr Loraine was now in the sea, the machine had sunk and Mr Loraine was drowning." "Vingt fois je lui ai dit, qu'il ne faut pas partir. Vingt fois. Vingt fois." ("Twenty times I told him not to go. Twenty times. Twenty times.").

Meanwhile, *Flight* continued, 'Jones flew out to sea, and in a very short time the expected rain descended in torrents, which caused those on the ground to take refuge in Jones' vacant shed, where they discussed with no little anxiety the probable effects of the drenching on Jones and his machine. Time passed, and he did not return, so that it became certain that he had either landed on the Isle of Wight or alighted in the sea. If the latter had happened, he would be dependent entirely on the assistance of various boats whose owners had volunteered to patrol the course, and it was with no little relief that a telegram was ultimately received from the Isle of Wight stating that an aeroplane had been observed on the cliffs.' (*Flight*, 23 July 1910).

Chapter Five: Isle of Wight Adventure, 16 July 1910

'It was just about 3 p.m. when Loraine made up his mind to try for the third prize in the "Needles and back" competition. The wind was then going down, but heavy rain clouds were banking up to windward, and everything looked gloomy. Loraine. being the first Britisher to make the attempt, was loudly cheered as he flew his lap of the course, and was out of sight in the dark mist to seaward in a few minutes. Five minutes later a terrific rainstorm burst over the ground, and we began to feel very anxious about Loraine's safety. Half an hour afterwards, when he should have returned, there was no sign of him; threequarters, then an hour, then an hour and a quarter, and the anxiety grew to a certainty that something was wrong. Those with experience of the sea said that no boat would be able to see him in the mist and gloom if he fell into the sea.' (*The Aero*, 20 July 1910).

Some accounts suggest that Robert was the first aviator to fly through a rainstorm. That distinction possibly fell to Frenchman Hubert Le Blon at Doncaster on the afternoon of 18 October 1909, during Britain's first air meeting. (Le Blon, born 21 March 1874, was giving

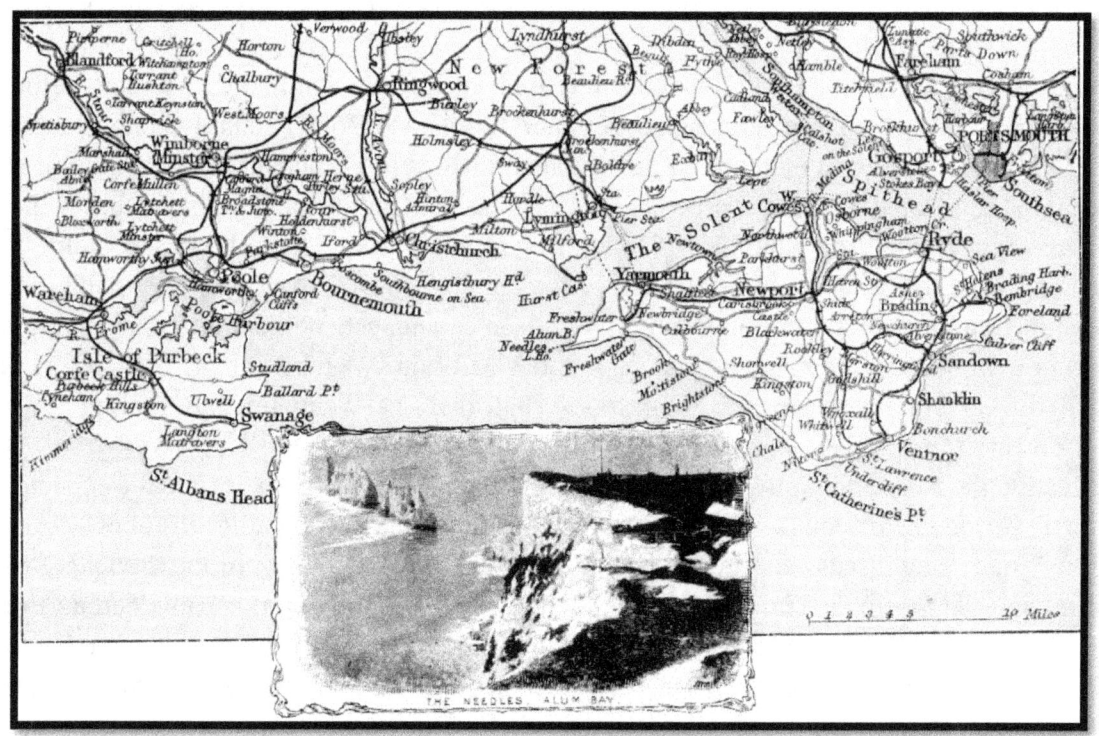

A 1905 postcard that illustrates the distance over water between Southbourne on Sea and The Needles. See the photograph on p.81 for where Robert actually landed on the narrow cliff top eastwards of The Needles.

Robert, wearing cork lifebelt, ready to go (photos Daily Telegraph, from Loraine archives)

exhibition flights at San Sebastián, northern Spain, on 2 April 1910 when, in stormy weather, he crashed onto some rocks in the sea at Ondarreta Beach, and was drowned.)

Though the Southbourne stewards had pleaded with Robert not to fly in the face of the approaching storm, he steadfastly took off in his attempt to win the £800 Sea-Flight first prize, the rules of which stated: 'Competitors to make one complete circuit of the Aviation Course, fly round a mark in the vicinity of the Needles Lighthouse, and return to the Aviation Ground, crossing the finishing line before alighting. Approximate distance, 21 miles, of which 18 miles are over the water.'[102] As Robert himself said: 'Here was the chance for me to show the world that aeroplanes were not just silly toys… A group of pilots, Cody, Morane and Dixon [*sic* – Dickson], came and urged me not to fly',[103] as did Védrines and George Smart, but Robert was determined: 'Je pars! Lancez l'helice, Védrines!' 'I'm going! Swing the propeller, Védrines!'

Jules hesitated, momentarily lost in thought as to his employer's impending fate, before Robert once again ordered Jules to start the engine – 'Loraine m'ordonna à nouveau de mettre son moteur en marche.'[104]

Worried spectators at Southbourne watched Robert flying round the course before disappearing, 'for the clouds were closing down like a pall and the headland in the distance

---

[102] Extract from *The Official Programme*, p.14.
[103] *Robert Loraine. Actor. Soldier. Airman*, p.115.
[104] *La vie d'un aviateur*, p.135.

was hidden in sweeping mist… He had achieved the compulsory double-circling [*sic*] of the aerodrome, and was now turning resolutely out to sea. Barely had he turned than the aeroplane was swallowed up in cloud.'[105] A moment later a thunderstorm broke over Southbourne.

Flying through the rain, Robert and his Farman were quickly soaked. With downward and horizontal visibility almost zero, and with no way of knowing the true direction of The Needles, he tried in vain to climb out of the storm. His plight worsened when his watch stopped and in desperation he turned back in the direction in which he thought Southbourne lay. Suddenly 'a rift in the mist disclosed a spot of green grassland, 1500 feet below me, to my left… I think I had given up all hope and was just waiting for the petrol to finish.'

Then, miraculously, he sighted land and managed to land on what proved to be the eighteenth green of the Needles Golf Club's links: 'I knew it was the first time I had ever

Two photos of Robert in his Farman passing over the last house on the mainland – next stop Isle of Wight (both from newspaper cuttings in Loraine archives, via Richard Holleyman)

---

[105] George Smart quoted *in Robert Loraine. Actor. Soldier. Airman*, p.117.

This photograph, looking east from The Needles, Isle of Wight, shows the narrowness of the strip of land towards the top right on which Robert landed. [Richard Holleyman]

done a golf-course in one.'[106] He had come down on the very western tip of the Isle of Wight.

His sensational arrival was reported in detail in *The Isle of Wight County Press* on Saturday, 23 July 1910: 'What was undoubtedly the most daring flight of the Bournemouth Week took place on Saturday afternoon, when Mr. Robert Loraine, the actor-aviator, who flies under the name of Jones, descended on the Needles golf links in his Farman biplane after a thrilling over-sea flight in pouring rain and a high wind. The few people who had braved the elements to keep watch on the Needles Cliffs had taken shelter under the walls of the Coastguards' observation-house, when at about a quarter to 4 a lady ran up from the cliff edge, pointed out to sea, and shouted the surprising message that a biplane was crossing the Channel about a mile out. Every eye was at once turned in the direction

---

[106] This and two previous quotes from *Robert Loraine. Actor. Soldier. Airman*, p.119.

Robert's Farman on the Isle of Wight. Note the two policemen (photo from newspaper cutting, Loraine family)

indicated by the lady and by the hum of the propellers, and the aeroplane could be seen just about due north of the Lighthouse, heading for St. Catherine's.[107]

'Great apprehension was felt when the machine was seen to swerve farther out to sea, and for a moment it was almost obscured by the mist, but just as it was passing from sight the pilot no doubt caught a glimpse of the high downs near the Tennyson Beacon and, bearing inwards, he was seen to plane down and alight on the golf links, about 2 miles from the Coastguard-station. Our representative was amongst the watchers at the station, and, after a hard run along the top of the downs, was one of the first to reach the aviator at five minutes to 4. Mr. Loraine was then standing some little distance from his machine and was being helped to remove his cork jacket by a gentleman, who had been the first to reach him.

'Soon the whole of the little band of people, including the Coastguards, arrived and every one was eager to greet Mr. "Jones" as the first pilot of a heavier-than-air [machine] to land in the Isle of Wight. Whilst awaiting the arrival of the Coastguards the brave aviator, though drenched to the skin and numbed with cold, calmly smoked a cigarette, and told our representative that he had had a very rough time. He said he started from Bournemouth about 3 o'clock and when about five minutes out from the shore ran into a terrific rainstorm,

---

[107] This was St. Catherine's Point, the southern tip of the isle, some 15 miles to the south-east of The Needles.

which completely blotted out all signs of land. He groped his way along by pure guess work, the rain half blinding him and making him very cold.

'For three-quarters of an hour he battled on, his engine, fortunately, working beautifully. At times he could tell he was being carried far out of his course, and tried to work his way back. He knew his petrol was becoming exhausted, but was afraid to descend lower than about 1500ft. for fear of striking the cliffs. "I was very thankful indeed," said Mr. Loraine, "to see these downs and descended at once. I don't know how much longer I should have been able to keep up." "This is a fine landing place. It could not have been better if especially made for me," continued Mr. Loraine as he hurried away with the Coastguards, who kindly provided him with clothing and food. He was anxious that a message should be sent to his friends at Southbourne, and this was done by the Coastguards, who also telegraphed for Mr. Loraine's mechanics, a few slight repairs being necessary before the return flight could be attempted.'

'After having some refreshment, Mr. Loraine appeared in a sailor's vest and a suit of civilian clothes, and, as his mechanics did not appear, he looked for a sheltered spot in which to place his machine for the night.

'During his absence the aeroplane had been guarded by Sergt. C. Ryall and P.C.'s Harris, Merritt, and Clark,[108] who were early on the scene, and a large crowd of people had assembled. About 6.45 their attention was diverted for a time from the silent aeroplane resting on the turf to another of the same type, piloted by Mr. Grahame White, which came up, made a graceful turn over the Needles, and sailed back again to Bournemouth. Favoured with better condition than Mr. Loraine, the second aerial visitor completed his trip and won the third prize.

'By this time Mr. Loraine had selected a chalk-pit on the opposite side of the down as a suitable shelter, and the aeroplane was wheeled thither by many willing hands, and by the kindness of the military authorities; men of the R.G.A. guarded it for the night. Mr. Loraine stayed at Alum Bay House.'

Back at Southbourne, after Robert's departure on the afternoon of 16 July, there was much consternation over his failure to re-appear. Lord Montagu of Beaulieu ordered motor boats to carry out a search and set out in his own yacht to look for him. Sir Thomas Lipton, too, took to the water in his yacht, just in case. There was great relief there when, at about 4.40 p.m., Major Lindsay Lloyd received a telegram, dispatched at 3.59 p.m. from a Mr. Taylor from The Needles: 'Biplane observed at 3.40 on cliff near Needles.' Another telegram was soon received 'from Alum Bay Heights that Robert had landed there safely at 3.55 p.m.' This was the telegraph sent by the helpful coastguards.

---

[108] Walter Charles Ryall, born c. 1869; James Merritt, 27 years old, married with two young daughters, lived at The Broadway, Totland Bay. Harris and Clark not identified.

Alum Bay House hotel. The disused chalkpit in which Robert's Farman was sheltered lies some 200 yards off to the right of this picture. [photo courtesy Freshwater & Totland Archive Group, via Richard Holleyman]

The chalk-pit where Robert's Farman was sheltered, photographed in May 2023

Having heard the good news, George Smart asked an official if there was any information as to the state of the Farman? On being told that there was none, George 'dispatched Védrines with petrol, oil and tools by a swift motor-car to Lymington, there to catch a steamer for Alum Bay.' George initially remained at Southbourne 'to establish a base', but arrived on the island on the following day, Sunday, 17 July, with further parts for which Robert had meanwhile telegraphed. 'He was', George recalled, 'waiting for me on a little wooden jetty, and I can never remember to have been so glad to see anyone before. He was unshaved and clothed in a sweater, leather-lined coat and breeches and crowned with a perfectly hideous brown leather cap, for which he has some inexplicable affection.'

In a waiting taxi-cab, George and Robert were driven to the Farman. There, said George, 'in a chalk-pit, partially protected by a few bits of sail, was the machine. A crowd of people, controlled by a guard of Garrison gunners,[109] were watching the antics of Védrines, who was pegging her down... After we had inspected the 18th green at the top of the hill, Robert and I had tea at the hotel near the chalk-pit.'[110] The hotel was Alum Bay House.

Robert instructed Védrines to continue with repairs, and sent George Smart back to Bournemouth to prepare for the return flight while he, with nothing to be done for his part, would head back to London until his aircraft was ready for the return voyage to the mainland.

'On Sunday morning [17 July] the biplane was covered with tarpaulins and despite the wet weather hundreds of people from all parts of the Island visited the spot. Photographers were very busy and a collection in aid of the local lifeboat funds, made by Mr. Barton, one of the aviation officials, who had come from Southbourne, realized 7s. 6d.' (This equates to around £55 today, 2023).

After the repairs had been completed on Monday, 18 July, George Smart notified Robert that the Farman was dry, and arranged to meet him at Brockenhurst railway station at two o'clock in the afternoon of the following day.

Tuesday, 19 July 'was beautifully fine and there was scarcely any wind. Mr. Loraine was in London, but he telegraphed that he would come down and make the return journey in the afternoon, between 4 and 6 o'clock.'

---

[109] The 'Garrison gunners' were from Nos. 11 and 33 Companies, Southern Group, RGA, quartered at Golden Hill Fort, to the north of Freshwater. The Commandant was Lieutenant-Colonel Julian Arthur Labalmondiere, RGA (8 Nov 1859–13 Nov 1913).

[110] George Smart quotes from *Robert Loraine. Actor. Soldier. Airman*, pp.120, 121 & 122. The Alum Bay House hotel to which Robert and George Smart went for tea 'was initially called Groves's Needles Hotel, but by the mid-1870s was renamed Alum Bay House.' The house was built in 1825 by James Groves of Freshwater. Information courtesy of Caroline Dudley, FATAG, email to author 7 Apr 2023.

The Farman Biplane of Robt Loraine Esqr sheltered in
Needles Down on 16 July 1910 - The first aviator to La

...okpit after his voyage from Bournemouth to the... in the Isle of Wight...

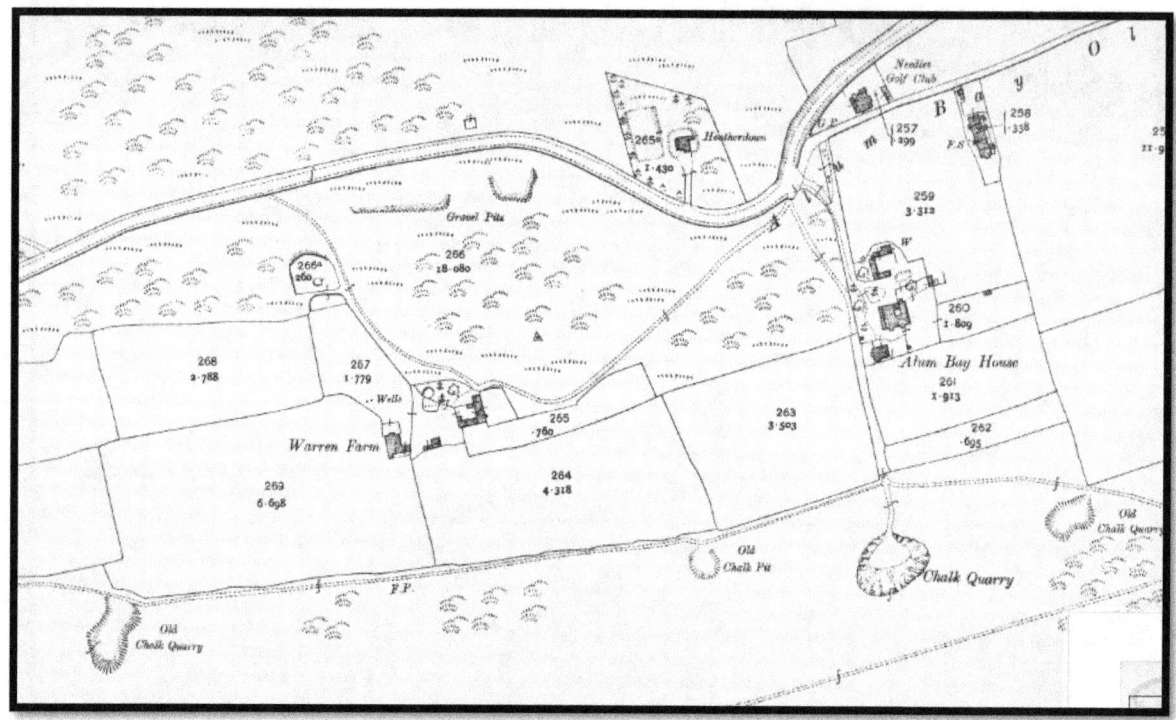

Part of 1907 OS map (scale: 1 to 2500) showing the Alum Bay House hotel to the right. The chalk pit in which Robert's Farman was sheltered is shown as "Chalk Quarry", immediately below Alum Bay House. The Needles Golf Club links ran along the bottom of the map, the '18th green' being close to the disused chalkpit. [via Caroline Dudley, Freshwater & Totland Archive Group]

Meeting as planned at Brockenhurst George noted that Robert 'was dressed in a blue suit and looked rather distraught. He has a dual personality and he changes from one person to another, with his clothes. Dressed in his blue suit, he was completely the artistic Robert, nice-looking, highly-strung and imaginative. When he changes into his knickerbocker suit with the leather lining and assumes the hideous leather cap, he becomes quite plain, morose and mechanical.'

As they motored to Lymington 'Robert explained how grateful he was for the confidence he had gained from his flight in the storm. But all the same I felt he was not confident; in fact, he was nervous.'

While George made his way back to Southbourne from Lymington, Robert crossed to Totland Bay on the Isle of Wight. 'On arrival at Totland Bay Pier in the afternoon this notable airman accepted the kindly offer to be conveyed in Mr. F.T. Mew's motor-car to the foot of the Needles down for his flight, and Mr. Jones, on alighting, expressed his grateful acknowledgments of the kindly consideration of Mr. and Mrs. Mew.'[111]

Jules Védrines had been 'very busy throughout the day getting the machine into trim, and the news of the proposed flight leaked out, with the result that during the afternoon crowds of people came on the scene by all kinds of conveyances, and a special excursion was run from Newport. There were roughly about a thousand people gathered around the edge of the pit, where, at about 4.30, Mr. Loraine put in an appearance. He was still wearing his leather motoring cap, and as he walked to his machine and tested the wires and planes he was loudly cheered. After going to the downs and studying the force and direction of the wind and the course he should take, the aviator ordered his machine to be brought to the level stretch in about the centre of the golf links.

'This was done by a number of artillerymen, whilst Mr. Loraine walked to Alum Bay House and had tea. Under the direction of Col. Labalmondiere and P.S. Ryall the aeroplane was got in position, facing inland towards the Tennyson Beacon, so that a start could be made with the wind. The crowd, which by this time must have numbered 2000, waited patiently and when at 6.15 Mr. Loraine was seen walking towards his machine with his secretary (Mr. Stanley Welsh) and his mechanic they cheered lustily.'

'For some minutes the aviator studied the sky, which had become rather overclouded, and he seemed loth to depart upon his journey. Exactly at 6.30, however, after a long talk with his mechanic he suddenly threw off his coat and jacket, and, amidst the applause of the crowd, donned his sweater, his wind jacket, and his cork lifebelt. A minute later he climbed to his seat, and after testing the working of the elevating and steering planes his mechanic started the engine. The 7-cylinder Gnome seemed to work splendidly, and the dozen or so artillerymen had a hard job to hold the straining machine back whilst the preliminary test was made.

'Just at 6.33, with a farewell wave of the hand and a shout to the men to let go from its brave pilot, the biplane darted over the soft down turf and after a run of about 100 yards rose gracefully into the air, amidst the clicking of a hundred cameras and the enthusiastic cheers of the crowd.

'Flying rather low Mr. Loraine went over the Golf holes, and with a pretty swerve passed directly over Totland and out to sea. Every eye watched him as he headed straight for Southbourne until he disappeared in the haze. No sooner had Mr. Loraine got well into the air than two other aeroplanes could be seen apparently making their way from Bournemouth towards Beaulieu. They were passing over Hurst Castle at a great altitude.

---

[111] The Mews may have been Francis T. Mew, brewery director, aged c. 52 years, and Olive K., aged c. 43. Presumably Mr. Mew was connected to W. B. Mew, Langton & Co. Ltd., the Newport brewery?

The people of Yarmouth had an excellent view of these machines, which, they state, were two monoplanes. Later the news was published that it was Mr. Drexel returning from Bournemouth.[112]

'Mr. Loraine, who accomplished his journey in 25 minutes, alighted at the aerodrome, within a short distance of his shed, where he was heartily cheered. He attained an altitude of 1500 feet.'

The monument to Lord Tennyson 'on the high downs'

---

[112] Also returning to Beaulieu in the other monoplane – a Blériot – was William McArdle.

Though the caption to this photograph, taken in the chalkpit on the Isle of Wight, says 'Loraine filling the tank', the man doing the filling is, unmistakably, Jules Védrines. Garrison gunners look on – the elderly gentleman does not!

Another view of the Farman in the chalk pit – same gentleman!

Left to right: three unknown ladies; PC Toomer of the local constabulary; Jules Védrines (back to camera); Robert Loraine (wearing spectacles); unknown (hands on hips); Lindsay McLennan (photographer) [photo from a leaflet in the possession of the author of www.shalfiow.demon.co.uk/, regrettably not identified]

'19 July 1910. First aeroplane voyage from the Isle of Wight – "Tuning up" Mr. Loraine's biplane in the chalkpit on Needles Down [50 ft – 3.10 p.m., - "C^B" - F.22 – 1/5"].' Jules Védrines is holding the rudder, on which, above the 12, is printed 'H:Farman/Constructeur/Camp de Châlons/Marne'.

3 p.m. '19 July 1910. First aeroplane voyage from the Isle of Wight – "Tuning up" Mr. Loraine's biplane [60ft – 3 p.m.- "D" – F.22 – 1"]'. A gunner corporal stands on top of the ladder.

'19 July 1910. First aeroplane voyage from I.W. – Needles Down chalkpit – Testing the engine – [3.20 p.m. – 50 ft – "B" – F.11 – 1/100"].' Garrison gunners hang on! Jules Védrines at the front of the Farman.

'19 July 1910. Chalkpit – Needles Down – First aeroplane voyage from I.W. Final inspection of Farman biplane by Robt. Loraine Esq. [4.27 pm. "D" – F16 – 1" – 50 ft.]'. Robert, in long coat with left hand on lower left mainplane, is talking to Jules Védrines, hand on hip.

yage from I.W. Final inspection of Farman [0.21 — 50ft.]

raine's Farman biplane for first aeroplane

No details on this postcard, but probably taken around the time of the one on the preceding page. Robert is in the centre, left arm pointing towards the Farman, with Jules Védrines (back to camera) standing next to him.

'*19 July 1910 – Needles Down – First aeroplane voyage from I.W. – awaiting arrival of owner, Robert Loraine Esq. for his 23 minute trip to Southbourne. [6 p.m. "D" F.8 – 1/25"]*'

Again, no details, but this photograph was taken at more or less the same time as the previous one. Note the closeness of the crowd to the Farman.

'*19 July 1910 – Needles Down – Robt. Loraine Esq. leaving on his Farman biplane for Southbourne – The first aeroplane voyage from the Isle of Wight. [6.30 pm – "D" – F.8 – 1/100.] He arrived at 6.53 p.m. safely.*'

Robert airborne for Southbourne just after 6.30 pm on Tuesday, 19 July 1910

When the time came for Robert to go to his aeroplane, he was nowhere to be found. Jules Védrines eventually found *le patron* at the hotel, staring out of a window, and realised that he was afraid. Robert had been thinking of the risk of flying out over the sea and how he would find himself 'in irretrievable trouble if anything went wrong. It seemed such a stupid risk to take. The aeroplane had been subjected to a severe strain during the storm [on 16 July] …'[113]

He further reasoned that 'it was more than likely that considerable adjustments would be necessary before she would be fit to fly over rough country, and from Alum Bay heights in whatever direction I started I would find myself immediately in trouble if the machine should prove to be distorted. I thought it was a foolish risk to take and was frankly disinclined to jump off that ledge of cliff in a machine which I had good reason to believe might have sustained hidden damage.

'I should have dismantled her and sent her back to the aerodrome for a thorough overhaul if I could have done so quietly and unobtrusively, but my flight from Bournemouth had attracted so much attention that this was impossible and to remove her by any other route than by the air would have given another weapon to her disbelievers.'

Védrines also suggested to him that the multitude of onlookers were expecting him to perform, and it was, therefore, with some reluctance that Robert followed the Frenchman to the Farman.

Meanwhile, at 6.10 p.m. on the afternoon of Tuesday, 19 July, Armstrong Drexel had taken off in his Blériot from Southbourne, heading for East Boldre airfield, in the New Forest, as Harry Delacombe, his passenger, described: 'Satisfied at last as to our height, he [Drexel] steered direct from Hengistbury Head towards the Needles. We could see Mr. Loraine's aeroplane, with people surrounding it, very distinctly on the high land over Alum Bay, and as we turned to the left over the promontory of Hurst Castle the view up the Solent as far as Southampton on the left and Cowes on the right was clearly mapped out underneath.' (*The Aero*, 27 July 1910).

Flight noted that Armstrong Drexel, having made two very wide circles, rose to a height of 600 feet and 'then started in the direction of Lymington, steadily rising to a height of 1,200 ft., passing the Needles meantime, and having a clear view of Loraine's biplane still at rest on the high land at Alum Bay. At 6.40 Beaulieu was in sight, and at 6.52 a safe descent was made on the grounds. Shortly after landing, Mr. McArdle was sighted, he passing on, having also flown over from Bournemouth on the other Blériot.' (*Flight*, 23 July 1910).

Presumably unaware of Drexel's Blériot passing the island Robert, at last having regained his self-control, was ready to take-off from the fairway of the third hole of The Needles

---

[113] *Robert Loraine. Actor. Soldier. Airman*, p.124.

Down golf course, and signalled to Jules to start the engine. Suddenly, at 6.30 p.m. on Tuesday, 19 July 1910, 'up went his hand. The Territorials holding on to the tail let go. The great bird rose into the sky while the sight-seers surged after her waving handkerchiefs and shouting hurrahs from the cliff-edge.'[114]

Védrines had urged Robert to head directly to the mainland visible in the distance but, once airborne, Robert's courage returned. Ignoring his mechanic's good advice, he headed for the nearest land-point and landed safely back at Southbourne at 6.53 p.m., after only twenty-three minutes in the air. As Jules Védrines said: 'Bravo Loraine!'[115]

As Robert approached the Southbourne field, those who had been watching and waiting for his return, George Smart among them, surged towards the Farman, where they found Robert calmly walking around it: 'He was still white with cold and his teeth were chattering, but he was in a state of great exultation.' After helping Robert with his lifebelt George superintended the housing of the Farman 'in our old hangar, whilst Robert signed autograph books. When I had at last put her snugly to bed and dropped the canvas curtains on her I went slowly across to Robert, who was sitting in a motor car, signing the last few books.'

---

[114] *Robert Loraine. Actor. Soldier. Airman*, p.125.
[115] *Jules Védrines*, p.140.

Chapter Six: Blackpool Flying Carnival, August 1910

Barely had the Bournemouth meeting finished than Robert and seven other aviators set off for the **Blackpool Flying Carnival** in the north-west of England. Again, the timing was unfortunate, as a larger Aviation Meeting was to be held from 6–13 August at Lanark, Scotland.

The Blackpool meeting would, therefore, be split into three parts. The first (28 July–3 August) and third parts (15–20 August) were for flying competitions, while the middle part (4–14 August) was reserved for static displays and exhibition flights.

This interval had been deliberately chosen to allow for the Lanark affair, the Blackpool organising committee being aware that some of those booked to fly in the first part of the Blackpool meeting were going on to Lanark. They hoped that some of them would return to Blackpool, and that some of the aviators who had gone directly to Lanark would attend the third part of the Blackpool meeting.

The prizes to be won at Blackpool were not huge, but were enough to entice, eventually, a baker's dozen of aviators of several nationalities: Harold Blackburn (did not fly); Bartolomeo Cattaneo (his aeroplane was identified by the letters AT); Florentin Champel (CL, but did not fly); Jorgé (Georges) Chávez (HZ); J. Armstrong Drexel (XL); Arthur Duray (did not fly); Cecil

Left: Howard Joseph Harding (1881–1947), striking an heroic pose at the Lyon Aviation Meeting in France, 7–15 May 1910. He was one of three aviators (Roe and Pixton being the others) who had not yet qualified for a flying licence and who were therefore not permitted to fly at Blackpool during official flying hours. In any case, the engine of his J.A.P. caught fire during a test the day before the start of the meeting, causing damage that kept him out for the week (www.thefirstairraces.net/) He finally qualified for his French ACF certificate, no. Fr.213, on 29 August 1910. Right: Harding's aeroplane at Lyons [photo www.thefirstairraces.net].

Grace (RE); Claude Grahame-White (his two aeroplanes were coded EE and EW); Robert Loraine ("Jones") (ON); William McArdle (MA); A.V. Roe (ER); and Maurice Tétard (AR). Also present at Blackpool, but not permitted to fly in any of the competitions, was H.J. Harding.

There, too, were C.H. Greswell, one of Grahame-White's mechanics, and C.H. Pixton, the latter in the employ of A.V. Roe at Brooklands.[116] Though neither flew competitively, the hard-working Howard Pixton was persuaded by H.V. Roe (A.V.'s younger brother) to have a turn on the triplane on the Bank Holiday Monday. As Pixton said: 'I flew an uneventful straight before returning it [the triplane] to him.'[117]

Pixton, who admitted that he didn't know how to turn corners, was fortunate to have been at Blackpool in the first place. He had been entrusted by A.V. Roe to pack-up two triplanes and everything else in the shed at Brooklands, and to have the whole lot sent by rail to Blackpool. This was done, everything being covered on the railway company's wagon by a large tarpaulin. Next day, Howard caught the train to Blackpool from Euston: 'I'd settled myself down to the nice, peaceful journey but halfway between Chorley and Preston the train unexpectedly pulled into a siding and stopped.' Curious to see why, Howard 'saw smoke billowing from the front of the train… There, at the front, next to the engines, were

---

[116] Greswell was to be awarded RAeC certificate no. 26 on 15 Nov 1910, and Pixton no. 50 on 24 Jan 1911.
[117] *Howard Pixton*, p.34.

our aeroplanes blazing merrily. Everything else was burning too, the bicycles and clothes…'[118] On the same train, but unaffected by the blaze, was Cecil Grace's aeroplane.

George Smart, also on his way to Blackpool, witnessed the blazing aeroplanes. Luckily, Robert's Farman, with Jules Védrines, had gone on ahead on the previous day.

'The first thing I did after arriving in Blackpool' George noted, 'was to engage rooms for Robert and myself at a small hotel on the front. All the other aviators were to stay at the Aero Club and a large hotel close by. But we wished to be alone. Robert is constitutionally a revolutionist. All forms of authority are to him anathema.'

The accommodation sorted, George went to the Blackpool flying ground (today, better known as Squire's Gate), where he was confronted by 'a forlorn little figure, limp and drooping, standing in the door of the paddock. It was Védrines.' Of Robert's Farman there was no sight. Védrines was once again a worried man: 'Ah mon Dieu! C'est terrible çe Blackpool! Rien n'est prêt! Ah, ces Anglais! Ces Anglais!' ('Oh my God! Blackpool is terrible! Nothing is ready! Oh, the English! The English!').

Further inspection by George proved Védrines to be right: 'Several wooden sheds were completed and two hangars at the far end had got as far as their green canvas roofs; the next were gaunt skeletons in various stages of construction. There was an army of tired, sulky workmen moving listlessly about and accomplishing next to nothing insubordinately. We inspected the completed sheds and discovered that one contained exhibits of Hovis bread, another Mr. Grahame-White's two biplanes already up, and the third, a bar at which somebody's special ales were sold.' George immediately had a word with the workers' foreman, and an effort of sorts was made to finish the construction of the hangar.

A room nearby was found for Védrines, and George retired to his hotel, to await Robert's arrival: 'Robert arrived at midnight. He detests travelling by train, in fact he is perfectly infantile on the subject. He goes first class and spares no money or trouble in making himself comfortable, but invariably becomes peevish. The Blackpool journey is a bad one, as I have already said, so that Robert was in a state bordering on tears when I met him. After I had told him my news he became sulky and announced his intention of going to bed and remaining there until further orders, at any rate until [his Farman] was ready to be flown. I did not try to pacify him; in fact I was secretly delighted. It is enough of a strain for the ordinary man to fly, but that is nothing to the strain Robert puts on himself and everybody else whenever he starts hurrying railway officials and British workmen.'

Thursday, 28 July 1910. At 4 a.m., with Robert still abed, George Smart was advised by a sleepy official at the goods station that Robert's missing Farman 'had been located seven miles down on a goods siding but could not be moved that day because of passenger

---

[118] This and previous quote from *Howard Pixton*, p.31. Also, 'sparks from the engine of the LNWR goods train set fire to their truck while puffing up an incline near Wigan on July 27.' *Avro Aircraft since 1908*, p.11.

Blackpool. Robert's hangar to the right; others still under construction

traffic!' George, as resourceful as ever, hired a traction-engine and driver, and the Farman, in its packing cases, was hauled to the flying ground in an operation taking seven hours.

On their way through Blackpool, George hired a motor car: 'Robert did not possess one and we had discovered that a motorcar is as necessary an adjunct to an aeroplane as the pilot fish to a shark. After some search I discovered a presentable looking machine and hired it and its chauffeur by the day until further orders. It was then I made the acquaintance of Gibbs. Gibbs was the chauffeur and, as he is inextricably bound up with the rest of the story, I will give both my first and last impressions of him. A tall, heavy man inclined to stoutness and with a florid complexion, Gibbs was completely mannerless and yet at the same time contrived never to offend or presume when dealing with his superiors. I always found him a willing worker even when under the influence of drink, which was usually the case.

'He invariably drove furiously, priding himself on the prowess of his car to go faster than anything else on the road. In his own estimation Gibbs is a person of universal popularity due to his jovial way of coarsely chaffing his equals whenever he comes in contact with them; the policeman on point duty, other drivers, tramcar conductors, Védrines, everyone who comes within range. His chaff never seemed to amuse anyone but himself; indeed, I know it has frequently given offence. But of this Gibbs is serenely unaware. In the opinion of decent persons like Robert and myself he was the last word in hoggish vulgarity. And yet I really believe that he was as loyal to us as it is in him to be loyal, and I must confess to a sneaking affection for Gibbs.'

Meanwhile, Védrines had located the Farman in its cases at the flying ground. George found that he had had them brought to the hangar, which was still unfinished late in the afternoon, though the foreman kept repeating that it would be ready in half an hour!

Robert's hangar was not the only one unfinished: 'The flying carnival at Blackpool opened with a state of unpreparedness in a measure difficult to account for altogether. The majority of the hangars were, firstly, not ready to receive the machines when they arrived, their construction having been delayed owing to the heavy rain during the two days prior

This photograph of Chávez's hangar at Blackpool gives an idea of their size

to the opening. Again, difficulties had also been encountered in the transportation of the machines, and this, combined with the unfortunate destruction by fire of A. V. Roe's two triplanes, gave one the impression that very little flying, if any, would take place on the opening day, and so it proved to be.'

The Aero explained the lack of sheds: 'Messrs. George Holloway and Webb, Ltd., who built the hangars at Blackpool, write us that only ten hangars were required for the first meeting, and all of these were ready for the reception of the aeroplanes forty-eight hours before the commencement of the meeting. The other hangars were not required until the second meeting, and were never intended for the first. In the report of this meeting which appeared in *The Aero*, it was noted that when some of the machines arrived there was no housing for them, in consequence of the hangars not being finished, and it is only fair to Messrs. Holloway and Webb that their statement should be made known. In view of the appalling weather which preceded the meeting, and must have prevented any work being done on the hangars for some time, it is remarkable that even the first ten should be finished by the specified time, and certainly the contractor's men worked excellently in getting one of the second set of hangars ready for Mr. Loraine's machine after he arrived and found that the finished hangars would not hold his machine.' (*The Aero*, 21 September 1910).

The shortage of hangars on the first day was matched by a shortage of aeroplanes. When the meeting started, only three had arrived – two Blériots owned by Claude Grahame-White and another jointly owned by Cecil Grace and G.H. Cockburn – and none of them was ready to fly.

Encouraged by the improvement in the weather after morning showers, some five thousand people had turned up and had paid an entrance fee. After waiting until half past five, they had had enough, and stormed the barriers of the hangar area: 'The crowd, or a section of it at any rate, pounced on Mr. Harry Delacombe, because he was wearing an official-looking badge, as Press Steward, though, as a matter of fact, he had nothing whatever to do with letting them into the aerodrome on that occasion. Mr. Delacombe tackled the crowd in a friendly way and soon had them in quite good humour with him, so that he was eventually able to send them away comparatively content with pass-out checks which admitted them on another day, and he arranged that those who were leaving Blackpool that day should have their money back'. (*The Aero*, 10 August 1910).

The star attraction, though, was Claude Grahame-White, who had himself arrived around mid-day on 28 July from Torbay, where he had been making exhibition flights in his Farman biplane. Getting to Blackpool was a remarkable effort: 'At 6 o'clock on Wednesday evening Grahame-White was flying at Torquay; shortly after that hour he landed, the machine was taken to pieces, put into a theatrical scenery van, which it fits exactly, and accompanied by Grahame-White and his crew it travelled straight through over the Great Western, Midland, and North-Western Railways to Blackpool, was taken out of the van, put on a lorry, and arrived at the ground at Blackpool exactly at 6 p.m. on Thursday. The crew which came with it, and the extra crew who brought Grahame-White's monoplanes from London, set to work on it at once, and at 7.40 p.m. precisely that machine was in the air, and remained there for twenty minutes. It is true that the wires were not very carefully adjusted, as some of the assistants working on the machine were distinctly volunteers for the occasion, but everything was firmly fixed, and nothing parted company.' (*The Aero*, 10 August 1910).

Grahame-White's crew of eight mechanics had performed wonders. Incredibly, with only twenty-one minutes left of the day's official flying time, Grahame-White was able to fly a couple of laps of the airfield, before heading out over nearby St. Anne's. Being the only one to fly, he won the day's endurance and general merit prizes.[119] Whether any of the angry crowd had stayed on to watch him fly is not known.

Grace's Blériot was also ready but, when the engine was run-up, not all cylinders were firing and, after some ten minutes, it was rolled back into the hangar.

There was a slight drizzle, but no wind, when, at six o'clock in the evening, Robert arrived. 'Are we ready?' he asked cheerily. George pointed at the unfinished hangar and at the packed Farman. As Grahame-White flew overhead, Robert turned and walked away.

---

[119] www.thefirstairraces.net/meetings/.

A Farman, possibly Claude Grahame-White's, flying over J & R Wilkinson's Beach Camp at Rossall Mount, Cleveleys, a mile or two north of Blackpool

In the distance George saw 'the foreman of works approaching. The sight of Grahame-White flying had made me furious; I ran at the foreman. "Where's our damned roof?" I enquired. "It is going to blow tonight", he remarked irreverently. I paused, searching for oaths. "These sheets cost fifty pounds", he said lugubriously. "I don't think I can take the responsibility of putting one up tonight if it blows – it might blow off."'

'For a moment I was too astonished even to swear.'

Then George 'saw Robert talking to one of the stewards a little distance off and hurried to tell him of the expensiveness of the sheet. He became white with rage and I really believe there were tears in his eyes. "Then I will pack up and go away at once", he said. "I can't risk their fifty pounds; it would be an outrage. Close the cases", he commanded. The steward protested, explained, cajoled. But Robert was cold to his pleadings. "I'm deeply affected", said Robert, "at the thought of the promoters of the meeting losing a sheet that cost fifty pounds."

'Goaded beyond endurance, the friendly steward took upon himself to order our roof to be fixed at once. He coaxed the foreman of works by promising to go bail for the £50. The foreman coaxed the morose working men by addressing them as "boys" in various tones and with various adjectives.'

At last Robert's team could unpack the Farman. It was eight o'clock, an hour after the first day's flying had finished.

McArdle (code letters "MA") on his Blériot

Friday, 29 July 1910 dawned bright and sunny, 'but the wind blew a gale the whole day, and it was absolutely impossible to go out.' Nothing 'whatever happened except that the carpenters managed to get rather further ahead with the hangars and the aerodrome enclosure.'

'In the hangar enclosure itself thousands of people assembled to look at such machines as had arrived, and during the day Cattaneo and Chavez arrived… By Friday evening the actual machines ready to fly were Grahame-White's Farman, Loraine's Farman, Grahame-White's new Blériot-cum-Gnôme, Cecil Grace's Blériot-cum-Gnôme bought from Morane, and Grahame-White's old Blériot-cum-Anzani, Drexel's Blériot-cum-Gnôme being laid up for want of a propeller, and the two-seater not assembled.

'By the way, it is interesting to note here that Cecil Grace and G. H. Cockburn have joined forces, and each own half a share in the Blériot machine.' (*The Aero*, 10 August 1910).

McArdle's Blériot had also arrived.

'Loraine's racing Farman machine was brought out at six o'clock, and the announcement was made that he would make an attempt in half an hour. The wind, however, increased in force, and flight became out of the question, Friday thereby proving a blank day.' (*Flight*, 6 August 1910).

Saturday, 30 July. Robert's Farman was ready at last, having been fitted with a new fuel tank which, it was hoped, would allow up to five hours in the air.

'The meeting on Saturday was opened by Loraine, who started off at 3.30 p.m. in a treacherous wind. After making one or two circuits of the course with great difficulty he came down in a field just beyond the flying ground.' (*Flight*, 6 August 1910).

Robert on his Farman, from a postcard sent from Blackpool on Sunday, 31 July 1910, part of its message reading: 'Had two fine days. Saw a flying machine this afternoon go round the Tower.'

Robert's Farman at Blackpool. He is standing far right. Next to him is George Smart with a flag for signalling to Robert that the Farman was 'behaving nicely or otherwise'. McArdle, hands on hips, is third from right. Robert's Blackpool identification letters, "ON" (for "Jones"), can just be seen on the right rudder.

Robert's Farman on the golf course

'Saturday morning was again too windy for flying, though nothing like as bad as the previous day, and after mid-day it seemed as if the wind were dropping still further, so about half-past three the public were admitted to the aerodrome, and at a quarter to four exactly Loraine started out on his Farman. He got round the bottom corner of the track all right, but when he reached the western end again he evidently found that a turn inside the aerodrome itself would involve the risk of being driven into the south-western pylon, so he flew out over the wall of the aerodrome and across the Golf Links, coming into the aerodrome again at the eastern end. The second time round he repeated the performance, but was caught by a gust of wind and forced down just behind a bunker on the golf course... He told me afterwards that he was really carrying more weight than he intended, as he had a very big petrol tank full of petrol. This was removed on the Golf Links, and, a lighter one having been put on, he flew back into the aerodrome quite safely and easily.' (*The Aero*, 10 August 1910).

Sunday, 31 July. No flying was scheduled on this day, but at five o'clock Grahame-White took off and flew northwards, following the promenade past Blackpool Tower to the North Pier. Turning back, he passed the Victoria Pier (now the South Pier) and landed on the beach in front of the Lancashire Aero Club's club house, where he had some refreshments.

Claude Grahame-White's Farman on Blackpool beach, 31 July 1910

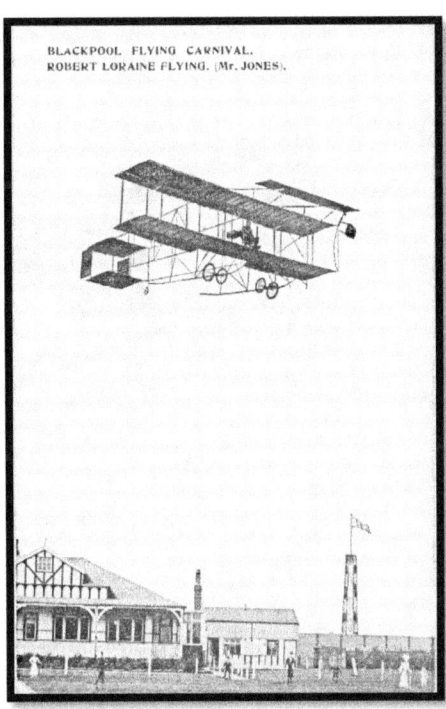

(Left) Robert on his Farman at Blackpool; (right) a faked photograph allegedly of Robert. It is in fact a photo of Louis Paulhan at Blackpool a year earlier! The pylon and a few figures have been added by A.P. Co.

A grumpy-looking Robert Lorraine [sic], inset, allegedly in flight at Blackpool, but note absence of identification letters "ON" on the rudder.

Published by E. R. G. & Co., Blackpool.—No. 19.

LORRAINE in F

...ht at Blackpool.

Inevitably, a large crowd had gathered and when Grahame-White tried to fly off, policemen and club members had to clear a space big enough for a safe take-off.

Monday, 1 August (Bank Holiday). Grace took off in his new Blériot and made a flight of eight and a half minutes. He started a second flight but, during the take-off run, the ignition control failed to work when he tried to shut down the engine. Although he shut-off the fuel supply, the engine kept turning until he had landed and crashed, breaking the wheels and propeller.

Robert had made plans the night before to make a flight away from the aerodrome, down the coast to the south. The plan was that after lunch ('...we had lunched amply off lobsters and cold beef') they would motor up to the hangar at 2 p.m., wheel out the Farman and, once in the air, Robert would circle the aerodrome once to give the impression that he was flying circuits. Meanwhile, George, Jules Védrines, and his brother Emile (who had days earlier been summoned to Blackpool to help), would pile into the car loaded with tools and petrol, and drive with Gibbs at the wheel to Lytham St. Anne's. From there, they would follow Robert's progress by telephone.

It was 2.15 p.m. when the conspirators arrived and, while Robert dressed for the flight, George gave warning to a steward that Robert was going to try for the Duration Prize: 'Loraine and the racing Farman became visible at 3 p.m., but no start was made until 3.15 p.m., owing to one of the wheel hubs seizing on its spindle. A fresh wheel being substituted, Loraine started, and having made a circuit of the aerodrome went off in the direction of Lytham. Various suggestions were made as to his ultimate goal, but it was not until a quarter past four that he was located, when a telephone message from Liverpool brought the news that he was flying over that city. A few minutes later we heard that he was rounding New Brighton town, and on his way back...'

In his own words, Robert 'took the occasion to fly along the coast and up the Mersey; it was a Bank Holiday and on the way I flew to the Cheshire side and over the place where I was born and had my childhood's dream of flight. I had always imagined Liverpool as an enormous town and was amused to find what little space it seemed as I looked down from my machine. The docks were full of shipping and as I was the first aeroplane ever to fly over Liverpool all the shipping and river traffic saluted me with their sirens and steam whistles, which I could hear above the roar of my engine.'

Over sixty years later, Robert's flight was remembered by Seth Forrester: '...August Bank Holiday 1910, was a red-letter day for us, for dad took us to New Brighton beach to see the first aeroplane to fly over the town. It was Mr R. Loraine (later Major) in his Farman biplane. It looked like a huge bird. As he drew direct for New Brighton Tower at a rapid pace the excitement of the spectators was intense.

New Brighton tower. In front is "Ham & Egg" terrace, 'a disgraceful collection of low eating-houses and oyster-stalls, where horseplay and vulgarity gained New Brighton an unenviable reputation all over the country.' (Sulley, writing in 1889).

This photograph clearly shows the shorter lower plane of a "Racing Farman"

'He glided in and out among the high buildings across the Mersey, accompanied by the lusty cheers of the trippers. History was made that day by Bob Loraine!' (*The Wallasey News*, 30 December, 1972).

Theodore J Bray had also spotted Robert's Farman: "Sir. As an item of news it may interest you to know that, while cycling along Harrison Drive, Wallasey, this morning, about seven o'clock, I saw an Aeroplane flying rapidly parallel with the coast line apparently making for Llandudno.' (*Wallasey News*, 13 August 1910).

George and the others, meanwhile, reached their target hotel at Lytham St. Anne's: 'I succeeded in getting news of Robert from three places along the coast some ten minutes after he had passed over each. The last place I heard of him was at New Brighton, which showed that he must be within sight of Liverpool, his goal and turning point.' Nothing was heard from Liverpool itself when, suddenly, 'the barmaid of the hotel came rushing through the hall. "He's fallen in the sea!", she screamed. "He's fallen in the sea!" I left the telephone and pursued her out across the road and on to the sand dunes. I inspected the sea fearfully but it was as still as glass; there was nothing to be seen.'

Cross-examination of the barmaid brought no clear evidence that Robert and his Farman were down in the sea, but eventually Robert was seen approaching Lytham. Gibbs hurriedly drove George and the Védrines brothers back to the aerodrome where, to George's dismay, there was no sign of Robert: 'Just before 7 o'clock a biplane was seen travelling over St. Anne's, and this proved to be the missing Loraine and his Farman. Hearty cheers greeted his landing in the aerodrome. It appears that after leaving New Brighton he had trouble with the lower plane of the tail. The oil from the motor had saturated the fabric, and this bellied upwards, reducing the lift of the tail so much that Loraine decided to come down, and landed on a sandbank at Fairhaven at 5.5 p.m., 6 miles away from the aerodrome. With the aid of Captain Smart and the mechanics the fabric was riveted down again, and the flight resumed at 6.45 p.m. It would be difficult to over-estimate the importance of this cross-country flight, and it must certainly be classed amongst the finest examples of such we have had in this country. As this flight did not count for the duration prize, the petrol tank was filled up again, and Loraine started off round the aerodrome, he and Tétard providing some very pretty flying.' (*Flight*, 6 August 1910).[120]

Robert had landed on a sandbank at Fairhaven, on the edge of yet another golf course – the Royal Lytham & St. Anne's – 'just round the Northern corner of St. Anne's'. Flying across the Mersey as far south as his birthplace, New Brighton, and over Birkenhead, he had returned via Formby, having been in the air for a record total of 2 hours 15 minutes. George and the Védrines, having gone to the golf club, watched Robert fly back to the aerodrome, after it had taken a full twenty minutes to clear the crowd from the flight path:

---

[120] Maurice Tétard (19 Oct 1879–21 Sep 1962) was a well-known "test pilot" of the time.

'We lost no time in following them. In fact, Gibbs was summonsed subsequently for furious driving on the Lytham St. Anne's road. But even so Robert had arrived at the aerodrome and had made a perfect landing in front of the judge's box long before we got there. He met us at the big gates and one glance at his face froze the congratulations on my lips. Robert was glowering. It was no longer the pleasant happy, successful Robert of half an hour ago. This was the fighting, kicking Robert – Robert in a towering rage.

'"What do you think?" asked he. I deemed it better to think nothing.

'"They have disqualified all the time I was out of sight of their dirty little aerodrome. I should have stayed here and flown around and around like a bumble bee in an epileptic fit, it seems!"'

Knowing that a further fifteen minutes' flying would qualify him for the second prize of £50, he immediately did what was required. Tétard won first prize of £100 with an overall time of 1 hour 59 minutes 25 seconds. Robert managed only 42 minutes 56 seconds.

The prizes for 1 August were:
£100 Duration Prize to Tétard, time 1h. 59m. 25s.
£50 Duration Prize to Loraine, time 42 mins. 56 secs.
£50 Altitude Prize to Chavez, height 2,550 ft.
£100 Merit Prize to Grahame-White.
£50 Special Merit Prize to A. V. Roe.

Official attendance for the day was 24,000. (*Flight*, 6 August 1910).

Tuesday, 2 August. On another very windy day at Blackpool, only Roe and Grahame-White made desultory efforts at flying. Robert did not fly.

Wednesday, 3 August was a good day for flying. 'The first part of the Blackpool Flying Carnival concluded to-day, the weather being ideal. During the morning Grahame-White's daring flight on the previous evening and the possibility of Loraine's flight to Douglas [on the Isle of Man] were eagerly discussed by those more intimately connected with the machines.' (*Flight*, 13 August 1910). This was based on sightings on 6 August of George Smart checking out possible landing grounds on the Isle of Man. It was, apparently, quite well-known back at the Bournemouth meeting that Robert was planning to fly from Anglesey to Ireland via Douglas.

Robert tried to get airborne again, but it was soon clear that the problems with the Farman's tail from two days previously had not been corrected, and he landed almost immediately. At least his earlier efforts were rewarded to some extent: 'The total prizes gained during the week's meeting are:— Mr. Grahame-White £650; M. Chavez £225; Mr. Drexel £175; Mr. Loraine £75; Mr. Roe £50.' (*Flight*, 13 August 1910).

Thursday, 4 August to Sunday, 7 August. On these four days there was little flying, the elements making life very difficult for the aviators. During this period Jules Védrines

The caption to this postcard, sent from Blackpool on 24 August 1910, read, simply: 'Farman racing'

announced that he had to go back to his family in Paris, his wife having upset a pot of scalding soup over their two children. Though Emile Védrines remained, he was a carpenter who knew next to nothing about aeroplanes. Jules promised to return in three days, and was as good as his word, returning with both his wife and Emile's.

It may have been at this time (he was hopeless with dates) that George Smart recorded the addition of a new member to the Loraine team, a certain H.J. Higgins, from Bradford. Higgins was confident that he could 'foretell the weather conditions minutely for every half hour throughout the day.' He was, he added, seldom wrong! George was unconvinced but, at Robert's insistence, engaged him as weather-forecaster for the forthcoming tour. Robert went to London.

Monday, 8 August. The weather was so good that a crowd estimated at ten thousand flocked to the aerodrome. Though Robert, back from London, did not take to the air, exhibition flights were given by Tétard, Roe, Harding, and Grahame-White.

Tuesday, 9 August. The strong wind 'prevented any flying until 3.30 p.m., when Grahame-White, Tétard, and Roe were all ready to come out. Roe, unfortunately, landed too quickly, and turned a complete somersault without, however, injuring himself. Grahame-White took up a lady passenger for a flight, which lasted a quarter of an hour, during which he rose to the height of 350 feet.' (*The Aero*, 17 August 1910). Roe, making a downwind landing, came in too fast and, losing control whilst turning, the triplane flipped onto its back. He escaped with only a slight injury to an ankle.

Robert again did no flying – he had other plans!

Financially, the Blackpool aviation meeting was a disaster, not least because the public had quickly realised that they could gain a perfectly good, free, view of the flying from the surrounding higher ground. *Flight* lamented that 'the financial loss is so great that the Lancashire Aero Club are not likely to undertake another meeting. Many things have contributed to this result, the weather being a large factor in preventing the success of the meeting. Lack of support from the municipality, and the thrift of those people who wished to see the flying without paying for the pleasure of doing so, have also handicapped the finances.

'Mr. Huntley Walker, who was chiefly responsible for the Carnival being held, estimates the deficiency at about £20,000 — a sum in which Lloyd's are considerably interested in finding.'

Years later, Winifred Loraine wrote scathingly about the meeting: 'The promoters were purely commercial. There were several large-scale caterers and brewers who had hired suitable ground two miles outside Blackpool and had converted it into an aerodrome.'[121]

---

[121] *Robert Loraine. Actor. Soldier. Airman*, p.126. This aerodrome became known as Squire's Gate.

The meeting, however, was far from being a disaster for Alliott Verdon Roe, who married Elizabeth Kirk on Saturday, 20 August at the South Shore Parish Church, Blackpool.[122] Two days later, while Mrs. Roe remained in England, Mr. Roe sailed for America, having been invited, along with Grahame-White, to compete in the Harvard/Boston Aero meeting in the USA.

Robert at Blackpool [photo: Flight]

---

[122] Miss Kirk's address at the time of her marriage was 84 Upper Richmond Road, Putney, London.

Chapter Seven: 'One of the most sensational flights in history.'

Robert's inactivity on 8 and 9 August 1910 at the Blackpool flying carnival was for the very good reason that he was preparing for his crossing to Ireland from Holyhead, Anglesey, North Wales.

Wednesday, 10 August. In readiness for this, George Smart had made his way overnight by train from Blackpool to Holyhead, booking into the Station Hotel.

Station Hotel, Holyhead

Meanwhile, back at Blackpool: 'It was a foggy morning at Blackpool, dead still and very cold. Robert had no difficulty in getting up at half past four that morning... Gibbs, who is physically incapable of being punctual, on this occasion managed to be only ten minutes late. Robert was waiting for him dressed in an ulster, his leather-lined tweed coat, breeches and stockings, a sweater, goggles and the abominable but beloved, leather cap. He also carried a handbag – he always does when he goes flying. It contains all sorts of things, mostly useless; novels, alternative goggles, alternative and more beautiful caps, and nowadays a compass. Robert greeted Gibbs coldly but politely. It is one of his finest qualities that he never fusses or blames, even under the most aggravating and nerve-wracking circumstances'.

They made their way to the Farman's hangar at Blackpool aerodrome: 'The Gnôme [engine] was soon started, and at 6.26 a.m. Mr. Loraine was in the air, and, climbing to a

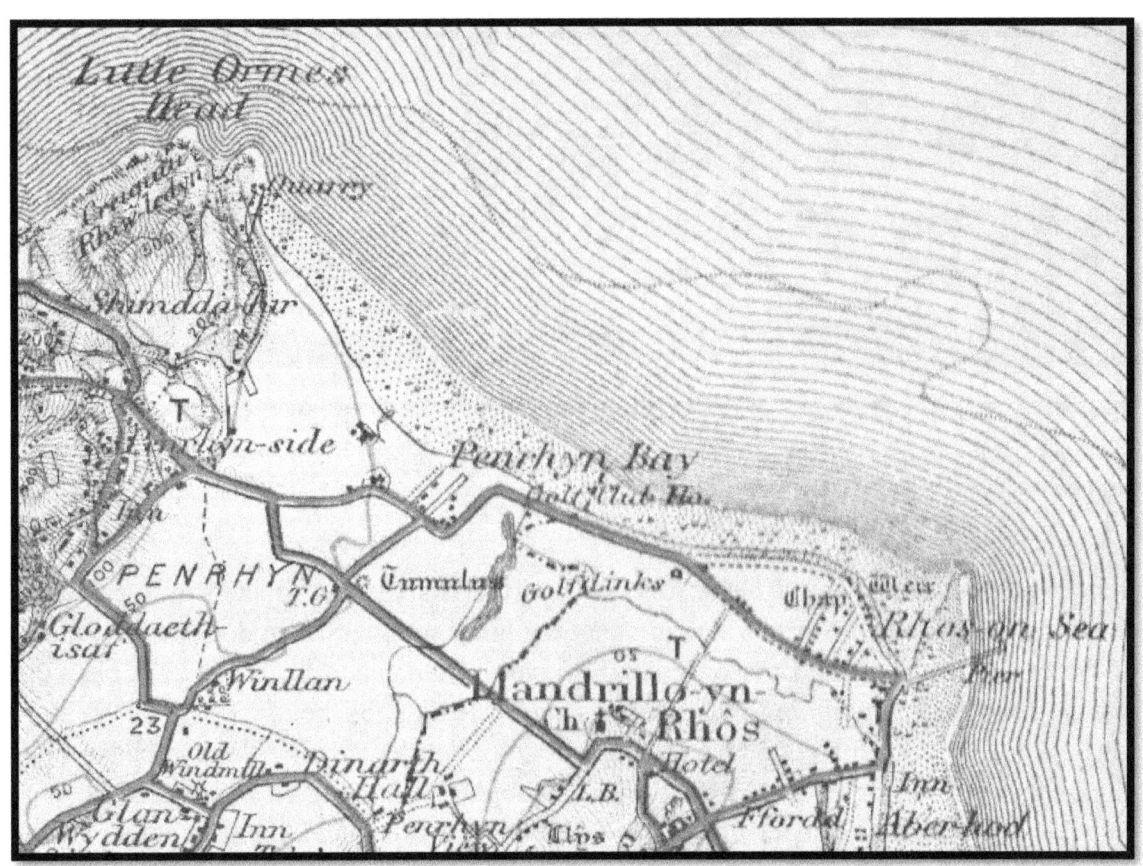

*Map showing Rhos-on-Sea, the golf links, Dinarth Hall, and Little Ormes Head
(OS map Llandudno, (Large Sheet Series) Sheet 42, pub. 1909)*

good altitude, he eventually darted off in the direction of Southport, and, crossing the town, turned out to sea, direct across to the Welsh coast, striking it at Rhos, and landing on the golf links there after a flight of about 60 miles. The time taken was a little over an hour and a half. Mr. Loraine intended to fly on to Holyhead later in the day.' (*Flight*, 13 August 1910).

The Aero also reported: 'Starting at 6.20 a.m., Loraine flew over St. Anne's to Southport and then across the mouth of the Mersey to Hoylake. From this, crossing the Dee, he flew parallel to the Welsh coast till he came within sight of the Great Orme's Head, eventually coming down on the golf links at Rhos-on-sea, within half a mile of Llandudno.' (*The Aero*, 17 August 1910).

♦ ♦ ♦

Hewitt's three photographs published in Flight, 25 June 1910. The aeroplane is unmistakably a Blériot. The car, registration number DM206, was registered in Flint.

It has been suggested that Robert was, in fact, the first person to land in a powered aeroplane from beyond North Wales *into* that region, if not the first to do so in the whole of Wales. Vivian Vaughan Davies Hewitt, however, a then uncertificated aviator, claimed to have been the first to fly *in* North Wales as per his letter published by *Flight* on 25 June 1910: 'I enclose some photographs of my Blériot monoplane and, as I claim to be the first one to fly on an aeroplane in North Wales, I thought they would be interesting to your valuable paper. I have been practising for some time on my machine, and had rather a nasty smash about two months ago, landing in the railway hedge from a height of about 30 feet. However, on the 26th of May [1910] I towed my machine to a large field, and succeeded in making a flight of half a mile, during which I attained a height of about 70 feet. The centre photograph shows the method of towing the Blériot behind my car. In the left-hand picture I am starting up prior to my flight, and that on the right was taken by my mechanic immediately after landing. The Blériot behaved very well during the flight, at the end of which I switched off and glided down, and, although it bumped a little on landing, nothing was damaged. Since then I have made numerous small flights, and hope to do better when I become more accustomed to the machine. [*signed*] Vivian V.D. Hewitt, Bodfari, North Wales.' (See Hewitt in Appendix IV).

Another claimant to be the first to fly in Wales was Cardiff-based engineer Horace Watkins (1884–1976) who, in his small, red monoplane, *Robin Gôch* (Red Robin), claimed to have made a few hops in 1909 and a more substantial flight in 1910. There appears to be no documentary evidence for any of these flights.

♦ ♦ ♦

Robert wrote his own account of the flight to Rhos: 'Leaving the Blackpool Aerodrome soon after dawn, in lovely weather I rose quickly to about 3,000 feet and I felt an unusual pressure on the elevator which became much stronger when I stopped climbing and commenced to fly in horizontal course.

'Owing to a wrong adjustment of the incidence of the planes the machine wanted to climb all the time and I could only prevent her from climbing by exerting all my strength on the elevator control lever which bent like a bow in the most alarming way.[123]

'I thought I should have to alight or fly back to the aerodrome to rectify the error of the adjustment as my arms were being numbed by the effort necessary to hold a level course and the strain set up throughout the whole structure was clearly very dangerous…'

Then 'a panorama of such sublime beauty was unveiled before me as the morning mists melted under the warmth of the rising sun that I forgot everything else as I gazed at the inspiring revelation of the wonders of the Lord. Through the ascending wreaths and wisps I saw beyond the sea the mountains of Snowdonia unveil their exquisite beauty. My spirit filled with heavenly joy as I could no more have turned my back on this glorious spectacle than a true believer could on paradise.

'In this exalted state I flew on entranced until I saw the golf course at Rhos on Sea near Llandudno where I alighted near the club house and was welcomed and given breakfast.

'Within an incredibly short time a crowd of such dimensions gathered around my biplane that it seemed as if all the inhabitants of Wales had come to see the first aeroplane to alight in their lovely land.'

Flight reported, too, that 10 August 'was remarkable for the magnificent effort made by Loraine, in flying to Cemlyn in Anglesey, with one stop at Rhos, near Llandudno. It was generally understood that Loraine was only waiting for favourable weather in order to put in some long distance flying, the opinion being held that he would probably try to reach some point on the Welsh coast, since he had abandoned the idea of flying to Douglas. His mechanics were very busy on Tuesday overhauling the machine and dismantling the engine. A start was made at 6.30 a.m. on Wednesday, just as the sun was breaking through the mist, and after making a circuit of the aerodrome to test the working of the motor, Loraine left in the direction of Liverpool, followed post haste by a car containing his mechanics and spares. Nothing further was heard of him until just before noon, when news came through that he had reached Rhos safely in time for breakfast.' (*Flight*, 20 August 1910).

After an hour and a half, approaching the Great Orme's Head, Robert had decided it was time to land and, fortuitously spotting Rhos-on-Sea golf course – his third in recent weeks – he landed on one of its fairways, to be met by a man in his pyjamas waving a toothbrush!

---

[123] The cause of this, it transpired, was faulty rigging by Emile Védrines.

Robert's Farman, Rhos-on-Sea golf course, 10 August 1910

BLACKPOOL
LORRAINE'S GRAND FLIGHT, FIRST

Robert's Farman at Rhos-on-Sea golf course. The placard invites a visit to 'Penrhyn Old Hall / near by / a rugged medieval manor...'

This apparition manifested himself as no less a personage than Henry Goldsmith, the owner of the golf course. Next on the scene were John Jones[124] and his son, Griffith Jones, of Dinarth Hall. Wishing to make a telephone call, Robert was offered a telephone at either Dinarth or, 200 yards away, at the Golf House. Choosing the latter, he sent a telegram for his support staff, and had his breakfast there, before lunching at Dinarth Hall and returning to the golf club for tea.

Arriving at Rhos-on-Sea with Gibbs in the support car was Jules Védrines who, reaching the golf course at around 3 p.m., had soon fixed the problem with the rigging caused by Emile's incompetence. Robert tried to fly off at 4.25 p.m., but was unable to do so as a large crowd, estimated at between ten and fifteen thousand, blocked his path, as Robert noted: 'There were of course the usual autograph collectors, but among the humbler folk there was an attitude of reverence, which was embarrassing. Hundreds of the women brought their children and begged me to let the little ones touch me…

'This was all very well but I wanted to get on with my journey to Holyhead and for two hours it was impossible to clear a lane in the crowd for my necessary run along the ground before I could get in to the air.

---

[124] John Jones' son, wife and two children were drowned in the sinking of the *Lusitania* in 1915.

At last they were made to understand that I could not rise vertically and they gave way and formed a passage. I gave the order to Védrines and my engine was started and I was off on my journey to Holyhead.'

After breakfast at the Station Hotel at Holyhead, George had made his way onto the roof of the hotel to look for a suitable landing ground for Robert. Through a pair of binoculars, he noticed that Holyhead's two harbours were divided by a green spit of land, Salt Island, the nearest point to the Irish mainland.

Deciding that Salt Island would be ideal, he sought permission to use it from the Captain of the Port of Holyhead, Rear-Admiral John Leslie Burr RN (1847–1917). Permission was enthusiastically granted, and work was at once put in hand for housing the Farman. All was ready by lunchtime.

Returning to the hotel, George was handed a telegram from Robert saying that all was well and that he was at Rhos-on-Sea golf links, having lunch. In the afternoon, in anticipation of the crossing to Ireland, George hired, at considerable expense, six tugs from a Liverpool firm – Alexandra Towing Company – each to be placed at seven-mile intervals across the Irish Sea under Robert's intended flightpath. He also arranged for a man with rocket flares to go on each tug.

A Mr. N.J. Hall wrote to *The Aero* (published on 24 August 1910): 'Enclosed you will find a few photographs taken by myself of Mr. Loraine's visit to the Rhos Golf Links, Colwyn Bay, yesterday, August 10th… Mr. Loraine arrived here at 8 a.m., having started from Blackpool at 6 a.m. He had intended alighting at Llandudno, but for some reason or other changed his mind and alighted at Rhos instead. After sending a telegram to Blackpool for his two mechanics he went to the Golf House to rest.

'The mechanics arrived in a motor car in the afternoon, and after cleaning and overhauling the Gnôme engine, and tightening the wires, pulled the Farman biplane to a level stretch of turf and waited there for Mr. Loraine to finish his tea.

'When Mr. "Jones" appeared he was enthusiastically cheered by the waiting crowds; having donned his lifebelt he climbed into his seat, the mechanics started the engine, let it run for a minute or two to see if all was in order, then let go.

'After running along the ground for about 100 yards Mr. Loraine rose beautifully into the air, turning in a wide circle he made out to sea high in the air, rounded the Little Orme, and was lost to view.'

Rhos-on-Sea to Holyhead. It was not until around 7 p.m. that the local constabulary had been able to clear a path, when Robert was able to take-off for Salt Island, where George Smart was waiting to greet his friend.

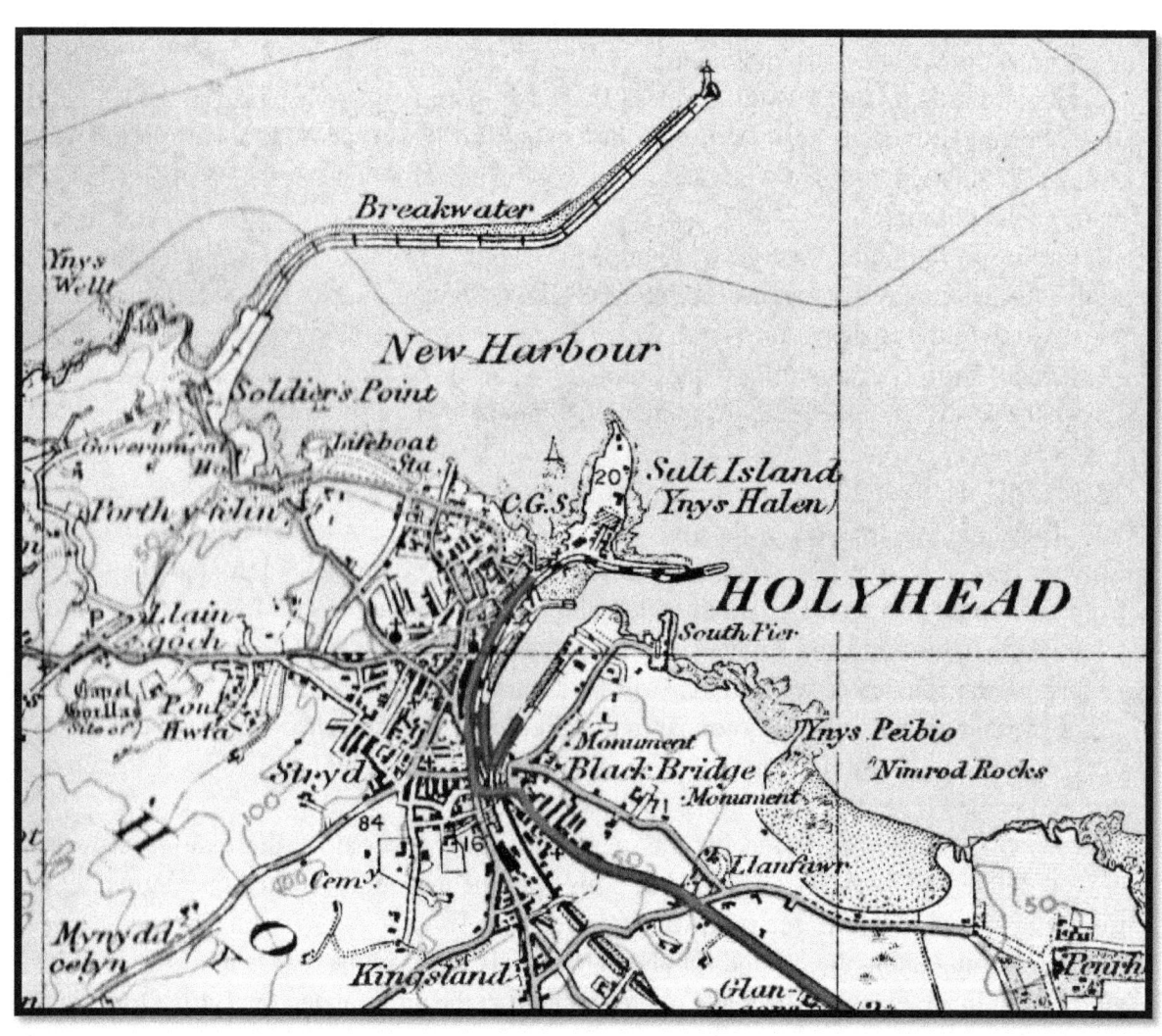

Holyhead and Salt Island (Ynys yr Halen) (OS map, Anglesey, Popular Edition, 1922)

Another view of the Farman and crowd at Rhos-on-Sea golf course, 10 August 1910

'Escaping from the crowd at Rhos-on-Sea, August 10th, 1910' [Loraine family]

Robert later described his flight from Rhos to Anglesey, Winifred giving a potted version of it on pages 148-150 of her book: 'I was flying above, high over the solitary sea which glistened here and there where the heat haze did not obscure it. No ships in sight to break the solitude, no land in view to call the mind to earth, no instruments to tell me what my course should be for the compass tied to my left hand strut was useless from the vibration and the deviation caused by the magneto. I felt rather a fool.

'It seemed to me that my intelligence was less than my enthusiasm, that I was justifying the many accusations made against me of recklessness, I was hopelessly lost and my wrist watch told me that the petrol tank was more than half empty. The only guide to my geographical position was a wonderful orange and crimson sunset which indicated the west but vaguely for the sun was behind the clouds. The illuminated gates of heaven stretched over a third of the horizon and the changes of light caused by the motion of the spheres struck the shifting atmosphere of earth, fantastic headlands came and went on the horizon line that the sunset did not occupy.

'A strange exaltation of spirit and a sense of cosmic serenity was induced by the sunset colours, but it did not prevent me from thinking hard and looking hard.

'When I left the ground at the golf course I had intended to fly down the [coast] straight to Holyhead. But as my departure had been delayed by the difficulty to getting the immense crowd to give me starting space and the summer evening was beginning to fade (summer time had not yet been adopted) I decided to try a short cut (almost always a foolish thing to do) so flying to the Little Orme I flew straight across the bay to the Great Orme and then turned right at a right angle and flew toward Point Lynas, which I expected to sight after about ten or fifteen minutes.

'The sea was partially obscured by the mist and also I must have flown to the north, but I was still hoping to find Point Lynas ahead, and wondering if I had miscalculated time and distance when I realized I must have passed the island on my left and that I was over the Irish Sea. What could be simpler, you will say, than to turn round and fly straight back and a little to my right?

'But I was like the desert traveller, only more so. With no fixed point to set my course by, the one thing certain is that it would not be straight. So I climbed in large circles, searching the widening horizon.

'With the sunset in its usual place you will think it should have been sufficient indication to show me where East by South East lay, but I wanted to see land, and I felt by climbing high enough and enlarging my radius of vision I must do so. And, sure enough I did, and a welcome sight it was—but it was in the wrong place.

'With my nose pointing to the sunset the land I sought must be behind me, to my left, but what I saw was behind me on my right—N. by N.E.

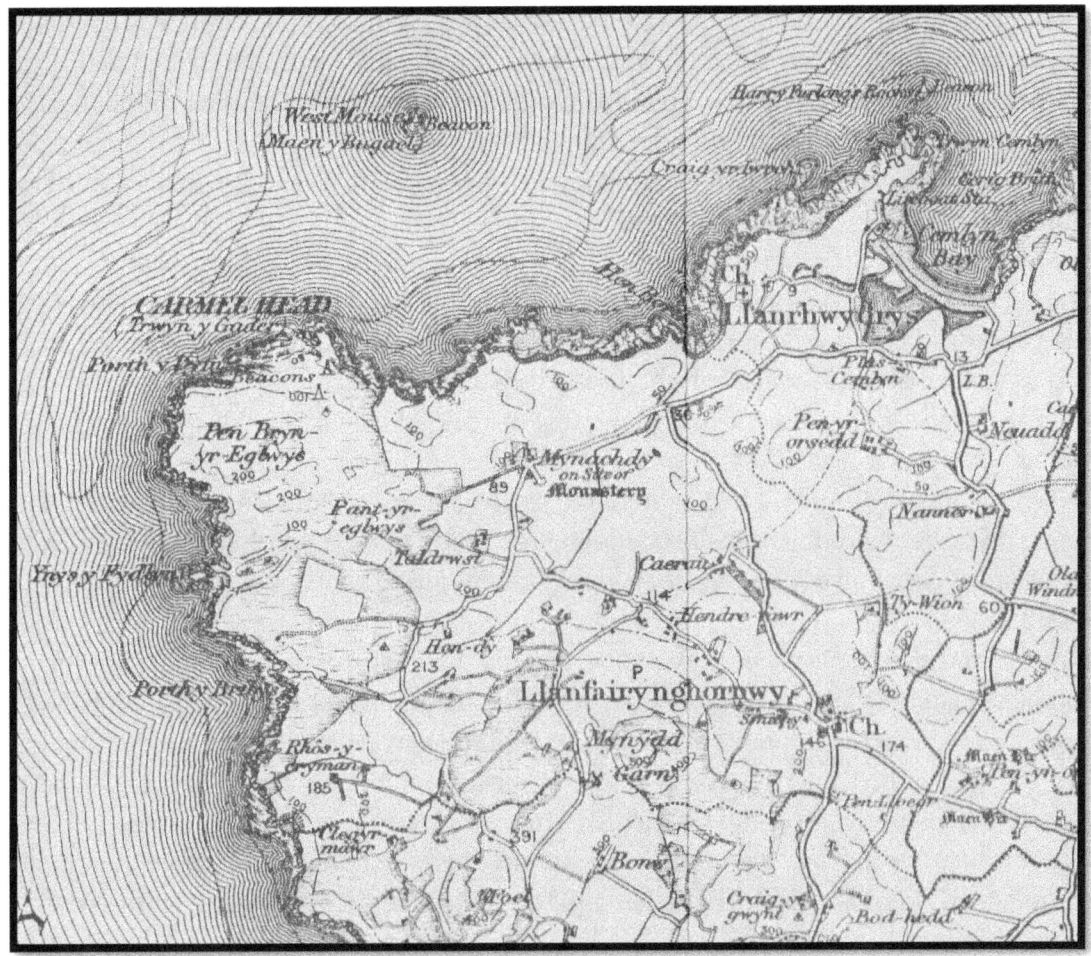
Part of 1905 OS map of north-west Anglesey; Llanfair-yng-hornwy in the centre

'Of course, it was the Isle of Man, or rather the Calf of Man, and as I made for it I remembered that my friend, George Smart, was waiting for me at Holyhead; that Holyhead was the place I meant to reach, and that if I flew straight away from the Calf of Man, keeping the sunset on my right, and watched carefully on my left, the range of vision from my great height must show me Anglesey if it was not hidden by fog.

'The surface of the sea was going into shadow as the earth revolved it away from the sun's rays.

'Then Anglesey jumped into view, just where I expected it to be, the whole island clearly outlined and unmistakable—in apparent size like that of a tea tray. Need I say I steered straight for the tea tray?

'I wondered if my petrol would hold out.

'As I drew nearer the island its green turned to umber, then to grey – night was overtaking the isle for, strange to say, the earth continued to revolve just as if nothing had happened.

'Nearer I flew, and the little problems of my daily life crept back into my mind and took the place of the calm serenity of impending death.

'My engine stopped about a mile from shore — the petrol was exhausted — but I was high enough to glide to land, and I made my first *vol plané*.'

Robert landed in the small field known as *Cae bendu* (*Black Field*) on Bryn Goelcerth farm,[125] near Llanfair-yng-hornwy, in north-west Anglesey, barely half a dozen miles from Salt Island as the crow flies. George Smart was to disparagingly describe the area as 'a strip of wilderness that could only be reached by eight miles of execrable cart tracks, up and down impossible gradients over outcrops of rock and shale. On every motor journey several tyres were burst.'[126]

When the inevitable crowd had gathered to see Robert's flying machine, the enterprising farmer on whose land Robert had landed (George Smart said it was Lloyd's farm)[127] seized the moment, charging three pence for a glass of local spring water, and a shilling for a glass of milk.[128]

Robert, meanwhile, was conveyed the sixteen long and winding miles by road to Holyhead on a farm cart, eventually arriving at the Station Hotel at 1 a.m. on Thursday, 11 August 1910. When his "crew" at the hotel heard the news, George wrote that they 'gave way to unrestrained hilarity which consisted in my joining in a war dance around the billiard table with the Védrines, whilst Mr Higgins so forgot himself as to clap his hands rhythmically. Of Gibbs, mercifully, I saw no more that night.' George had earlier 'commanded Gibbs to drive off into the night to find Robert. Gibbs was drunk – too drunk to speak, but not too drunk to drive.'

Holyhead to Ireland. As noted, Robert had been planning to make a flight from Blackpool to Ireland across the Irish Sea, with a stop at Douglas on the Isle of Man. Though George Smart had been seen surveying landing areas on the isle on 6 August, a new plan was made – Robert would now fly non-stop across the Irish Sea from Holyhead to Dublin. Thanks largely to George's industry, matters were well in hand by the time that Robert had reached Holyhead, where George and the Védrines brothers had also now gathered, conveyed thither by Gibbs.

Robert intended making the crossing to Ireland that very Thursday, 11 August, but strong winds would cause the flight to be postponed. Before the postponement, however, George, at the early hour of five o'clock in the morning, had 'interviewed six tired rocket operators,

---

[125] The farm was occupied by Ishmael and Margaret Jones, and their son Thomas, aged 4.
[126] *Robert Loraine. Actor. Soldier. Airman*, p.152.
[127] 'A clerk at Cemaes reports that a flying machine has come down on Lloyd's farm.'
[128] *Early Aviation in North Wales*, p.72.

together with six surly sea dogs, each of whom commanded a tug. The operators were tired because they had travelled all night with the rockets and had on that account been refused all shelter – even that of a station waiting room; the sea dogs were surly for no reason that I know of unless it be that tug commanding has embittering limitations. I paired them off, a rocketeer to a captain, and sent them away to take up station across the channel between Holyhead and Dublin.'

The six tugboats headed for their positions in the Irish Sea: 'Shortly after 8 o'clock last evening the *Andrew Jolliffe* and the *Alexandra*, two Liverpool tug boats, entered Kingstown Harbour [today Dún Laoghaire]. Their arrival was connected with the flight of Mr. Lorraine [*sic*] from Holyhead to Dublin.

'A representative of the "Daily Express" had an interview with the captains of both vessels, and learned from them that the *Andrew Jolliffe* had left Holyhead at 9 a.m. on Thursday morning [11 August] and had taken up her station three miles on the seaward side of the Kish lightship. The *Alexandra* followed her, and at hour intervals the tugs *Wallasey*, *Harrington*, *Hornby* and *Toxteth* left Holyhead and remained at stations seven miles apart. They were instructed to be at their stations at 2 p.m., and told that "Jones" would probably start his flight from Holyhead at 3 o'clock. The tug boats waited, but no sign of the aviator appeared, and the *Andrew Jolliffe*, *Alexandra*, and *Wallasey* came into Kingstown Harbour, while the *Harrington*, *Hornby*, and *Toxteth* put back to Holyhead.

'These tug boats were all supplied with red smoke rockets, for the purpose of signalling to "Jones" during his flight. The whole of the arrangements connected with the flight are in the hands of Lloyds' agent at Holyhead. According to instructions from him the tug boats in Kingstown Harbour are ordered to be at their stations at 6 o'clock this morning.

'It is expected that Mr. Lorraine will make an early flight and reach Dublin about 9 a.m.

'He had contemplated landing at Bray, but it is expected that this morning he will land on the strand at Sandymount, the tide being dead low and there being a splendid piece of sand stretching for a considerable number of miles. Failing this he will go inshore to land. It is stated that Captain Smart, Mr. Lorraine's agent, crossed to Kingstown last evening to make arrangements for the landing on the Irish coast.' (*Dublin Express*, Friday, 12 August 1910).

Sandymount, noted for its long, sandy beach, is a south-east suburb of Dublin. Bray lies a dozen miles to the south of Dublin, with Kingstown halfway between Sandymount and Bray.

While the tugs were busily engaged, Robert yet had to extricate his Farman from the field at Bryn Goelcerth, and another day was lost due to strong winds, as George Smart noted: 'The wind continued to rise throughout the afternoon and evening and the sky became more and more overcast. At seven o'clock I received a telegram from Robert saying that he had been obliged to abandon the idea of flying for the day. I recalled the tugs and returned moodily to the hotel. We dined in a state of considerable depression and afterwards Robert wrote a cheque for the horrible tugs, which had been lying out at sea all day. This operation almost brought tears to our eyes, for tug-hiring is one of the most expensive sports I've met. We went to bed early, wrapped in an atmosphere of opaque gloom.'

Friday, 12 August. They were up early in the morning, but their weatherman, Higgins, who had been with them all this time, gave them his prognostication that there would be a fierce storm that afternoon. George Smart was not convinced: 'By now I had lost all faith in Mr Higgins. He had never been wrong yet, certainly, but he was indubitably mad. Robert, on the other hand, still had a sneaking belief in him. He knew the man's methods to be questionable on scientific grounds, but he felt that Mr Higgins might have some gift in regard to the weather. I telephoned to the tug captains and the rocket men to stand by in Holyhead harbour, for we couldn't risk a second blank day – and a second cheque for the same. The retaining fee was bad enough but it was only one sixth of the amount of that haunting cheque.'

As the Védrines brothers were already 'established at the farm of Ishmael Jones', Robert, George and Mr. Higgins were driven by Gibbs to Llanfair-yng-hornwy. They were greeted by an upset Jules Védrines, who explained that, during the night, a pig had drunk a bucket of *col du pâte* (varnish) intended for the fabric covering the Farman's wings.[129] The wretched creature had also rubbed its back against the Farman's tail, and broken it. George was driven back to Salt Island for another bucket of varnish, 'leaving Robert surrounded by autograph books.'

George was back just in time to see Robert attempting to take-off with the wind behind him. As the Farman was going away from those watching, they 'could not see Robert or the elevating plane. At the bottom of the field, they left the ground and, keeping very low, sped across the ground to the opposite hills.

'A hundred yards and they hadn't risen an inch and in front of them was an abrupt slope 300 feet high and intersected by a stone wall. Of course, Robert was working like a madman to get her up and of course the wind, which was imperceptible on the ground, formed a solid lip over the cup-like hollow and forced them down. The end came soon. After a few seconds of terrible suspense, the white planes [*wings*], caught in some furious eddy, tilted over to an angle of forty-five degrees, the lip of the lower plane struck a stone wall, twisting the machine entirely around like a top. Then they smashed down to earth. The propeller and various bits of wood flew into the air in all directions and the planes collapsed flat on the ground, one on the top of the other like a falling house of cards.'

Everyone ran to the scene, to find 'Robert standing up by the wreck and waving his hand to us. We pulled up and looked at each other. The relief was nearly choking me, and the

---

[129] The concoction was starch-based – as in shirts and maids' aprons etc. – and was no doubt a great delicacy for pigs! Thanks to Richard Holleyman for this information.

tears began to roll down the cheeks of the excitable little Védrines. When we got up to Robert, he was calmly examining the damage. He was not hurt he told us a little brusquely, but brusqueness was the only sign he evinced of his shock and disappointment, otherwise he was the calmest person present.'

Jules Védrines' description of the crash is memorable: '… Patatras… Boum… Paf… Bing!... Le voilà par terre… En morceaux…' Crash, bang, wallop… on the ground… in pieces.[130]

This was *Flight*'s version of events: 'By his fine flights already achieved, Mr. Loraine ranks amongst the best pioneers of the day, and that he is mainly prompted in following up the art for itself is clearly evidenced by his exceptional avoidance of self-advertisement in regard to the work which he is accomplishing. Quite quietly and almost secretly on Saturday last he arrived at Holyhead from Cemlyn, where his Henry Farman machine is stored since his mishap when attempting to fly from that point to the Anglesey port.

'The weather being all that was desirable for a successful flight, Mr. Loraine determined to attempt the journey across the water to Dublin, with the intention of returning to Holyhead as soon as possible, anticipating the time the journey each way would occupy to be about 1½ hours. At six o'clock he was ready, and in spite of all precautions a goodly number of the public had somehow got wind of his intentions and gave voice to their enthusiasm at the apparently successful consummation of the project. The recent heavy rains, however, were against the attempt, having saturated the ground to such an extent that it was impossible to get the aeroplane up to a sufficient speed to enable it to get clear of terra firma.

'In the attempt, unfortunately, the machine came into contact with a boulder, smashing the lower part of the aeroplane, and necessitating considerable repairs. Mr. Loraine, who was somewhat mixed up with the wires through the sudden shock, was not hurt in any other way, although he came to the ground with a fair amount of force. Further attempt for the moment was therefore out of the question, and Mr. Loraine returned by car to Holyhead a very disappointed man. When he makes his next attempt in all probability his starting point will be from Salt Island, which spot he hopes to make for also on his return journey.' (*Flight*, 10 September 1910).

Robert had found a carpenter in the crowd, and the man agreed to build a hangar by the following night. With nothing further to be done, it was time to go. George 'took Robert's arm and turned away. "Are you sure you are all right, old man?" I asked. "Perfectly", he answered. He walked in silence for a while, then turned to me. "For a few seconds I thought I was going to be killed", he said simply.'

---

[130] *La vie d'un aviateur*, p.142.

'We were very silent going home, each of us busy trying to conquer our miserable disappointment. Our little drama had failed, utterly and completely failed. Our sudden appearance over Ireland could no longer take place. The papers would tell in many columns of the smash, and the repairs would take a week to perform. Robert would still fly the Irish Sea, of course; in fact, he was now bound to do so, but it would be an anti-climax. Dramatically speaking, we had already failed.

"'Why did you start?" I asked at last. "Outside there was a forty-mile [an hour] wind."

"'Good heavens! Was there?" Robert said, surprised. I regarded the pitifully drooping back of Mr Higgins in the front seat ferociously.

"'Did he tell you it was calm?"

"'No, no, it wasn't his fault", Robert, ever generous, hastened to assure me.

Again we were silent for a while.

"'What a lucky thing you smashed where you did, instead of getting out into the gale," I said.

"'By Jove, wasn't it?" he replied gratefully.

'Thereafter we discussed our plans for the repairs and future flights with the utmost optimism.'

That evening it was George's painful duty to dismiss the useless weatherman. Given his rail fare plus five shillings for expenses, Mr. Higgins was sent back whence he had come, to Bradford, Yorkshire.

Saturday, 13 August. Returning to the crashed Farman, they were accosted by a farmer, the owner of the field in which Robert had crashed. Not only was the farmer demanding payment for the damage caused, but he made it clear that the hangar would not be completed on his land until such a payment had been made. Robert had no choice but to agree to the man's demands, and signed an agreement for the damage to be duly assessed. With that, they hurried back to Holyhead for Robert to catch the train to London.

Jules Védrines set about re-building the wrecked aeroplane in the temporary hangar on lower, flatter ground near Mynachdy farm.[131] Robert had given him one week to complete the job. New parts were ordered, and slowly the Védrines brothers began to put the Farman back into the required shape, ably assisted by two intelligent boys, David and Dick ("Daveed" and "Deeck" according to Jules), who had been hired by George.

While all this was going on, Jules and Emile wrote to their wives, inviting them to their farmhouse. Soon the four were happily installed there, and everyone was very kind ('tout le monde est très gentil pour nous.') It was Gibbs who let the cat out of the bag when he told George that he had taken two French women to the farm where the Védrines were

---

[131] The 1911 Census shows four occupants of Mynachdy Farm: Hugh Jones (aged 39, unmarried); a housekeeper (39); a farm labourer in his mid-twenties; and a female domestic servant (16). (Via Richard Holleyman).

staying. To Gibbs they were, simply, 'a fine pair of lasses… "Madams" they call 'em, and they may be and they mayn't – but they're a bit of orl right any road.'

Robert was back after a week away. Not happy to find the Farman's repairs not yet completed, he decided to get rid of the Védrines brothers. George pleaded the case for Jules to be retained and, in the end, Robert agreed that Emile should go. Leaving the problem with George, Robert went off to London again, though when Emile and his wife departed is unclear. Jules was to write that Robert had hired a boat to take him and his brother to Dublin ['… de fréter spécialement un bateau pour nous conduire à Dublin, mon frère et moi.'][132] According to George Smart only Jules, his wife and George himself were actually on the boat to Dublin on 11 September – see page 146 below.

On 4 September, having returned from London, Robert tried to fly out of the field. This time the wind was blowing strongly from the east, in his favour, and would greatly assist his passage across to Ireland. No sooner had he begun his take-off, however, than the wheels stuck in the boggy ground and the Farman came to a sudden halt. George heard a loud detonation, 'followed by silence as the engine ceased. A shower of spars and splinters shot up in all directions. A bit of the propeller went up like a rocket', and the Farman 'subsided gently on the grass.'

Running to the crash, George 'observed with horror that Robert had not risen. I could see him kneeling on his hands and knees, with his back to us. Védrines and I raced each other across the oozing turf. Robert was in the same position when we got to him. I dived in through the wires to him.'

'"My ankles", he said, and immediately I noticed that he had become very pale.'

Robert's Farman and canvas and wood hangar at Mynachdy Farm (via Richard Holleyman)

---

[132] *La vie d'un aviateur*, p.143.

'Jules joined me and we saw that the front boom of the lower main planes, with all the weight of the engine, had fallen across his ankles. We managed to raise it a little and Robert crawled forward and sat down. We removed his shoes and stockings quickly and to our infinite relief were unable to discover a broken bone. Fortunately, the very softness of the ground, which had been his ruin, had also been the salvation of his ankle bones.'

A reporter from the *Freemasons Journal* saw the crash slightly differently: 'Unfortunately owing to the boggy state of the ground, caused by the recent rains, he failed to raise the machine. It went at a moderate speed until it struck a rock, which completely damaged the lower portion of the machine. Loraine himself became entangled in the biplane and injured his right leg rather badly. He was taken from under the machine by friends, and immediately attended to by a Holyhead doctor. Later he was conveyed by motor to Holyhead.'

George and others 'helped Robert across to the hangar and the doctor, after making a careful examination, was able to pronounce the injury no worse than a slight sprain.' Leaving him bathing Robert's ankles in a bucket, George went back to the Farman which, this time, had suffered only a broken undercarriage and a couple of bends to the main wing. It was Jules's task to get the Farman back to the hangar and to repair it once more.

It was all too much for Robert, a little bruised and battered, and he told George that he was all for giving up: '"I shall have to chuck it", he said at last. I made no answer.'

'"There is no way out of it, is there?" he asked anxiously.'

The mood brightened after dinner, and after the doctor had bandaged Robert's ankles, he 'spoke hopefully of a quick recovery. That was enough for Robert.'

'"Can we get her in?" he asked suddenly. "I think so", I answered.'

'"Get her in somewhere nearby, where the luck is better", he said. "By Gad, I must have one more dart at it".'

And so, in better spirits, Robert again took the night train from Holyhead to London. The keen reporter from the *Freemasons Journal* found Robert 'on the railway platform awaiting the arrival of the Irish mail which leaves at 12.15 a.m. He was assisted to the sleeping saloon portion of the train by Captain Smart, who superintends the flight. Asked as to what caused the mishap he replied – "The state of the ground and nothing else."

'"How was the wind?" I asked him, to which came the reply, "There was no wind at the time."'

'Further questioned as to whether he was badly injured, he said he could not say exactly what was the extent of the injury to his right leg… He looked pale and rather disappointed.' (*Freemasons Journal*, 5 September 1910).

On the morning of Monday, 5 September, in view of Robert's regained optimism for the flight to Ireland, George hired a number of carts and sent them out to Mynachdy with instructions for Jules to load the Farman onto them. George, meanwhile, would look for a

Penrhôs Park

suitable new home for it. With nothing suitable near Holyhead, he found a spot on the coast at Penrhôs Park, home of Lord Sheffield,[133] two miles east of Holyhead. Seeking, and getting, permission to use the site, a temporary shelter was erected under some trees in the park, near the shore on Holyhead Bay.

George soon received news that there was trouble brewing at Mynachdy, and went there only to find that Jules was insisting that the Farman be put into proper crates before being carted off somewhere. He wanted these huge boxes – or else! George ignored the volatile Frenchman, and supervised the packing of the Farman onto the carts himself. It was six in the evening before the job was finished. Before them lay the journey of a dozen miles or so to Penrhôs Park, through Llanfair-yng-hornwy, on to Valley and then by the London Road to Penrhôs.

Back in Holyhead, George was handed a letter from the farmer on whose field Robert had landed. The man was demanding considerable recompense. Leaving that aside for the time being, George set off in search of the Farman-bearing carts and eventually found the first, at ten o'clock that night, on the London Road (today the A5) heading slowly for its destination: 'By one o'clock the following morning we had parked all the lorries [*carts*] besides the half-completed hangar. The rest of the week was spent in unceasing labour.'

These were trying times, not helped by Gibbs's behaviour, with Robert's chauffeur basking in the reflected glory of his master's deeds: 'He also had friends, who showered favours upon him and as there is only one form of appreciation that appeals to him, I am

---

[133] Edward Lyulph Stanley (1839-1925), 4th Baron Stanley, had become Earl of Sheffield in 1909.

sorry to say that Gibbs was now almost perpetually intoxicated. The car began to fail at psychological moments and my temper began to give out.'

Friday, 9 September. Nevertheless, by Friday night, Jules, with the help of his young assistants, "Daveed" and "Deeck", had finished the repairs to the Farman. Robert was again summoned from London.

Saturday, 10 September. Returning to Holyhead in time for dinner with Rear-Admiral Burr, Robert, having been teetotal all summer, partook of a glass or two of the admiral's excellent port.

Sunday, 11 September. Robert was impatient to take the Farman for a test flight. George 'ran forward to the brow of the hill to see if the tide was out and our sand aerodrome visible, but to my horror there was scarcely any sand at all. We were too early; only a vast expanse of smooth water faced me.' Robert was off anyway, and the Farman flew beautifully, its engine not missing a beat. As he flew back, George 'turned to Jules, who had run up and was standing close to me, staring with parted lips and shining eyes. I put my hand on his shoulder. "Good, good", I said in French. "You are a marvel, Jules." Tears sprang into his eyes.'

'"C'est bien. Il marche très bien ("It's good. It's going very well") he said, turning away.

'Robert made a wide circle towards Holyhead Mountain, and then turned back along the wharves. Then he bore out into the bay a little, so as to approach the field end on. When he was some 100 yards from the cliff, he cut the engine and began to glide down towards us.'

Robert landed, got out of the aeroplane and walked towards George:

'"She's perfect", he said. "You have all done wonders."

'"I am glad," I answered.

'"A little breakfast and I'll be off," he said. The big house opened its arms to us, and we went in to breakfast. Whilst we fed leisurely and sumptuously three things happened. The crowd outside in the Park grew larger and larger, a strongish wind got up, and our car broke down.'

Soon, though, it was time to leave Penrhôs Park for distant Ireland. 'The wind had increased to a strength of between fifteen and twenty miles an hour when we emerged from the big house, but it was due east and therefore rather an advantage than otherwise, for the rest of the weather was propitious; it was one of those blue and white days, clear and cold for the time of year, with a sky covered with puffy patches of cotton-wool cloud.'

'Thoroughly alive to the lack of shipping in the channel on Sunday mornings, I sought out Gibbs, with the idea of sending him down to the harbour to endeavour to persuade any yachts or tugs that might be in to put out.' George found him perspiring, very red in the face, and peering underneath the bonnet of the car. Gibbs was not in a good mood. Not only did he not know why the car wouldn't start, but he hadn't had any breakfast yet!

Robert and his Farman at Penrhôs Park, 11 September 1910 (via Richard Holleyman)

George 'borrowed a car, sent it off with a note to the Admiral, and then joined a consultation that was going on between Robert and Védrines respecting the strength of the wind. We decided that it was not too bad, and Robert announced his intention of pushing off at once.'

'"There are no boats out. Hadn't you better wait and see if we can get hold of some?" I said.

'"It is better not to wait", Robert answered. "If you can find any, send them along after me to pick me up."'

So, they dressed Robert 'up in two sweaters, a padded waistcoat and a patent jacket which was made of reindeer hair and was warranted to keep him afloat for five days. And over all we fixed on his old cork lifebelt. Robert is not in the least superstitious, but he will never fly across water without that lifebelt.' On his head he wore 'the leather cap which, in addition to its original hideousness, was now dirty and stained from much wear.'

'He climbed up into his seat whilst the crowd cheered and waved hats and handkerchiefs frantically. Then we fixed the new compass to his [right] knee, which was the most suitable place for it, as we had discovered from our experiments.'

Just as they were discussing the position of the sun with regard to Robert's intended course, and whilst Jules was giving the engine a final pat, the Admiral hurried up. He was greatly concerned. There was not a ship of any sort in the harbour that could put out into the channel except his own launch, with a radius of operation of ten miles only, and a motor-boat which was given to breaking down.'

'"That's all right," said Robert cheerily. "Send the motor boat after me, but I'm pretty sure I shall be all right,"'

'"Come on – let's get off."'

And so, at 11.05 a.m., on Sunday, 11 September 1910, the compass on his right knee, and a map on his left, he took off in the direction of Ireland. As for the cork lifebelt, it would, in the event, prove to be more of a hindrance than a help.

Left: Robert at Penrhôs Park, about to set off for Ireland. Note the cork lifebelt around his middle, compass on his right knee and map case on his left. (The Sphere, 17 September 1910, via Richard Holleyman). Right: Robert's compass, made by Ross of London, now owned by Roy Sloan. [photo via Richard Holleyman]

When it was all over, and Robert was safe in Dublin, he gave his account of the flight. At first he made good progress being able, he said, to verify 'the relative position of the sun and my compass needle' by following the wake of the mail boat making for Holyhead. However, about a third of the way across and flying at 4,000 feet, his engine suddenly malfunctioned and, most alarmingly, stopped. The Farman headed down to the empty sea below but, just as he had managed to pull up with a few hundred feet to spare, the engine coughed back into life.

Listening all the while, Jules 'gave the solution. The big petrol tank had lately been opened, to be fitted with baffle plates, and no doubt a little pellet of solder had been left in. This would roll back and close the feed pipe when the machine was tilted upwards and would likewise roll away when the glide became steep and the machine tilted downwards.'

Robert continued: 'Between whiles I set my course, keeping my eyes almost continuously on the compass on my knee and feeling the most desolate of all living human beings in that dreary isolation of empty space. There was nothing to be seen but a blue sea and a blue sky. Neither ship nor land did I sight for over forty minutes, also there was nothing to assure me that I was steering right except the sun, and that only gave me a rough idea. I had to rely implicitly on the compass and, of course, 1 was haunted every second by the dread of that failing engine.'

Height would be gained and lost six times before the flight came to an end. To add to his worries, Robert had to fly through a rain squall, and visibility worsened. Looking at his watch, he noted that he had been up for an hour: 'If I was on my right course, I must be half-way across I thought, and at the altitude I was, I ought to see land.'[134]

If he saw nothing below, he 'was observed near the Kish light vessel, off Kingstown, going along at a very great altitude, and with every prospect of a safe landing.' Making its way from Dublin was the steamer *Snowdon*, whose master, Captain Bulmer, had 'sighted the aeroplane… and at the time it was proceeding in a most graceful and easy manner.' (*Western Daily Mail*, 12 September 1910). (This steamer was George's "Butter boat" – see page 158).

Worryingly for Robert, though, he had seen nothing until spotting the lightship moored on the Kish Bank, some seven miles east of Dublin. Now, at least, he knew where he was: 'It was with considerable relief, under the circumstances, that he ultimately discerned the Howth promontory through the bank of cloud and mist which hung over the Irish coast.'

Elated, Robert looked at his watch again, and saw that it was 12.15 p.m.: 'So I had done the sixty-four miles in an hour and ten minutes, record going for a record crossing'.

---

[134] *Robert Loraine. Actor. Soldier. Airman*, p.169.

The Kish lightship Cormorant, June 1908 (withdrawn from service on 9 November 1965) [photo: National Library of Ireland]

Robert was not far from his intended landing-place when something went wrong with the Farman's controls. Struggling to keep it in level flight, he headed for the nearest point of land off to his right – Howth Head. He was low over the water when 'something else went… Whatever it was we plunged straight into the sea.'[135] Jules Védrines, interjecting again, was certain that the wire on the small tailplane had parted: 'C'est le petit cellule. C'est le petit cellule. C'est le fil du fer Anglais...' ('It's the small tailplane. It's the small tailplane. It's the English wire…'). Jules despised the poor quality of British-made goods compared with the excellent French ones!

---

[135] *Robert Loraine. Actor. Soldier. Airman*, pp.170-1.

Robert continued his account: 'I managed to straighten her a little at the last moment, and splash! We were in the sea!'

'I dived as deep as 1 could to clear the wires and it seemed ages before I came to the surface. When I did, I found 1 was just outside the machine, which looked as if it was going to sink immediately. 1 struck out at once, to avoid being caught by the end of the wings, and as I did so she turned slowly over on her back. She sunk as far as her lower plane and then floated with her two wheels and skids sticking forlornly up in the air, like a dead wild duck. I made for the shore, and as I swam I cursed myself for having put on so many clothes, for I could scarcely strike out at all. When I was within fifty yards of the rocks at the foot of the cliff I saw the lighthouse man removing his coat and waistcoat, evidently with the idea of rescuing me, but naturally I didn't want to be rescued; the best I could do now was to get ashore unaided. But I had the greatest difficulty in preventing him, in fact I had to tread water and swear at him.'

Robert had come down a hundred yards or so from Irish soil, and almost in the shadow of the Baily lighthouse on Howth Head.

The "lighthouse man", Mr. J. Natson, reported to his superiors: 'I respectfully beg to report that today at noon I observed a biplane passing this Station from the Eastward. When about 500 yards N.W. of the lighthouse it circled round and dropped into the sea about 100 yards on the Dublin side of here. After a short time the aviator, who turned out to be Mr. Lorraine [sic] swam towards the rocks and I assisted him to land. One of Tedcastle's

The Baily lighthouse on Howth Head

steamers, the Adela, came along shortly after and we directed her attention to the machine in the water, she lowered a boat and took the machine in tow, brought it alongside the ship and hoisted it on board. Mr. Lorraine asked me to put him on board the steamer so that he could look after his machine, which I did in the boat that has been here for some time back for the workmen's use… J. Natson (Lighthouse Keeper)'.

Badge of the Loraine Club cyclists [by kind permission of Bob Montgomery, via Guy Warner]

Among the witnesses to Robert's watery arrival were 'members of a local cycle club who were out for a spin. They decided to honour the occasion by adopting the name "The Loraine Cycle Club", with the good-natured agreement of Loraine himself.'[136]

Robert was happy to become President and Patron of the Loraine Club. On his death in 1935, his widow, Winifred, became their (Honorary) Life Vice-President and kept up a correspondence with them until the outbreak of the Second World War in 1939. She also gave the Club a gift of £30 (equivalent to £2,650 approx. in 2023).

Inevitably, there were any number of accounts in various newspapers of the momentous event, including this one: 'Mr. Loraine, the aviator, just fell short by about a hundred yards of the jetty near the Irish coast. Shortly before one o'clock he suddenly appeared from amid the haze over the sea some distance from Howth Head. There were but few people about the cliffs, as the morning had been hazy and rain was falling. Mr. Loraine's intention was, apparently, to effect a landing on one of the slopes on the head, but when about a couple of hundred yards off the cliffs his gnome engine [*sic* – Gnôme] did not work well, and he could not get the aeroplane to rise. It subsided, and at the tantalizingly distance of about a hundred yards from the shore it dropped quietly into the water.

'Those on shore who saw the occurrence were greatly alarmed for the aviator's safety, but their fears were relieved when they saw him detaching himself from the machine and pluckily striking out for the shore. He reached the rocks close to the Bailey [*sic* – Baily] Lighthouse without difficulty, and clambered up clear of the sea. The water was very calm at the time.'

'Meanwhile, the ss *Adela*, of the Tedcastle McCormick Co., which was coming into Dublin, picked up the aeroplane which had floated. By the time Mr. Loraine himself had

---

[136] *Pioneers, Showmen and the RFC*, p.62.

The Adela

got into a small rowing boat, and was rowing to the rescue of his machine, and he was taken on board by the *Adela*. He found the aeroplane very little damaged.

'The *Adela* then resumed her voyage to Dublin, and arrived in the port at about 2 o'clock.' (*Cork Examiner*, 12 September 1910).

Robert was taken by Mr. Natson by boat from the lighthouse to the *Adela*, where his Farman 'had already been practically salved, and he was able to have the satisfaction of personally ascertaining the amount of damage it had sustained.'[137]

Once aboard the *Adela*, Robert was delivered in triumph up the River Liffey to Sir John Rogerson's Quay, Dublin.

The Stage published an interview with Robert on 15 September 1910: 'Congratulations to Mr. Robert Loraine on his plucky flight on Sunday from Holyhead across the Irish Sea to within sixty yards of the Irish coast. Just as he neared his goal Mr. Loraine's aeroplane fell in a slanting direction, and struck the water about sixty yards from the shore near the Baily Lighthouse. Mr. Loraine, who wore a lifebelt, swam to the lighthouse, and his aeroplane was afterwards rescued by a steamer. His achievement constitutes by far the finest oversea flight yet performed.'

---

[137] *Flight*, 17 Sep 1910. The *Adela*, built in 1878, was nearly 200 feet long with a gross weight of 685 tons. On 27 Dec 1917, making for Liverpool, she was torpedoed by the German U-boat, U-100, with the loss of twenty-four crew. The skipper, Captain Tyrell, intending to go down with her, somehow survived, the only one to do so.

Robert's broken Farman on its way to Dublin [photo Daily Mirror, courtesy of Rob Schmidt]

The Adela at Sir John Rogerson's Quay, Dublin (date not known) (photo: eastwallforall.ie)

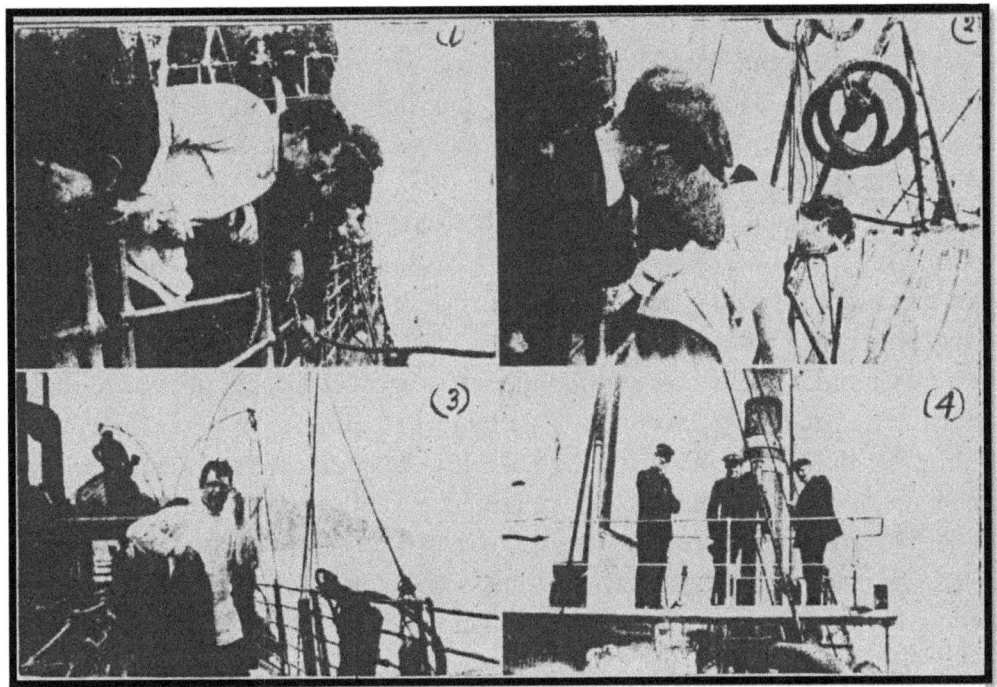

Robert aboard the Adela, 11 September 1910:

'(1) On board the "Adela." Mr. Loraine (in the white sweater) is not sea-sick—he is superintending the making fast of his biplane alongside. (2) Loraine, standing outside the ship's rail, is directing the hauling up of his machine. It may be seen how much the skids are dislocated. (3) The job finished, Mr. Loraine proceeded to don his coat. Behind him is Howth Head. He swam ashore at the extreme point on the right, and afterwards came out to the "Adela." (4) Mr. Loraine on the bridge of the "Adela" with the skipper, Captain Kinch, and

The Anglia rounding Admiralty Pier, Holyhead, date unknown

Robert made it clear in the interview that 'he had no intention of ceasing to fly on account of his theatrical engagements. "There is no reason why one should not fly in the daytime and act at night," he added, "and flying is infinitely more important, apart from its fascination. I am only afraid that some flying plans I now have under consideration may prevent my acting much in the future."'

Robert also commented particularly on the Irish Sea crossing: 'I regard the discovery I made during my sixty-mile oversea flight that frequent stopping of the engine of a biplane does not inevitably mean the death of the airman and ruin to the machine as the most important result of my journey. Six times the engine stopped, and I made controlled flights downward each time, finally coming into the water because I could not rise to the cliffs. I was able to steer successfully by compass, getting what sailors term a good landfall, as well as a safe "waterfall," for I made for the Kish Lightship and kept my course accurately. Airmen have done this before overland, steering by compass, but never when out of sight of landmark of any kind. There were no tugs to help me and there is no steamer on Sunday morning. I had made a trial flight, and the time to make my attempt seemed to have arrived so I started. I wore only a cork lifebelt over my clothes and this I found a great nuisance, of course, when I had to swim, but I should have been very glad of it if I had fallen into the sea further from land.

'Perhaps I am the first airman who has had to choose between his flying and a profession in which he has become established, for most airmen are men of leisure. Certainly I do not intend to give up flying, so I fear I may have to give up acting. It is the preparations for flights that take so much time.' (*The Stage*, 15 September 1910).

Having watched Robert depart, George Smart, Jules and Madame Védrines made their way to Holyhead, where George was given lunch at his hotel by Rear-Admiral Burr. Afterwards, George, Jules and his wife caught the 2 p.m. mail boat to Dublin. About halfway across, they were informed by a ship heading east (George called it "the Butter boat") that a biplane had been seen over the Kish lightship, barely six miles from Dublin, and assumed, with great rejoicing, that Robert had successfully completed the crossing. After the mail boat had docked at Kingstown around 5 p.m., and George and the Védrines had learnt from a policeman that Robert had had to swim ashore at Howth Head, the trio caught the train to Dublin. There, with some difficulty, they located Robert hiding from the Press aboard the Holyhead mail boat, the *Anglia*:[138] 'He was dressed in a pair of sailor's blue trousers and a blue jersey, inscribed across the chest with the insignia *SS Adela*.' His own clothes were drying, he explained.

The four returned that night to Holyhead on the *Anglia*.

---

[138] Thanks to *Pioneers, Showmen and the RFC*, pp.62-3, for these details.

Irrespective of the outcome, Robert's achievement was regarded as monumentally brave. Whereas Blériot had flown twenty-one miles or so over water just over a year earlier, Robert had now flown three times that distance.

After Robert's Farman had been off-loaded from the *Adela* in Dublin it was, according to one newspaper report, 'taken on board the s.s. *Slieve Gallion* for shipment to England.'[139] Another newspaper, the *Irish Independent*, said that the ship was the ss. *Slieve Bloom*.[140] (Whichever, both ships were owned by the London and North Western Railway). The broken Farman was never re-assembled. Packed away, it was sent over to Hendon, north London, while Robert returned to London for the opening of the aptly-named play *The Man from The Sea*.

A year and a half later, at the RAeC's annual general meeting on 21 March 1912, Robert 'received a medal for his flight across the Irish Sea in 1910. Sir Edward Seymour remarked that this performance would always rank high amongst sporting feats, as it was done without any prospect of reward. As a matter of fact, in the

Robert's RAeC Silver Medal [photo by Richard Holleyman]

opinion of many good judges, Mr. Loraine's performance is reckoned as one worthy to be commemorated in some very much more substantial manner than by the presentation of a silver medal. Curiously enough, the feat is much more highly thought of on the Continent than it was, even at the time, in this country.' (*The Aeroplane*, 28 March 1912).

The editor of *Flight*, too, described Robert's crossing of St. George's Channel as 'one of the most sensational flights in history'. He added: 'No pioneer ever attempted a more dangerous task and none ever had so many successive escapes from death in so short a time.'[141]

---

[139] From an article by, or in the, "D.M.P.", 13 Sep 1910, via Richard Holleyman.
[140] Information on the Slieve Bloom via Pioneers, Showmen and the RFC, p.63.
[141] *History of British Aviation 1908-1914*, quoted pp. 57 and 58.

Robert's flight was commemorated many years later on a Carreras Ltd cigarette packet. No doubts, then, as to who was the first to fly across the Irish Sea!

Robert was further honoured by the celebrated actor Sir Herbert Beerbohm Tree (1852–1917) who, on behalf of the Green Room Club, presented him with 'a magnificent silver statuette representing the marriage of Art and Aviation… It was inscribed with the motto *Sic itur ad astra*.'[142]

Controversy exists to this day as to whether or not Robert was the first person to fly a powered aircraft to Ireland, given that he did not actually land on *Irish soil*. Author William Hywel was to write that no race is ever won without breaking the finishing tape and that it was never Robert's intention to come down in the sea short of the finish. He had made a valiant effort, but had not quite achieved that which he had intended to do.

Some argued, though, that he *had* succeeded, as he had passed *beyond* Irish soil before coming down in Irish waters but as C.G. Grey, as unequivocal as always, was to write: 'Strangely enough, the papers, in commenting on these flights [*those of Corbett Wilson and Hewitt to Ireland – see Appendix IV*], write as if the Irish Channel had not yet been flown, ignoring Mr. Robert Loraine's fine flight from Holyhead to Ireland in September, 1910. It is true that Mr. Loraine did not actually land in Ireland, but legally and practically he flew from England to Ireland, for not only did he land inside the three-mile limit, but actually crossed over the Bailey [*sic*] Lighthouse on the end of Howth Head before he fell into the sea. When he did fall into the sea he was well inside the line drawn from the Bailey light to Bray Head at the opposite extremity of Dublin Bay, and he was only prevented from landing in Ireland by the fact that his machine refused to rise high enough for him to land on the top of Howth Head, and that the cliffs thereabouts have no beach at the foot on which he could land, so that to Mr. Robert Loraine will always belong the honour of being the first man to fly from England to Ireland.' (*The Aeroplane*, 25 April 1912).

---

[142] *Robert Loraine. Actor. Soldier. Airman*, p.172. '*Sic itur ad astra*' ('*Thus one journeys to the stars*') was taken from Virgil's *Aeneid*, book IX, line 641. Robert would also use this quote in a tribute to fallen airmen in the 1926 series *Allied Memorial*.

Chapter Eight: Autumn Manoeuvres, Salisbury Plain, September 1910.

It was testament to Robert's strength of purpose that, barely a week after his Irish adventure, he should volunteer to fly in the British Army's manoeuvres on and around Salisbury Plain.

Following the ending of the Second Boer War in 1902, the British Army undertook a series of large-scale military manoeuvres across the south of England. The latest in the series, the Great Autumn Manoeuvres, scheduled to begin on 19 September 1910, would involve two opposing forces, Red and Blue, with 'up to 75,000 troops. Simulating a "Prussian" invasion force,'[143] the Blues were to advance on London from the south, while the defenders, the Red force, deployed on a defensive line from Salisbury to Bath would try to stop them. So vast was the area to be covered by the manoeuvres that the Ordnance Survey had to produce two map sheets, Eastern and Western, at 2 miles to the inch, for the soldiers' use.

The manoeuvres excited great interest, as noted by the *Salisbury Journal*: 'These manoeuvres, centered on Salisbury, were on a scale never before attempted. The Director was General Sir John French and the Chief Umpire Lt. Gen. Sir Horace Smith-Dorrien, commanding Southern Command. The Blue Army was commanded by Lt. Gen. Sir Charles Douglas,[144] and the Red by Lt. Gen. Sir Herbert Plumer…

'The Red Army, 27,000 strong, marched from Aldershot, preceded by 1st Cavalry Brigade, which was joined by 1st South Western Mounted Brigade who had concentrated at Windmill Hill…'

Following the example of the French Army's manoeuvres in Picardy earlier in the same month, in which aerial scouting was involved, the British Army Council was persuaded to keep in touch with aviation by inviting 'a few individual pilots to participate, entirely at their own risk and expense, in the 1910 Autumn Manoeuvres on Salisbury Plain.'[145] The Council agreed that up to four aeroplanes could be used. Initially, two pilots – Captain Bertram Dickson and Launcelot Gibbs – stepped forward and made their way to Amesbury, taking rooms at *The George Hotel*.

Gibbs had already taken his clipped-wing racing Farman down to Lark Hill, barely three miles away to the north-west of Amesbury, while Dickson was there thanks largely to the initiative of the British & Colonial Aircraft Company ("Bristol"), which provided two of its new "Boxkite" aeroplanes, factory numbers 8 and 9. Dickson took over No. 9.

---

[143] *Flying with the Larks*, p.52.
[144] General Sir Charles Whittingham Horsley Douglas, born 17 Jul 1850, Chief of the Imperial General Staff for the first three months of the First World War, died of strain and overwork on 25 Oct 1914.
[145] *Bristol Fashion*, p. 39.

The George Hotel, High Street, Amesbury, as Dickson & co would have known it.

Flight noted: 'On Tuesday last [13 September] at the flying school of the British and Colonial Aeroplane Co., Ltd., at Lark Hill, Salisbury Plain, some trial tests were carried out by Captain Dickson, the well-known aviator, with the "Bristol" biplane he will use in the forthcoming Army manoeuvres. This aeroplane was specially built for the purpose at the Filton works of the British and Colonial Aeroplane Co., and is fitted with a 50-h.p. Gnôme engine. It was only commenced on August 17th, and yet it was delivered on Saturday last [10 September]. Early on Tuesday Captain Dickson took it out for its first trial, when it did a fine flight and showed great stability in the air. A few minor adjustments were then made, and the trials were resumed in the evening, when the wind had moderated to about 12 miles an hour. On this occasion Captain Dickson made some magnificent flights for a long distance over the surrounding country at a height of about 200 ft., finishing several of them with very fine *vol planés*, landing on each occasion with great skill and smoothness.' (*Flight*, 17 September 1910).

Dickson and Gibbs were joined at *The George* by the *Daily Mail*'s reporter Harry Harper (and his motorbike), who had been instructed by his boss, Lord Northcliffe, to follow Dickson wherever he went. Harper found 'Dickson in a mood of deep despondency'.[146]

---

[146] *British Aviation. The Pioneer Years*, p.240.

Another of the *Daily Mail* staff, Holt Thomas, 'special envoy to Salisbury Plain', 'discovered Captain Dickson and Mr. Gibbs both looking for instructions, but no General concerned in the manoeuvres and none of the high officials had apparently sufficient interest to see that any instructions whatever were given.' The two airmen had, according to Mr. Thomas, been 'plumped down on Salisbury Plain ten miles from the seat of operations and left there.'

Charles Grey, too, was furious at the Army's lack of interest: 'The only things at the hangars to tell him [Thomas] that manoeuvres were taking place were three press photographers; not a British uniform was in sight; not a sign of a soldier. He [Thomas] says very properly: "The absurdity of asking officers to provide their own machines if the Government provide sheds and permit them to fly over Salisbury Plain is gross."

'The final indictment by Mr. Thomas is the most bitter, and probably gets perilously near the truth when he says: "It seems to me that the only object in having aviators here must be in case any question is asked in the House. Certainly it is not to use them. Nobody could be keener on being of service than Captain Dickson and Mr. Gibbs, but it was obvious to me that they were not wanted. Nobody cared two pins about aviation or aerial scouts."' (*The Aero*, 28 September 1910).

As neither pilot had had any instructions from the Red staff officers as to what might be expected of them during the manoeuvres, they 'agreed a plan of action for the following morning. Dickson would take off first and attempt to locate Blue Force'.[147] He would then go on to a field that would be clearly marked and land to report to Red force HQ at Codford St. Peter. Gibbs would then, as planned, fly afterwards.

Arriving on Salisbury Plain on Wednesday, 21 September 1910 were Field Marshal the Duke of Connaught, Earl Roberts, and Field Marshal Sir Evelyn Wood VC, no doubt too late to see Dickson depart on his historic reconnaissance flight. Earlier that morning Dickson had made his way to Lark Hill: 'As soon as it became light enough to get away Capt. Bertram Dickson... muffled himself up with scarves, leggings, and extra sweaters',[148] and 'borrowed Harry Harper's motor-cycle gaiters – for his seat on the naked lower wing of the Boxkite provided no more protection than an airborne kitchen chair against the chill autumnal mist.'[149]

Leaving his hangar at 5.30 a.m. on a misty morning, Dickson flew off beyond Stonehenge in a south-westerly direction hoping to locate Blue Force. This he duly did, after flying some ten miles or so. Witnessing this historic moment was Corporal A.G. Edwards, North

---

[147] *Flying With the Larks*, p.54.
[148] *Ace Air Reporter*, p.96.
[149] *Bristol Fashion*, p.40.

*Dickson's No. 9 "Boxkite" captured by North Somerset Yeomanry, Blue Force, 21 September 1910.
[The Aero, 28 September 1910; Flight, 1 October 1910]*

'Captain Dickson, on his biplane, reconnoitering over the Somerset Yeomanry.'
(Flight, 1 October 1910)

The former George Inn, Codford, today used for other purposes

Somerset Yeomanry: 'We had camped for the night in the valley of the River Wylye and next morning were up at the crack of dawn to feed and groom our horses. Before we had finished we heard a noise overhead – an aeroplane.' As Edwards says, military discipline thereupon collapsed, the troopers waving and cheering at the aeroplane, and making no effort to conceal themselves.[150]

Dickson, landing to ascertain whether the troops that he had seen were Blue or Red, was promptly captured by the Blues. When he pointed out that he was a neutral, and could not therefore be made a prisoner, he went off to report to Red headquarters, leaving his aeroplane in the hands of Blue Force.

Finding a telephone, Dickson reported his observations to Red officers, who 'were breakfasting at the George Inn at the village of Codford.'[151]

'Captain Dickson returned to his aeroplane only to discover that in the meantime the Blue forces had retired and the position had been recaptured by the Reds; consequently he was able to start again from that point on a proper tour of observation. On returning the first men to meet him were two or three officers who had been pronounced by the Umpire as killed, and Captain Dickson, not knowing this, proceeded to make his report to the "dead men," only to find that he had to do it all over again because, as he put it himself, he had "inadvertently confided in an officer a moment or two after he had been shot by the enemy."

---

[150] *Bristol Fashion*, p.42.
[151] *Pioneering Places of British Aviation*, p.188. *The George* is in neighbouring Codford St. Peter. Dickson's flight has been well detailed in *Flying with the Larks* on pp.53-9.

Captain Dickson talking with General Sir John French, 21 September 1910 [The Aero, 11 January 1911]

'During the day General French had a conversation with Captain Dickson and expressed his interest in the work he was doing, and it is understood that General French also spoke of the keen, practical attention with which all far-seeing military authorities had taken up aviation. In view of this it is all the more difficult to understand the attitude of the War Office authorities respecting aviation in general.

'On Thursday more scouting was done both by Captain Dickson and Mr. Gibbs, both of them locating detachments of Blue Cavalry. The *Beta* from Aldershot also came across to Amesbury and manoeuvred over the heads of the opposing armies.' (*The Aero*, 28 September 1910). The dirigible airship *Beta*, which was to cover over 700 miles in all, 'was equipped with wireless and was able to pass messages to the ground'.[152]

After Dickson's aerial scouting, 'over at the aeroplane sheds, an urgent message reached us from Headquarters. They wanted a 'plane to go out at once in a certain direction to find out what it could about some new and threatening movements by the "enemy." This time our second pioneer air-scout, Lieut. Lancelot Gibbs, took the air in the other Boxkite biplane; and, the weather now being much clearer, he was able to supply a more detailed report than Capt. Dickson had done.'[153] In fact, Launcelot Gibbs also flew in Dickson's Bristol "Boxkite" No. 9.

Back in London, meanwhile, having read Harry Harper's report in the *Daily Mail* that Dickson was going to fly as an aerial scout for the Red Force, Robert Loraine offered his services to Blue Force in a similar role. These were accepted for, after a performance of *The Man from The Sea* had finished at the Queen's Theatre on the evening of 20 September, Robert left 'his understudy to cope with his part in *The Man from The Sea*',[154] and set off by car 'with two friends' to Amesbury, 'where we had supper and a short sleep, and soon after dawn I inspected the aeroplane [at Lark Hill].'

---

[152] *Pioneering Places of British Aviation*, p.188.
[153] *Ace Air Reporter*, pp.97-8.
[154] *Bristol Fashion*, p.44.

Beta, the Army airship, at Farnborough

Robert's "Boxkite" No. 8 at Shrewton, Wiltshire, 21 September 1910. The words "The Bristol" are just visible on the right rudder.

Another view of "Boxkite" No. 8 at Shrewton, 21 September 1910

Robert had had the foresight to send Jules Védrines 'to Lark Hill two days ahead to see that the 50 hp Gnôme engine with which the machine was fitted was in good order.' Early on the morning of Wednesday, 21 September 1910, Robert went to Lark Hill. Finding that Boxkite No. 8 was ready for flight, he took to the air in it, with George Smart as a passenger. However, 'an unknown technical problem forced them to land near Shrewton just 7 miles away.'[155]

Also present at Lark Hill on 21 September were members of the Bristol and West of England Aero Club, who had been invited for lunch by the BCAC's directors, 'admirable arrangements' having been made by the club secretary, Mr. A. Alan Jenkins. Just 'as the Aero Club members had finished a lunch provided by the Aeroplane Company's directors the whirr of Mr. Loraine's Gnôme engine was heard', on his return from Shrewton.[156]

Shortly afterwards, Robert was off again: 'He this time took up another passenger, and after a flight he came down and set off again, this time unaccompanied. The easy manner in which he raised himself from the ground, and the way in which he landed in practically the same spot, aroused the warmest admiration of the considerable crowd.' (*The Aero*, 5 October 1910).

'Later in the afternoon after luncheon, following a proposal and unable to be present—a visit was paid to Wylie [*sic* - Wylye], several miles further on. Here Captain Dickson went

---

[155] *Flying with the Larks*, p.58.
[156] See *Power for the Pioneers*, pp. 51, 62; *Bristol Aircraft since 1910*, p.48.

up in another Bristol machine for the purpose of taking observations. Captain Dickson made a magnificent flight across a wide expanse of country, and after he had descended Mr. Gibbs went up in the same machine. On landing he described the Bristol biplane as the best machine he had ever been in—a striking compliment to a locally produced article.' (*The Aero*, 5 October 1910).

Shortly afterwards, Dickson went back to London, and then on to an aviation meeting in Milan, Italy, where a mid-air collision would change forever what little was left of his life. Robert, too, playing no further part in the day's proceedings, returned to London by train in time for the evening performance of his play.

Having acquired a working knowledge of Morse code during his service with the Yeomanry in South Africa, Robert was persuaded to return to Lark Hill to carry out experimental flights in "Boxkite" No. 8, 'which had been equipped with a Thorne-Baker wireless transmitter'.[157] Brushing up on his Morse Code skills, Robert 'caught the first morning train out of London on Monday 26 September'. Arriving at Salisbury station at 8 a.m.,[158] he was driven to Lark Hill.

Aware of the history that he was about to make, and seeing the considerable crowd and many photographers, Robert 'asked those who wanted to take pictures to go down to Stonehenge about five miles away [*sic – nearer two miles*], and to photograph me as I flew low over the druidical monuments.' So it was that, flying No. 8 later that day, he was near Stonehenge when he transmitted the message: 'Enemy in sight'.

The message was received by the inventor of the apparatus, Thomas Thorne Baker,[159] who was standing outside one of the Bristol company's sheds at Lark Hill with his receiver balanced on the rung of a step ladder. Though the distance from air to ground was only a few hundred yards, it was a start. Also present, and particularly interested in the aerial activity at Lark Hill, was the Home Secretary, Mr. Winston Churchill.

The portable Thorne Baker wireless spark-gap transmitter, weighing fourteen pounds, was attached to No. 8's passenger seat, while the 'Morse key for tapping out the messages was fixed at the airman's left hand.'[160] The transmitter's aerial 'was about 65-feet long and was rigged from the aircraft's nose to its tail via the wing tip with the ground wire mounted similarly on the other side of the machine. At Larkhill a crystal detector was used in the receiver.'[161]

---

[157] *Bristol Aircraft since 1910*, p.48. The equipment was apparently paid for by the *Daily Mail*.
[158] *Flying with the Larks*, p.59.
[159] Thomas Thorne Baker (no hyphen between Thorne and Baker) was born at Barkston, Yorkshire, on 19 Mar 1881, to John, a practising solicitor, and Julia (née Thorne) Baker. Thomas died on 19 May 1962.
[160] marconiheritage.org/ww1-air.html.
[161] *The Dawn of the Drone*, p.96.

Purportedly a photograph of Robert over Stonehenge. The wooden props were positioned in 1902.

Thomas Thorne Baker, Salisbury Plain, with the receiver balanced on a step of the ladder [photo courtesy of Mr. Reed Harmer]

 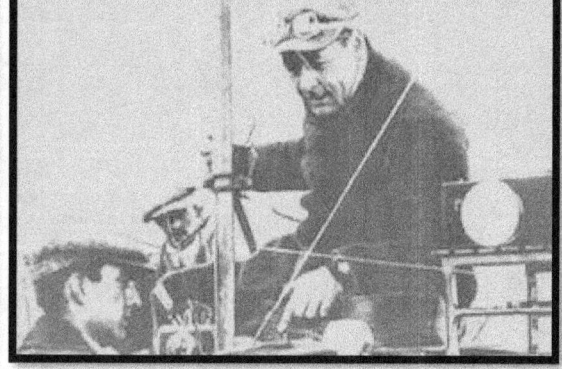

Robert receiving instruction from Thomas Thorne Baker at Lark Hill, September 1910 (via Richard Holleyman)

Robert on his wireless-equipped Boxkite outside the Bristol & Colonial sheds, Lark Hill, September 1910 [from Wakefield & Co. "Castrol" oil booklet, via Richard Holleyman]

'The receiving station on the ground consisted of improvised masts with aerial wires stretched across parallel to the ground in different directions. The electromagnetic Marconi detector was used by Thorne Baker with a headphone and telephones to pick up the signals. This was linked to two sets of aerials; one set could always present itself broadside to the plane.'[162]

This experiment 'marked the first use in this country (though just antedated by McCurdy in America) of air to ground radio communication, using a spark and coherer apparatus designed by T. Thorne Baker of Cricklewood.'[163]

---

[162] Mary Thorne-Baker, via Reed Harmer.
[163] *Bristol Aircraft since 1910*, p.15. On 27 Aug 1910, Canadian aviator John Alexander Douglas McCurdy (1887–1961) transmitted a Morse code message to Henry M. Horton, whilst flying over the Sheepshead Bay race track, Brooklyn, New York, USA – see http://marconiheritage.org/ww1-air.html.

Robert was back at Lark Hill on 30 September when, again in the wireless-equipped machine, No. 8, he was able to transmit a wireless signal in excess of one mile. Mr. Barron, a representative of the Marconi Company, was present at the time and commented 'that, with a tuned Marconi receiver, communication should be easy with the present transmitter up to ten or twenty, or perhaps, fifty miles.'[164]

The Baron de Forest Prize, December 1910. Moving on from his historic flights over Salisbury Plain, Robert's next aviation interest was the Baron de Forest Prize, to be awarded for the longest cross-channel flight from England to anywhere on the Continent. In 1909 Baron de Forest had offered a prize of £2,000 to the first Englishman to fly across the English Channel in an English-built aeroplane, but when Frenchman Louis Blériot, in his own French-built flying machine, successfully did so in July that year, Baron de Forest doubled the prize to £4,000, but with the stipulation that it had to be won by 31 December 1910.

In anticipation, therefore, of their flights over the English Channel to the Continent, several aviators took their aeroplanes to various places in Kent in the south-east of England. Lieutenant Hugh Evelyn Watkins (1882–1942), Essex Regiment, took Captain Maitland's Howard Wright to Shorncliffe, while Tom Sopwith took his Howard Wright to Eastchurch. Clement Greswell[165] with his Grahame-White "Bristol-Farman" and Grahame-White and his "Military Bristol" (Boxkite No. 16, with an E.N.V. engine) both went to Swingate Downs, near Dover, just about the nearest point in England to the Continent. Also at Swingate Downs was Robert with Bristol "Boxkite" No. 8, the one that he had flown at Lark Hill in September: 'Loraine had also entered the competition, flying No. 8.' (*Bristol Aircraft since 1910,* p. 50). It was not, as some suggest, a Howard Wright, but see below.

Swingate Downs was hit by a storm on 16 December, so fierce that three hangars, each sheltering an aeroplane, were blown down: 'The exposed position of the hangars and their somewhat flimsy construction obviously placed too much confidence in luck, for when the writer visited them earlier in the week they were straining badly even in a 35 m.p.h. wind, and would have done with a good deal more roping down.' (*The Aero*, 21 December 1910).

Robert's and Gresswell's aeroplanes were very severely damaged. Grahame-White's "Military Bristol", escaping with comparatively slight damage, was repaired in time to fly again on 18 December. Unfortunately, it crashed when caught by a down-draught over the cliffs of Dover. It was not a lucky aeroplane for, having landed after testing earlier in the month, a dog ran into the blades of the still-turning propeller, and was killed. The propeller, badly damaged, was replaced. A replacement Boxkite, factory No.17, was rushed down from Brooklands to Grahame-White, but that 'caught fire soon after arrival at Dover.'

---

[164] From an unattributed newspaper report displayed in *Flying with the Larks*, p.60.
[165] Clement Hugh Greswell (5 Dec 1890–1 Dec 1968) was awarded RAeC certificate no. 26 on 15 Nov 1910.

The wreckage of the hangars, Swingate Down [Flight, 24 December 1910]

With Boxkite No. 8 unrepairable in time Robert immediately bought himself a Howard Wright aeroplane to replace it: 'Robert Loraine's Bristol Boxkite with E.N.V. [engine] was damaged in its shed during a gale at Swingate Down, Dover… Loraine acquired, urgently, a Howard Wright… fitted with E.N.V.' (*Power for the Pioneers*, page 51).

This was confirmed in *The Aero*'s report of 21 December 1910: 'At the time of writing the following competitors have still to make their attempts: Frank McClean (Short), Colmore (Short), Ogilvie (Short Wright), Cody (Cody), Loraine (Howard Wright), Watkins (Howard Wright). All are using E.N.V. engines except Cody (Green) and Ogilvie (N.E.C.).'

Robert, well wrapped-up on his Howard Wright, late December 1910. Note cork lifebelt, and compass and map on knees [photo courtesy Rob Schmidt]

Though Robert's new biplane, the Howard Wright, had been prepared by 22 December, the weather at Dover was still so bad that he moved it north to the RAeC's Eastchurch flying ground on the Isle of Sheppey, Kent. Again, fate was to rear its ugly head. After engine trouble had been rectified on 27 December, Robert took off on 28 December, only for the engine to fail once more. Landing on rough ground, he hit a ditch and, though he was flung out unhurt, the Howard Wright was wrecked.[166]

Flight reported: 'On the 28th ult. Mr. Loraine got his machine ready at Eastchurch in view of an attempt to cross the Channel, but engine trouble intervened, causing him to delay his departure until the following morning. Then the weather conditions were again favourable, and the actor-aviator decided to make a preliminary trial before actually starting off. The engine, however, was again obstinate, and forced Mr. Loraine to land on bad ground, with the result that the machine ran into a dyke. The right-hand side of the main planes was badly damaged and Mr. Loraine was thrown out of his machine, but fortunately he escaped injury.' (*Flight*, 7 January 1911).

The Aero also reported on Robert's misfortune, but they had totally failed to grasp the fact that it was Boxkite No. 8 that had been destroyed in the gale, not the Howard Wright that he had acquired immediately afterwards to replace it: 'Wednesday, December 28th. With only three more days available for flights for the de Forest, excitement is reaching a climax. Determined to wrest the prize from Mr. T. Sopwith, who is at present in a winning position, is Mr. Robert Loraine, who now has his headquarters at Eastchurch. Undeterred by the recent destruction of a new [sic] Howard Wright biplane in the gale which blew down the temporary sheds on Swingate Downs, Mr. Loraine has been busy ever since equipping himself with a new machine of similar make. [*There was, of course, only ever one Howard Wright in Robert's possession at this time.*] Yesterday he telegraphed us that he was ready again. This morning, receiving a fairly favourable weather report from here (north-west wind, rather high, accompanied by mist in places on the Channel), he sent wires to the harbour people here and also to Calais, ordering out tugs to take up positions between Calais and Dover. The sun began to shine brilliantly, and the mist cleared away to some extent. But there was no sign of Mr. Loraine, who was expected to fly over Dover on his way into France. His non-appearance was explained when, after lunch, a telegram came from him explaining that engine troubles had delayed his start until it became too late.'

'Thursday, December 29th. To-day has again emphasised the extraordinary chapter of accidents which has attended attempts for the prize. Pluckily refusing to be discouraged by the destruction of his Howard Wright biplane in the recent gale, Mr. Robert Loraine has been moving heaven and earth to procure another machine. Yesterday evening, after carburation troubles with his E.N.V. at Eastchurch, he telegraphed to us here that his

---

[166] It may well have been this aeroplane that Lewis Turner used at Hendon in later months.

second [*sic – first and only*] Howard Wright was in "fighting trim." At 10 a.m., therefore, with capital weather conditions and steam tugs out in the Channel, his advent over Dover was eagerly awaited. Hopes were soon dashed by the receipt of a telegram, however, which read: "Machine smashed in trial. Self unhurt. Loraine."

'Subsequently Mr. Loraine telegraphed a fuller account of his accident, as follows: "Engine at fault in my fall and narrow escape to-day – not the biplane, which is splendid. Carburation being very bad yesterday. I wired for experts from carburettor and engine makers, who worked all night, but could not make her go.[167] I was forced to descend bad ground. Machine ran into dyke; smashed right main planes." Mr. Loraine gave it up and returned to London.' (*The Aero*, 4 January 1911).

Notwithstanding Robert's problems at the end of the year, the editor of *Flight*, Stanley Spooner, and author R. Dallas Brett considered Robert and T.O.M. Sopwith to have been 'the outstanding newcomers to the game' in 1910, and they decided that, of the ten best English pilots at the end of that year, Robert was fourth on the list behind, in an illustrious order of merit, Grahame-White, Sopwith, and Cody.

Romance in the air. Away from flying, Robert was embroiled in another romantic entanglement in 1910, this time with Marie Löhr, an actress fourteen years his junior, whom he had first met in May 1908 playing G.B. Shaw's *Getting Married*. In 1909 both were in Somerset Maugham's play *Smith*, at the Comedy Theatre, in which the title character, Smith, a parlour-maid (Marie Löhr), confesses her love for Tom Freeman (Robert).

Later in 1909 the part of Smith was played by Irene Vanbrugh, who had married the play's director, Dion Boucicault junior, in 1901.[168] Now, having become engaged on 15 October 1910, it seemed that Robert and Marie Löhr would follow a similar path but it was not to be. Putting her foot down, Marie's mother, the actress Kate Bishop, 'made it a condition of the marriage that Robert give up flying',[169] rightly believing that aviation was both costly and potentially deadly. This put Robert in a quandary, for he had already been invited to fly at the prestigious flying demonstration at Hendon Aerodrome in May 1911. Faced with the choice of marriage or flying, he chose the latter, the report of the dissolution of their betrothal being reported on 12 February 1911.

---

[167] Robert's engine was an E.N.V. and could be fitted with either a Zenith or a White & Poppe carburettor. The engine, of 7,623 cc, was capable of 88 hp at 1,500 rpm. It cost £450 (10,000 FF) in 1910.
[168] Irene Vanbrugh, born Barnes in 1872, took Vanbrugh as her stage name. She became a good friend of Robert's.
[169] *The Life of Robert Loraine*, pp.113, 114. Marie Löhr (28 Jul 1890–21 Jan 1975) was a stage and film actress. Her Australian father, Lewis John Löhr, treasurer of Melbourne Opera House, had married Kate Alice Bishop (1 Oct 1848 – 12 Jun 1923) in 1885.

Sopwith, winner of the de Forest prize, on his Howard Wright biplane with E.N.V. Type F engine, with White and Poppe carburettor [photo © IWM Q67498]

Scenes from Smith, showing (left) "Tom" (Robert) telling his "sister" that he has asked Smith to marry him; (upper right) Robert and Edyth Latimer; and (lower right) Marie Löhr as Smith confessing her love for "Tom". (The Illustrated Sporting and Dramatic News, 30 October 1909).

Marie Löhr (left) and her mother, Kate Alice Bishop

Robert and canine companion, in his Austro-Daimler outside the Criterion Theatre, Piccadilly, London

Kate Bishop may well have seen the article entitled "Suicides in the Air", published in early 1911 by the *Daily Express* newspaper as a protest against the number of aviation-related deaths in 1910 (a list of which is given in Appendix III). Robert had told a *Daily Express* reporter that many of the accidents were due to carelessness and over-confidence, as he himself had realised: 'Eternal vigilance is the pilot's price of safety', adding that 'a series of deaths, far from making aviators who are still uninjured more careful, has precisely the opposite effect. On the old theory possibly that lightning does not strike twice in the same place those left imagine that the gods are appeased for a season. They, therefore, consider themselves immune from possible disaster, and do not fail to act accordingly.' (Quoted in *The Aero*, 11 January 1911).

After the break-up with Marie, Robert 'fitted an extra-large arc-lamp above the driver's seat to his Austro-Daimler car, and charged about the country at 80 and 90 miles an hour every night after the theatre, for several weeks.'[170]

The Hendon Demonstration. A man with a keen business-sense, Claude Grahame-White was eager to show to the British Government that these new flying machines were capable of warlike intentions. Accordingly, on Friday, 12 May 1911, at the invitation of 'the Parliamentary Aerial Defence Committee—with Mr. Arthur Lee, M.P., at its head, and Mr. Arthur Du Cros, M.P., as its indefatigable hon. Secretary,' he arranged for a flying demonstration to be held at Hendon in which, as seen, Robert had been invited to fly.

Also attending were 'some 300 Members of Parliament and some hundreds of Army and Navy officers, the Duke and Duchess of Connaught, Prince Arthur of Connaught, members of the Cabinet and Opposition, including Mr. Asquith, Mr. Balfour, Mr. Lloyd George, Mr. McKenna, the First Lord of the Admiralty, Mr. Winston Churchill, Sir Rufus Isaacs, Sir Herbert Samuel, the Postmaster General, Lord Lansdowne, Colonel Seely—in fact practically every Minister who was not in duty attendance upon King George during his official visit to the Crystal Palace. Other notable attendances were Lord Northcliffe, Lord Charles Beresford, Lord Roberts, the Lord Chief Justice, Lord Rothschild, Lord Fisher, Sir Ernest Shackleton, Sir Philip Watts, Lord Denman, Mr. Gerald Balfour and Mr. Burdett-Coutts.' (*Flight*, 20 May 1911).

Later in the day, after several interesting aerial displays of flying and "bombing" with bags of flour, 'Greswell on a Blériot got away for a spin round the aerodrome, followed almost immediately by Pixton on the Avro, which had also arrived by way of the air from Brooklands earlier in the day. These flights were in connection with the item for rising and alighting quickly, in which also Mr. Loraine took part on his Howard Wright biplane. An excellent flight followed the get off of the Avro machine, Mr. Pixton finishing up with a splendid *vol plané* from over the hangars across the enclosures.'

If Robert was fortunate to have been allowed to fly at all, poor Cody, having flown over from Laffan's Plain, was not called upon to fly and was, understandably, furious.

Robert, hitherto a devotee of the biplane, saw the debate as to whether the monoplane or the biplane was the safer and faster aircraft. Even though he had had no experience of flying one, he decided to buy an Antoinette VIII monoplane, intending to enter it for the 1911 *Daily Mail* Circuit of Britain air race. Accordingly, in June 1911, he went to Mourmelon-le-Grand, France, to learn how to fly an Antoinette.

In early July, however, it was reported that 'James Radley and Robert Loraine, who both intended to fly Antoinettes in the "Circuit of Britain," have now given up this idea. Loraine

---

[170] *Actor, Soldier, Airman*, p.178. The designer of the Austro-Daimler was a certain Ferdinand Porsche.

Robert flying at Hendon, 2 October 1913 (photo via Richard Holleyman)

will probably be flying a Nieuport.' (*The Aeroplane,* 6 July 1911). This proved to be the case for, when the entries for the *Daily Mail* race had been declared, Robert was listed as flying a Nieuport aeroplane with a 70 h.p. Gnôme engine and was given race number 26.

Involved in yet another accident with his troublesome Nieuport, however, he never started the race, and sold the flying machine 'to settle some theatre debts'.[171] The Nieuport ended-up in the hands of Captain Eustace Broke Loraine (no relation), who sometime later went to Lark Hill with the '70-h.p. Nieuport, with intention of competing for Mortimer Singer [Prize].' 'He intended to start with Robert's Nieuport, but had had no previous experience of this type of machine, though he is a remarkably fine flier on both the Blériot and Deperdussin.' (*The Aeroplane*, 28 March & 4 April 1912).

Robert was to do little more flying before the First World War. Gustav Hamel (see Appendix IV) took him up as a passenger in his Blériot two-seater at the end of December 1911 'for a long flight across country, much to the satisfaction of the well-known actor, who said he had never flown in such a steady machine.' (*The Aeroplane*, 4 January 1912). On 22 February 1912 he flew, probably at Brooklands, with Tom Sopwith in a dual-control Wright aeroplane, and again, on 2 October 1913, at Hendon in a Grahame-White "Baby", as noted by *The Aeroplane* on Thursday, 9 October 1913: 'An interesting incident of the

---

[171] *The Life of Robert Loraine,* note 65, p.116.

afternoon was the first flight for two and a half years of Mr. Robert Loraine in a G.-W. box-kite; he had lost none of his skill.'

Flying was an expensive business, as Robert well knew from experience, and now he was short of money. Attempting to recoup some funds 'he presented a play called *98.9* in which the production – self-financed – cost £7,000.' The play was a flop and, to pay for it, Robert had to sell 'his car and luxuriously appointed home at 51 Conduit Street – a place that was minute but exquisite'.[172]

As further income was promised from a tour of the USA with Bernard Shaw plays, he sailed First Class from Southampton to New York on the White Star Line's RMS *Oceanic* on Wednesday, 11 September 1912: 'The date on which he sailed is the second anniversary of his famous flight on his old Farman biplane across the Irish Channel, when he landed in Dublin Bay, a flight which was certainly the pluckiest that had ever been made and was the world's record for a flight over water. It is interesting to note that Miss Irene Milton,[173] Mr. Loraine's secretary, has made a collection from among the company Mr. Loraine is taking to America, and the proceeds are being handed to the Aerial League's National Shilling Fund. Everyone will wish Mr. Loraine and his colleagues all the success they deserve.' (*The Aeroplane*, 12 September 1912).

A USA promotional postcard of Robert for Man and Superman

Robert played in George Bernard Shaw's *Man and Superman* on Broadway, New York, from 30 September to 23 October 1912, after which the play toured the USA and Canada until 15 February 1913. He returned to England on the *Cedric*, landing at Liverpool on 17 May 1913, and 'took a flat at the Albany, a posh apartment complex on Piccadilly'.[174] Also resident at some point in one of the Albany's bachelor apartments (known as "sets") was actor/manager Sir Herbert Beerbohm Tree (1852–1917).

Robert was one of several well-known aviation personalities invited to attend "The Topsy-Turvy" dinner at the Royal Automobile Club, London on 16 January 1914. Organised by Richard Gates and Bernard Isaac, it was to commemorate the achievement of B.C. Hucks and Gustav

---

[172] *Actor, Soldier, Airman*, pp.177, 178. The address, in the 1911 Census, was given as 51^A Conduit Street.
[173] According to the 1911 Census, Irene Milton was a private secretary, aged 21; she and her widowed mother (aged 47) were "boarders" in a house in Upper Tooting, London. An Irene Milton, spinster, died at The Royal Free Hospital, Hampstead, London, on 20 Jan 1959.
[174] *The Life of Robert Loraine*, p.112.

'The Centre of the Loop at the Topsy-Turvy Dinner.' Hanging from the ceiling is the "looping model". Claude Grahame-White is standing centre, with Hamel on his right and Hucks on his left. [The Aeroplane, 22 January 1914]

Hamel 'as the first two Englishmen to fly upside-down under control.'[175] As Charles Grey noted: 'The names of those present at this historic curiosity of a function deserve to be placed on record... Messrs. Grahame-White, Hamel, Holt Thomas, Orde, Isaac, Chéreau, Perrin, Whittaker, Savage, Willows, Reynolds, Strange, Manton, Walton, Ledeboer, Beatty, Brock, Desoutter, Gates, Spooner, Capt. Bass, Messrs. Withers, Forrestier, Whitehouse, Goodden, Baumann, Marty, Carr, Handley Page, Grey, Loraine, Noel, Ramsay, Verrier, Biss, Birchenough, Greswell, North, Sir Bryan Leighton, Bart., Lieut. Porte, R.N., Messrs. Gates and Hucks. It was a truly merry evening, and none of us will easily forget it.' (*The Aeroplane*, 22 January 1914).

Robert's name, with seven others, was put forward in February for election to the RAeC's committee at the annual general meeting of the members of the RAeC to be held on 24 March 1914. He was not successful.

---

[175] *History of British Aviation 1908-1914*, Vol. 2, p.95. Hucks had done so in France on 15 and 16 Nov 1913, while Hamel had finally succeeded on 26 Dec 1913.

Clearly still in close contact with the aviation world, Robert made his way to Hendon during the Easter Holidays and, during the afternoon of Easter Sunday, 12 April 1914, was taken for a flight by Gustav Hamel, with whom he looped the loop.

On Wednesday, 3 June, 'wishing to show them the aerial power of the Empire in full blast,' Robert 'inveigled a certain famous American author and his charming wife' to take him and Charles Grey 'in a large Pierce-Arrow automobile of comprehensive comfort and speed' to the RFC's Concentration Camp then being held at Netheravon on Salisbury Plain. What nobody had realised was that Wednesday was 'observed by the R.F.C. as a half-holiday' and so, on arriving, they 'found an atmosphere of Sabbath calm over everything. The camp slept under a blazing sun. The sheds were shut. A few strenuous officers and men played cricket in a hollow of the downs. No suggestion of an aeroplane could be seen.' (*The Aeroplane*, 11 June 1914).

Whether there was any connection to the Americans mentioned above with the following is doubtful, but in June 1914 it was announced in a newspaper in the USA that Robert was to marry 18-year-old Marie Hegenbusch, the daughter of a wealthy Dutch stockbroker. The parents, however, whose daughter was training to be a singer, disapproved of Marie's marriage to Robert.[176] Perhaps they were concerned that Robert, now 38, was more than twice the age of his intended!

Weightier matters, though, were in the offing.

---

[176] *The Spokesman Review*, Spokane, Washington, 12 Jun 1914, from *The Life of Robert Loraine*, p.114. Little seems to be known of the Hegenbusch family, but was there a connection with the Hagenbuch family living in Nazareth, Pennsylvania, USA? The Hagenbuch family today are convinced that they are Pennsylvania Dutch.

Chapter Nine: The First World War, 1914–1918

The origins of the First World War have been well documented. Suffice it to say that Britain declared war on Germany on 4 August 1914. Two days prior to this, Robert, aged 38, had offered his services to My Lords of the Admiralty and also to the War Office through the RAeC. By the time that My Lords had replied to him on 5 August, he had received a telegram from the War Office on 3 August asking him if he would accept a commission in the Royal Flying Corps' Special Reserve? He replied that he would. The Admiralty's response, 'offering me higher commission in the Royal Naval Air Service than the one I have accepted in the Royal Flying Corps' was too late.[177]

◆ ◆ ◆

Established by the Royal Warrant of 13 April 1912, the Royal Flying Corps (Military Wing) ("RFC") was officially inaugurated on 13 May 1912 as a component of the British Army. Until then, military aviation, such as it was, had been in the hands of the Air Battalion, Royal Engineers. By the time that war on Germany was declared the RFC had precious few pilots and precious few aeroplanes for them to fly.

The RFC component of the British Expeditionary Force that went to France in August 1914, therefore, comprised just four squadrons – Nos. 2, 3, 4, and 5. They would be commanded in the field by Brigadier-General Sir David Henderson KCB, DSO. Other Headquarters officers were:

Lieutenant-Colonel F. H. Sykes, 15th Hussars – GSO 1;[178]
Major H. R. M. Brooke-Popham, Ox & Bucks LI – Deputy Assistant Quartermaster General;
Captain W.G.H. Salmond, RA – GSO II;
Lieutenant B. H. Barrington-Kennett, Grenadier Guards – Deputy Assistant Adjutant (Staff Captain);
Captain C.G. Buchanan, Indian Army – Camp Commandant;
Captain R.H.L. Cordner, RAMC – Medical Officer;
Lieutenant the Hon M. Baring, Intelligence Corps – Intelligence Officer;
Second Lieutenant O.G.W.G. Lywood, Norfolk Regiment – Wireless Duty.

HQ RFC, with its NCOs and men for clerical, transport and domestic duties, left Farnborough for France on 11 August 1914, via Southampton, and reached Amiens two days later.[179]

---

[177] Quoted from Robert's diary in *Actor, Soldier, Airman*, p.179.
[178] Later Major-General Sir Frederick Sykes GBE, KCB, CMG (1877-1954), Chief of the Air Staff.
[179] *The Army and Aviation. A Pictorial History.*

Sykes had been Commandant of the RFC's Military Wing at South Farnborough. His post was now filled by (Temp.) Lieutenant-Colonel H.M. Trenchard CB, DSO, who had been promoted from major with effect from 7 August 1914 (granted the temporary rank of Lieutenant-Colonel whilst so employed).[180] Trenchard, desperate to see action, considered Sykes to have taken his rightful place in France and 'would soon develop a visceral loathing' for the man.[181]

◆ ◆ ◆

Robert's fate was to lie in Trenchard's hands after the RFC announced in *The London Gazette* (no. 28867) on 11 August 1914 that the seven 'undermentioned gentlemen [were] to be Second Lieutenants (on probation). Dated 12th August, 1914. Mark Dawson. John G. Miller. James Valentine. Leonard Parker. Thomas F. Rutledge. Robert Loraine. John R. Howett.' Dawson, Miller, Parker and Rutledge had gained their flying certificates between April and July 1914 (nos. 768, 825, 795, and 841 respectively), while 17-year-old John Reginald Howett would be awarded certificate no. 896 on 8 September 1914. For James Valentine, see Appendix IV.

Robert goes to war – again. On 12 August 1914 Robert 'joined at Farnborough' (*from his War diary – hereinafter "War diary"*). He was one of the first men to be assigned to No. 1 Reserve Squadron at South Farnborough, where their flying proficiency was to be assessed. Lieutenant-Colonel Sefton Brancker remembered 'some of the first pupils – Bob Loraine, Rickards (more commonly known as "The Blighter") ... Jimmy Weir (the younger brother of Lord Weir), and Conway Jenkins (one of our "push and go" men on the Equipment side later).'[182] (See Appendix IV for more on these men).

Robert, who had not flown for a while, was given the opportunity to demonstrate his flying ability, but 'neither his eyesight nor his landing skills had improved in the meantime. In his first practice flights he destroyed the undercarriages of two planes.'[183] It was left to Brancker to give Robert the bad news: 'On one of my first visits to Farnborough, Trenchard deftly saddled me with the unpleasant task of telling Loraine that he couldn't be allowed to fly any more because he had damaged two of our all too precious machines. He had done a lot of flying during peace, and he was nearly heart-broken at this decision; but his

---

[180] *The London Gazette*, 18 Aug 1914, no. 28873. Later Marshal of the Royal Air Force Lord Trenchard GCB, GCVO, KCB, DSO.
[181] *Boom*, p.100.
[182] *Sir Sefton Brancker*, p.70. In August 1914 he was a major at the Air Section of the War Office. Later Air Vice-Marshal Sir Sefton Brancker KCB, AFC (22 Mar 1877–5 Oct 1930). He was one of the forty-eight tragically killed when airship R.101 crashed near Beauvais, France early in the morning of 5 October 1930. There were six survivors.
[183] *The Life of Robert Loraine*, p.121.

RFC Headquarters, South Farnborough

enthusiasm and keenness were such that I sent him out to France as an observer. Loraine was short-sighted, and I promptly got a letter complaining that I was sending out observers who couldn't see!'[184]

Brancker added: 'Some of our very best pilots started very badly. For instance, [Albert] Ball, who was one of the finest fighting pilots ever seen, was very heavy-handed at first… Robert Loraine was another who at the beginning of the War was sent out as an observer, because he was considered too difficult to train as a pilot *on the few machines we had at our disposal*. Later, as a reward for his services as an observer, he was allowed to learn to fly, and eventually turned into a very fine fighting pilot.'[185] Brancker, perhaps, was writing at some remove from the reality for, in no way denigrating Robert's undoubted courage, events later in the war would show that Robert never had the skills of the much younger scout pilots (or fighter pilots as they were later known) such as Mannock, McCudden and Ball and numerous other high scorers.

---

[184] *Sir Sefton Brancker*, pp.70-1.
[185] *Sir Sefton Brancker*, pp.39-40. *Italics* are the author's.

Following his poor start at Farnborough, Robert was ordered by Trenchard on 30 August to report to the War Office on the following morning, where he would 'receive final orders to proceed at once to front as an observer.' (*War diary*).

A War Office letter dated 17 September 1914 identified 'all officers who had been ordered to join the Military Wing (in any capacity) since the beginning of the war. Annex C listed the eight men who had been sent to the Expeditionary Force as observers, including 2/Lt. R. Loraine, the only pilot among them.'[186]

At the War Office on 31 August Robert was told to report to the Embarkation Officer at Southampton with this typed order: 'Please send this officer overseas as soon as possible.' Making final preparations, and his Will, on 1 September, Robert 'left personal luggage at Purves-Stewarts. Slept at Royal Aero Club.' (*War diary*).

On the following day, after lunch at Waterloo Station, Robert caught the 2.10 p.m. train to Southampton, where he arrived around 4.30 p.m. His departure for France was delayed as le Havre was considered "dangerous", and no troops were to be sent there.

Having been told by the Embarkation Officer to report back at 6.30, Robert found on his return that another officer, Major J.D.B. Fulton (see Appendix IV), was also waiting to

The Alberta

---

[186] Observers and Navigators, fn4, p.7.

Rue Gambetta, Pont-Audemer. The Hôtel Lion d'Or is the building on the right nearest the camera

cross to France. He had 'just arrived from Farnborough with his Daimler car and two serjeant Inspectors of A.I.D. Fulton and I were told to return at 8.30.' (*War diary*).

Back once again at the docks, the Embarkation Officer said that only Fulton and his car, with the two sergeants, were to leave for le Havre at 4 a.m. on the passenger ship *Alberta*, while Robert was to leave on the first available transport. Deciding that he would reach his destination more quickly if he travelled with Major Fulton, Robert bought a ticket for the *Alberta*, and left with the major, the two sergeants and car at 4 a.m. on 3 September.

In France. The *Alberta* reached le Havre at around 11 a.m., but not only had to wait for the American 14,500-ton cruiser USS *Tennessee*[187] to clear its berth but also 'for a floating crane to take off the car'. The two officers, therefore, 'strolled in the town and had tea, returning to *Alberta* about 5 p.m.' (*War diary*).

Eventually making their way along the north bank of the Seine estuary, they reached the small town of Quillebeuf-sur-Seine where, amidst much applause from the French citizenry, they caught the ferry across to the Seine's southern bank. It was 9 p.m. and dark before they were over. A dozen kilometres or so later they 'arrived at Pont-Audemer, very late, and had dinner specially prepared for us by the Hostess of the Lion d'Or [*a two-star hotel on the rue Gambetta*], who insisted on opening a bottle of the family Burgundy in

---

[187] The *Tennessee* was bringing over around $6 million in gold, some of it to support the Bank of England.

which she joined us, and we drank standing to: "Success à nos armées." ["*Success to our armies.*"]

'Fulton slept in a room vacated by the hostess, and I was billeted in a good room in a house over a bicycle shop across the street. The two serjeants were in other houses in the village.' (*War diary*).

4 September. Woken-up at 5 a.m., Robert and his companions enjoyed a good day's drive to their destination, the RFC's Aircraft Park at the Le Mans flying ground. Commanded by Major A.D. Carden RE, the Aircraft Park 'provided the field base for the RFC; it comprised of 12 officers and 162 other ranks and was equipped with 20 spare aircraft. The bulk of the personnel and four crated Sopwith Tabloids entrained at Farnborough 15th August for Avonmouth Docks and shipment to Boulogne. Their remaining 9 BE2s, 3 BE8s and a BE2c were flown to Amiens by Park and supernumerary squadron pilots.'[188]

Also at the Aircraft Park was flight commander Captain W.D. Beatty RE.[189]

5 September. Robert rose at 4.30 a.m. 'and got Beatty, who was proceeding by car, to give me a lift to Melun[190] to R.F.C. [HQ]… Lunched at Hotel Grand Monarque. Saw Maurice Baring. Reported to General H. [Henderson] who was very pleasant. Col S. [Sykes] appointed me to Squadron B [No. 3].' (*War diary*).

Brigadier-General Sir David Henderson KCB, DSO, the RFC's commander in the field, had established his HQ at the 40-room *Hôtel du Grand Monarque* on the Rue du Miroir, Melun. It was left to Colonel Sykes to post Robert to No. 3 Squadron commanded by Major J.M. Salmond: 'Reported to Major Salmond at Mess,

(Left) Major A.D. Carden; (right) Captain W.D. Beatty

---

[188] The Army and Aviation. A Pictorial History.
[189] William Dawson Beatty, born 16 May 1884 at Darjeeling, India, was awarded RAeC certificate no. 89 on 30 May 1911. He would replace Fulton at the A.I.D. on the latter's promotion to be Assistant Director of Military Aeronautics. Resident in Cairo, W/Cdr. W.D. Beatty CBE, AFC died 18 May 1941.
[190] Melun lies some 50 kms. / 30 miles south-east of Paris.

Hôtel du Grand Monarque

tea-time. Dined Hotel Commerce. Could not find the right girls' school where we [3 Squadron] were billeted, so slept on Floor at Grand Monarque.' (*War diary*).

6 September. Rising early on Sunday, Robert eventually found 3 Squadron which, since arriving in France on 13 August 1914, had moved from one landing-ground to another: Amiens, Maubeuge, Le Cateau, St. Quentin, La Fère, Compiègne, Senlis, Juilly, and Serris. For the slow RFC aeroplanes, with their ability to take-off and land in any suitably-sized flat field, a landing-ground could be practically anywhere: 'A field became an aerodrome by the simple process of having some tin huts and canvas hangars erected on it.'[191]

Robert was probably at Serris when Lieutenant E.L. Conran (see Appendix V) returned from a reconnaissance in his Blériot Parasol with the startling news that the Germans had been halted at a village near Meaux, a few miles to the north, on the river Marne. Robert stayed the night 'with squadron officers at École Jeanne d'Arc.'

His arrival coincided with the start of the Battle of the Marne (6–12 September 1914) when the German armies, having broken through Belgium into France, were advancing towards the French capital, Paris. French troops under General Joffre and the BEF stopped the Germans on the River Marne, and Paris was saved.

---

[191] *Swifter Than Eagles*, pp.53-4, & p.54.

7 September. No. 3 Squadron were on the move again, this time to Pézarches, on the road to Coulommiers, the squadron's tenth base since arriving in France, Pézarches having only very recently been evacuated by the Germans: 'The dead still lay in the streets of the village.' Tents were erected 'on ground enemy had occupied night previous.' (*War Diary*).

First, however, there was the important matter of food: 'Moutrie Read [*sic* – Moutray-Read, see Appendix IV] and I went to buy carrots for the mess at Château of the Marquis de Mun.'[192] Though the Count complained about the state of his property after the Scots Fusiliers and RA had been there, he gave the airmen a glass of wine.

8 September. As Orderly Officer of the day, Robert had the unpleasant duty of having to deal with Private Boyd RAMC, who had been handed-in as a deserter. Also brought in for his attention were 'Two drunken men of ours also prisoners'. (*War Diary*).

9 September. No. 3 Squadron moved again, this time to Coulommiers. Though Robert's duty as Orderly Officer had ended, he was still not required for flying duties. RFC HQ 'were billeted in a large empty school, and the Aerodrome was outside the town on the top of a hill.'

On this day, No. 3 Squadron took delivery of Blériot XI no. 1810, seen in the photograph below with its original number, 810. This number was changed when it was realised that 810 had already been allocated to the RNAS's Sopwith Admiralty type 807. 3 Squadron had the distinction of being the only one of the four squadrons that went to France in mid-August 1914 to have been equipped with Blériot XI's. Together with Blériot 810/1810, 3

This photograph of some of 3 Squadron, near Amiens, shows Blériot no. 810/1810 (nearer) and Morane Parasol no. 616 [RAF Museum]

---

[192] The Château de Lumigny, Seine-et-Marne, barely 2 kms from 3 Squadron's aerodrome, was the property of Comte Adrien Albert Marie, Marquis de Mun who, born 28 Feb 1841, died at Bordeaux 6 Oct 1914.

Squadron also took on charge Blériot XI's 1808, 1809, 1811, 1812, 1815, 1816, 1819 and 1820.

10 September, 'Allen and I went to Saacy [*sic* – Saâcy-sur-Marne] to find landing-ground and place T. Then on to Montreuil-aux-Lions for same duty. Back to Coulommiers. Bivouacked.' (*War Diary*). (The "T" was made up of strips of material displayed in the form of a "T" to show the direction of the wind to landing pilots.) Allen was 1AM C.F. Allen (Service no. 99), who had been with 3 Squadron since 27 June 1912, when he transferred from 2nd Battalion Grenadier Guards, in which he had enlisted on 13 June 1906.

11 September. Further leg-work was required of Robert: 'Poel [*sic*] and I ordered to find landing-ground and next day's Head Quarters at Marigny. Warned at Nanteuil that Germans in wood ahead had just killed a peasant woman. Proceeded, after reporting to officer commanding ammunition column. Made a mistake of memory and went in error to Montigny. Then to General Poulteney 3rd Army at Loges-aux-Boeufs. Realised mistake and went to Marigny. Pouring with rain. Dead horses thicker than yesterday. Graves by roadside. 3rd Army looking tired but still cheery. Bridge at Ferté destroyed, so crossed by pontoon back to Coulommiers.' (*War Diary*). Robert's colleague Poel was probably 2AM Jack Peter Powell, who had been with 3 Squadron since 1912. (It was a common affectation of speech at the time to pronounce Powell as "Poel".)

12 September. The Battle of the Aisne (12–15 September 1914) began. With the Germans on the retreat from the Marne, the four RFC squadrons were sent north-east from Coulommiers to an aerodrome at Saponay, a mile or so north-west of Fère-en-Tardenois. RFC HQ left Coulommiers with all its impedimenta packed into a van emblazoned with the name of Maple & Co., the well-known London furniture and upholstery manufacturer. The over-loaded van 'broke down irrevocably just as we were starting.'[193]

Devastation was everywhere to be seen: 'More killed horses and more graves. Saw Devons skirmishing. Arrived at Fere in heavy rainstorm. Christy, Jackson and I went to Zig-Zag-um. No dinner at camp because of rain. Made tea at Zig-zag-um and eat bully beef. Slept on floor of a school under heavy artillery fire.' (*War Diary*). (Christy not found, but Jackson may have been Corporal Ernest Douglas Jackson, who had been with the RFC since 7 November 1912. The Devonshire Regiment was defending Lines of Communication.)

'The squadrons were now comfortably established at Saponay: No. 2 commanded by Major Burke; No. 3 by Major J. Salmond; No. 4 by Major Rawleigh [*sic* – Major G.H. Raleigh]; No. 5 by Major Higgins.'

---

[193] R.F.C. H.Q. 1914-1918, pp. 39-40.

'Most of the pilots were billeted in the village. One Squadron (No. 3) was billeted on the Aerodrome itself, the messes being in kind of dug-outs made in haystacks.'[194]

Disaster, however, was soon to strike Saponay: 'We've had the devil of a doing... a terrific storm and a gale of wind proved our undoing! The machines got here before the transport had come in: so pilots and observers had to shift for themselves as best they could. The ever-ingenious [Lieutenant L.A.] Strange saved his own machine from destruction by pushing it under the lee of a haystack, laying a ladder which he piled up with paving stones across the front skids, and pegging it down with ropes made of twisted hay. Others were not so provident. A gust of wind caught one Henri Farman, lifted it thirty feet into the air, and deposited it plump on the top of another... to their mutual detriment! It was a fearful night! The B.E.'s romped across the aerodrome like dinosaurs at play. Some finished on their noses; others rolled over on their backs, and yet others sat upon their tails. Morning broke upon a scene of horrid shambles. There were scarcely ten machines fit to take the air that day.'[195]

Of course, Robert's sleep was interrupted: 'Goss called us at 4 a.m. Very high wind. On arriving at camp found eight machines had been blown over during the night and smashed. But for timely action of pickets, who wrenched down the tent-hangars – which were acting as balloons, bellying up and taking machines with them – every plane would have been destroyed, and Air Force out of action. Such planes as were saved were pegged down, and went out on reconnaissance just as usual later in spite of bad weather.' (*War Diary*).

Another member of 3 Squadron, Lieutenant W.R. Read (see Appendix IV), wrote in his diary that the 'sudden squall got up and turned over 5 BEs and two Henris [Farmans].'[196] Such was the shortage of aeroplanes following the storm that No. 3 and No. 4 Squadrons were temporarily amalgamated. As for No. 5 Squadron, 'they had four Henri Farmans completely wrecked.' (*Flying Fury*, p.46).

13 September. Robert made his first reconnaissance on this day. His pilot was Lieutenant D.S. Lewis (see Appendix IV), commander of the wireless flight attached to 4 Squadron. Robert noted that they flew for one hour thirty minutes: 'Went through heavy rifle-fire at Filain Wood. Found fourteen bullet holes in the machine, two of them within a foot of my head. Archie greeted us on east of the enemy's position. Soissons in flames. Heavy artillery fire on both sides. Could scarcely recover from my excitement.' (*War Diary*).

It was during the Battle of the Aisne that the art of aerial artillery observation was born, as Lieutenant R.S. Wortley was to note on 19 September 1914: 'Wireless signalling for the registration of artillery targets from an aeroplane has become the rage. The gunners are wildly enthusiastic about it, and the competition to secure the services of the wireless

---

[194] R.F.C. H.Q. 1914-1918, p. 44.
[195] *Letters from a Flying Officer*, pp.26-7.
[196] Quoted in *Three's Company*, p.56.

machines is simply terrific. Alas, there are too few of them. The credit for the introduction of this new form of artillery co-operation is due to two Sapper [RE] officers, Lewis and [B.T.] James… They have both installed wireless sets in their machines, and they spend hours over the enemy lines, communicating direct with receiving sets placed in the gun positions themselves. Lewis returned from one of these expeditions this afternoon with his machine shot full of holes.'[197] This "expedition" might well have been his flight with Robert on 13 September.

"**Archie**" was the RFC's name for German anti-aircraft artillery, a shortened form of Archibald. The man who claimed to have coined the word was 5 Squadron's Lieutenant A.E. "Biffy" Borton, who wrote to his father sometime in the early autumn of 1914: 'I claim the honour of having christened ARCHIBALD the anti-aircraft gun, which I have seen mentioned of late in the papers. He is an excellent fellow who by his uncertainty prevents any chance of a flight over the scene of the fighting becoming dull … one has only to wander over the haunts of ARCHIBALD to be sure of a warm welcome…'

Borton had worked out that, whenever he saw the flash from the anti-aircraft gun, all he had to do to avoid being hit was to make a sharp turn left or right. As the shells exploded harmlessly in the recently-vacated spaces, he 'and his observer broke into a chorus of a popular music-hall song of the day 'Archibald – certainly not!' The full chorus, as sung by George Robey, was: 'Archibald – certainly not / Get back to work, sir, like a shot / When single you could waste time spooning / But lose work now for honeymooning / Archibald – certainly not.'[198]

14 September. Major John M. "Jack" Salmond agreed for Lieutenant Lewis to carry out an experiment with a Royal Artillery gun battery using a radio transmitter to communicate the fall of artillery shells. This squadron was also proving to be quite innovative, using lamps for Morse signalling to gun batteries, and, on 15 September, the British Third Corps assigned its RFC squadrons to support the divisional heavy and howitzer batteries.

Robert was still on probation as an Observer but, becoming more experienced, he flew more reconnaissance patrols, notwithstanding his less than perfect eyesight. The enemy, now well-entrenched along the Aisne, were proving hard to find anyway.

No. 3 Squadron was now using several landing-grounds, including one at Serches, a few kilometres east of Soissons.

15 September. 'Battle continues. Still at Fère.'

16 September. 'Wadham returning from reconnaissance at Serches with Charlton as observer side-slipped and completely smashed Blériot. Cut his head and hurt Charlton's

---

[197] *Letters from a Flying Officer*, p.29.
[198] Thanks to Guy Slater and to his editing in *My Warrior Sons*, p.15.

foot. Charlton sent [to] hospital [at] Braine.' (*War diary*). Charlton was sent back to England for further treatment.

17 September. Robert flew his second and third reconnaissances from Serches as observer with Lieutenant G.F. Pretyman (see Appendix IV) in a Blériot. They were up for one hour fifteen minutes in the morning and then, after lunch, '1 hour and 45 minutes, observing troops and chasing Aviatic [sic – *Aviatik*, German aeroplane].' (*War diary*).

18 September 1914. Though Robert noted only 'Rain and battle continue', it was on this day that 'the first experiments with dropping bombs from the air were made by Major Herbert Musgrave (see Appendix IV) of the RFC HQ Flight. One bomb was dropped, and it exploded but not exactly where nor how it was expected to explode.' He was a man full of new ideas (see entry for 27 September 1914 below), as were his two lieutenants – D.S. Lewis and B.T. James (see Appendix IV).

19 September. Robert went 'out with light tender to various landing-grounds.'

20 September. The war was closer once again: 'Batteries at Brenelle shelled. Some casualties. Went to see the squadrons wounded, at Braine.' Brenelle and Braine were ten to twelve miles or so north of Saponay.

22 September. Robert, replacing the injured Charlton, went up on his fourth reconnaissance, with Second Lieutenant V.H.N. Wadham (see Appendix IV), flying for an uneventful ninety-minutes to Braine.

23 September 1914. Robert went to Serches, a dozen miles north of Saponay, and to Muret (where HQ Second Corps was located) half that distance to the north-west of Saponay.

24 September. Made 'First flight on Blériot.'

25 and 26 September. Returned to Muret, though why is unclear.

27 September. 'Church Parade.'

On this day, the Experimental Wireless Unit, comprising the Wireless Flight of No. 4 Squadron, was formed under Major Musgrave at Saponay, to work for RFC HQ, using 'wireless-equipped B.E.2a's.'[199] Other officers were the afore-mentioned Lieutenants Lewis and James, Lieutenant S.C. Winfield-Smith, and Second Lieutenant O.G.W.G. Lywood (see Appendix IV for last two).[200] Lywood, Norfolk Regiment (Special Reserve), 'was in charge of ground stations, motor transport and technical stores' and, as more and better equipment was needed, was sent to Paris 'early in October to purchase wireless apparatus.'[201]

---

[199] *The History of 9 Squadron Royal Air Force*, p.5.
[200] See *Observers and Navigators*, p.7.
[201] *The History of 9 Squadron Royal Air Force*, p.5.

A wireless-equipped B.E.2a of 4 Squadron in French lines (from postcard dated 30 April 1915)

28 September. Fifth reconnaissance. Robert was flown from Serches by Second Lieutenant A.L. Bryan (see Appendix IV). They were airborne for one hour twenty minutes.
29 September 1914. Went with the squadron CO, Major Salmond, 'to landing grounds.'
2 October. Sixth reconnaissance. Robert's pilot was Second Lieutenant Harold Blackburn (see Appendix IV).
3 October. A blank day, though Robert noted: 'Sergeant Brown left for England.' 428 Sgt G.C. Brown, another "old soldier" who had enlisted in the Royal Artillery on 7 October 1903, had been posted to 3 Squadron on transfer to the RFC on 10 September 1912.
  It is interesting that Robert, a junior officer, should make this observation of an Other Ranker. No doubt his time in the Boer War had made him feel comfortable with "other ranks", but any such familiarity was frowned upon by most officers and Robert was put under open arrest by Lieutenant G.W.R. Mapplebeck, 4 Squadron, for drinking with NCOs.
4 October. More mundane, but nonetheless useful, matters occupied Robert on this Sunday: 'I took eleven motor lorries to Mont Notre Dame where I loaded with 9000

blankets and took these to Villers [-en-Prayères, *just south of the Aisne*] unloading blankets for troops of 1ˢᵗ Division… Fierce fighting to North.' (*War diary*).

5 October. With the enemy now advancing towards the Belgian coast in the so-called "race to the sea", 3 Squadron was ordered to move some distance north to Abbeville, near the mouth of the Somme. Robert travelled with the squadron's heavy transport along roads in such awful condition that the Maple & Co. van (last seen breaking-down irrevocably on 12 September) had to be abandoned east of Villers. The convoy halted for the night.

6 October. 'Continued march until nightfall. Then billeted at La Ferme du Bel Air, north-east of Clermont. Very comfortable billet, but unwholesome man in kitchen.' (*War diary*).

7 October. At 6 a.m. they set off for Amiens, arriving at 11 a.m. Robert sought solace in a local hotel: 'Had bath. Did shopping. Dined at Hotel du Rhin. Was ever War conducted in such comfort.'[202] He then retired to a 'comfortable billet on the Rue Lamarck.' It was, incidentally, at the Hôtel du Rhin that HQ officers had been billeted on their arrival in France on 13 August, before they and the RFC squadrons moved to Maubeuge on 16 August.

The Hôtel du Rhin was located on the Place St. Denis, Amiens, here as Robert might have seen it

---

[202] The *Hôtel du Rhin*, place Saint-Denis, Amiens, rated two stars in the *Guide Michelin* 1900.

8 October. 3 Squadron's aeroplanes were now at Abbeville, a few miles north-west of Amiens, for Robert flew from there on his seventh operation, with George Pretyman again, for 3 hours 45 minutes: 'St Omer and back to Abbeville. Reported area clear of enemy. Slept billet in Abbeville.'

9 October. 'Moved to Moyenville, south of Abbeville. Billet in village.'

10 October. 'Motored to Abbeville for shopping.'

11 October. Flew on his eighth reconnaissance with pilot Sergeant R.H. Carr (see Appendix IV), who had arrived in France on 30 September. Up for 3 hours 35 minutes, they flew from Abbeville to Poperinghe: 'Saw masses of enemy. Landed St. Pol at dark. Reported to Salmond by telephone. Slept St Pol.'

12 October. Robert was flown to St. Omer in readiness for his next operational flight. Billets were at Longuenesse, a small village just to the west of St. Omer.

13 October. On his ninth reconnaissance, he observed for Lieutenant W.C.K. Birch (see Appendix IV) for 3 hours 15 minutes: 'Between Aire and Armentières was clear. Heavy mists and low clouds later made it impossible to find Lille. Flew East and descended to 500 feet in order to land and inquire whereabouts, when we ran slap into three regiments of German infantry [*just north of Quesnoy*], who opened fire on us. Rose from this hornet's nest and flew by compass South-West. By luck sighted St. Omer and came down. Only one bullet hole in wing!' (*War diary*).

14 October. St. Omer.

15 October. St. Omer.

16 October. 'Joined detachment "A" Flight at Hinges, taking heavy transport with me.' Hinges was a way to the south-east of St. Omer, near Béthune.

17 October. He attempted a flight with Wadham but they had to give up after half an hour due to low clouds.

18 October. 'Walker being sick, I took his job with 5th Division Artillery.'

Robert was observing, with Wadham again, to the south of la Bassée, where "Archibalds" were very active. According to his diary, he did his 'best reconnaissance... Generals Headlam, Charles Ferguson and Smith-Dorrien all very pleased.' He was then detailed in the afternoon for artillery observation, requiring a ninety-minute flight over German targets. Unfortunately, the British Gunner-Major to whom Robert sent the various signals by Very lights apparently failed to understand them, and Robert's ability as a short-sighted observer was called into question. He could have been sent home, superfluous to requirements, but it is testament to his undoubted courage that he continued to be allowed to fly and observe.

19 October. He was up with Wadham again for his eleventh operation, and they found a new enemy battery and trenches: 'Did second artillery observation. About 3 hours flying altogether.'

20 October. Tuesday. 'Returned to St. Omer. Orderly Officer until Sunday.'
22 October. 'Salmond told me of unofficial complaint regarding Very Light signals. Gunner Major evidently trying to excuse his own indifferent work.'
24 October. Twelfth reconnaissance, with George Pretyman, for 3 hrs. 10 mins.
25 October. Thirteenth reconnaissance, with Pretyman again – 2 hrs. 45 mins – to 'Armentières, Courtrai, Lille, La Bassée.'
27 October. Fourteenth reconnaissance, with Carr, 2 hrs. 45 mins., in the morning, and fifteenth, again with Carr, in the evening.
28 October. Sixteenth reconnaissance, with Wadham, 2 hrs. 20 mins. 'Found Comines bridge down. Menin packed with enemy infantry. At Turcoing and Lille about 5,000 cavalry and much rolling stock and transport at Courtrai and Lille. Took charge of Hotchkiss machine gun.'
29 October. Seventeenth reconnaissance, with Birch, 2 hrs. 40 mins. 'Same area. Heavy fog. Came down to 2,000 feet at Lille and could not get height again.'
30 October. Eighteenth reconnaissance, with Wadham, 2 hrs. 45 mins. Robert noted that there was a battle at Deulemont: 'Reported enemy reserves. Motored to north of Hazebrooke [*sic* – Hazebrouck] to find out about guns in action I reported yesterday. Found these guns were French troops firing at the aeroplane with rifles, the flashes evidently being much magnified by the fog.'
31 October. Nineteenth reconnaissance, with Second Lieutenant Alan Hartree (see Appendix IV), 3 hrs. 'Rudder action impeded, landed Bailleul. Restarted. Carburettor froze. Returned St. Omer.'
1 November. Twentieth reconnaissance, with Hartree again, 2 hrs. 45 mins., in the 'Lod area. Motor started missing at Courtrai. Losing height, could not attack enemy's observation balloon.'

There was to be no Sunday afternoon off for No. 3 Squadron: 'Orders came at lunch for every machine to go with bombs to Gheluwe, as Kaiser was there. I had reported 2,500 cavalry there on dawn reconnaissance. Left at 2 p.m. with Pilot Birch on a Blériot. The machine could not climb well with weight of bombs. Dropped bombs on Gheluwe at a height of 3,700 feet at 3.30 p.m. …flew 5 hrs. 45 mins all day.'

About twelve machines took off on the 36-mile flight 'bristling with bombs.' There was no official information that Kaiser Wilhelm had breathed his last, having, apparently, departed before 3 Squadron arrived![203]

2 November. Robert's twenty-first sortie, on the other hand, proved to be quite dramatic. He and his pilot, Lieutenant W.R. Read, set off at 7.08 a.m. in their Farman. On these fighting machines the observer sat below the pilot.

---

[203] *Three's Company*, p.59.

Pilot and observer positions on a Farman

All went well until, just over an hour later, at around 5,000 feet over Courtrai, Read was hit in the leg. Blood dripped onto Robert who, without hesitation, climbed up and over to help Read, who was strong enough to land the Farman at a casualty clearing station near Ypres. With Read in safe hands, Robert returned to the Farman and resumed the reconnaissance until the engine failed, forcing him to descend at Dickebusch, behind French lines: 'Thought I was in enemy lines at first, owing to blue of French uniforms. 2 hrs. flying.'

Robert gave a somewhat distant account of this drama to the *Daily Mail* newspaper, published on 28 December 1917: 'The anti-aircraft guns of the Germans are excellent. They have many batteries of them, and although in the early days of the war their shooting was poor it is no longer so. They can send shells to burst at 8,000 ft. above the ground, and as effective observations cannot be made at a greater height than 6,000 ft. the batteries get a chance of hitting us.'

'Sometimes we descend as low as 4,000 ft. to make sure of certain things, and one day when I was about that height the machine I was in suddenly dived on to its nose. I thought for a second that a shell that burst close to us had smashed the rudder, and I glanced back. There was nothing wrong there, however, and the machine was up again in a moment. When I looked at the man with the levers [*i.e., Read*] I saw blood dripping from him, falling into the air, and I clambered over to help him should he relax his hold on the levers, but he was strong enough to keep control till he brought her down.' (*War diary*).

3 and 4 November 1914. Fog too dense to permit flying.

5 November. Twenty-second reconnaissance. Robert 'with Wadham, 2 hrs. 45 mins. Fog and thick low clouds. Courtrai, Lille and around. Had difference of opinion regarding route with pilot'. (*War diary*).

After Wadham had returned to Hinges aerodrome, Robert went up again with Birch in the driving seat: 'Did 3 hrs. reconnaissance, reporting signs of enemy's infantry retirement at Menin. Trains leaving Courtrai eastward. Transport at station at Tourcoing and activity. 2 enemy planes made half-hearted attempts to attack us over Lille. 5 hrs. 45 mins. flying in a day. Ordered on detachment for artillery observation. So motored there in evening.' (*War diary*).

6 November. 'Hinges. Fog. No flying. Motored to H.Q. Royal Artillery Lahore Division at Estaires. And also to battery 109th four 4.7 guns under Major Phillips. Also saw Colonel.'

7 November. Twenty-fourth reconnaissance. Although still misty, Robert flew with Sergeant F.G. Dunn (see Appendix IV) for 2 hrs. 15 mins.

8 November. Twenty-fifth reconnaissance. Though the fog persisted, Dunn and Robert managed to fly for 3 hours 30 minutes on 'artillery reconnaissance and observation'.

9 November. The weather was even worse, 'fog and low clouds down to 400ft'. As there was no flying, Robert went to Béthune for a haircut.

10 November. A storm blew up and blew down one of the squadron's tents.

11 November. 'On patrol duty to protect [Lord] Roberts who is at Lacon.' Lord Roberts had arrived at St. Omer on this day, and walked round the aerodrome on a bitterly cold afternoon.

12 November. 'Storm continues. Motored [to] Estaires, reported to General Johnson.'

13 November. 'Storm continues. Motored to St Omer; got 125 francs, second payment.' Lord Roberts 'caught cold, and on Saturday evening [14 November] he died.'[204]

14 November. The storm having abated, Dunn and Robert carried out an artillery reconnaissance and observation, Robert's twenty-seventh operation. Flying over a German battery 'two shrapnel bullets from Archie passed between Dunn's feet. He remained circling, and I dropped a note on the German gunner, telling him he couldn't hit the sky.'

---

[204] *R.F.C. H.Q. 1914-1918*, p.65. Lord Roberts of Kandahar VC, 30 Sep 1832–14 Nov 1914.

(*War diary*). They were at least able to get the 109th Battery's heavy guns on target during their 4 hours 45 minutes in the air.

After this flight, Robert went to the HQ of the 8th Gurkha Rifles, Bareilly Brigade, Indian Expeditionary Force, in the hopes of finding Ralph Walter Maude, younger brother of his friend Cyril Maude, actor and manager.

As no-one there had ever heard of Maude, Robert was arrested as a spy! A 'mechanic had to be sent from No. 3 Squadron to identify 2nd Lieut. Loraine and at the same time as the mechanic arrived, Maude turned up from a visit to Béthune!'[205] It transpired that Maude, an Interpreter in the Intelligence Corps, had been away from his regiment for some time, and had returned during the confusion of a fierce battle in the Neuve Chapelle area, which had begun on 13 October 1914, and which had lasted for three weeks or so.[206]

Major Ralph Walter Maude DSO (right), when Assistant Provost Marshal of Cologne, with his Sergeant-Major, in Cologne, 6 March 1919 [photo: IWM]

15 November. 'Storm worse. No flying. Saw General Scott and Major Poole, 114th Heavy Battery.'

16 November. Robert flew with Dunn again on Artillery Fire Control, but when an inlet valve broke over enemy lines Dunn was forced to land near Béthune. Robert borrowed a horse from the gunners and rode back to Hinges.

17 November. Up again with Dunn, they were forced down once more, this time by a snowstorm. Coming down at Bailleul, they had lunch with No. 4 Squadron, after which they flew back through further snow, total flying for the day adding up to 3 hours.

18 and 19 November. Both blank days due to the storm.

20 November. Robert flew a reconnaissance, his thirtieth, (pilot not stated), for 2 hours 15 minutes. His brief diary entry for the day ends with the cryptic comment: 'Drury shot self in machine.'

---

[205] *Actor, Soldier, Airman*, p.195.
[206] Ralph Walter Maude was born on 1 October 1873, his father, Charles, being an Indian Army Officer (born c. 1831). Ralph died on 17 January 1922 at the Villa Marie Marguerite, Hyères, Var, France.

21 November. Though the atrocious weather continued, Robert went up with Dunn on patrol duty over Loos, guarding the Prince of Wales.

Having received a note from George Smart, Robert replied to him at Hazebrouck, arranging dinner with him on the following day. Sadly, it was not to be. Robert also added the laconic note: 'Stoddart died in Avro.'

22 November. Robert flew with Lieutenant Denys Corbett Wilson (see Appendix IV) on Artillery Fire Control on behalf of the 114th (Heavy) Battery, RGA. So strong was the westerly wind into which they had to fly that they were practically hovering over the German guns at Fromelles. In another display of bravado, Robert, very rashly as events were to prove, dropped a message on the Germans: 'Keep your eye in; we will be back this afternoon.'

Sure enough, after a visit to the 114th (H) Battery to find out what had gone wrong, Corbett Wilson and Loraine returned to the enemy guns. After three-quarters of an hour of further "hovering" over Fromelles, the German gunners had their range and, at 3.10 p.m., Robert was hit by a ball from an exploding shrapnel shell. He later wrote to a friend: 'I had been working daily over the enemy's lines but they bagged me at last. An anti-aircraft battery, with which I had had previous dealings, interrupted me by sending a shrapnel ball into my back between the liver and the spine. It came out near my neck in front, after traversing en route the right lung from bottom to top.'[207]

A fuller description appeared in an unnamed American newspaper on 16 January 1915: 'I was doing a reconnaissance in a very strong and tricky wind which compelled me to direct my pilot along a course which, in order to get over certain of my objectives, necessitated standing into wind exactly over a battery of very efficient anti-aeroplane howitzers with which I had had previous dealings – standing into the wind in such a manner that I was practically motionless over a two [gun] a-a battery. So I was not in the least bit surprised when he got me.

'I was flying at 4,800 feet over [Fromelles] and marking on my map with great accuracy the precise position of a new battery of heavy guns the enemy had brought up when he hit me with a double knock just below my right shoulder blade. A large flat spent piece of this shell, probably the base, nearly knocked me out of the machine. It just hit me and glanced off, but at the same time I realized that the shrapnel bullet had just missed my spine and had sizzled through my right lung from bottom to top.

'Had I been standing, walking or running I should have gone out at once, as the excessive bleeding would have suffocated me. But being seated I found that by leaning forward and

---

[207] Quoted on p.153 of *Aircraft in the Great War* – Claude Grahame-White and Harry Harper (T. Fisher Unwin, London, 1915).

to the right and not attempting to breathe with the injured lung – being content with very small gasps with the uninjured one – I could conquer suffocation at least for a time.

'My reconnaissance was of immediate importance. I found, however, on trying to observe that details were quite impossibly beyond me, so I directed my pilot to go straight back to our landing ground, telling him I was hit. As there was nothing else to do then for the moment, I fainted.'

Denys Corbett Wilson wrote home to his mother: 'Had a rattling day today, over five hours in the air. Poor Loraine, my observer, was slightly, I hope, wounded. We got him to Hospital as quickly as possible and he's quite comfy now though in some pain. Of course we had to give it up when he was hit, but the reconnaissance was important, the French thought they were going to try a very strong attack from La Bassée way, and information was much wanted as regards movements of troops on the railway. The wind was so strong we couldn't get against it, but had to sidle up the position as far as Armentières and then drift across keeping her head to wind more or less.

'We saw very little movement really on the line, all clear as far as Wavrin, but I should not be surprised if they are thinking of attacking again there, as we were very much fired at. This was the last reconnaissance for the day, and there was a delay at the start owing to my right-hand shock absorber having perished in the frost. It had stretched and let the machine down on one side so had to be replaced at the last moment, and as we had so little time before dark, we hadn't time to climb more than 5,000 feet, still I hope he's not too bad. I got him home very quickly down wind, 5,000 [feet] is usually fairly safe, but standing against the wind made it easier for them to make some good shooting. Today, it was a job to get him out of the machine, he kept saying all the time we were getting him out "all clear as far as Wavrin".

'He is the actor Robert Loraine, the once flying man now turned observer. He joined the Corps at the beginning of the war and has been doing good work, I believe, observing… Loraine has taken great trouble and studied it up, and is very keen.'[208]

Robert was rushed to a casualty clearing station as soon as Corbett Wilson had landed. Next day, 23 November, he was transferred to the Lahore Division's Field Hospital in the *Mairie* at Lillers, where an RAMC major wrote: 'I have an interesting personage in my hospital—Loraine, aviator and actor. I have often seen him act in London in "Man and Superman." He was out making a sketch of the enemy's position, and, whilst doing so, a bullet from a shell hit him below the shoulder-blade and traversed the lung and came out just below the collar-bone in front. He was very bad when brought to my hospital, but is doing well now. He is convinced that our treatment of him when he was brought in saved

---

[208] *Letters from an Early Bird*, pp.85-6.

his life, and is correspondingly grateful. I think he will be all right now.' (*The Aeroplane*, 9 December 1914).

It was, nevertheless, touch and go.

Hovering between life and death for nearly a week, Robert was visited by several senior officers including, on Saturday, 28 November, his squadron commander, Major John Salmond, who wrote a short letter in pencil to the patient on a thin, torn scrap of paper from a Field Service notebook: 'My dear Loraine, I was awfully sorry to hear about you, but am v glad indeed to hear you are getting on well. I came to see you your first night, but they would not let me in… We all miss you very much in the Mess, and just as much in the field. Cheerio, old boy, and buck up and get well. Yrs. – Jack Salmond.'

'P.S. Smart has been informed.'

Aldford House, 1918 [photo: Wikipedia]

Considered strong enough to begin the journey to England, via Boulogne, on 8 December 1914, Robert was taken to the hospital at Aldford House, 26 Park Lane, Mayfair, London on 11 December.[209]

The Aeroplane's editor, Charles Grey, took a close interest in the patient: 'Apropos Mr. Loraine's wound, it is reported from another source that the machine he was flying disappeared into a cloud, and that the German guns then ranged on the cloud, and hit the machine when it came out, luckily doing only slight damage. It is not clear, however, whether he was wounded on this occasion, or afterwards.' (*The Aeroplane*, 9 December 1914).

Again: 'Everybody will be glad to learn that Mr. Robert Loraine is in London making excellent progress towards recovery after his injuries recently received at the front, but for the moment it is not permitted to say where he is being nursed. He is reported in the "[Daily] Telegraph" to have given the following account of his casualty: "I was wounded on November 22nd, in the middle of an important reconnaissance, by an anti-aircraft shrapnel shell (commonly known as an Archibald), when I was flying at a height of 5,000 ft. above the enemy's lines. My right lung was pierced from the base of my back, the ball coming out near my neck in front. As I had done daily three to six hours' work in the air over the enemy for nearly three months I think I may consider myself pretty lucky. Although I was not expected to recover, I am now, as you see, doing extremely well, getting on, indeed, quite rapidly, and the doctors assure me my recovery will in the end be absolutely complete. I am returning to the front in about two months' time, with a beautiful single-seated long-distance machine, fitted with wireless, which will do about ten miles an hour more than the swiftest German Taube." [One publishes this with all reserve, as it bears no resemblance to Mr. Loraine's usual manner of speech.]' (*The Aeroplane*, 30 December 1914).

Yet another account, published in *Lloyds Weekly Newspaper* on 3 January 1915, ends: 'Mr Robert Loraine, the well known actor and aviator, says he is romping along towards recovery, and hopes soon to be "up and about again" as he puts it.'

Four weeks after being wounded, Robert was allowed visitors and on 15 December 1914, still *hors de combat*, was confirmed in the rank of Second Lieutenant, Special Reserve. Then, on 18 December, he was promoted to Flying Officer with seniority of 3 September 1914 (*The London Gazette*, no. 29011). With this good news came the awful news that his old friend, Captain George Henry Smart, had been killed in action.

---

[209] Aldford House was built in 1894-97 for the gold and diamond magnate Alfred Beit. The house was demolished in 1929 and a block of flats built in its place. Not far from Aldford House was the 20-bed Harold Fink Memorial Hospital, at 17 Park Lane, London.

Martinsyde no. 710 at Farnborough, 28 October 1914. Robert flew it on 29 June 1915

After several weeks had passed, during which time he had lost half his bodyweight, Robert was advised by his old friend Dr. James Purves-Stewart to take a sea cruise to recover his strength, and so took passage on the RMS *Alcantara*.

In April 1915, immediately after Robert's voyage, the ship was requisitioned by the Admiralty. Converted into an Armed Merchant Cruiser, she was lost in action on 29 February 1916.

RMS Alcantara.

Pilot training. On his return in April 1915 Robert was posted to the flying school at Le Crotoy, on the Baie de la Somme, France, but this was soon changed when, on 29 April, he was attached to No. 3 (Reserve) Aeroplane Squadron at Shoreham, Sussex, for flying training. After spending two weeks there – 29 April to 11 May 1915 – flying Maurice Farman S.7 Longhorns Nos. 526 and 529 he was posted on 19 May to No. 14 Squadron at Hounslow. There, from 21 May to 6 July, he flew a variety of aeroplanes: Blériot Parasol no. 574; Avro 500 nos. 406 and 430; Blériot Tractor nos. 4655 and 4656; Maurice Farman S.7 Longhorn no. 2963; Maurice Farman S.11 Shorthorn no. 2943; Martinsyde S.1 Scouts nos. 710 and 2826; and B.E.2c no. 1693, in which he practised bomb dropping.

Robert's total time in the air amounted to 18 hours 54 minutes, with his logbook being signed-off by Major George Eardley "Sweeney" Todd, OC 14 Squadron.

No. 2 Squadron. Though at this point Robert's official military service record (TNA file AIR 76/306/110) is confused, he was, after his instructional course with 3 RAS and 14 Squadron had finished in early July 1915, posted as a pilot to No. 2 Squadron at Hesdigneul-lès-Béthune (south-west of Béthune), France.

Over the forthcoming weeks, Robert would fly with several observers, including Lieutenants R.N. Marshall and Russell, and Second Lieutenants R.L. Chidlaw-Roberts (see Appendix IV), Davies and Ellison.[210] From 16 July 1915 to the end of that month he usually flew either B.E.2c no. 1659 or no. 1660. He was on a patrol on 27 July in B.E.2c 1660 with Ellison when, after only fifteen minutes, the petrol-pipe union broke, and he was obliged to return to the aerodrome. Mended, the patrol was resumed, at 8,000 feet.

No. 2 Squadron, 1915. Lt. R.N. Marshall (sitting) and Robert Loraine (courtesy www.airwar1.org.uk, from the collection of Major F.W. Smith)

---

[210] www.apw.airwar1.org.uk/no2sqn3.htm.

A B.E.2c of No. 2 Squadron at Hesdigneul, Summer 1915 (www.airwar1.org.uk)

German shells bursting on Béthune

On the morning of 19 July 1915 'Béthune was shelled in the vicinity of the station. Lt. R. Loraine had tea in Béthune and afterwards walked round to see the damage caused by shell fire. Several houses were demolished & many injured. The British replied this evening by shelling La Bassée with 9.2 howitzers.'

FLIGHT COMMANDER LORAINE

The public generally will be pleased to hear that Mr. Robert Loraine, the well-known actor-airman, has been promoted to a flight commander. In matters aviatic his keenness is proverbial. None of those little mishaps of the air which have befallen him, as they do all airmen from time to time, damp his ardour in the slightest.

Captain Robert Maxwell Pike

Robert was promoted captain on 1 September 1915 and a fortnight later made a '*Flight Commander* — Lieutenant Robert Loraine, Special Reserve, from a Flying Officer, and to be temporary Captain whilst so employed. Dated 15th September, 1915.' (*The London Gazette*, 8 October 1915, no. 29322).

No. 5 Squadron. Following his promotion, Captain Robert Loraine was appointed as "B" Flight commander, No. 5 Squadron, to replace Captain R.M. Pike, killed in action on 9 August 1915.

No. 5 Squadron, which had formed at Farnborough on 26 July 1913, and had made RFC history by forcing down the first German aircraft of the war on 24 August 1914, was to serve on the Western front from 15 August 1914 until the end of the war. The squadron's Commanding Officer when Robert joined on 15 September 1915, the day of his promotion, was Major A.G. Board (see Appendix IV).

The Battle of Loos (25 Sep–13 Oct 1915). Ten days after Robert's arrival, the Battle of Loos began: 'No. 5, like the other Squadron in the 2nd Wing [No. 6 Squadron], was kept fully employed doing tactical reconnaissances for its Corps, and such artillery observation as was called for day-by-day.' The CO of the 2nd Wing, Lieutenant-Colonel J.M. Salmond, Robert's erstwhile 3 Squadron CO, issued a Standing Order that No. 5 Squadron, on top of its reconnaissance and observation duties, was also to patrol 'the line from Wytschaete to Boesinghe, during the hours 5.30 – 9.30 a.m., the same area being patrolled by No. 6 Squadron (No. 5's stable-companion at Abeele) from 4 to 6 in the evening.' (TNA file AIR 27/63).

Robert was up on 26 September 1915 with Lieutenant Cyril Porri (see Appendix IV) as observer. Flying in Vickers "Gunbus" F.B.5 no, 5459, they were over Zonnebeke at 12.50 p.m. and Poelcappelle two minutes later. Then, at Langemarck at 12.55, they saw 'about 10 detached open trucks in new [railway] station… No movement on railway visible. Town appeared clear of M.T.'[211]

On 11 October 1915 Robert was confirmed in the rank of captain from lieutenant (temp. captain),[212] and on the same day he and his Observer, Corporal George Fineran (see Appendix IV), had an inconclusive combat with a Fokker near Voormezele, as recorded in RFC Communiqué No.14: 'Capt Loraine and Cpl Fineran of 5 Sqn in a Vickers with two Lewis guns, when patrolling north-east of Vormozelle [sic] at 10.50 a.m. saw a Fokker diving at a B.E.2c. Capt Loraine flying towards the Fokker opened fire at it while about 1,000 feet below it. The hostile machine passed directly over the Vickers and tried to get behind it. By turning sharply this was prevented. The Fokker then turned north-east and disappeared in the direction of Polygon Wood.'[213]

This was Robert's report: 'Vickers was between Voormezeele and Zillebeke at 8,000 feet when I saw the Fokker come from an Easterly direction at about 12,000 feet high. He dived at a B.E.2.c which was about 10,000 feet high and passed about 400 feet behind it. I climbed towards the Fokker and when he was still about 1,000 feet above me I fired at him. He passed directly over me and tried to dive behind me. I kept turning sharply so that he could not get behind. I then climbed towards him and he headed N.E. and disappeared to the North of Polygon Wood.'

No. 5 was the first squadron to operate the Vickers F.B.5 two-seater "Gunbus" fighters in any numbers but, having received a total of nine between 19 March and 21 June 1915, only three had survived to 30 June 1915.[214]

---

[211] TNA file AIR 1/2159/209/4/17.
[212] In the same list Gilbert Braithwaite Rickards was similarly promoted.
[213] Royal Flying Corps Communiqués 1915-1916, p.59.
[214] *The Aeroplanes of the Royal Flying Corps Military Wing*, p.571.

Robert had been given a new "Gunbus", but found it too slow to catch the German fighters that were then the scourge of the RFC. In the hope of improving its performance, Vickers installed a 110 h.p. le Rhône engine and a larger-pitch propeller into one of the production models. This 'produced a slight improvement in performance but was not followed up.'[215] It was probably this very aeroplane, F.B.5 no. 5459, that found its way into Robert's hands.

Robert was, in the words of one of his junior officers, 'bored stiff flying there while his observer was able to fire at the Germans and he had nothing to do. So he said: "I'm going to have another gun" and he brought one in and fixed it on the nacelle between himself and the observer, so that now he had two guns to fire, which was quite an advance.'[216]

The modifications to 5459 were, however, sufficient to allow Robert to get after the Hun. He and Lieutenant The Hon. Eric Lubbock (see Appendix IV), observer, were on patrol near Houthem on 26 October 1915 when they 'engaged and shot down one of two enemy aeroplanes which were attempting to cross the lines near the Ypres–Comines Canal.' (TNA file AIR 27/63).

Robert reported: 'While patrolling I observed two German Machines approaching from the East.

'I attacked the first one and fired half a drum at him at 15 yards. He dived almost vertically and I followed him firing nearly the whole of the remaining half of the drum. While my Observer fired nearly a whole drum.

'I followed the enemy down and saw him crash and turn completely over at U. 13.a.5.6, Sheet 28, within our lines. I then found I was 700 ft. high, and climbed to attack the second German. At 6,000 ft. my engine stopped and I landed on good plough 8 kilometres E. of Godewaersvelde. The pilot was shot by machine gun fire and the Observer wounded.' (TNA file AIR 1217/204/5/2634).

Their action against an Albatross B.II was also reported in RFC Communiqué No.16.[217] For their destruction of the Albatross of the 33rd *Feldflieger Abteilung*, both Robert and Lubbock were awarded the MC: 'Captain Robert Loraine, Royal Flying Corps, Special Reserve. For conspicuous gallantry and skill on 26th October, 1915, when he attacked a German Albatross biplane, getting within fifteen yards of it. When the hostile machine dived he dived after it, and followed it from a height of 9,000 feet to 600 feet. The enemy pilot was hit, and his camera, and wireless transmitter were subsequently found to have bullet-holes through them.'

---

[215] *The Aeroplanes of the Royal Flying Corps Military Wing*, p.572.
[216] W/Cdr F.J. Powell in IWM interview 25 Jan 1973.
[217] See Royal Flying Corps Communiques 1915-1916, p.67.

First production Vickers F.B.5 "Gunbus" No. 1616, at Farnborough, 24 December 1914, with Frank Gooden, pilot. This machine was issued from the Aircraft Park to 5 Squadron on 14 April 1915.

Robert Loraine (left) and Eric Lubbock

The above photograph of Robert was published in *The War Illustrated* on 18 December 1915, with the caption: 'Captain Robert Loraine, Royal Flying Corps, who is well known as an actor, was awarded the Military Cross for his conspicuous gallantry and skill in attacking a German Albatross biplane.' Robert then 'had the honour of being received by the King' at Buckingham Palace on 29 March 1916, 'when His Majesty conferred on him the Military Cross.' (*The Aeroplane*, 5 April 1916).

Eric Lubbock had already been presented with his MC on Saturday, 15 January 1916 when the King 'held an Investiture at Buckingham Palace'. Lieutenant Eric Lubbock was 'introduced into the presence of the Sovereign' and presented with his MC. (*The Aeroplane*, 19 January 1916). The citation for Lubbock's MC read: 'Temporary Lieutenant The Honourable Eric Fox Pitt Lubbock, Army Service Corps, attached Royal Flying Corps. For conspicuous gallantry and skill on 26th October, 1915, when he attacked a German Albatross machine at a height of 9,000 feet with machine-gun fire. The hostile pilot was shot and the aeroplane was brought to the ground within our lines. The attack finished at a height of only 600 feet, and during an almost vertical dive, when the pilot was fully occupied, Lieutenant Lubbock fired deliberately and with effect.'[218]

Lubbock's own account of the action was published in the *Daily Telegraph* on 11 November 1915, and also in the *Eton College Chronicle*: 'Yesterday Loraine and I had an exciting adventure. We sighted a German about four miles off and attacked. We both

---

[218] *The London Gazette*, 16 Nov 1915, no. 29371. Note British spelling of *Albatros*.

opened fire at about fifty yards. I fired again at about twenty-five, firing twenty-six rounds, and then my gun jammed. I heard Loraine give a great shout, but felt neither fear nor triumph. Then our machine turned downwards. As I had fired my last shot I had seen the German turn down. I knew that if he got below us, my machine-gun was the only one that could fire at him. We were diving, I standing almost on the front of the body. Then we turned level. I finished my gun, but there was no German! But our guns (Loraine's and mine) had jammed at the same moment. I spent another five minutes at Loraine's gun, and finally got both done.

'We saw another enemy aeroplane coming in the distance. Loraine went all out to climb and attack, while I put my stiff and aching hands in my mouth praying for sufficient life to come back to them—they were frozen. Then our engine stopped, and we were helpless, so we turned and glided homewards. Unable to reach the aerodrome we landed in plough, a beautiful landing. The luckless Boche fell twenty yards behind our front line trench. The pilot was shot through the stomach; the observer, a boy of 17, had his head grazed. In spite of his fall he will be all right, but yesterday he was crying and absolutely nerve broken. No wonder, poor thing. The pilot was dead before they got him away.

Albatross B.II

'On the machine was found an old machine-gun. It had been taken from the Canadians months ago, and now has come back to them. It is absolutely unfit for aeroplane work, being three times as heavy as the one we use, and having lots of other technical drawbacks. There was a camera with a Zeiss lens, which will be most valuable to us; although the camera was pierced by two bullets. There were some plates which are being developed at this moment. The camera is heavy and clumsy, not a patch on ours. It is such that you cannot take a vertical photograph. There was a carbine, a very nice weapon, and a pistol for firing coloured lights, which had been hit by us and spoiled. There was also a priceless pair of binoculars, magnifying eighteen times. I am to take all these things myself to the General Headquarters, which makes me very shy.

'The German observer says he was given to understand that we tortured all our prisoners, and wondered when it was going to be over. He was also much surprised to hear that he was going to be taken to England, as the German Navy has control of all the seas, and

England is completely cut off! Now one can understand why they go on fighting.' (*The Aeroplane*, 14 Nov 1915).

Robert's victory, recorded in RFC Communiqué 16, notes that the German pilot, Unteroffizier Gereld, severely wounded in the groin, was killed and that his observer, seventeen-year-old Second Lieutenant Buchholz, was wounded in the head and was in hospital. He 'had won the Iron Cross [2nd Class] when serving as an infantry officer in the IXth Corps.'[219] RFC Communiqué No. 17 was mainly devoted to an interrogation report on Buchholz, who provided useful Intelligence on his squadron and on the German Air Force.

Along with many others, Robert and Eric Lubbock were Mentioned in Dispatches in the 1916 New Year's Honours List. (*The London Gazette*, 1 January 1916, no. 29422).

Robert's bravery was never in question, but the manner of his leadership was. Though popular with the other ranks – Robert had, of course, been a "ranker" in the Second Boer War – the officers who served under him in 5 Squadron's "B" Flight were, according to Lieutenant F.J. "Fred" Powell,[220] 'most awfully sick at the way we were being ordered about by this old man of thirty-nine. His record as a pilot before he came to us did not impress us, and in private life he was an actor! This made everyone eye him with suspicion.'

Robert had also had the temerity to order, unilaterally, modifications and alterations to be made to his pilots' aeroplanes. Each pilot usually looked after his own machine and became obsessively possessive of it. It was unthinkable, therefore, for anyone else to tamper with one's "own" machine. In the end, the officers of "B" Flight had had enough of Robert's interfering. Fred Powell, being the youngest – he was only twenty (see Appendix IV) – was, as he said, 'delegated by the other officers to tackle Loraine on it. I remember walking across the aerodrome with him and I said: "Look, Sir. I have a complaint to make and I'm not speaking only for myself but for everybody in the Flight – all the pilots – and they don't like the way you're autocratically ordering modifications to be done to the aircraft in the Flight." He said: "Alright, Powell. In future I'll give my orders to the officer. Woe betide any officer who doesn't carry them out."'[221]

Thus was the matter resolved, though Powell records that, though 'Loraine, the man, was full of understanding… outwardly he remained a disciplinarian to the last inch of him.'[222]

(It is also worth noting that a certain Squadron Leader A.T. Harris, displaying a similar, necessary toughness when CO of 45 Squadron, 1922-24, was described as 'a strict

---

[219] Royal Flying Corps Communiqués 1915-1916, p.69.
[220] Later Major Frederick James Powell MC. Born 13 Aug 1895.
[221] Reel 4, interview with FJ Powell on 25 Jan 1973, Imperial War Museum.
[222] *Actor, Soldier, Airman*, pp.217, 218. It is clear, from Powell's future actions overall, that he had a high opinion of Robert. – *author*.

disciplinarian, a martinet according to his detractors, but he understood that being a CO was not a popularity contest and that laxity was inherently dangerous in a military organisation, especially one on active service.')[223]

In due course, when Robert was given command of 5 Squadron's "A" Flight, Fred Powell took over "B" Flight. Unsure of himself, he asked Robert for advice. Robert's reply gave Fred 'confidence as no one else could.'

Early in 1916, as flight commanders, Robert and Fred Powell were each given a "pusher" aircraft to evaluate. Robert got Airco D.H.2, no. 5917: 'The first production D.H.2s appeared in November 1915. On 24 November Nos. 5917 and 5918 were at Hendon, waiting to go to the RFC in France, but a change of allocation on 28 November sent them to CFS instead. Probably the first to go to France was [D.H.2, no.] 5919, which was flown over by Lt Breeze on 8 January 1916'.[224]

D.H.2s 5917 and 5920 were allocated to 5 Squadron early in 1916, for Robert reported using the former on a patrol over Polygon and Houthulst Woods on 8 February 1916, when he attacked an Aviatik scout at 9,000 feet over Hooge, keeping his subsequent report to the bare minimum: 'During Patrol, the hostile machine was sighted over Polygon Wood going N.W. at about 9,000 ft. The De Haviland pursued and got within 350 yards over Houthulst Forest. The prospects of coming to close quarters within a reasonable time were small, and so fire was opened at this range. The Aviatik then turned S.E. and over Polygon Wood the range had decreased to about 250 yards, when the Aviatik dived in the direction of Zwandhoek. Tracer bullets appeared to strike the fuselage of the Aviatik.'[225]

Fred Powell was allocated a single-seat R.A.F. F.E.8, no. 7457, the model's second prototype. It was flown to France by the factory's test-pilot, Frank Goodden, on 19 December 1915 'for evaluation by operational pilots of the RFC.'[226] No. 7457 'had a spinner mounted when it was sent to No. 5 Squadron RFC at Abeele for evaluation on 26 December 1915; this spinner was removed before mid-January 1916. No. 7457 became the nearly exclusive mount of Captain Frederick Powell.'[227]

---

[223] *The Flying Camels*, p.78. Harris was later Air Chief Marshal Sir A.T., OC RAF Bomber Command 1942-45.
[224] *The Aeroplanes of the Royal Flying Corps Military Wing*, p.43. Was "Breeze" 2nd. Lt. N.G. Breeze – see p. 261.
[225] TNA file AIR 1/1217/204/5/2634. Note that mis-spelt words are as per the original.
[226] The Aeroplanes of the Royal Flying Corps Military Wing, p.432.
[227] From website military-history.fandom.com/wiki/Royal_Aircraft_Factory_F.E.8.

D.H.2 no. 5943, from the same production batch (nos. 5916–6015) as Robert's 5917.

On the afternoon of 5 February 1916, Powell went off on his own in 7457 and had a fight with an enemy aircraft. Others of the squadron, meanwhile, undertook their duties in their B.E.2.c aeroplanes, Robert flying B.E.2.c 4093 with Lieutenant Harold Hemming (see Appendix IV) observing. They departed at 1.35 p.m. on an artillery engagement and a brief report was made after they had landed at 2.40 p.m.: 'Six shots observed falling on target further observation impossible owing to clouds. Batteries engaging target [were] 39th Siege, 13th, Bde., 7th Siege.'

As a result of developments in the war on the ground, 5 Squadron's 'participation was confined very largely to patrols to ward off enemy aircraft. Some of these patrols resulted in engagements of an indecisive character, and Captain G.J. [sic – F.J.] Powell, in particular, flying the Squadron's F.E.8, had several such encounters. On the last day of February, over Bailleul, Powell joined issue with two enemy two-seaters, driving them back to their lines with expenditure of all his ammunition, but without effecting any apparent damage.'[228]

Instructing in England. Robert was now recalled to England as part of the drive to bring new squadrons up to the required standard for active service in France, and on 11 March 1916 was posted to 2 (Reserve) Squadron at Brooklands as an instructor. Although there was no lack of willing volunteer pilots, 'there were insufficient instructors; many of them were pilots who had been sent home for a rest after cracking up under the strain of operations in France and held a jaundiced view of the joys of flying. The result was that newly-qualified pilots arriving in France after the statutory 15 hours of solo flying were far from ready to face action.'[229]

40 Squadron. After his spell with No. 2 (Reserve) Squadron, Robert was briefly posted to No. 45 Squadron, before going to No. 40 Squadron on 6 April, then to No. 1 (Reserve) Squadron at Farnborough with effect from 24 April.

He was there less than a week before being posted back to No. 40 Squadron, which was slowly being built-up. Sometime later in the year, 'No. 902 F/Sgt. Oliver Day reported in at Fort Grange, Gosport with a party of senior N.C.O.'s, direct from France. Marching the party across the parade ground to a line of offices he had a few words with an old friend, D.S. Jillings, the R.F.C.'s first casualty in [the] war, then entered one of the buildings as Major Lorraine [sic] called for F/Sgt. Day [see Appendix IV]. Coming to attention the N.C.O. reported his arrival and Major Lorraine looked at him and said – "You're for 40 Squadron."'

'"Forty" at this time took a little finding. Formed under the command of Captain G.R. Howard from a nucleus of No. 23 Squadron on February 26th, 1916, its original training

---

[228] TNA file AIR 27/63.
[229] *Boom*, p.129.

Officers of 40 Squadron at Gosport. Major Robert Loraine MC is seated centre, with Captain G.D. Hill on his right, and Captain D.O. Mulholland on his left. Captain F.J. Powell is seated second from right.

syllabus was based on photographic and artillery observation patrols with B.E.2c's and Avro's. Early in March a body of men were posted in from a recruits training school near Brighton, [and] the command passed to Major "Bob" Lorraine, and a change in aircraft and duties was recorded.

'Training switched to D.H.2's and the pilots put in many hours on these aircraft before they began to take on charge the F.E.8 in readiness for more serious work.'[230]

40 Squadron's first commander, Captain G.R. Howard DSO (see Appendix IV), was to have been replaced by Major Louis Arbon Strange (*below*),[231] but the latter was unable to take-up the appointment following a botched operation for an appendectomy at Cosham Military Hospital, when the surgeon accidentally left a swab inside him.[232]

Robert, 40 Squadron's only Flight Commander at the time, was promoted and given command of the squadron *vice* Major Strange: '*Squadron Comdrs.*, and to be temp. Majors whilst so empld… Capt. R. Loraine, Spec. Res., from a Flight Comdr. 24th Apr. 1916.'[233]

---

[230] From *40 Squadron History* compiled by James L. Dixon in TNA file AIR 27/2698.
[231] Later Wing Commander RAF, DSO, OBE, MC, DFC & Bar (27 Jul 1891–15 Nov 1966): 'No other fighter pilot saw combat in the Great War for the full duration', from 1914 to 1918 (*Dorset Flight*, p.3).
[232] *Recollections of an Airman*, p. 134.
[233] *The London Gazette*, 9 May 1916, no. 29573.

Major Louis Arbon Strange

The squadron was, however, short of officers, as most had already gone to France: 'How massive the turn-over was can be seen from the fact that, of the twenty-five officers on the squadron on 16 March, only the CO, Loraine, and Lt D. O. Mulholland remained at the time the Squadron went to France in August.'[234] The three Flight Commanders were Captains D. O. Mulholland (see Appendix IV), G.D. Hill (joined in the second week of July), and F.J. "Fred" Powell (joined 6 August).

To help make up the numbers, Robert had sent a telegram to his fellow flight-commander on No. 5 Squadron, Fred Powell: 'I am leaving overseas week after next. I am at Gosport now. I have a Flight for you. Can you come?' Though recovering from an accident in which he had broken an ankle, Fred's reply was in the affirmative and, having persuaded a doctor that his ankle had mended, joined 40 Squadron – still on crutches.

Fred Powell would remember how Robert, having just been promoted to major, took to wearing an eyeglass, as that was what every major in a play on the stage always wore: 'When I went on leave in London I bought from Harrods a whole box of plain glass eyeglasses with broad black ribbons.' On his return from leave (date not known), Fred issued every officer on the squadron with one of these eyeglasses: 'That night at dinner everybody wore an eyeglass. I must say that Loraine was quite good. He took it in good part. He didn't comment at all. He didn't even try to say that he had a defective eye, but he paid no attention to that, and for that I admired him.'[235]

40 Squadron's motor transport left Fort Grange for France on 30 July, while six pilots of "A" Flight, under Captain Mulholland, flew in their F.E.8 aeroplanes from Gosport to Folkestone and thence across the English Channel to St. Omer, France on 1 August 1916. With Mulholland were Second Lieutenants M. Jacks, H.C. Davis, H.A. Rigby and P.V. Tanner (these last two Australians – see Appendix IV), and Sergeant F.E. Darvell who had been posted in for training on 10 April (see Appendix IV). Robert, Mulholland and Darvell were the longest-serving pilots on the squadron.[236]

The pilots of "A" Flight, 40 Squadron, then flew from St. Omer to their new base at Treizennes on 2 August 1916. "B" and "C" Flights crossed to St. Omer on 19 August, joining "A" at Treizennes six days later. Attached to 10th Wing, 40 Squadron patrolled the

---

[234] *Sweeping the Skies*, p.17.
[235] From transcript of undated interview with "RGL" at the IWM, quoted in *Bloody April*, pp.299-300.
[236] *Sweeping the Skies*, p.17.

3rd Army's sector of the Western Front, its main duties being to provide escorts for 25 Squadron (with the F.E.2d), and 'to carry out line and offensive patrols with the aim of destroying or driving off German reconnaissance aircraft.'[237]

40 Squadron's first combat victories came on 22 September whilst on escort duty, when Mulholland and Second Lieutenant J. Hay were successful.[238] The claim that Second Lieutenant K.S. Henderson, an Australian (see Appendix IV), scored a victory on 9 September appears to be erroneous: '2/Lt. K.S. Henderson arrived, a strip of a lad of nineteen, brought down a Halberstadt the day after arriving, and was then himself crashed.'[239]

F.E.8 no. 6390 [courtesy www.militaryfactory.com/aircraft/]

---

[237] *Sweeping the Skies,* p.17.
[238] James L. Dixon in his *History*, and *Sweeping the Skies*, p.18.
[239] *Robert Loraine, Actor, Soldier, Airman*, p.222.

Tom (left) and Gilbert W.R. Mapplebeck

The two Australian junior officers, Second Lieutenants P.V. Tanner and H.A. Rigby, were not altogether enjoying life on the squadron. Joining on 1 August, Rigby wrote that we 'were soon made to feel we were Colonials by the Commanding Officer Major Robert Lorrain [*sic*]. During the short time I was with the Squadron in France, he [Robert] did not leave the ground,[240] but spent a lot of time at night crawling over beetroot fields trying to pass the guards without being challenged. The unfortunate guard then got 21 days field punishment. This was ended one night when I was orderly officer, and the guard commander marched in and announced he had a prisoner found in suspicious circumstances on the edge of the aerodrome. What is a poor 2nd. Lt. with just over two months service to do when his own C.O. is marched in between four hefty guards? I recognised the prisoner and released him.'[241]

Rigby's actions had upset a plan carefully hatched by the squadron's other officers, who knew that only a senior officer was entitled to release a prisoner. Thus, Rigby found himself unpopular not only with his CO but also with his fellow officers!

Joining 40 Squadron 'as a supernumerary Flight Commander on 3 October'[242] was Captain T.G. "Tom" Mapplebeck,[243] whose elder brother Robert had encountered earlier in the war (see page 203).[244]

---

[240] It should be made quite clear that by not flying on operations Robert was obeying the direct order not to do so.
[241] Letter 16 Jan 1960 to a Mr H. Russell.
[242] *Sweeping the Skies,* p.18.
[243] RAeC no. 2754, 18 Mar 1916.
[244] *Sweeping the Skies*, pp.19, 20.

Though Robert may not have been popular with some of the 40 Squadron officers, Major-General "Boom" Trenchard had a high opinion of the squadron and of its CO, as evidenced by RFC Communiqué No. 59 issued on 27 October 1916: 'I visited 40 Squadron yesterday, and was much struck by the extraordinarily fine organisation in the Squadron, also by the excellent method and cleanliness in regard to machines, workshops, transport and sheds.'

Trenchard's visit to 40 Squadron on 26 October had been prompted by the squadron's successes over the three days of 20, 21 and 22 October 1916. On 20 October, Mulholland, Benbow and Second Lieutenant S.A. Sharpe[245] had each claimed a German aircraft shot down; on 21 October Tom Mapplebeck claimed a victory, while Lieutenant G.C.O. Usborne and Second Lieutenant R.E. Neve (see both Appendix IV) 'claimed two others out of control, Usborne's going down in a spin, smoking'.[246] On 22 October, Australian Second Lieutenant John Hay, Second Lieutenant Edwin Benbow, and Lieutenant Henry Cuthbert Todd (see Appendix IV for these three) also claimed one each.

Five weeks after joining 40 Squadron, Tom Mapplebeck became a prisoner of war. He had only just returned from leave when, on 9 November 1916, he flew an offensive patrol in his usual F.E.8 no. 7624.[247] For some reason he was unable to climb above 5,000 feet, and handed over the flight to Robert Gregory (see Appendix IV). On the way home, he destroyed a German observation balloon over the La Bassée sector, but was then attacked by two German machines. With his fuel pipe severed by a bullet, he was forced to land on a German aerodrome and was taken prisoner of war. He later managed to escape from (Canabrück) Clausthal, but was recaptured and sent to Schweidnitz. Eventually sent to the awful camp at Holzminden, where he saw out the war, he was not repatriated until 29 January 1919.

No. 40 Squadron more than evened the score for their recent losses when, on 4 December 1916, Mulholland and Benbow each shot down one of the three Jasta 12 aircraft that were attacking a B.E.2c of 16 Squadron.

Early in December 1916 Robert was invited to a farewell dinner given for Major R.R. Smith-Barry,[248] the outgoing commander of 60 Squadron, based at Savy, a couple of miles west of St. Quentin: 'The guests included General Higgins (the brigade commander), [George] Pretyman (the wing commander), Col. Lewis and Barnaby of the "archie" gunners, Robert Loraine and several other squadron commanders.'[249]

---

[245] Sharpe's "Graduation Certificate" was dated 22 Sep 1916, making him a newly-qualified pilot. He became a POW on 3 Apr 1917 when shot down in Nieuport 17 no. A6674 by Gustav Nernst, in Albatros D.III 2147/16.
[246] *Sweeping the Skies*, p.18.
[247] TNA file AIR 1/1405/204/28/5.
[248] On returning from France, Major Robert Raymond Smith-Barry (1886–1949), later (temp.) Brigadier-General, ran a special flying training school at Gosport.
[249] *Sixty Squadron R.A.F. 1916–1919*, p.22 – A.J.L. Scott (Greenhill Books, London, 1990).

The following officers were among those serving on 40 Squadron in early 1917: Captain D.O. Mulholland; Captain W.R. Gregory; Lieutenants E.L. Benbow; D. de Burgh; C.G. Gilbert; W. Morrice; T. Shephard; G.C.O. Usborne; Second Lieutenants L. Blaxland; W.H. Cox; G.F. Haseler; K.S. Henderson; W.B. Hills; R.E. Neve; H.S. Pell (see page 237); S.A. Sharpe; P.H. Smith. Also on the squadron was pilot Sergeant W.T. Walder (see Appendix IV).

The weather during the winter of 1916/17 was severe, a bitter blow to the men of the newly-arrived 43 Squadron with its Sopwith 1½-Strutters, who were to share the bleak amenities of Treizennes aerodrome in January 1917 with 40 Squadron. The CO of 43 Squadron, Major William Sholto Douglas MC,[250] wrote: 'That winter of 1916-17 was a brutal one, and it was bitterly cold at Treizennes. The ground was snow-covered – the first six weeks of the new year was a period of hard frost – and we had to camp out in bare, empty huts with only our flying kit to keep us warm. Never in my life have I been so cold as I was during the first forty-eight hours'.[251]

Captain Harold Balfour,[252] another of 43's officers, agreed: 'That winter was one of the hardest for many years. Added to the dangers of flying and fighting was the very real one of frost-bite. We covered our faces, hands and wrists with whale oil but even so had a number of aircrew invalided home with acute frost-bite. The day we arrived at our new airfield the temperature was far below zero'.

On arrival at Treizennes 43 Squadron were given a taste of Robert's thoughtfulness: 'A messenger came up and saluted. "Major Loraine's compliments and hot lunch is ready in the mess." That was hospitality that was.'[253]

Major Douglas was clear that their 'miserable introduction to life at Treizennes was made just bearable by the kindness of the other squadron – No. 40 – with which we were to share the airfield... and the squadron was under the command of Robert Loraine. A handsome and very well-known actor of middle age [*he was 41 in January 1917*], Loraine was also a first-rate airman.'

'The whole atmosphere of the aerodrome at Treizennes was dominated by the character of Robert Loraine... I came to know Loraine very well both as an airman and, through going to the theatre and enjoying his work, as an actor.'[254]

Balfour, too, thought that Robert 'was always the actor. The whole of his organisation was stage-managed with a masterly touch. The officers' mess was filled with patent bells

---

[250] Douglas, born 23 Dec 1893, awarded RAeC certificate no. 1301, 2 Jun 1915. Later MRAF 1st Baron Douglas of Kirtleside GCB, MC, DFC. Died 29 Oct 1969.
[251] *Years of Combat*, p.165.
[252] Harold Harington Balfour, born 1 Nov 1897, awarded RAeC certificate no 1399, 5 Jul 1915. Later MC, Under Secretary of State for Air, and 1st Baron of Inchrye (1945) died 21 Sep 1988.
[253] *Wings Over Westminster*, p.36.
[254] *Years of Combat*, p.165.

and alarms liable to go off at any moment, each indicating some different happening like a patrol taking off or an enemy sighted. When this happened his pose was to be quite undisturbed, continuing his conversation, only pausing to say over his shoulder to one of his Flight Commanders, "I think there may be an enemy around. Perhaps you had better see to it." He would then go on with his game of Bridge.' Robert did, though, try to be "one of the boys", 'and let himself be rolled about on the floor by his junior officers.'[255]

Robert's theatrical behaviour was not confined to his own squadron, as witness a visit to 60 Squadron recorded by an unknown officer: 'I can still see Peter Portal behind the actor-airman Robert Lorraine [sic] in the mess, and copying all his actions, much to our amusement.'[256]

When Higher Authority decreed that squadron commanders were no longer permitted to fly offensive patrols, Robert knew that his operational flying career was, in theory, all but over. In any case, he would have had neither the lung capacity nor the reflexes to be a fighter pilot, even though Air Vice-Marshal Sir Sefton Brancker thought that Robert 'eventually turned into a very fine fighting pilot.'[257]

On days when flying was not possible, and there were many of them, Robert made sure that the men on the squadron did not remain idle, and ordered practice moves. 'It was not' as Corporal (later Flight Sergeant) Robert Muir recalled 'a popular event, but as an aid to 100% Efficiency, it could not have been surpassed.'[258] Robert also looked after his own men's catering, making as sure as he could that everyone ate as well as could be expected under prevailing wartime conditions. Muir again: 'I state emphatically that no body of men were better fed or looked after than the men of 40 Squadron.'[259]

And there was entertainment, too. After George Bernard Shaw had sent the scripts for two of his plays – *O'Flaherty V.C.* and *The Inca of Perusalem* – to Robert, Robert decided to produce them for the delectation of his squadron. Lieutenant William Morrice, who was returning on leave to England in December 1916, was tasked with obtaining the necessary costumes from L. & H. Nathan's, the leading theatrical costumiers. Having obtained Morrice's signature for them, Nathan's obligingly sent the costumes to France on 5 January 1917. This would come back to haunt Robert and Morrice a couple of years later, when Nathan's sued for damages for the loss of the costumes. *The Stage*, on 24 April 1919, reported on the court case in which Robert and Morrice gave evidence. The judge, in deciding that all the officers of the squadron should foot the bill, regretted that he had to order Morrice himself to pay £140 plus costs.

---

[255] *Wings Over Westminster*, pp.36-7.
[256] Quoted in *Portal of Hungerford*, p.50 – Denis Richards (William Heinemann Ltd, London, 1977).
[257] *Sir Sefton Brancker*, p.40.
[258] *Actor, Soldier, Airman*, p.227.
[259] *Actor, Soldier, Airman*, p.227.

As it happened, Shaw was invited by General Sir Douglas Haig to visit the Western front. Arriving in France on 28 January 1917 for a nine-day visit, he managed to get to 40 Squadron at Treizennes on 3 February thus, albeit briefly, renewing his friendship with Robert. Shaw, impressed by the way in which Robert handled his squadron, was able to attend a dress rehearsal of *The Inca of Perusalem*, which was being held in 'an abandoned Red Cross hut' called the *Theatre Royal*, which the squadron 'had moved piece by piece.'[260]

Sitting with Shaw during the comedy's performance was Fred Powell, who couldn't fail to notice that Shaw was laughing until he cried. After the performance, Powell said to Shaw: 'I am so glad, Sir, that you appreciate our poor efforts at your play.' Still wiping his eyes, Shaw replied: 'Do you know? If I had thought it was going to be anything like that, I wouldn't have written it!'[261]

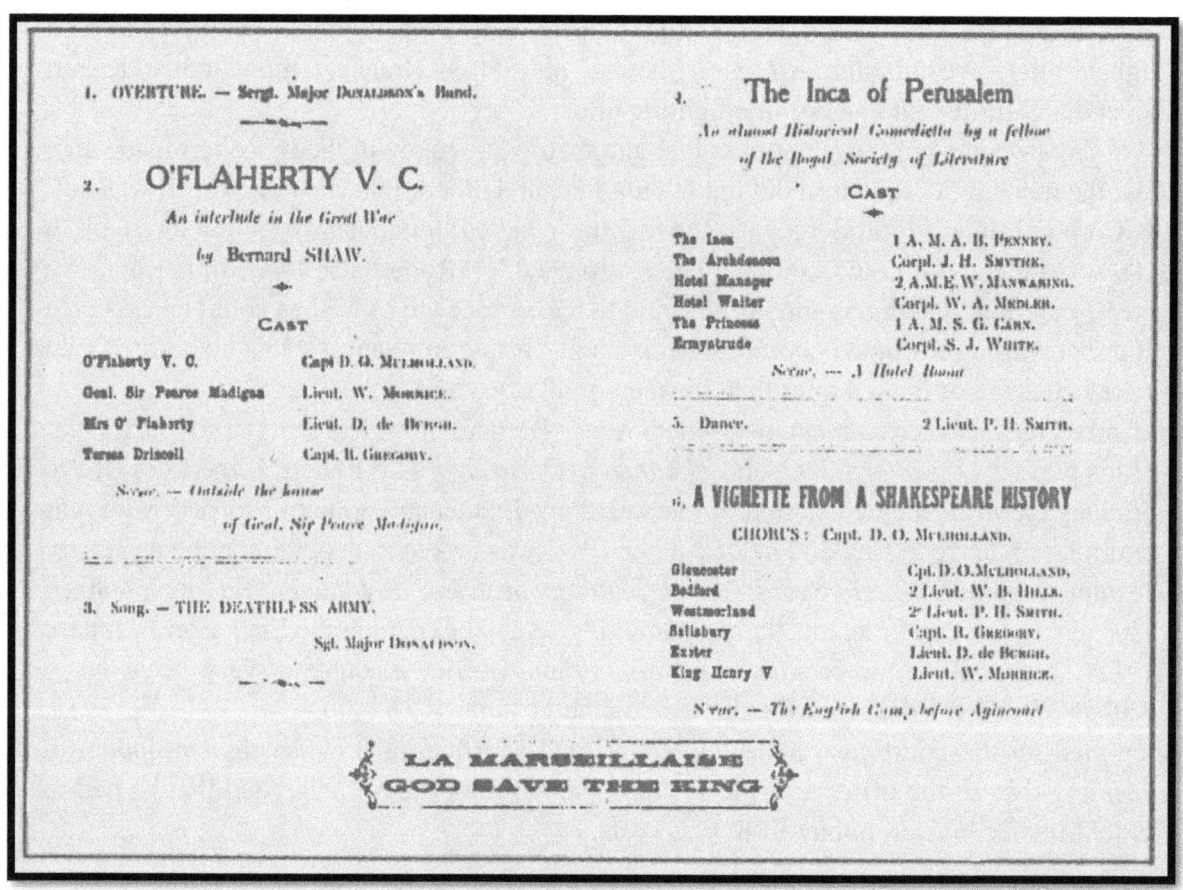

Programme of 40 Squadron's plays (www.airwar19141918.wordpress.com/tag/robert-gregory/)

---

[260] *The Life of Robert Loraine*, p.141.
[261] Quoted in *Bloody April*, p.300.

Promotion. Shortly after Shaw's visit, Robert was promoted to temporary lieutenant-colonel with effect from 12 February 1917: '*Wing Comdr. From Sqdn. Comdr., and to be temp. Lt.-Col. whilst so empld. Capt. (temp. Maj.) R. Loraine, M.C., Spec. Res. 13th Feb. 1917.*'[262]

Robert's time in command of 40 Squadron was now at an end but, before he left, there was an incident remembered by everyone. During dinner one night, fire broke out in one of the sheds, with four aeroplanes in it, as Captain Balfour recalled: 'Fire pickets had doubled to the spot but there was nothing to be done except to form a semi-circle round the blazing hangar and let the fire burn itself out… The hangar had a lean-to shed in which mechanics kept their tools. It had not yet caught fire and a little sergeant thought he could help by going to the lean-to and starting to throw out spanners, vices and screwdrivers. Hardly had he begun this rather futile task than Robert Loraine strode into the centre of the firelit ring of men, seized the little sergeant by the coat collar and pushed him aside. In a large stage voice he cried out, "Away! Away! Away, my man! If this is anybody's place, it is mine." … and there, in the full glare of the light, performed a perfectly natural function to the admiring eyes of the assembled pilots and mechanics.'[263]

Sholto Douglas added: 'I could never have attempted to offer leadership with the touches of sheer flamboyance that Loraine displayed, but there was never any question about the devotion that his style inspired in those under his command.'[264] None doubted that Robert, ever the actor, was a brave man.

After Robert's departure as CO of 40 Squadron, the Squadron continued to flourish, and several fine pilots were posted to it. On 6 April 1917, a replacement pilot, a certain Edward Corringham Mannock, arrived. On his first night, joining the other officers at the dinner table, he saw an empty chair and asked if it was taken. There was a stunned silence, until someone said: 'It was. It belonged to Pell. He didn't come back this afternoon.' Luck had run out for the long-serving Harry Saxon Pell on 6 April 1917. Unaware of the custom of leaving an empty chair in the Mess as a mark of respect for one of the squadron who had failed to return, Mannock 'nodded coolly and sat down.'[265] He would later be known as "Mick" Mannock VC, DSO**, MC*, with sixty-one aerial victories to his credit (24 May 1887–26 July 1918).

Back to England. On 13 February 1917, on promotion, Robert was posted as wing commander to 23rd (Training) Wing, Home Establishment, at South Carlton, Lincolnshire, a mile or two north-west of Lincoln itself: 'South Carlton aerodrome… was equipped with seven permanent hangars of the RFC 1916 pattern, one of which served as an Aeroplane

---

[262] *The London Gazette*, 27 Feb 1917, no. 29965.
[263] *Wings Over Westminster*, p.37.
[264] *Years of Combat*, p.166.
[265] *They Fought For The Sky*, (Pan edition) p.186.

Avro 504 trainer no. D174 has landed in the wrong place at South Carlton (photo from an album compiled by Frank Saunders, who trained with 23rd (T) Wing. (www.walkingthebattlefields.com/2020/03/south-carlton-airfield-1918)

Repair Shed. In addition there were several temporary hangars of the Bessonneau type and living accommodation was provided for by rows of wooden huts.'[266]

During Robert's brief time at South Carlton, four crashes ended in the death of the pilot, the last being on the very day on which he was posted away, 11 April 1917. Three were members of No. 45 (Reserve) Squadron, the fourth of No. 69 (Reserve) Squadron.

France again. With the war not going well for the Allies in France, both on the ground and in the air, Robert's time at South Carlton was cut short by the need for experienced wing commanders in France. With effect from 11 April 1917, therefore, he was given command of the 14th Wing, which had been under the temporary command of Major L.W. Learmount DSO, MC, who was simultaneously the CO of 22 Squadron at Chipilly aerodrome.[267]

As at 31 March 1917, the RFC's Wings were distributed over the Western Front as follows:[268]

Unit	**Location**
HQ, RFC	Château de St. André
9th (GHQ) Wing – 19, 27, 35, 55, 66, 70 Squadrons	Fienvillers
I Brigade	Château de Réveillon
1st Wing – 2, 5, 10, 16 Squadrons	
10th Wing – 25, 40, 43, Naval 8 Squadrons	
II Brigade	Cassel
2nd Wing – 6, 21, 42, 46, 53 Squadrons	
11th Wing – 1, 20, 41, 45 Squadrons	
III Brigade	Château de Sains
12th Wing – 8, 12, 13, 59 Squadrons	
13th Wing – 11, 29, 48, 60, 100, Naval 6 Squadrons	
IV Brigade	Misery
3rd Wing – 7, 9, 34, 52 Squadrons	
14th Wing – 22, 24, 54, Naval 1 Squadrons	
V Brigade	Albert
15th Wing – 3, 4, 15 Squadrons	
22nd Wing – 18, 23, 32, Naval 3 Squadrons.	

---

[266] *Action Stations 2. Military airfields of Lincolnshire and the East Midlands*, p.170 – Bruce Barrymore Halpenny (Patrick Stephens Ltd, Cambridge, 1981).
[267] Chipilly is located on the north of the River Somme, a dozen kilometres south of Albert. Leonard Wright Learmount, born 21 Nov 1889 at Gateshead-on-Tyne, was awarded RAeC certificate no. 1146 on 2 Apr 1915.
[268] From *Letters from a Flying Officer*, pp.116-7.

14th Wing. At this time, No. 22 Squadron had an establishment of eighteen F.E.2bs; 24 Squadron eighteen D.H.2s, (replaced in May 1917 by D.H.5s); 54 Squadron with eighteen Sopwith Pups; and No. 1 RNAS with Sopwith Triplanes. By 11 April 1917, Naval 1 and Naval 6 Squadrons, the latter equipped with the Nieuport 17, had swapped Brigades. It had been recognised that Naval 6 had been under-performing, and was to be strengthened by 'a complete flight from No. 11 Squadron under acting Squadron Commander Draper.' Morale cannot have been improved when, two days after arriving at its new aerodrome at Chipilly, Naval 6's Acting Squadron Commander, John Joseph Petre DSC, was killed in Nieuport Scout N3206 whilst diving at a practice target on the ground.[269]

Major K.K. Horn, 54 Squadron CO (photo courtesy www.saam.org.au/history_group)

54 Squadron, on the other hand, were fortunate to have a CO, Australian-born Major Kelham Kirk Horn, who believed in being as comfortable as possible. As well as possessing a cow, the squadron also 'had fifty-four chickens and one cock. The cock was called Robert after a famous actor who was also in the Corps, though the imputation that the latter had fifty-four wives was a base libel.'[270] Robert Loraine's reputation, however true, had clearly gone before him!

A week or so after his arrival Robert received orders to move the Wing from Misery back to Flez, some fifteen kilometres west of St. Quentin, as the French were planning a "push" as far as the latter town. In the event, the French offensive, which began on 16 April 1917, was a failure. While much of the French Army mutinied, the British, under Sir Douglas Haig, attacked Messines Ridge, and the Canadians wrote their names in history with their heroic assault on Vimy Ridge.

---

[269] *A History of No. 6 Squadron RNAS*, pp.44 & 45. J.J. Petre, born 11 Apr 1894, was the youngest of three brothers, each an aviator, the other two being Henry Aloysius (1884–1962) and Edward (1886–1912).
[270] Quoted in *Bloody April*, p.288, from TNA file AIR 1/2388/228/11/83 R.M. Foster.

F.E.2b, no. A5548

One of 14th Wing's aerodromes (photo courtesy Rob Schmidt)

During the chaos, 14th Wing's aircraft were occupied in various ways. One of 54 Squadron's pilots, Lieutenant Oliver Stewart,[271] posted to Chipilly in early 1917 from 22 Squadron, wrote: 'The FEs were having a bad time on their photographic patrols. They were going down in flames on a large scale. The pilots of 22 were asked to face fearful conditions. And now the Albatros V-strutters were after them. Most of the FE pilots, as they seemed to us of 54 Squadron, were old men. Many were over thirty. Some… were over forty. But they continued to go out and make themselves sitting targets for hours on end for the anti-aircraft guns.'

'… But the FE casualty rate was seen even by those who sat at desks a good way away from the fighting to be excessive. So escorts were decided upon.'[272]

---

[271] Born 26 Nov 1896, awarded RAeC certificate no. 2630, 30 Mar 1916.
[272] *Words and Music for a Mechanical Man*, p.124.

At least the escorts, though they could do nothing about "Archie", might be able to minimise losses from the German fighters. This, then, would be the job of 54's Sopwith Pups. Oliver Stewart noted that it was Robert 'who received the demands from the FEs for protection and from our artillery observation machines for protection.'[273]

It proved, however, to be not that simple. The canny Germans began by attacking in two layers, the upper one keeping the Pups quiet while the lower one went for the slow and clumsy FEs. So, the D.H.5s were added to the mix at lower altitudes as the Pups easily outflew them at heights above 10,000 feet. Inevitably, the Germans countered the new RFC tactics by adding their own third layer and, inevitably, the RFC added their own third layer, this time bringing in No. 1 Squadron RNAS, commanded by Major Christopher Draper,[274] with their Nieuport scouts. Even then, in a formation of some sixty aircraft, 'the FEs were murdered'.

To add to the RFC's problems, von Richthofen and his Jasta 11 were still dangerously active on 14th Wing's front – Richthofen alone had scored forty "kills" by the time Robert took command of the 14th Wing on 11 April – and the Germans were enjoying aerial supremacy. The Battle of Arras (9 April–6 May 1917) gave Jasta 11 the opportunity to claim eighty-nine Allied aircraft destroyed in those four weeks (from a total of 298 claims made by *all* German fighter units for that period). Not for nothing was April 1917 known to the RFC as "Bloody April".

The pressure now on Robert, who had been in action one way or another since August 1914, was growing, the gaps in his squadrons' ranks affecting him badly: 'He hated waiting on the tarmac for the dawn reconnaissance to return, standing next to the Sergeant-Major, who would also be counting the machines in…'

As the commanding officer of the 14th Wing, it is unlikely that Robert got to know many of the young airmen who daily went out to face the enemy but, of the four squadrons in the Wing, it was 22 Squadron, with its F.E.2bs, that suffered the most casualties during "Bloody April," 1917. Four of its airmen were killed in action, four more were wounded, and another four became prisoners of war.[275] The Squadron's first losses that month were Second Lieutenant Patrick Alfred Russell (pilot) and Lieutenant Henry William Victor Loveland (observer) (see Appendix IV), who took-off at 6.35 a.m. on 2 April 1917 for a photographic sortie in F.E.2b no. 6953. Attacked by eighteen German aeroplanes over Gouzeaucourt, 6953 was shot down in flames by Offizierstellverstreter Edmund Nathanael of Jasta 5, for his sixth victory.

---

[273] *Words and Music for a Mechanical Man*, p.130.
[274] Major Draper DSC (15 Apr 1892–16 Jan 1979) was nicknamed "The Mad Major" for his *penchant* for flying under London's bridges.
[275] See the authoritative book *Bloody April 1917*.

The other two of 22 Squadron to be killed were Lieutenant E.A. Barltrop RE and Second Lieutenant F. O'Sullivan. On the afternoon of 23 April, flying in F.E.2b no. 6929, they collided with a D.H.2 flown by Second Lieutenant M.A. White, 24 Squadron (see just below and Appendix IV).

24 Squadron lost Second Lieutenant J.K. Ross, RFC, and Lieutenant E. Kent, 2nd Battalion Essex Regiment, both members of "A" Flight. On the morning of 5 April 1917 Ross, in D.H.2 no. A2592, was attacked by four hostile aircraft and 'brought down east of Honnecourt by Leutnant Wolluhn and Unteroffizier Mackeprang'.[276] He was last seen in a spin and out of control. He had joined the squadron only three weeks earlier, on 16 March 1917.

Second Lieutenant Ernest Kent died on 8 April 1917 allegedly 'from wounds received in action.'[277] He was buried in Cerisy Gailly New French Military Cemetery, half a dozen miles south-west of Albert, in the Somme. 'The grave… is marked by a durable wooden cross with an inscription bearing full particulars.'[278] However, in the telegram dated 9 April 1917 to his mother, Sarah, informing her of her son's death, it is stated that he 'died of accidental injuries.' As no aeroplane loss is attributed to him (see *Bloody April 1917*, p.53), it would seem likely that he died in some other, unfortunate way. Kent's personal file has, therefore, contradictory causes of death but in the history of 24 Squadron he is listed in the section 'Accidentally Killed Whilst Flying'. He had been on the squadron for just three days, joining on 6 April. (See Appendix IV for brief details of Ross and Kent).

24 Squadron's Second Lieutenant Melville Arthur White, flying D.H.2 no. 7909, was trying to avoid an attack by Kurt Schneider of Jasta 5 in an Albatros when he collided with Barltrop and O'Sullivan.[279] White, of "B" Flight, had arrived on 24 Squadron on 14 April.

54 Squadron's only casualty was Lieutenant R.N. Smith, who was wounded.

Naval 1 Squadron lost Flight Sub-Lieutenant L.M.B. Weil (see Appendix IV) on 6 April: 'Flt. Sub-Lt. Louis Marcus Basil Weil, R.N.A.S., attached R.F.C., was … reported missing by the Admiralty on April 7th, and news unofficially received on May 11th states that he died on April 6th, having been shot through the head by enemy fighting machines.' (*The Aeroplane*, 16 May 1917).

Naval 6 lost one pilot – Flight Sub-Lieutenant A.H.V. Fletcher (see Appendix IV). On 29 April, at 5.45 p.m., he took off in N3192 in a "C" Flight patrol of three Nieuport aeroplanes led by Flight Commander Ernest William Norton DSC in N3208. Just before 7 p.m. they were attacked over Guise by twelve Albatros scouts. Norton and the third man, Rupert

---

[276] *Bloody April 1917*, p.29.
[277] TNA file WO 339/35607.
[278] TNA file WO 339/35607 – letter of 1 May 1917 from Army to Mrs Sarah Kent (mother).
[279] *Bloody April 1917*, p.97. For brief details of White, see Appendix IV.

Randolph Winter, in N3195, managed to get away,[280] but Fletcher, wounded in the fight and forced to land, was taken prisoner.

The events of 8 May 1917, for example, were probably typical for this time. On this day all the squadrons of 14th Wing were detailed for a variety of operations under Operation Orders No. 103. The target in the morning for six aeroplanes of 22 Squadron, each carrying six 20lb. bombs, was 'huts in the wood 600 yards East of Fontaine Uterte.' They would be escorted by another six aeroplanes of 54 Squadron, while Naval Squadron 6 would, earlier, fly offensive patrols, also with six aeroplanes. Further offensive patrols would be mounted during the afternoon.

Ernest William Norton *Rupert Randolph Winter*

Robert's orders for the day's operations were signed on his behalf by Lieutenant John Joseph Breen, Royal Irish Regiment who, having qualified for his RAeC "ticket", no, 2103, on 18 November 1915, had transferred from Flying Officer to Adjutant on 15 January 1917.[281]

Home again. Robert may have been given a temporary lift with another MiD, on 15 May 1917, but each passing day was slowly taking its toll on him. After so many months at war he was weary of it all, and the 'ever-increasing death-roll was breaking him up in spirit'.[282] His latest spell in France would soon, however, be coming to an end and, undoubtedly held in high regard by his seniors, his contribution was recognised by

Lieutenant John Joseph Breen, Adjutant, 14th Wing

another, high, award: 'War Office, 4 June, 1917. His Majesty the King has been graciously pleased to approve of the undermentioned rewards for distinguished service in the field: —

---

[280] Norton, born 14 May 1893, awarded the DSC on 1 Jan 1917, later served in the RAF, rising to Air Commodore. He died on 23 May 1966. Winter was KIA on 3 Feb 1918.
[281] Later AVM J.J. Breen CB, OBE (8 Mar 1896–9 May 1964).
[282] *Actor, Soldier, Airman,* pp.237-8.

'To be Companion of the Distinguished Service Order. Capt. (temp. Lt.-Col.) Robert Loraine, M.C., R.F.C., Spec. Res.'[283] It was not, however, until 2 January 1918 that he 'had the honour of being received by His Majesty at Buckingham Palace, when the King invested him with the Insignia of Companion of the Order into which he had been admitted.'

On 25 June 1917 Robert was once again put on the strength of Home Establishment, and given command of the new 18th (Training) Wing, tasked with both Home Defence and training. At this time, appreciating that these two functions could not be adequately completed by a unit on its own, High Command split them and thus Robert found himself at Training HQ in London, dealing with pilots' applications.

One such application came from Lieutenant G.B.S. Fuller who, after crashing at Gosport was ordered to report to Robert, OC 18th (T) Wing: 'Despite the very bad report and the recommendation of Major Smith that my services were of no further value, instead of being severely rebuked I was given a very sympathetic hearing. At the end of the interview I was told not to worry; I would still have the opportunity to fly. He [Robert] was recommending me for a course at the Wireless and Observers' School to train as an observer.'[284] George Fuller would serve as an observer on No. 9 Squadron at Proven, Belgium, from 10 September 1917 to 9 March 1918.

Though away from flying and removed from the immediate horrors of the Western Front, Robert's depression did not improve, as fellow squadron commander Sholto Douglas observed about some of the pilots who were sent home: 'They were casualties not listed as officially wounded, but they were nevertheless still casualties, and some of them were wrecked in health for the rest of their lives.'[285] In Robert's case, doctors decided that he was suffering from the first stages of neurasthenia, as it was then called, a condition considered to be the result of exhaustion of the central nervous system's reserves. He was admitted to the Mount Vernon military hospital[286] in Hampstead, north London, with the comment on his Medical Record that, from 26 September 1917, he was unfit for General Service ["G.S."] for three months.

---

[283] *The London Gazette*, 4 Jun 1917, no. 30111.
[284] From his article *9 Sqn. Observer* in *Cross and Cockade*, Vol. 9, Autumn 1978.
[285] *Years of Combat*, p.253.
[286] In December 1917 it became the RFC Central Hospital [https://ezitis.myzen.co.uk/...].

Mount Vernon Hospital, North London

The next entry on his medical record states: 'Unfit G.S. 2 months. HS [*Home Service*] 1 month. Fit L.D [*Light Duties*] no flying.' Four weeks later, his record was amended: 'Fit G.S. in a warm climate or fit HS.'

Andover, 36th (Training) Wing. Such were the exigencies of war, however, that on 31 October 1917, though not fully recovered, Robert found himself posted to command the Southern Training Brigade's 36th (Training) Wing located at the 54th Training Depot Station, Andover, Hampshire, in southern England.

Andover aerodrome, which had only opened in August 1917, covered '400 acres of nearly flat pasture land bounded by three roads, the most important now the A303.' As not all of the aerodrome's buildings had been completed, at first some of the personnel 'lived in tents with the aircraft housed in a row of Bessonneau canvas hangars erected along the northern boundary.'[287] The Wing's HQ was located at "Upper Croft", a large house in the village of Goodworth Clatford, some 2½ miles from the aerodrome.

---

[287] *Action Stations 9. Military airfields of the Central South and South-East,* p.40 – Chris Ashworth (Patrick Stephens Ltd, Wellingborough, 1985).

Andover aerodrome, looking north (photo taken 16 Jan 1947) [wikipedia.org/wiki/RAF Andover]

Making-up the 36th (Training) Wing were three, newly-formed bomber squadrons: Nos. 104 (CO: Major W.R. Read – see page 384; 105 (Captain H.G. Bowen); and 106 (Captain E.J. Garland – see Appendix IV).[288] The build-up of personnel and flying machines, however, was slow. Garland found on arrival at Andover on 6 October that he was one of only three to have arrived there, and that there was not a single aeroplane anywhere. In his diary, he noted that on 14 October a few more officers had arrived, but still no aeroplanes.

It was Garland's task, when flying personnel did arrive, to find accommodation for them in and around Andover, but they were such a rowdy bunch that this proved difficult, with

---

[288] 104 Squadron formed at Wyton, Cambs., on 4 Sep 1917 before moving to Andover on 16 Sep. Nos. 105 and 106 Squadrons were formed at Andover, on 14 Sep 1917 and 30 Sep 1917 respectively.

a good number finding their way into the local police station. All were colonials, so Garland was told!

Robert arrived at Andover on 31 October 1917 to find 'only three students in attendance; the rest reportedly had some vague medical disorder.'[289]

Robert at this time was still far from well, and undoubtedly vented his spleen on everyone, not least on one very junior airman, Cadet 178074 Harold Arthur French (see also page 261). An actor before enlisting in the RFC, he had had a tough *ab initio* training: 'At last they took us to an aerodrome where they taught us to fly. In charge of that aerodrome was Lieut.-Colonel Robert Loraine, whom I had last seen giving a fine performance in *The Tyranny of Tears*.[290] I longed to get to know him so that we might talk theatre together – I was missing the theatre badly – but what chance had I, a humble flight cadet, of getting near this "God".'[291]

One of the requirements for pilots under training was to fly three circuits of the aerodrome and land. Harold, unfortunately, was unsure as to whether he should land *into* the wind (correct) or *down*wind (wrong). He chose the latter: 'I landed with a series of bumps and a final crunch two feet from a hedge I had never seen on the aerodrome before.' He was immediately summoned by Robert: 'What the devil did you think you were doing?'

'I'm sorry, sir; first night nerves, sir.'

'If I had been expecting a cosy theatrical chat, I was mistaken. He gave me a bleak stare.'

'I suppose you've been trying to tell me that you have been an actor.'

'Yes, sir.'

'Well, you are not an actor now … Sergeant.' He addressed my instructor. 'Take this man to the field. Let him make three circuits, landing after each one. If he makes one idiotic mistake, let me know, and the poor bloody infantry can have him… Dismiss.' These were the only words I had with Lieut.-Colonel Robert Loraine while I was under his command.'

Harold's contribution to the war effort was a negative one: 'I pottered about from aerodrome to aerodrome, hardly fired a gun in anger, and ended up upside down in Finsbury Park [in London] … They put me into a charming hospital [St. John's, Hastings on 29 June 1918] and kept me there until the end of the war. I was then demobbed [demobilized, on 9 January 1919], given quite a large sum of money as gratuity, and turned loose.'[292] He would, however, meet Robert again in more pleasant circumstances soon after the war.

The following selection from Captain Garland's diary highlights Robert's *malaise*:

---

[289] *The Life of Robert Loraine*, p.149.
[290] Robert had opened in *The Tyranny of Tears* in February 1914.
[291] *I Swore I Never Would*, p.180.
[292] *I Swore I Never Would*, pp.180-1.

'Nov. 12 [1917]. Our Colonel is Robert Loraine and he is making himself felt. Thank goodness am staying the weekend at the Suttons. Doing a lot of instructing on R.E.8s.'

'Nov. 18. Frightfully busy these days – hardly time to feed – we are expected to do impossibilities in the way of flying time, in that there is not enough "personnel or material" to do so. Have done about three hours instruction the last couple of days.'

'Nov 19–25. Colonel Loraine away on a course in France so I am acting for him though with rank of Capt. I also have my duties as O.C. 106 Sqdn. I am therefore "acting" three commands, Colonel, also Station Commdr, as well as Squadron Commander.'

'Nov. 25. Am having the busiest time of my life – this treble command is no joke – everyone finds fault and no-one helps. The Station is the most difficult to run chiefly on account of the serious lack of manpower. To add to my troubles there is a gale raging and our hangar is ripped to bits, also stores and workshop tents, mess marquees etc. The entire Station is just about blown down. Today is a holiday and I am the only officer in the camp with a few men…'

Robert returned from France on the evening of 30 November 1917. Though relieved of one of his onerous duties, Garland's woes continued:

'Dec. 20. … The Colonel continues to make life a worry and has driven one Squadron cmdr. away already. We now have about six machines in each squadron – B.E.s, R.E.8.s. About 90% of our officer pupils are Canadian, good keen pilots but anything but "good officers". One of mine appeared in spats for instance. I don't do much flying myself now as there is not time with the whole station to keep going. It is very hard to find billets for the men, and more so as the people of Andover look on us as their natural enemies rather than otherwise. There is little or no Xmas leave owing to our "dear Colonel". There is supposed to be a day off once a fortnight but not for me as I have to organize men's sports, etc.'

'Dec. 24. Can hardly believe it is Xmas Day tomorrow. We are "graciously" given a day off, but there isn't much holiday for me as I have to attend the men's sports, meals, concerts etc. … Every day now is a mass of trouble and I am beginning to feel the strain… Things wouldn't be so bad if it wasn't for the exorbitant demands made by the Colonel…'

'… So far there haven't been many casualties, though there are many crashes. We buried a chap the other day who collided in the air,[293] and several fellows are in hospital on and off – but on the whole things aren't too bad.'

Garland continued writing his diary into 1918.

1 January 1918: 'The first day of 1918 has dawned with a snow storm. We saw the old year out in pretty good style and finished up by leaving the White Hart at 7 a.m. this morning. Walmisley is my second in command now – he was with me in No. 10 in France.'

---

[293] This was Second Lieutenant J. E. Ransome, 104 Squadron (see Appendix IV).

2–4 January 1918: 'Major [J.C.] Quinnell has arrived to take 104 Sdn. and is also Station C.O. which I am very glad to hand over. I will now be able to concentrate on the Squadron and do more flying.' (Re Quinnell, see Appendix IV).

6–11 January 1918: 'Things much the same at Andover – there are now about 50 officer pupils in my squadron and 6 to 12 machines according to crashes. Two of my machines were written off in one day this week, so with three squadrons the average of crashes is pretty high.'

There is little doubt that Robert was at his wits' end regarding the pupils. He 'forced those he reckoned shirkers into the air, over-ruled medical reports that pupils were too ill to fly and was to some extent responsible for the high casualty rate. Nobody could accuse him of hanging back himself; were he to be told that a machine was unserviceable he would take it up himself, arguing that if a pilot as clumsy as he could fly it then anybody could.'

On 11 January 1918 the Station held a dance. Plenty of girls 'turned up and of course there was plenty to drink – we carried on till 5 a.m.' (Garland diary).

13–18 January: 'Same old routine going on – everyone getting more and more fed up. Weather wintry with falls of snow. The Colonel is worse and worse and makes things unbearable sometimes. It appears he is furious with me about something, so I expect I will be chucked out any time now. The relief of responsibility will be restful at all events. If it were not for the odd dance and party in the evenings one would die of "fed-upness". I hardly get time to fly – my total time in the air since coming here is only 40 hrs. Some D.H.4s have arrived – Tysoe, one of my old pupils, took me up in one…'

19–21 January 1918: 'There is nothing much worth entering – one gets to accept events as ordinary, although sometimes rather unusual things occur. Crashes are so usual now I don't think to mention them. The Col. persists in demanding impossibilities and then strafing if not carried out.'

22 January: 'Things are worse than ever as regards the Col. He asks the most impossible things and strafes the heart out of you for not doing what is humanly impossible. Can't make out why I havn't lost the sqdn. yet. I have all these worries with no extra pay and rank. "I don't wish him any harm, but."'

Captain Garland added a Comment to the above diary entry: 'Col. Robert Loraine was famous both as an actor and airman… To us he was a real tyrant and finally the commanders under him got together and by a dirty trick got him in front of a court of inquiry on charges of being drunk on duty. It was a nasty business, and I was very thankful to be out of it, as I was in hospital dangerously ill [*requiring an appendectomy*]. He was a holy terror as a C.O. but I found him good company off duty. He was a brave flying man and a great actor and producer. His Cyrano was a classic.'

The charge, brought by Major J.C. Quinnell, CO of 104 Squadron, was so serious that it could not be swept under the carpet. Accordingly, on 5 April 1918, Robert was brought before a court-martial. The result of the trial was an acquittal for Robert.

Life for the squadrons under training continued to be traumatic, not least for Captain Garland who bemoaned the fact that there 'has been nothing but troubles in the squadron [106] lately', with not a few crashes dotted over the southern English landscape.

Though the high casualty rate in the Wing earned Robert 'a reputation for sheer unmitigated brutality,'[294] C.G. Grey, editor of *The Aeroplane*, wrote of Robert in 1938: 'The RAF could do with a few disciplinarians of his type to-day, now that all sorts of unlicked youngsters are coming into it.'[295]

In a way that would seem to be supportive of Robert's methods, it was Quinnell himself who would later observe that: 'The man power of England was feeling the stress of war. There was difficulty in getting suitable personnel for the Flying Service'. He added that a 'number of these people came from a category that had rather vague ideas of honour. They were attracted to the Flying Corps by the pay. Their one idea seemed to be to draw their pay and avoid service in France.'[296]

The three squadrons at Andover may well have suffered numerous training accidents, but a trawl of one archive[297] revealed seven deaths from the end of January 1918 to the end of April 1918:

30 January 1918. Second Lieutenant Thomas Le Messurier (aged 20), Canadian, killed in D.H.4 no. B5472, 106 Sqn, which broke up in a spin coming out of a loop in the Weyhill area. A note sent to his parents in Nanaimo, Canada, stated that he was looping the loop at 6,000 feet, and that he was unconscious before he hit the ground. He was buried with full military honours in Andover cemetery.

28 February 1918. Second Lieutenant Albert Augustus Gerow (22), Canadian, killed in D.H.4 no. A7980, 104 Sqn, which had spun on a flat turn in the Weyhill area. 'He was appointed Instructor at the Andover aerodrome, being the first cadet out of a class of 36 to receive his wings.'[298] He is buried in Penton Mewsey (Holy Trinity) churchyard, Hampshire.

3 March 1918. Lieutenant Llewellyn Crighton Davies MC (29) (see Appendix IV) crashed on landing, near Culham Bridge, Abingdon, Oxon., in D.H.4 no. B5495, 105 Sqn. He died of his injuries on 16 March 1918 in the Somerville Section, 3rd Southern General Hospital, Oxford. '"Accidental death" was the verdict recorded at Oxford on March 18th

---

[294] *Actor, Soldier, Airman*, p.239.
[295] *Wonder Aces of the Air*, p.44.
[296] Quoted by auctioneers Noonans on www.noonans.co.uk/auctions/archive/lot-archive/results/59246/.
[297] R.C. Cawsey.
[298] The *Daily Colonist*, 3 March 1918.

on Lt. Llewellyn C. Davies, R.F.C, who died in hospital of injuries received in a bad landing at Abingdon.'

17 March 1918. Second Lieutenant Walter George Cottrell Jones (39) (see Appendix IV) killed when B.E.12 no. C3238, 105 Sqn, side slipped, crashed and caught fire on Ramridge Farm, Weyhill. The subsequent enquiry into his accident decided that it was 'entirely due to carelessness on the part of the pilot'.

17 March 1918. Second Lieutenant Herbert Nelson (23) in D.H.9 no. C6075, 105 Sqn, stalled on landing, near Hemel Hempstead. He died of his injuries on 19 March 1918. Born on 28 January 1895 in Coventry, Warwickshire, he enlisted in the RFC as 2AM (Service no. 52902), and began his flying training at Reading on 29 June 1917. After further training, he was posted to 104 Squadron on 4 November 1917 and to 105 Squadron on 1 February 1918. He is buried in Coventry (London Road) Cemetery.

(Coincidentally, another pilot named Nelson, born on 13 November 1891 in New York, USA to Jewish parents, with sixty-seven flying hours under his belt, was also killed in a freak accident, in Warwickshire. Second Lieutenant Harold Griffith Nelson, a member of the American Air Service, attached to 59 (T) Squadron at Lilbourne, Warwickshire was flying at a height of 2,000 feet in Bristol F.2B B1236 on 22 January 1918 when he pulled the machine into a vertical stall. When the machine nose-dived violently out of control, Nelson fell out of the aeroplane, which came down a few fields away.[299])

25 April 1918. Lieutenant Harry Morley Whitcut (25) (born 16 June 1892), 5th S. Staffs. Regt., att. RAF, was stunting over Perham Down, Wiltshire in D.H.4 no. B5489, 106 Sqn, and crashed when overstraining the aeroplane. With him were two army officers as passengers – Lieutenant George Jamieson Downey (24), 3rd King's Own (R. Lancaster Regt.) (Canadian) and Second Lieutenant Frank Arnold Richardson (22), 1st E. Yorks Regt. All three were killed and are buried in Tidworth Military Cemetery.

Whitcut had been involved in another fatal accident on 11 January 1918. Flying B.E.2e A8635, 98 Squadron, from Old Sarum he hit a steel mast on take-off. He was injured, but 19-year old Lieutenant Azariah Phillips died next day.

27 April 1918. Lieutenant Norman Charles Kearney (26) (see Appendix IV) was killed when R.E.8 no. C2424, 106 Sqn, stalled on a turn, spun, crashed and caught fire near Penton Mewsey, Andover: 'Lt. Norman Charles Kearney. R.A.F. (late East Surrey Regt. and R.F.C.), was killed at Andover, Hants, on Saturday, April 27th. Mr. Kearney had just left the ground when apparently engine trouble developed. The machine stalled when fifty feet from the ground and nose-dived to earth. Death was instantaneous. The machine caught fire and was completely destroyed, but owing to the promptness of Major Joy, who rushed to the spot, his body was rescued.' (*The Aeroplane*, 15 May 1918).

---

[299] Researched by Dr Ronnie Fraser for *We Were There Too*.

The high casualty rate among airmen under training everywhere was so well-known outside RFC circles that E. R. Calthrop's Aerial Patents, Ltd. were prompted to say in a March 1918 advertisement for their "Guardian Angel" parachute: 'Let the year 1918 be signalised by a great reduction of the fatal casualties upon our Training Grounds.'

After the nasty business, as Garland called it, Robert was keen to escape from the 36th Wing and requested a drop in rank to major, which would allow him to return to the Western Front as a squadron commander. His wish was granted: '… *Sqdn. Comdr.*—Capt. (temp. Lt.-Col.) R. Loraine, D.S.O., M.C., Spec. Res., to revert from a Wing Comdr., to relinquish his temp. rank of Lt.-Col., and to be temp. Maj. whilst so empld. 3rd Mar. 1918, with seniority from 24th Apr. 1916.'[300] He returned to France on 26 May 1918, stating on Form A.S.D. 28 (Particulars of Newly Joined Officers) that his next-of-kin (as always) was George Bernard Shaw (friend), of 10 Adelphi Terrace, London.

No. 211 Squadron. Robert made his way to Petite-Synthe aerodrome, some 2½ miles west of Dunkirk on the north-east coast of France, where he assumed command of No. 211 Squadron RAF, formerly No. 11 Squadron RNAS. On 1 April 1918 the RFC and RNAS were amalgamated, the naval squadrons simply being re-numbered with a "2" in front of their old squadron number. 211 Squadron RAF was equipped with the two-seater Airco D.H.9 bomber.

Also at Petite-Synthe was 85 Squadron, whose seventeen pilots had arrived on 22 May from Hounslow, via Lympne, England, with nothing but their aeroplanes and whatever they could cram into them. 85's CO was Major Billy Bishop VC, DSO, MC, who would officially become the highest-scoring pilot of the British Empire with seventy-two victories during the war. He wrote to his wife, Margaret (née Burden), on the day he arrived: 'There is a Naval bombing squadron on this aerodrome & they have been awfully good to us, putting all of us up and being very nice in every way. Of course we have nothing at all of our own. I am sleeping in one blanket on an Army mattress.'[301]

Bishop wrote again to his wife, on 23 May: 'We're still sponging on 211 Squadron for meals etc.' He added a postscript: '211 have a goat which eats cigarettes & fights bow-wows.'

On the night of 23/24 May 'a terrible gale came up, and in the middle of the night it commenced to pour & rain, continuing until noon.' (Bishop letter, 24 May 1918). The dud weather at least gave the men a chance to have a party. One of 85's pilots was Lieutenant John McGavock Grider, an American: 'We arrived at our airdrome about six. It's two miles south of Dunkirk and is an old R.N.A.S. 214 Wing station called Petit Synthe. We are about three miles from the coast and there are two other squadrons on this same airdrome. They

---

[300] *The London Gazette*, 19 Mar 1918, no. 30589.
[301] Extract from Bishop's letter of 22 May 1918, from Lannie Liggera, via Richard Holleyman.

are bombers and have D.H. Nines. We had dinner at the 211th squadron which used to be No. 11 R.N.A.S., and they are very nicely fixed in semi-permanent quarters…'

'We are in the 65th wing, which is a part of the 5th brigade…'

'211 is a good outfit and we had quite a party. [Elliott White] Springs and I got a couple of motorcycles and went out in search of eggs and cream. We found plenty and made a big tub of eggnog. 88 squadron came over to see us with a band and we had a regular binge.'[302] Had he been there, Robert would no doubt have enjoyed the party, as he was 'able to drink the whole world under the table.' If invited to other squadrons and challenged to a drinking competition, he always won.

The third squadron at Petite-Synthe was No. 87, equipped with the Sopwith 5F.1 Dolphin, which had arrived there in April 1918 under the command of Major J.C. Callaghan (see Appendix IV).

No. 211 Squadron continued to co-operate with the Royal Navy, undertaking 'bombing and reconnaissance in the area bounded by the Flanders coast and the line Dixmude-Thourout-Bruges, the majority of its bombing raids being made against Bruges docks, Zeebrugge and Ostend.'[303] (It should be noted that Bruges (Brugge) is linked by the Boudewijn Kanal to Zeebrugge ("Bruges-on-Sea"), a dozen kilometres to the north.) The squadron also flew in support of the Belgian Army, its targets including enemy airfields, bomb and ammunition dumps.

Though Robert's duties as CO of 211 Squadron would restrict his time in the air, he flew his first operation, as an Observer, with Canadian-born pilot Captain H. M. Ireland (see Appendix IV) on 27 May 1918, only his second day with the squadron. They flew in Ireland's regular aeroplane, D.H.9 no. B7624, on an evening bombing raid on Engel Dump, dropping eight 25lb Cooper bombs from a height of 16,000 feet. Three enemy aeroplanes 'came up in front but always kept off in vicinity of Ostend.' B7624 was accompanied on this raid by D.H.9's B7629 (Lt. H.N. Lett and F/O H.W. Newsham) and B7626 (Lt. E.S. Morgan and 2nd. Lt. R. Simpson).

Robert and Ireland flew B7624 again on 7 June with the squadron – six D.H.9's – on a bombing raid on Ghistelles aerodrome,[304] seven or eight kilometres south of Ostend. Five aeroplanes dropped eight 25lb Cooper bombs from a height of 16,000 feet, while the sixth, Morgan and Simpson in D2781, dropped six from 12,000 feet. Various bursts were noted across various parts of the aerodrome. There were no casualties, though D2782 (Lt. H. Axford and R. Dawson) was hit in two places by "Archie", which they noted as 'heavy'.

---

[302] *War Birds. Diary of an Unknown Aviator.* p.153 – ed. by Elliott White Springs (John Hamilton Ltd, London, 1927). Grider, born 18 May 1892, was KIA 18 Jun 1918 in SE5a no. C1883.
[303] *Bomber Squadrons of the R.A.F. and Their Aircraft*, p.199 – Philip Moyes (Macdonald & Co (Publishers) Ltd, London, 1964).
[304] Ghistelles is the French spelling, Gistel the Flemish.

The Airco D.H.9 was designed to replace the D.H.4 but, mostly fitted with the unreliable Siddeley Puma engine, actually had a worse performance than the D.H.4.

Robert and Ireland flew again on 22 June in B7624, accompanied by B7679, D1021, B7598, D2782 and D7204, their target being Bruges docks. The Squadron diary noted that three of the pilots, apart from Ireland, were Canadians. All carried two 112lb bombs. A strong westerly wind blew them past their target, and they were almost over the Scheldt into Holland before they got their bearings through the clouds: 'We were lucky to sight our objective through about the only hole there was in the clouds and we dropped our bombs and took an hour to get back against the wind.' (From Ireland's diary).

Robert reported: 'Bombs dropped flying South West. Target just visible through hole in clouds immediately previous to dropping bombs. No reconnaissance owing to dense clouds.'

Robert's next operation was on 7 July, but this time his pilot was newly-promoted Captain H.N. Lett (see Appendix IV) in C1168. It was the turn of Ostend docks to receive 211 Squadron's bombs, six D.H.9's – the other aeroplanes being B9346, C1182, D2782, B7581, B7603 – taking-off at 12 noon, all dropping two 112lb bombs from 14,000 feet. Robert also exposed eighteen photographs, even though visibility was very poor. At least others did see their bombs burst.

Two days later, on 9 July, taking-off at around 11.40 a.m., Lett and Robert in C1168 led B7598, C6348, B7581, B9346 and D1701 to Bruges docks again, all again dropping two 112lb bombs. Robert reported: 'Dropped bombs flying west. 3 E.A. at rear of formation

Officers and mechanics with Airco D.H.9, A-Acme, 211 Squadron (Norrie Collection, 211 Newbury Squadron ATC; http://www.211squadron.org/world_war_i.html)

Petite-Synthe. Three 211 Squadron D.H.9's, September 1918, in front of a wood and canvas hangar. (Picture courtesy of HISPASEC, via https://www.49squadron.co.uk/airfields/af1_psynthe)

between Bruges & Ostend. A.A. heavy. 18 plates exposed.' B7581 (Lt. J.F. Drake and 2/Lt. H.G. Breeze) was attacked by three enemy aeroplanes, one of which was 'driven down.' (Ten days later Drake and Breeze were 'shot up' in B7581. Breeze was wounded, and his place would be taken by 2/Lt. G.J. Moore.)

At 10 a.m. on 20 July Robert, back with Ireland in B7624, "P", took-off to bomb Bruges docks again with five other D.H.9's: D1701 (Lt. A.F. Bonnalie (see Appendix IV) & 2/Lt. J.B. Blundell); B7626 (2/Lt. C.H. Dickins & 2/Lt. A.M. Adam); B7603 (Lt. W.D. Gairdner & 2/Lt. H.M. Moodie); C6270 (Lt. E.R.L. Sproule & Sgt. Obs. P.C. Sivertsen); B7614 (Lt. F.C. Leonard & 2/Lt. E.D. Deck).

They were interrupted during their bombing of Bruges by several enemy aeroplanes. B7626 was attacked by four of them, with 2/Lt. Adam firing off two drums at 500-600 yards range. D1701 and B7614 were both attacked by three of the enemy. In some confusion, all six D.H.9's managed to head for home, five landing safely at base.

Ireland and Robert, however, were missing, as Ireland reported in Squadron records: 'After dropping bombs on Bruges, we proceeded out to sea over Blankenberge [*some nine miles to the north-north-west*] where we were attacked by an enemy seaplane scout coming from the direction of Ostend. Got a good burst at E.A. with front gun as he crossed in front of us and Major Loraine engaged E.A. as he turned behind us. E.A.s first burst wounded Major Loraine in the leg and punctured my water pump above the cowling.'

'E.A. continued to attack from behind but then broke off the engagement but returned to the attack immediately. E.A. was again engaged by Major Loraine who finally sent E.A. down decidedly out of control. (We watched E.A. fall for about 2,000 feet.) Owing to the continuous loss of water and a boiling engine we carried on straight for Nieuport and therefore lost sight of E.A.'

'Engine seized up on reaching Nieuport and I was able to glide on to the beach opposite La Panne.'

Ireland also noted in his diary: 'Saturday, July 20 1918: Carried out a good raid on Bruges this a.m. Photographed the vicinity of Thourout and Artrycke on way home [*sic – on way out?*].[305] Formation never followed me after dropped bombs and I found myself alone after crossing Zeebrugge. Was attacked by a Hun seaplane and had a running fight from the mole to Ostende before Major Loraine knocked the Hun down [*with his Lewis gun*]. The major was wounded in the leg by an explosive bullet and my water-cooling system was down at the same time. After losing water, engine started to heat up and boiled quickly. Almost decided to make for Holland but carried on with the Hun in pursuit on the chance of reaching our lines. A second attack by the Hun shot gun gear and put gun [*the front Vickers gun*] out of business but the CO sent him off to Ostende and we reached our side without further fighting. Engine seized up off Nieuport and I landed on beach at La Panne and had the Major taken to the hospital there where they immediately extracted the bullet and found his hip bone cracked...'

'Monday, July 22 1918: Drove to La Panne to see Major Loraine and found him suffering a lot. Sent him up some Chlorodyne later.' (Chlorodyne is 'a drug, containing chloroform among other ingredients, with sedative, narcotic and pain-relieving properties.')

Robert's operational war had come to an end.

Some years ago, a certain Stewart K. Taylor said that he once knew Robert's pilot, Captain Ireland, and that Ireland had told him a thing or two about Robert. For example, when Robert took command of 211 Squadron he was 'heavily into Morphine and it showed'. Taylor also claimed that Harold Ireland gave him 'a couple of illustrations as to what kind of a skittish guy he [Robert] was.' Once, 'under the influence [of Morphine] he [Robert] set out in the observer's cockpit of Ireland's DH9 from where he liked nothing better to do than direct the flight of aircraft following Ireland, the leader, to take up proper station in the sky preparatory to flying in their bomb raid formation. He worked the pilots like an

---

[305] Thourout (Fr) = Torhout (Flemish) and Artrycke = Aartrijke (Flem.) are a few kms SSW of Bruges.

orchestra leader with all the movement of the professional. The result was not what he expected. Aircraft were scattered all over the sky and only when Ireland delivered the correct wing movement did they read his signals correctly. Loraine was a laughing stock. Ireland pitied him.'[306]

It should not be forgotten that Robert was 42 years of age, and that he had, effectively, only one lung. Furthermore, flying at heights of up to 16,000 feet, where the air contains fifty per cent less oxygen than at ground level, might, in Robert's case, have led to hypoxia, which can result in 'symptoms like confusion, restlessness, difficulty breathing, rapid heart rate' etc.

Robert would not have been overly troubled by what others thought of him when he took what he believed to be the right action. For instance, as they were not that far from the Germans, he ordered that the ground crew be taught how to fight as infantrymen. They laughed at him. In fairness, this was not the sort of behaviour that would have been demonstrated by other squadron commanders.

Hospitalised. Three of the bullets fired by the enemy seaplane on 20 July had hit Robert in his left leg and hip, which was broken. Taken to the Queen Alexandra Hospital, Dunkirk, run by the Friends' Ambulance Unit,[307] he was also found to have a shattered knee cap. The over-worked surgeons wanted to amputate his leg, but Robert was not prepared to go on living 'as a crock. So when the doctors in France wished to cut off his leg, on the grounds that it would save him from gangrene and a host of complications, he fought like a madman to keep the stump, and declared he would prefer a London opinion.' The surgeons were emphatic that his leg would have to come off: 'Not only had his knee-cap been shot clean away, but also the knuckle end of the bones, so that there was no knee joint.' Robert was, however, prepared to let the surgeons 'extract three sharp twisted bullets and that was all.'[308] Following the surgery, Robert was put on the strength of 88 Squadron on 5 August, and shipped back to "Blighty" on 7 August.

Back in London he was taken to the Royal Flying Corps Hospital for officers at 37 Bryanston Square, London W. During the Great War several privileged members of society offered their properties and wealth for the benefit of wounded officers. The hospital in which Robert now found himself had been opened in May 1916 in a large house lent by Lady Katherine, Viscountess Tredegar (1867-1949), with a Convalescent Home also being established at Freshwater, on the Isle of Wight.

---

[306] From information supplied to Lanayre Liggera's agent by Stewart K. Taylor.
[307] Society of Friends, the Quakers. The FAU came under the British Red Cross's umbrella.
[308] *Actor, Soldier, Airman*, p.243.

'The Leave-Boat will be a great memory of the war for our soldiers, for whom a trip home from "blood and mud" has been an unspeakable joy.'

An earlier patient at 37 Bryanston Square was A.J. Insall, an Observer, who remembered 'a young pilot occupying a bed in the ward I was in… whom none of us had so far actually seen, for the simple and distressing reason that the only thing visible, apart from the slender outline of his body under his bedclothes, was three snow-white cocoons of bandages – one indicating his motionless head and the other two his motionless hands. There were the inevitable cavities over the eyes, nose, and mouth, and we knew that he could speak. He had been admitted to the hospital one afternoon direct from France… The extraordinary thing about this lad was that, of all of us there (and there were quite a number) he appeared to be the cheeriest.'[309] Happily, to much rejoicing, this lad recovered, though badly burnt, having been pulled from the wreckage of his aeroplane by the infantry.

The hospital, affiliated to Queen Alexandra's Military Hospital, had twenty beds, twelve of which had been donated by Lady Tredegar, who also contributed to the maintenance fund for the running costs. Princess Christian of Schleswig-Holstein[310] also gave a substantial donation towards the cost of the equipment.

---

[309] *Observer*, p.163 – A.J. Insall (William Kimber & Co. Ltd., London, 1970).
[310] Born Princess Helena (25 May 1846–9 Jun 1923) she was the third daughter of Queen Victoria and Prince Albert.

Lady Katherine, Viscountess Tredegar   *Irene Vanbrugh*

Another benefactor was Baroness St. Helier,[311] who presented beds and other practical gifts, and also obtained financial assistance. (It was she, incidentally, who arranged for a Canadian patient at the hospital, a certain Billy Bishop, to be accepted for pilot training. He was at the time, May 1916, an RFC observer who had sustained a knee injury).

With the numbers of sick and wounded RFC officers increasing dramatically, and the accommodation at the hospital proving insufficient, the Committee appealed for funds for expansion. Lady Tredegar, who had already had a ward named after her for her generosity in allowing the use of her house, contributed £375 to cover maintenance of the hospital for six months and one additional bed.

♦   ♦   ♦

---

[311] Baroness St. Helier – Susan Elizabeth Mary Jeune DBE (18 May 1845–25 Jan 1931).

Still very much worried as to his wounded leg, Robert wrote to his old friend, George Bernard Shaw, for advice as to what to do, Shaw having been nominated by Robert on his Service Record as the 'Person to be Informed of Casualties'. In reply Robert received a 'jolly letter; but, as far as practical advice was concerned, no help at all.' Better news, though, was that doctors had found no gangrene in his leg, but anyway thought it best to encase it in Plaster of Paris for five months. Robert learned in conversation with a doctor that, at the end of this period, 'his muscles would have knit in such a manner that the limb would be stiff forever and he would be unable to bend it at the knee.'[312]

Horrified at the prospect, Robert removed the plaster cast and somehow managed to bend inwards what was left of his knee in the hope that muscle-stiffness would not set in. Coming to his rescue that very afternoon, however, was the actress Irene Vanbrugh,[313] calling to see how he was getting on.

As luck would have it, she knew the very eminent surgeon Sir Alfred Fripp,[314] and determined that he should see Robert. Ignoring the etiquette that existed between surgeons and their cases, Sir Alfred pulled rank. Taking over Robert's case, he operated on the damaged knee in such a way that, though Robert would be lame for a long time, 'the knee would not be stiff, nor crooked'.[315] And so it was to prove.

On 8 September 1918 Robert was moved to Swanage Hospital to convalesce and recuperate.[316] Three months later the war to end all wars was over, and so were Robert's days as a warrior. All that was left to do was to resign his commission: 'Maj. R. Loraine relinquishes his commn. on account of ill-health caused by wounds, and is granted the hon. rank of Maj. 11th Dec. 1918.'[317]

Finally, on 24 January 1919, as a reward for his service to King and country, 'R. Loraine, D.S.O., M C. (late Maj., R.A.F.), is granted the rank of Lt.-Col., Dec. 11th, 1918.'

---

[312] *Actor, Soldier, Airman*, p.245.
[313] Irene Vanbrugh (2 Dec 1872–30 Nov 1949) was made DBE in 1941.
[314] Sir Alfred Downing Fripp KCVO (12 Sep 1865–25 Feb 1930) was Surgeon to Edward VII and George V.
[315] *Actor, Soldier, Airman*, p.246.
[316] He was either at the Cluny Auxiliary Hospital at 20 Cluny Crescent, Swanage, today YHA Swanage, or the Grosvenor Hotel, Swanage, which was also in use as a convalescent hospital at the end of the war.
[317] *The London Gazette*, 10 Dec 1918, no. 31058. See also TNA file AIR 76/306/110.

Robert, his medals and other pieces.

Medals – top row (left to right): DSO; MC; Queen's South Africa Medal, with Bars for Wittebergen, Transvaal, Cape Colony; 1914-15 Star, with Mons Bar; British War Medal, 1914-20; Allied Victory Medal, 1914-18, with Oak Leaf for Mention in Dispatches.

Middle row: Tunic buttons; RFC and RAF "Wings".

Bottom row: RAeC Silver Medal (presented 21 March 1912); dress medals (same as top row); South African Campaign 1901 medal. [Photo: Richard Holleyman, November 2011].

Chapter Ten: The Last Act

The cover of the menu for the dinner, the menu being printed before Robert's official elevation from honorary major to lieutenant-colonel [via Richard Holleyman].

Robert Bilcliffe Loraine DSO, MC, MiD***, a civilian once again, was well enough to take the chair at the Green Room Club's annual dinner at the Criterion, Piccadilly Circus, on 22 December 1918. The London-based Green Room Club, primarily for actors, was established in 1877 at the Criterion restaurant.

Robert, though, was not fully recovered from his war-time injuries. For a while, he continued to use crutches in his daily life, and G.B. Shaw, aware of this, wrote another letter to him in which he suggested that he could play the part of Higgins in *Pygmalion*: 'Now, there is not the least reason why Higgins should not be lame... So long as you have a mouth left and one lung to keep it going, you will still be better than the next best'.[318]

Robert, however, with his eyes fixed on Rostand's *Cyrano de Bergerac*, agreed a contract with Charles B. Cochran, 'the great hearted showman', that would keep him, Robert, in funds for the next three years at £135 per week (around £8,000 in today's money). The deal was signed on 21 November 1918. After a short spell in the provinces, *Cyrano* opened at the Garrick Theatre, London, at the end of March 1919. The theatre, however, proved to be too small for a cost-effective audience and, after four weeks, *Cyrano* was moved to the much larger Theatre Royal on Drury Lane.

In his book *Distinguished Company* the later and much celebrated actor Sir John Gielgud devoted several pages to Robert in the chapter *Two Forceful Actors*, describing him as 'a powerful, expressive actor, broadshouldered and possessed of a noble presence and a deep resonant voice.'[319] He also gave examples of Robert's strong, stage personality, implying that he thought highly of himself and cared little for what those around him thought of him.

---

[318] Quoted in *Actor, Soldier, Airman*, p.247.
[319] *Distinguished Company*, p.91. Claude Rains (10 Nov 1889–30 May 1967) was the other forceful actor.

He concludes his piece on Robert thus: '... on the first night of his revival [*in 1927*] of *Cyrano* in London, the stage-hands, resenting his rude treatment of them at the dress rehearsals, deliberately omitted to fasten the cleats holding up the stage tree under which Cyrano has to sit in the final scene, and the poor actor was forced to hold up the sagging piece of scenery with his back and finish the play as best he could.'[320] Sir John, nevertheless, 'thought his Cyrano perfection, and was greatly moved by his performance of Strindberg's *The Father*.'

Robert, date unknown.

Robert's hopes of playing *Cyrano* had been recorded as far back as 1911 in *The Aeroplane*: 'Mr. Loraine's Suggestions for *Cyrano*... Concerning his future plans Mr. Loraine is full of ideas. "I hope to appear one day as Cyrano de Bergerac," he says. But "the translation of Rostand's alexandrines into English appears to me a most difficult task. So far I have not read a version that satisfies me completely. To be perfect the translation should be apportioned to different people, giving, for example, the first act to Mr. Bernard Shaw, the second to Mr. Maugham, the third—the love scene—to Mr. W. B. Yeats, the fourth—the episode of the Siege of Arras—to Mr. Kipling, and the last act—the death of Cyrano in the convent—to Mr. Barrie." ... In spite of all this work he has by no means given up his interest in aviation, and hopes to be flying again next spring.' (*The Aeroplane*, 30 November 1911).

Now, eight years later, one of the men chosen to play three parts in *Cyrano* was Harold French,[321] who, it will be recalled, had encountered Robert at Andover in late 1917 (see page 251). Released from hospital in January 1919, Harold was keen to get back into acting and, seeing that C.B. Cochran and Robert were producing *Cyrano* at the Garrick, wrote to Cochran for a part. Receiving no reply, he decided to waylay Robert at the theatre, and was fortunate one day when Robert stepped out of a taxi. Both were in uniform and, properly, Harold saluted his superior officer: 'He stopped, gave me a puzzled look, the memory stirred.'

'"Good Lord, are you still alive?"'

'"Yes, sir."'

'He grinned, then held out his hand.'

'"Do you know, I'm astonished."'

'"The luck of the Irish, sir."' (Harold's father, William Joseph, was born in Dublin).

---

[320] Distinguished Company, p.93.

[321] Harold – full name Harold Arthur George French – was born on 23 Apr 1900. After a long career as a film director, he died on 19 October 1997.

Handley Page O/400 airliner G-EAKG (ex RAF J2250) taking off from Cricklewood for Paris, 1919 [photo: 40 Years On..., p.33]

 Harold then asked if Robert had a part for him in *Cyrano*? Robert did and, after a reading of a part, said: '"Yes, yes, I think you'll be alright."'[322] Harold clearly was, for he played the parts of Athos; Baron de Malgouyre Estressac Lésbas d'Escarabiot; and Baron de Casterae de Cahuzac.

 At one point, wishing to see for himself what Cyrano looked like from the audience point of view, Robert asked Harold to play the part, extra-large nose and all. Bobby, as the other players called him, watched the performance, until something happened.

 '"What the hell's going on up there?" came Loraine's voice from the stalls.' It was quickly explained that Harold's nose had fallen off! 'There was silence for a moment. Then the sound of muffled footsteps, the clang of a pass door, and Loraine strode on to the stage. Had he attempted to throw me into the orchestra pit, I don't think I could have resisted. But he did no such thing. He took one look at that wobbly nose, then, to my astonishment, took my arm. "What a bloody shame, just when you were doing so well." Then a smile spread across his face, "I told you you'd be a better actor than airman." He turned to actor Nicholas Hannen. "Thanks for pointing out my stupidity. I don't think. That's my trouble. I just don't think." Again that smile, and when Loraine smiled, one wondered why he didn't

---

[322] *I Swore I Never Would,* pp.182-3.

smile more often. "Shall I carry on, sir?" I ventured. "Yes, do, Harold. But I think without the nose, don't you?"'[323]

The Dawn of Civil Aviation. On 1 November 1919 'a Handley Page aeroplane carried twelve passengers, 500 lb. of freight, and nearly 400 lb. of personal luggage to Paris through driving rain. Lieut.-Col. Robert Loraine, the aviator actor, was one of the passengers.' (*The Aeroplane*, 12 November 1919).

♦ ♦ ♦

During the war the firm Handley Page had produced two massive bombers, the HP O/100 and O/400, each with a 100-foot wingspan, nearly 63 feet long and with a maximum weight of 14,000lbs. Their potential as carriers of passengers was realised when the Peace Conference talks officially opened in Paris on 18 January 1919. Beginning on 10 January, an air service was provided between London and Paris for the members of HM Government who would be participating in the talks. Flights were made using Airco D.H.4 and two military HP O/400 aeroplanes, *Great Britain* and *Silver Star*, both fitted with saloon interiors. One of them handled seven hundred passengers in a month of average winter weather.

It was also in February 1919 that the Civil Aviation Department of the Air Ministry was formed, and the Air Navigation Act 1911–19 was passed, giving the power to 'the Secretary of State for Air to prepare air traffic regulations which included the first airworthiness and registration regulations ever formulated. They were issued on 30 April 1919 and civil flying began on the next day.'[324]

Commercial flying for profit in Britain was under way, and on 25 August 1919 Aircraft Transport & Travel Ltd 'inaugurated the first sustained international air services, between London and Paris.'[325] AT&T Ltd had been flying D.H.9's from Hawkinge, Kent, since February 1919 to an airfield near Ghent in Belgium at the request of the Belgian government. Flown by ex-RAF pilots, they carried 'woollen and cotton goods, foodstuffs and other necessities of life urgently needed by the Belgian people.' (*The Aeroplane*, 12 February 1919).

Handley Page, too, undertook flights for civilians over the same route, using adapted HP O/400 bombers: 'Handley Page, Ltd., are starting a regular service to Paris and Brussels on Sept. 1st. Machines will leave at 12 noon for Paris on Tuesdays, Wednesdays and Fridays, and will return on alternate days. For Brussels they will leave on Mondays, Wednesdays and Fridays, also returning on alternate days.'

---

[323] *I Swore I Never Would*, pp.185-6.
[324] *British Civil Aircraft 1919-1972: Volume I*, p.7 – A.J. Jackson (Putnam, London, 1987).
[325] *The Evolution of the Transport Aircraft*, John Stroud, in *Biplane to Monoplane*, p.29.

Cricklewood Airport, probably in 1920, as aircraft G-EASY (ex RAF D4614) was not ready for civilian flights until March 1920 at the earliest [photo: 40 Years On..., p.32]

'The fare for the single journey ... is 15 guineas. Goods will be carried at 2s. 6d. per lb., with a minimum charge of 5s. The O.400 twin-engined type of machine will be used, with covered-in limousine fuselage, having seating accommodation for 14 passengers inside and two outside... The journey will take three hours.'

'For Paris the machines will land at the Le Bourget aerodrome.' (*The Aeroplane*, 27 August 1919).

◆ ◆ ◆

Robert's visit to the French capital in November 1919 may have been connected to his forthcoming production of Shaw's play *Arms and the Man*, which opened at the Duke of York's theatre on 11 December 1919. Robert's great admirer, Charles Grey, wrote: 'Mr. Robert Loraine, actor-manager (better known, perhaps, to readers of this paper as Lieut.-Col. Robert Loraine, D.S.O., M.C., late R.F.C.), has achieved, at the Duke of York's Theatre, another success in "Arms and the Man," which, if not perhaps equal as a *tour de force* to "Cyrano," is, in one's personal opinion, an even better piece of acting. Mr. Loraine shows his ability as a manager no less than as an actor in selecting this particular play for production at this particular moment when a little of the glamour of soldiering has passed and when people are more inclined to regard the soldier as an integral part of the composition of the nation and as a man who follows a profession as a profession, free from high falutin' ideas. Both the play and the acting will do good...

'One is a trifle doubtful as to whether the fashions of the Servo-Bulgarian war period were precisely those worn by the ladies of the cast. They struck one as belonging to an earlier date, but perhaps the Paris fashions took a year or two to reach Sofia. Also one has doubts as to whether the Servian officers wore French kepis. One's personal recollection of the pictures of the period is that the Servians wore a head-dress resembling the Austrian shako, but one assumes that Mr. Loraine made the necessary research into the costumes of the period before dressing the parts. Be that as it may, the performance is wholly excellent, and Mr. Bernard Shaw's pitiless logic and biting humour will probably be better appreciated to-day, now that everybody has been closely in touch with militarism in one form or another, than it was when the play was last staged in London.' (*The Aeroplane*, 17 December 1919).

The production was otherwise well-reviewed, but not so much by Shaw himself who, having seen the play two days after it had opened, 'went through the roof and wrote Robert a scathing letter about playing for laughs.'[326] Shortly afterwards, in the New Year, their friendship of twenty years or more became seriously strained. Curious as to some of Robert's actions in the play, Shaw asked: 'Was it morphia? I know that you keep up appearances extraordinarily well…' Robert was furious, replying 'in language that was excessively forceful. This in turn reinforced Shaw's suspicions that Loraine was addicted to morphine.'[327] Author Lannie Liggera, however, is clear that their friendship *did* survive, albeit on a reduced scale, not least because Shaw found Robert too expensive. Whatever level their relationship had reached, Shaw would be a witness at Robert's marriage in July 1921.

The Palace Hotel (front right), Saint Moritz, overlooking Lake St. Moritz

---

[326] *The Life of Robert Loraine*, p.167.
[327] Quotes from *The First Flight to Ireland*, p.18.

St. Moritz, Switzerland. When *Arms and the Man* closed on 7 February 1920, Robert took himself off to the Palace Hotel at Saint Moritz, Switzerland: 'His knee was worse, his nightcaps stronger'.[328]

There he received a letter from Sir James Barrie,[329] asking him to act in his new play *Mary Rose*. Robert at first declined but, so flattered was he by a subsequent telegram from Barrie, that he decided to return. As the quickest way home was by aeroplane, he hired Swiss aviator Alfred Comte[330] to fly him back to England across the Alps in, probably, an ex-German air force LVG C.V two-seater reconnaissance biplane. (Croydon airport recorded Comte leaving for Switzerland on 29 March 1920 in a *Contor* [*sic* – *"Kondor"*] aeroplane with the Swiss markings "CH2". (*The Aeroplane*, 7 April 1920). "CH2" on the Swiss aeroplane register was an LVG C.V biplane.)

This un-annotated photograph, found amongst Robert's papers, is believed to show Swiss aviator Alfred Comte, with a lady passenger in the front seat (via Richard Holleyman).

---

[328] *Actor, Soldier, Airman*, p.274.
[329] Sir James Matthew Barrie OM (9 May 1860–19 Jun 1937).
[330] Alfred Comte – born at Delémont, Switzerland, 4 Jun 1895; died Zürich 1 Nov 1965 – was awarded an ACF certificate in 1913.

The Aeroplane (10 March 1920) also reported on their journey: 'Colonel Robert Loraine (late R.A.F.) with a Swiss pilot, Lieut. Comte, attempted to fly from St. Moritz to Hounslow on March 4th. But owing to clouds and a faulty compass, after leaving Zurich, a landing was made at Marburg, in the heart of Prussia, where the population were inclined to be hostile. Some bad petrol was secured at Marburg, which enabled them to fly to Elsenborn in the new territory ceded to Belgium by Germany. The next stop was Antwerp. On March 6th the weather was too bad to continue the flight, so Colonel Loraine completed his journey by boat and train.'

Flight (11 March 1920) added: 'Wishing to get home from Switzerland in quick time Lieut.-Col. Robert Loraine on March 4 left St. Moritz in a Condor machine, piloted by Comte. Unfortunately, owing to heavy mist and low clouds and the use of a very poor map, the pilot lost his way after leaving Zurich and landed at Marburg, in Prussia, where their reception was none too cordial. On the next day another stop was necessary at Elsenborn, and finally the machine reached Antwerp, where as the weather was too bad for flying, Col. Loraine decided to complete his journey to London by boat and train. Col. Loraine says in flying over Germany he was very much impressed by the extreme activity that was everywhere noticeable. At all the manufacturing towns chimneys were belching forth smoke and quarries were being worked very actively.'

Leaving in thick fog and with a faulty compass, Alfred Comte had become hopelessly lost and ran out of petrol. Without realizing it, he had flown some 480 kms (300 miles) slightly west of north into Germany, being forced to land near the town of Marburg, in the German province of Hesse. To the quickly-assembled crowd Robert announced that he was a French-speaking Swiss, a fact of which they approved, until someone noticed small Union Jacks painted on the aircraft![331]

With anti-British feeling still running strongly in post-war Germany, Robert was interned for five hours by the Bürgermeister on the pretence of being a spy. By the time that the matter had been sorted out, it was too dark for Robert and Comte to continue. All was set for the flight to continue to England next morning, when it was found that the aeroplane's tanks had been filled with benzene instead of higher-grade aviation fuel. Comte was, therefore, obliged to land at Elsenborn after a further 175 kms (110 miles), just inside Belgium. Another 160 kms (100 miles) were then flown to Antwerp, where weather conditions were too poor to permit a crossing to Hounslow, England.

Robert, in a hurry to get home, abandoned the aeroplane, and made his way to 'the Hook [of Holland] by canal and road and proceeded by night-boat to England, arriving in London at 10 a.m. the next morning, dog-tired.'[332]

---

[331] One wonders why the Swiss owner would put Union Jacks on his Swiss-registered aeroplane.
[332] *Actor, Soldier, Airman*, p.275.

With the aeroplane long overdue, it and Robert were presumed lost. Consequently, when he turned up at the Haymarket Theatre just as the cast were rehearsing the first ghost scene in *Mary Rose*, they got the shock of their lives!

Charles Grey reviewed *Mary Rose*: 'Lieut.-Col. Loraine plays three parts—the Australian soldier, the sub-lieutenant, and the latter when captain. He lives his characters, each with its subtle distinction of manner and age. Boisterous when necessary, in repose he shows equal skill. His perfect acting needs no gloss. He is well supported by Mr. Norman Forbes, Miss Mary Jerrold, Mr. Thesiger, Mr. Whitby, and Miss Jean Cadell. The play should have a long run if genius in writing and in acting obtain full recognition.' (*The Aeroplane*, 28 April 1920). The play was still going strong when, in September 1920, Robert decided to move on.

Herbert George Brackley

Away from the stage, not yet forgotten for his derring-do as a pioneer aviator, Robert was one of some two hundred and fifty guests invited to a dinner at the Connaught Rooms in London on 12 July 1920, organised by Benn Brothers Ltd, the proprietors of *Aeronautics* magazine. Of those present, about forty-five were in the first hundred certificated pilots, and some sixty or so more were among the true pioneers. Robert shared Table K with Horatio Barber; the Hon. Alan Boyle; H.G. Brackley DSO, DSC;[333] Harry Delacombe; H.G. Hawker; H. Jullerot AFC; Tom Sopwith; Stanley Spooner; and C.C. Turner.

'The gathering was very representative of the early days of aviation and of the present-day British Aircraft industry. His Royal Highness the Duke of York honoured the gathering with his presence, and the Chair was taken by Major-General J. E. B. Seely.' (*The Aeroplane*, 14 July 1920).

An impressive feature of the occasion was a silent toast to the twenty-five of the First Hundred Pilots, the pioneers, who had died, and to seventeen other non-pioneers, but including several pilots (including W.B. Rhodes-Moorhouse VC), who had also perished.

Major-General Sir F. H. Sykes, GBE, KCB, CMG, replying to a toast, said that 'he would like to say a few things with which he hoped the real pioneers in the hardest work would agree. When he saw around him friends of these old days he felt that an almost impossible task was imposed upon him. He referred to Roe, Sopwith, Ogilvie, Loraine, Jullerot, and one of the best pilots of the time, Samson, who started the Naval Wing, Brooke-Popham,

---

[333] Herbert George Brackley, born 4 Oct 1894, drowned whilst swimming at Copacabana, Brazil on 15 Nov 1948.

Maitland, Longmore, and many others.' (*Flight*, 22 July 1920). To have had their names mentioned in such distinguished company must have given Robert and his fellow pioneers great satisfaction.

World cruise. A few weeks later, still troubled by the pain in his knee, a post-war *wanderlust* took Robert on a trip around the world. Leaving Southampton on 29 September 1920 on the RMS *Olympic*, he arrived at New York on 6 October, where he met Jesse L. Lasky, one of the founders of Paramount Pictures.[334]

Though Robert was in great demand, and had been offered several plays, Lasky whisked him off to California, "home" of the "talkies", but Robert

In the USA. Left to right: Lasky; Avery Hopwood and Edward Knoblock (playwrights); Robert Loraine. [Exhibitors Herald, 18 Dec 1920, p.67]

decided that the time was not yet right for him to play in a movie. He left San Francisco on 24 November 1920 on the SS *Wilhelmina, a*rriving at Honolulu, Hawaii, six days later, where 'he was awed by the fire-crater of Kilauea'.[335]

Continuing his voyage to China, where he dabbled in Buddhism, Robert visited his friend Sun Yat-sen, whom he had last met in London in 1910.[336] From China, Robert went on to Sarawak, Burma and India, until 'May 12th, 1921, found him taking leave of the East, bidding farewell to its noisy sunsets and pungent dawns, leaning over the deck-rails of a P. and O. mail ship steaming out of Bombay harbour…'[337] Robert, a First Class passenger aboard the RMS *Naldera*, was on his way home, via the Suez Canal and the Mediterranean, to London's Tilbury docks, reached on 3 June 1921.

At some point on the voyage, Robert 'caught sight of a girl… looking in his direction', though *she* was not looking at *him*. Robert went towards her, as if to speak to her, but the young woman turned and went through the door into the saloon. He followed, but she was nowhere to be seen. Somewhere in the Red Sea, though, she – her name was Winifred

---

[334] Lasky, born 13 Sep 1880, died of a heart attack in Beverley Hills on 13 Jan 1958.
[335] Nearly a century later, we, too, were awed by *Kilauea*'s eruptions on 3 May 2018 and in Jun & Sep 2023.
[336] Sun Yat-sen (12 Nov 1866–12 Mar 1925) was the first leader of a Republican China.
[337] Actor, Soldier, Airman, p.284.

Lydia Strangman[338] – with a subaltern as escort engaged him in conversation. The word was out that Robert Loraine DSO, MC, the actor, was on board ship, and she and her escort had been detailed to find him.

Winifred sought out Robert once more, and though twice her age (he was 45 at the time, she was 22), a liaison was formed. Telling him that she was thinking of marrying her subaltern escort (he was, in the event, barred from so doing by his Regiment), Robert generously offered £2,000 to the couple, money that he did not have. Winifred was now even more impressed by his sincerity and generosity.

The voyage over, Robert went home to 36 St. James Street, London. Meanwhile, young Winifred and her family – parents Thomas Joseph and Winifred (née Warneford) Strangman,[339] and sister Josephine, younger than Winifred by two years – were heading home to 12 Cork Street, London, to prepare for Mr. Strangman's impending knighthood. For his services in India, King George V was 'pleased to confer the honour of Knighthood upon… Thomas Joseph Strangman, Esq., Advocate General, Bombay' at Buckingham

A very smart-looking RMS Naldera. Launched in December 1917, Naldera, 16,088 tons, the first three-funnelled P&O liner, entered service with P&O on 25 March 1920. She was broken-up on 19 November 1938.

---

[338] Born 25 Oct 1898, Winifred was a cousin of the late Sub-Lieutenant R.A.J. Warneford VC.
[339] Thomas Joseph Strangman and Winifred Warneford Warneford were married on 25 Jul 1896.

Palace on 25 June 1921.[340] A barrister and Advocate-General of Bombay, Thomas Strangman was the first lawyer to successfully prosecute Mahatma Gandhi.

After a whirlwind romance, Winifred and Robert announced their engagement on the very day on which her father was to be knighted. Less than three weeks later, on 14 July 1921, they were married at the fashionable Parish Church of St. George, Hanover Square, Mayfair, London.

The marriage certificate states that the marriage was solemnized in the presence of: R.R. Strangman; Lady Winifred Warneford Strangman; George Bernard Shaw; Blanche Lloyd (an actress); B. Scott; and J. Pitcher [*sic*]. This last-named person, Air Commodore Duncan Le Geyt Pitcher (see Appendix IV), an old and close friend of Robert, 'was best man.' (*Flight*, 21 July 1921). Winifred's father, Sir Thomas, was not present at the proceedings. He was "old-school" and, so the Loraine family say, disinherited Winifred for marrying 'an actor, not a gentleman.'

'ACTOR AIRMAN AND HIS BRIDE

'*Mr Robert Loraine, D.S.O., the well-known actor-airman, and Winifred Lydia, daughter of Sir Thomas and Lady Strangman, of Bombay, photographed with the bride's attendant, Miss Josephine Strangman, at the reception after their wedding at St. George's, Hanover-square, London.*'

By the end of 1921 Robert was in financial straits. Finding it difficult to get work, and drinking and smoking more, his relations with Winifred became strained. There was some hope, though, when he got a part in the comedy play *Deburau* at the Ambassadors Theatre later in the year. But it 'was a failure. It was off in three weeks.'[341] Making his stage debut in *Deburau* as "The Young Man" was Ivor Novello.[342]

---

[340] *The London Gazette*, 20 Sep 1921, no. 32461. His Majesty's intention to confer the knighthood on Strangman had been announced on 1 Jan 1920. Sir Thomas Joseph Strangman QC, born 7 Jan 1873, died 8 Oct 1971.
[341] The play was based on the life of the mime artist Jean-Gaspard Deburau (born Jan Kašpar Dvořák), 1796–1846.
[342] Born David Ivor Davies on 15 Jan 1893, he died on 6 Mar 1951.

Winifred Loraine, 1921 [Photo by Bassano Ltd. © National Portrait Gallery, London]

The upside of the play, however, was that Robert temporarily stopped drinking and smoking, and made his first film, the 1922 British silent drama film *Bentley's Conscience*.

On 5 July 1922, again for reasons unknown, 'Lt.-Col. Robert Loraine went to Paris in a D.H.18 with Mr. Robins. He returned on Friday in a [Handley Page] W.8b with Major Foot.' (*The Aeroplane*, 12 July 1922). With a crew of two, the W.8b could carry twelve to fourteen passengers. (For brief details of A.C. Robins and of Major E.L. Foot, see Appendix IV).

(left) Robert as a "Pierrot" in Deburau; (right) Ivor Novello (then in his late 20's)

The outward trip may have been flown in one of Instone Air Line Ltd.'s aeroplanes – D.H.18A G-EARO, or either of D.H. 18B's G-EAWW and G-EAWX – the airline having been 'appointed, in open competition, exclusive contractors by the Postmaster-General for the carriage of the Air Parcel Post to Paris.' The D.H.18 biplanes, with a 450 h.p. Napier Lion engine, could carry up to eight passengers, but would soon be replaced by the D.H.34, while Instone itself would be absorbed into the newly-created Imperial Airways in 1924.

As for Robert's return trip, he might well have flown in W.8b G-EAPJ: 'Handley Page Transport have now got the Napier W.8, G-EAPJ, running on the [Paris] service again and on Wednesday with a good wind behind she lowered the twin-engine record for the trip, occupying only 1 hour 42 minutes, with Major Foot as the pilot. The previous best "twin-engine" time was made by the same machine in December, 1919, on her maiden trip, which she completed in 1 hour 50 minutes.' (*The Aeroplane*, 26 July 1922). G-EAPJ was noted as being the fastest of the four of its type.

DH18a G-EARO City of Cardiff of Instone Air Lines, Croydon, 1922 [photo courtesy L.T. Mason]

Robert (fourth from right) in front of an Imperial Airways aeroplane. Date and place unknown, but possibly as late as 1929. Note the two pilots – helmets and goggles – who flew in an open cockpit! [photo via Richard Holleyman]

A charming shot of the three girls – Alice, Joan and "Pixie" [Loraine family, via Richard Holleyman]

Family man. Between 1922 and 1926 Robert and Winifred had three daughters. Their first, Roberte Winifred Alice, always known as Alice, was born on 14 August 1922 at Horsley Towers, East Horsley, Surrey;[343] Beatrice Joan, "Joan", was born on 17 April 1924; and Mary Elisabeth, "Pixie", on 6 March 1926. (Alice Loraine (1922–1982) lived and worked in Lausanne, Switzerland; Joan Beatrice Loraine (1924–2016) became a teacher in Turkey and Africa, then horticulturalist at Greencombe, Somerset, England; Mary Elizabeth Loraine (1926–1977) trained and toured in ballet and then briefly theatre. She taught at Cornell and then Principia College, Elsah, USA. Married to James K. Schmidt (1925-2013), they had three children: Penny, Rob (Robert) and Ben (Bennet).

---

[343] Horsley Towers was then owned by Tommy Sopwith, who designed the Hawker Horsley bomber aeroplane, which first flew in 1925.

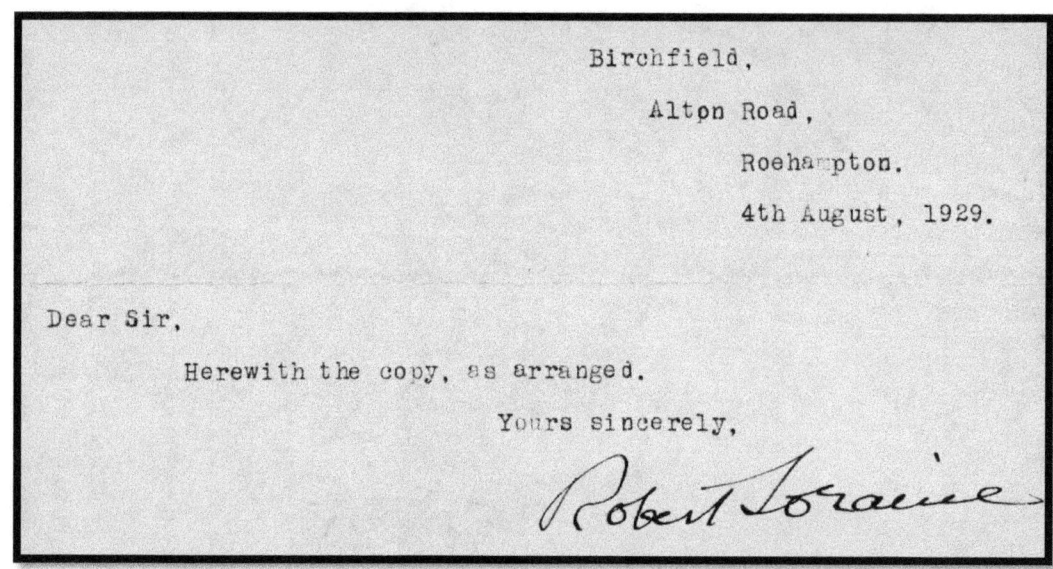

Very short letter signed by Robert at "Birchfield", 4 August 1929

In the summer of 1923, from the proceeds of an insurance claim, Robert and Winifred were able to buy "Birchfield", a large house on Alton Road, Roehampton, London SW15, (telephone number PUTney 3481), standing 'in beautifully-timbered grounds of nearly 1½ acres in extent', which backed on to the east side of Richmond Park. Robert managed to get the purchase price down from the £8,000 asking price to £6,000 (around £450,000 in today's money). The house, which had been tenanted by Mr. F.A. Capper, was sold by its owner, Stanley Borton Brown, a member of The Stock Exchange, then living at 79 Clarence Gate Gardens, Regents Park.

As the nearest entrance to the park, Chohole Gate, was two or three hundred yards away on the Portsmouth Road, Robert understandably wanted to put a gate in the garden wall to gain access to the park. His hopes were dashed when, on 12 November 1923, in a letter addressed to him at the Theatre Royal, Haymarket, the Office of Works refused to grant permission.

On 19 September 1923, Robert wrote to the Ministry of Pensions re his war pension: 'I beg to apply for a reinstatement of my wounds pension which was discontinued two years ago, on the grounds that though the disability resulting from my wounds was somewhat less at the time the award was withdrawn on account of my having had to take a year's complete rest and a voyage round the world in an attempt to recover from my disabilities, these are now more pronounced than ever since my actual recovery from the wounds. I am unable to do a quarter of the work which I did formerly; I am compelled to rest for long and frequent periods; I have recently been compelled to refuse work which I would normally have been able to do with ease, and which would have very materially increased my income. I am severely handicapped in my profession as a direct result of my wounds. I suffer extremely from insomnia in addition to enduring a great deal of pain.'

'Under these circumstances I hope that my application may receive your favourable consideration.'

Summoned to attend the Central Medical Board for an examination on 5 December, Robert was informed by the Director General of Awards, Ministry of Pensions, Officers' Branch, on 19 December 1923 that he had been 'granted a renewal of wound pension at the rate of £100 a year from the 20th July, 1920, to the 24th July, 1924, and the following amended award has been authorised in your case:- Temporary Retired Pay and Wound Pension at the combined rate of £108 a year / from the 20th July, 1920, to the 24th July, 1924.' They added that the award was 'made in respect of the rank of Major.' The extra £8 was temporary retired pay in addition to his wound pension, his disability having been assessed at 40 per cent.

With the pain in his knees continuing, Robert visited Doctors W.H. Coldwell and F.M. Allchin at 52 Welbeck Street, London W1, on 21 August 1924 where his limbs were radiographed:

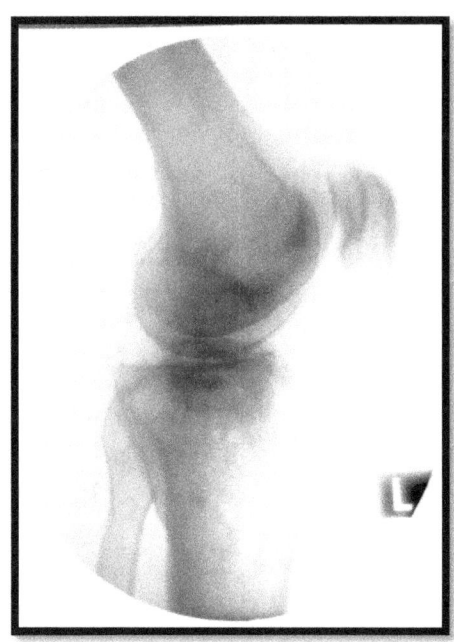 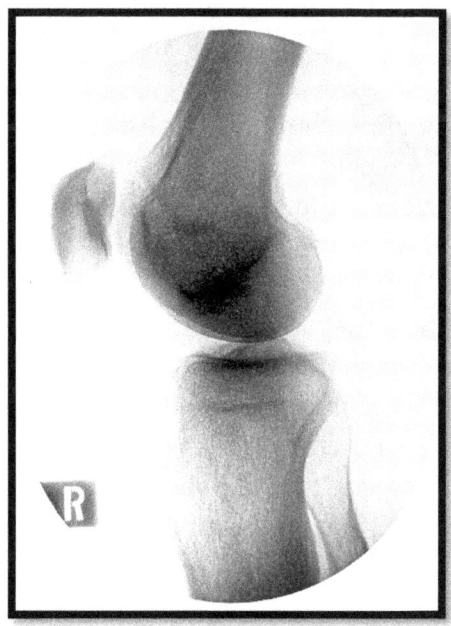

Radiographs of Robert's knees [photos courtesy Rob Schmidt]

Shortly afterwards, he was offered the part in the play *Tiger Cats*, which was to be launched in New York, and in which he had starred with Edith Evans.[344] Accordingly, on 9 September 1924, he crossed the Atlantic on the *Aquitania*, with Winifred, Alice and Joan following from Liverpool on the *Aurania* on 11 October. When the play closed after six weeks, the Loraine family came home on the *Mauretania*, arriving at Southampton on 23 January 1925.[345]

Robert returned to North America on the SS *France* on 3 September 1925 for the play *The Man with a Load of Mischief*. It opened in Toronto, Canada, on 28 September 1925, before going to Detroit, USA.

Winifred, once again pregnant, and the two girls remained in England, subsisting on monies paid to Robert by an Italian film company which wanted English sub-titles for its film *Cyrano*. Robert, returning on the *Berengaria*, landed at Southampton on 28 June 1926.

Film, Epic of the Skies. With no theatre work in the offing, Robert thought that it might be profitable were he to write the script for a film about the brief history of the RAF. He hoped it would be a 'film epic of the skies' dealing with 'the activities of the R.F.C. and the R.A.F. in the recent war'. It was to be 'a romance as well as a chronicle of flying heroism and achievement.' He stressed: 'This picture must be done in colour, and the scenes showing aeroplanes in flight must have a background of clouds…'[346]

A scenario, prepared by Charles Lapworth and R.C. Fogwell, was approved by the Air Council. These two would assist Robert in the film's directing, though the technical director would be Maurice Elvey. The financier of the picture was to be A.E. Bundy, and the making of the film and its subsequent distribution would be placed in the hands of the Gaumont Company. Robert estimated that £15,000 would be sufficient to cover all costs. The length of the film would be eight reels.[347]

Approval was given by the Air Council for the Gaumont Company to take it on but, on 7 April 1927, the Air Ministry informed Robert that 'they do not desire to accept the offer made to them by you for the construction of such a film.' A further nail was put in the coffin by Gaumont in their letter of 5 May 1927 to Robert in which they said, inter alia, that 'it is better that we should disassociate ourselves from the complications that have unfortunately arisen.' Mr. Soman, a senior director of the Gaumont Company, was proving difficult, however, and, to Robert, Soman's demands for a third of what he, Robert, would make from the film was tantamount to blackmail.

---

[344] Edith Mary Evans (8 Feb 1888–14 Oct 1976) was made DBE in 1946.
[345] The *Mauretania*, all 31,938 tons of her, held the Atlantic westbound speed record, the Blue Riband, from 1909 to 1929, and the eastbound record from 1907 to 1909, and again from 1924 to 1929.
[346] From Robert's *Rough Draft of a Preliminary Scenario* (no date), Loraine family via Richard Holleyman.
[347] Robert's letter of 5 Mar 1926 to unknown.

Eventually the Air Ministry had had enough of the behind-the-scenes wrangling, and A.H. Self, Director of Contracts, wrote to Robert on 22 July 1927: 'I am directed to inform you that full consideration has been given to the matter in all its aspects and it is regretted that the Department has been unable to accept the proposals of Messrs. The Gaumont Company Limited.'

That should have been the end of the matter, but Robert tried again in June 1930, even trying to persuade his old RAF boss, Jack Salmond, that the film should be revived. Salmond, by this time an Air-Marshal and Chief of the Air Staff at the Air Ministry, declined, and Robert was again rebuffed, in a letter of 16 July 1930, regretting that 'the facilities required cannot be afforded'.

Another potential string to Robert's bow for the making of his film had involved the attempted purchase of the airship, the R.33 (civil identification G-FAAG, the "R" of R.33 standing for Rigid), then in storage at Pulham, Norfolk. He wrote to the Air Ministry on 13

The R.33 at Pulham, Norfolk. She 'cost £350,000, and she flew for 800 hours and burst...' [Frank Herbert Rose (5 July 1857–10 July 1928), MP for Aberdeen North, quoted in The Millionth Chance, p.57]. After almost nine months under construction, the R.33 was launched on 6 March 1919. The forward part of R.33's control car can now be seen at the RAF Museum, Hendon.

April 1927: 'As I understand the R.33 is about to be demolished I should be obliged if you would inform me on what terms I could acquire the airship at a breaking up price, for the purpose of using her for a cinematograph film story.' The Director of Contracts replied on 3 May: 'I am to state that no decision has been arrived at that the airship is to be demolished.'

Robert's proposal, somehow leaked to the Press, was published by, inter alia, the *Newcastle Evening Chronicle* on 10 May 1927. It was read by James Jamieson, a former sheet metal worker on the construction of R.33's gondola in Northumberland around 1918. He wrote to Robert on 12 May advising him that he owned a sheet of the metal – Duralumin – that had been used on a gondola. The sheet in question, having been exposed to the atmosphere but not to the weather, was now, eight years on, 'encrusted with a substance that looks something like Lime.' He added that 'it cannot be making the metal any stronger.'

Mr. Jamieson's amateur analysis was to prove correct. The R.33 had been put into storage in a shed at Pulham in November 1926, where it had languished until 'metal fatigue was detected in the framework; [and] she was forced to be dismantled during 1928…'[348]

Coincidentally, a year later, on 18 July 1928, the directors of the Airship Development Co. Ltd. wrote to Robert to ask if he might be interested in 'taking a financial interest in a proposition which has an assured future, and is unique in the aviation world?' They wanted to use their airship – yet to be built (at a cost of £4,000) – for aerial advertising. Records are silent as to Robert's reply which was, no doubt, in the negative given his financial state.

♦ ♦ ♦

In the event, the Airship Development Company Ltd., formerly British Airships Ltd., *did* manufacture a small non-rigid airship in the former RN airship shed at Cramlington, Northumberland. Designated the A.D.1 and registered G-FAAX, it made its first flight on 13 September 1929. Flying over Belgium, however, on 5 October 1930, the airship was destroyed in a storm and the Airship Development Company was liquidated at the end of 1930.[349]

It is worth noting Robert's changing thoughts with regard to airships. Some years earlier, on 24 September 1911, His Majesty's Airship No. 1 "The Mayfly" had broken its back when being moved out of its shed at Barrow-in-Furness. Robert was quoted as saying that it was 'only what everybody had been expecting. The whole history of the machine has been a chapter of accidents. Why the authorities persist in these experiments with dirigibles

---

[348] www.airshipsonline.com/airships/r33/R33-breakway.
[349] www.airshipsonline.com/sheds/Cramlington.htm.

is a mystery to me. There has not been a single test in recent years in which the aeroplane's superiority has not been constantly apparent…'[350]

Robert's thoughts were echoed by the Editor of *Flight*, who declared that 'we do not seem to have made a single step in advance so far as the airship proper is concerned. It scarcely needed the lesson of the collapse of "Naval Dirigible No. 1" to demonstrate the elementary fact that the big dirigible is a failure.' (*Flight*, 30 September 1911).

♦ ♦ ♦

In 1927, after his film project had failed to materialise, further attempts by Robert to find employment also came to nought and so, deeply depressed, he took to locking himself away in a darkened room. When, however, he heard that Edgar Wallace[351] was looking for someone to appear in his play *The Squeaker*, he put his name forward, only for Wallace to turn him down, and for his depression to continue.

A break came when he took the title rôle in August Strindberg's play *The Father*. Opening at the Everyman theatre on 3 August 1927, it moved to the Savoy three weeks later. After a further three weeks, the lease at the Savoy expired, and the play transferred to the Apollo theatre. Robert was involved in arranging the next lease and, on 30 October 1927, the Apollo 'passed into his hands.'[352]

Robert and Winifred decided to revive *Cyrano* at the Apollo and it opened on 9 November 1927. It was not a success and other plays in which he performed over the ensuing months, including one by Edgar Wallace, also failed.

From the front cover of the programme for The Father. Theatregoers would enjoy a double bill, with J.M. Barrie's Barbara's Wedding, produced by, and starring, Robert as The Colonel, opening the entertainment.

During his "ownership" of the Apollo, Robert's second film, *S.O.S.*, a British silent adventure movie, was released in 1928. In 1929 he leased the Apollo Theatre.

---

[350] Quoted in *The Millionth Chance*, p.54.
[351] Richard Horatio Edgar Wallace (1 Apr 1875–10 Feb 1932) became a famous writer of "thrillers".
[352] *The Life of Robert Loraine*, p.199.

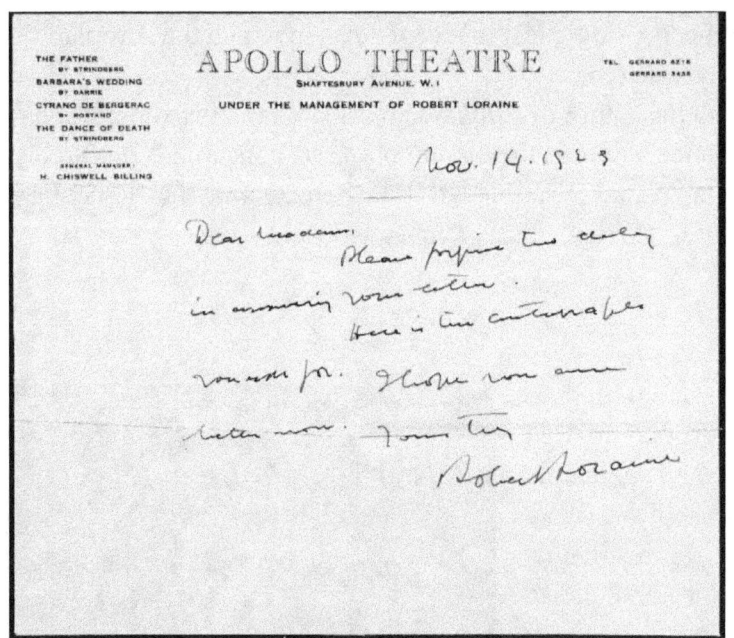

Letter from Robert, dated 14 November 1929: 'Dear Madam / Please forgive the delay in answering your letter. / Here is the concertina file you ask for. / I hope you are better now. / Yours truly / Robert Loraine.'

He spent several weeks during 1929 in crossing the Atlantic in search of work and by December 1929 had run up an overdraft of £7,000. He was not the only one in financial straits. The USA's Great Depression, which began in October 1929, was followed by the world market crash and, in Britain, the Great Slump as the financial disaster there was called. This, and the stress of being out of work, caused him and Winifred to separate, though continuing to see each other for business purposes. Even though he, himself, was still heavily in debt, Robert was happy to broadcast an appeal on behalf of St. John's Hospital, Lewisham on 23 February 1930.

He decided to try his luck once again in the USA but, after a short stay, returned to England. He managed to get a part in another film, *Birds of Prey*, which was released in Britain on 18 November 1930 and in the USA, under the title *The Perfect Alibi*, on 1 April 1931. Making his screen debut in the film was a young Jack Hawkins (1910–1973).

The "flyers" for the film Birds of Prey / The Perfect Alibi (via Richard Holleyman)

 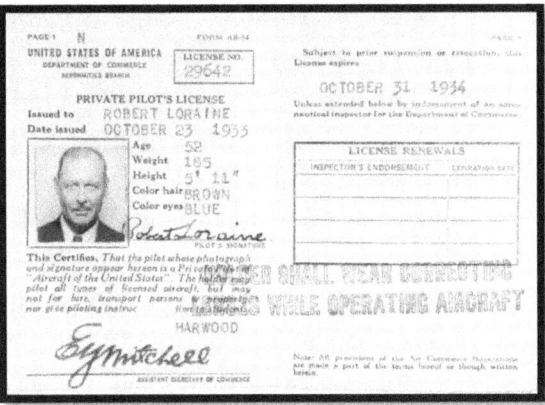

[Left] The front cover of Robert's USA 1933-issued log book; [right] his USA flying licence. Note his age is given as 52, not 57, and that he was required to wear 'correcting lenses while operating aircraft.' [via Richard Holleyman]

Robert in the USA, and the last two types of aeroplane that he flew over there (via Richard Holleyman)

Flying interest revived. Further visits to the USA and Canada followed over the years, all adding to Robert's financial distress but, while living at 130 West 44th Street, New York City, his interest in flying was re-kindled. The first entry in his American logbook is dated 17 August 1933, when he flew a Taylor E-2 Cub for fifty minutes from Nobadeer, Massachusetts, on the East Coast. Issued with USA pilot's licence No. 29642 on 23 October 1933, he flew regularly until 4 November 1933, when he returned to acting.

He then flew six times between 28 May and 3 June 1934, but did not do so again until 11 October 1934. Flying occasionally until 18 January 1935, he made his last eight, short, flights over the six days of 5 to 10 August 1935. On 9 August he flew a Waco 10 aeroplane non-stop for three hours from Roosevelt Field, New York,[353] and on his last flight, in a Fairchild 24, was up for twenty minutes doing 'loops and spins'.

At the end of his USA log book, he wrote: 'Previous to this log book I have had no less than 1200 hours solo flying time. [*signed*] Robert Loraine.'

Early 1934 found Robert still in the USA and in a play at a Boston theatre, which ended after a short run. He then went to Canada, returning from St. Hubert Airport, Montreal, on 28 February 1934. Flying in tri-motored Stinson Model U aircraft register no. NC12115, piloted by S.T.B. Cripps DFC (see Appendix IV), he landed at the Albany Municipal Airport, New York.

Hollywood. Robert's next move, in 1934, was to go to Hollywood, where he made three movies – *Outcast Lady*; *Marie Galante*; and *Limehouse Blues*[354] – before flying back to New York soon after 18 January 1935.

Robert's fortunes revived when he sold the film rights of *Cyrano* to Robert Korda for $60,000, equivalent to £38,500 at the time. After a stay in the Bahamas, he sailed on 23 April 1935 aboard the *Carinthia*, on a five-day voyage to New York. He made one last movie in the States, playing Inspector Valentine in *Father Brown, Detective*.

Returning to England on the French ship *Normandie*, he arrived at Plymouth on 14 October 1935.

Sometime after his return he was given a flying certificate by the RAeC in what seems to have been some form of reciprocal agreement, the index card (see below) giving no indication of his having taken a further test in England.

---

[353] It was from this airfield that Charles Lindbergh left on his flight across the Atlantic on 20 May 1927.
[354] In *Outcast Lady* (lead actor Constance Bennett) Robert played the character Hilary; in *Marie Galante* (Spencer Tracy) he played Ratcliff; and in *Limehouse Blues* (George Raft) he played Inspector Sheridan.

Four stills (above) of Robert (now aged 58) as the serious "Mr. Ratcliff" in Marie Galante (1934). Ratcliff arrives at the US military intelligence office in the Panama Canal Zone, where he is announced as 'Mr. Ratcliff, from London, England.' He was there to help uncover a plot by certain persons bent on destroying the Panama Canal and several US Navy ships stuck in it. With Spencer Tracy (lower left), and with monocle (bottom right)!

Four "stills" from Limehouse Blues (also known as East End Chant) (1934), set in London. Robert, sporting a moustache, plays Inspector Sheridan, who is determined to bring a smuggler, Harry Young (played by George Raft, the villain of the piece), to justice (seen talking to each other bottom left). Top right, Robert is seen talking to the heroine, "Toni" (played by Jean Parker). Believing that he needs a gun of some sort with which to tackle Young, Sheridan asks his superior (top left) for one, with the classic words: 'You can't go after wild game with a butterfly net!' He gets his gun – a Thompson gun – and in a boat chase in the dark, presumably on the Thames, shoots at Young, who gets away. Eventually catching-up with Young in his den, Sheridan tells him that he can't get away from him now. 'Yes I can' replies Young, and promptly dies, clearly having been shot by Robert in the boat chase earlier!

Four stills, from Father Brown, Detective: (top left) Inspector Valentine (Robert) talking to the villain, Flambeau (Paul Lukas); (top right) Inspector Valentine with the heroine, Evelyn Fischer (Gertrude Michael); (bottom left) Flambeau talks to Inspector Valentine, while Sergeant Dawes (E.E. Clive) and Sir Leopold Fischer (Halliwell Hobbes) look on; (bottom right) Inspector Valentine, Evelyn Fischer and Father Brown (Walter Connolly).

```
                                                              13329
    LORAINE, Robert,
                36, St. James' Street,
                              London, S.W.1.


    Born        14th Jan. 1876    at  Liscard.
    Nationality    British.
    Rank, Regiment, Profession    -
    Certificate taken on
    At          22.10.35.   (American Licence 9642.31.10.35.)
    Date
```

The RAeC index card. Note that the date of the USA licence, 31.10.35, was that for its annual re-issue from 1933 and that his date and place of birth are correct.

On 15 November 1935, the British Broadcasting Corporation (founded on 18 October 1922) offered Robert the part of Scrooge in two readings of Charles Dickens' *A Christmas Carol*, to be broadcast on 26 and 27 December 1935. He was looking forward to the broadcasts but, ominously, was having throat problems.

Robert, who been away from his family for several years, was now presented by Winifred with divorce papers. In her petition for the divorce, filed on 3 December 1935, she prayed that his Lordship 'will decree that her said marriage may be dissolved and that she may have custody of the children…' It was further noted 'that on the 20th, 21st, and 22nd days of November 1935 at the Jules Hotel Jermyn Street in the County of London the Respondent committed adultery with a woman whose name is unknown to your petitioner.'[355] Robert, once again, was doing the gentlemanly thing, going through the legal routine for an uncontested divorce. Winifred filed for alimony on 18 December.

With his throat problems worsening, Robert had only a few days left in which to live. Winifred wrote that 'the lung hæmorrhages were worse, and other complications set in.

---

[355] TNA file J77/3536/7868.

The fight had lasted four months.'[356] On the morning of 23 December, Robert telephoned Winifred to tell her that he was going to the Royal National Throat Nose & Ear Hospital at 32-33 Golden Square, London W1, near Piccadilly Circus, London, for an immediate operation. Afterwards, even though his temperature had risen to an alarming 104°F, he appeared to be quite lively but, that same day, he died of a heart attack, three weeks short of his sixtieth birthday. His death certificate states: 'Cause of Death 1a. Cardiac failure. b. Acute oedema of larynx. c. Peritonsillar abscess. Certified by R.A. Marshall MB.'

After a funeral service at Roehampton's Holy Trinity Church, conducted by the Reverend Henry Elkerton, Robert was buried in Putney Vale Cemetery on 29 December 1935.

Winifred filed a Notice of Abatement on 4 January 1936 withdrawing her divorce petition. As Lord Justice Bowen was to observe in another, earlier case: 'A man can no more be divorced after his death than he can after his death be married or sentenced to death.'

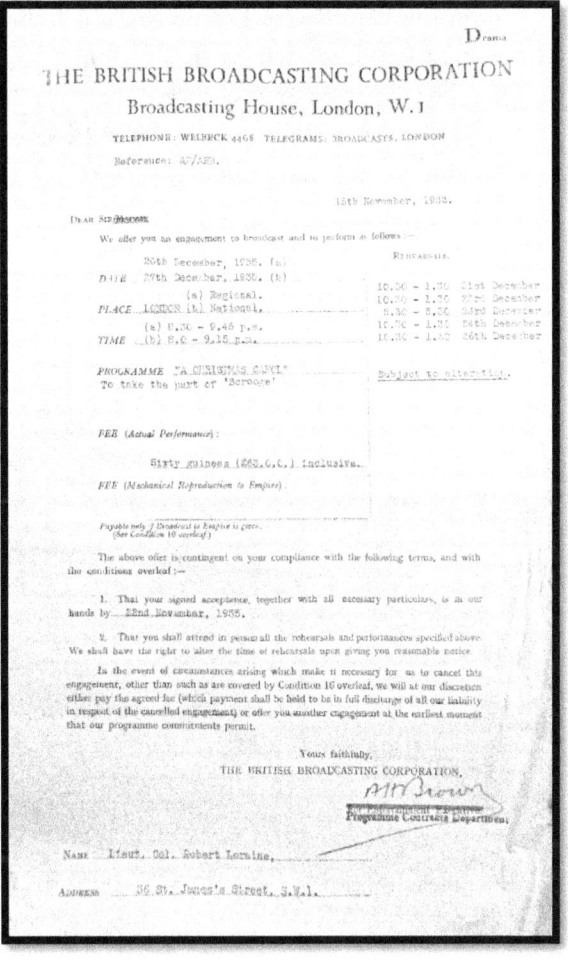

The BBC's letter to Robert inviting him to "play" Scrooge on 26 & 27 December 1935 (Loraine family via Richard Holleyman)

Though Robert's flying adventures had begun a quarter of a century earlier, he had not been forgotten: 'Robert had lived and flown in exalted company but he, together with Moore-Brabazon, Cockburn, Mortimer-Singer, ... McArdle, Gibbs, Radley, Colmore, Rawlinson, Valentine, Morison, Greswell, Barber, Paterson, Fleming, Hewitt, Corbett-Wilson, Ewen and Turner had blazed into prominence and faded away.'[357]

---

[356] *Actor, Soldier, Airman*, p.378.
[357] *History of British Aviation 1908-1914, Vol 2*, p.143.

Flight, too, was moved to write on 2 January 1936: 'It seems a very long time ago since Robert Loraine, who died in a nursing home just before Christmas, was astounding the embryonic flying world with his daring feats in a Henry Farman biplane... Since the war one has thought of him almost exclusively as an eminent actor and theatrical manager, but in the pages of *Flight* of the year 1910 he appears constantly as one of the most notable of the flying pioneers.'

Holy Trinity Church, Roehampton

In the beginning: Robert on his Henry Farman biplane, 1910 ...

... and at the end (photos courtesy Rob Schmidt)

Appendix I: Some significant dates in the life of Robert Bilcliffe Loraine

1876, January 14	Born in New Brighton, Cheshire, to Henry Bilcliffe and Mary Ellen Loraine.
1889	Began acting career in *The Armada*, in Liverpool.
1894, 22 May	Made London stage debut, at the Strand Theatre.
1895, 1 August	His mother, Mary Ellen, died in London.
1897, 4 November	Married American actress Julie Opp.
1899, 10 July	His father, Henry, died in London.
1899, 11 October	Start of the Second Boer War, South Africa.
1899, 20 December	Enlisted in Montgomeryshire Imperial Yeomanry.
1900, 16 January	Began military training.
1900, 13 March	Sailed to South Africa with the 49th MIY.
1900, 8 April	Disembarked at Cape Town, South Africa.
1900, c. October	Hospitalised after drinking contaminated water.
1900, 15 November	Arrived back in England on hospital ship.
1901, 13 January	Discharged from the Army at own request.
1901, 16 January	Sailed to New York, USA for acting engagement.
1901, 4 March	First appearance on the New York stage, at the Knickerbocker Theatre.
1901, 22 May	Resumed acting career in London.
1901, 26 July	Julie Loraine (née Opp) filed Petition for Divorce.
1902, 18 December	Final Decree (Absolute) signed.
1905–1907	Made a fortune from G.B. Shaw's play *Man and Superman*.
1906, 3 July	First flight, with George Bernard Shaw, in the balloon *Norfolk*.
1908, January	Ordered an aeroplane from Henry Farman in France. Not delivered.
1909	Became friends with George Henry Smart.
1909, July	In France to watch first crossing of English Channel by aeroplane.
1910, March	Learning to fly at Pont-Long aerodrome, Pau, south-west France.
1910, 4 April	Resumed acting in London, in *The Rivals*.
1910	To France, to see Henry Farman at Mourmelon-le-Grand, to continue flying lessons. Bought a flying machine. Hired mechanic Jules Védrines.
1910, 21 June	Awarded pilot's certificate no. 126 by the Aéro-Club de France.
1910, 11 July	At the Bournemouth International Aviation Meeting, Southbourne.
1910, 16 July	Flew in rainstorm to Isle of Wight. First aeroplane to land there.

1910, 19 July	Flew back to Southbourne.
1910, 29 July	At the Blackpool Aviation Carnival.
1910, 10 August	Flew from Blackpool, via Rhos-on-Sea golf course, North Wales, to north Anglesey.
1910, 11 September	Flew from Anglesey in attempt to reach Ireland. Came down in Dublin Bay sixty yards short of land.
1910, 20 September	To Lark Hill, Salisbury Plain to fly in Army's Autumn Manoeuvres.
1910, 21 September	Flew with George Smart to Shrewton, Wiltshire. Returned to London.
1910, 26 September	Flew Bristol "Boxkite" aeroplane fitted with wireless apparatus; transmitted message over a short distance. Returned to London.
1910, 30 September	Back to Lark Hill from London to fly the wireless-equipped aeroplane. Transmitted message, this time over a distance of one mile.
1910, 15 October	Became engaged to actress Marie Löhr.
1910, 16 December	Aeroplane destroyed in a gale at Dover. Bought another machine.
1910, 29 December	Crashed new aeroplane.
1911, 12 February	Romantic entanglement with Marie Löhr ended after ultimatum from her mother to choose flying or marriage.
1911, 12 May	Flew his new Howard Wright biplane at the Hendon Demonstration.
1911, June	Bought new monoplane. Went to Mourmelon-le-Grand, France, to learn to fly it. Bought a Nieuport aeroplane instead. Crashed it. Sold it to Captain E.B. Loraine, Grenadier Guards (no relation).
1912-13	Continued acting career on both sides of the Atlantic.
1914, August	Hoped to marry 18-year-old Dutch heiress, Marie Hegenbusch, but parents disapproved.
1914, 4 August	Joined the RFC on declaration of war with Germany.
1914, 11 August	Appointed 2nd Lieutenant (on probation) in RFC.
1914, 2 September	Posted as Observer to 3rd Squadron RFC, France.
1914, 14 September	Flew first reconnaissance as Observer over enemy lines.
1914, 2 November	Helped land aeroplane after pilot was wounded.
1914, 22 November	Badly wounded in right lung by shrapnel ball.
1914, 11 December	In hospital in Mayfair, London.
1914, 15 December	Confirmed as Second Lieutenant, Special Reserve, RFC.
1914, 18 December	Promoted Flying Officer, seniority 3 September 1914.
1914, 22 December	Captain George Henry Smart, his great friend, killed in action.
1915	Went on five-week cruise to regain full health.
1915, April	Sent to Le Crotoy, France, for training, but recalled to England.

1915, 29 April	Reported to Shoreham; attached 3 RAS for instruction.
1915, 19 May	Posted to 14th Squadron. To Hounslow, for further training.
1915, July	Posted to 2nd Squadron, RFC.
1915, 1 September	Promoted Temporary Captain.
1915, 15 September	Graded Flight Commander. Posted as pilot to command "B" Flight, 5th Squadron RFC.
1915, 11 October	Promoted Captain from Lieutenant (temp. Captain).
1915, 26 October	Shot down enemy aircraft with Observer, Lieutenant Eric Lubbock.
1915, 16 November	He and Lubbock awarded Military Cross.
1916, 1 January	Mentioned in Despatches.
1916, February	Recalled to England. Given several postings.
1916, 29 March	Invested with MC by King George V at Buckingham Palace.
1916, 26 April	Promoted to Temporary Major and to command 40th Squadron RFC.
1916, 1 August	First 40 Squadron aircraft flew to France.
1917, 12 February	Left 40 Squadron on promotion to Temporary Lieutenant-Colonel, and graded Wing Commander.
1917, 13 February	Assigned as wing commander to 23 (Training) Wing, Lincolnshire.
1917, 11 April	Given command of 14th Wing, France.
1917, 15 May	Mentioned in Dispatches.
1917, 4 June	Admitted Companion of the Distinguished Service Order.
1917, 25 June	Given command of the new 18th (Training) Wing.
1917, 26 September	Admitted to Mount Vernon hospital, Hampstead, London, with neurasthenia. Declared unfit for General Service for three months.
1917, 31 October	Posted to command 36th (Training) Wing, Andover, Hampshire.
1918, January	Court-martialled on trumped-up charge of being drunk on duty.
1918, 19 March	Reverted at own request to Major wef 3 March 1918, seniority 24 April 1916.
1918, 5 April	Acquitted by Court-Martial of all charges.
1918, 26 May	Returned to France.
1918, 29 May	Given command of 211th Squadron (formerly No. 11 RNAS).
1918, 20 July	Flew as Observer on bombing raid to Bruges. Attacked by enemy seaplane; hit in left leg, and hip (broken). In hospital, Dunkirk.
1918, 7 August	Shipped to RFC hospital, Bryanston Square, London.
1918, 8 September	Moved to Swanage Hospital to convalesce.
1918, 11 December	Relinquished commission. Granted rank of lieutenant-colonel.
1920, c. February	Went to St. Moritz, Switzerland, for a rest. Asked by J.M. Barrie to play a part in new production in London. Accepted offer.

1920, 4 March	Chartered an aeroplane to fly back to England. Pilot landed off course near Marburg, Germany. Crossed to England by boat from The Netherlands.
1920, 29 September	Left on round-the-world trip.
1921, 12 May	Sailed from India to England. Met future wife on board ship.
1921, 3 June	Arrived Tilbury Docks, London.
1921, 14 July	Married Winifred Lydia Strangman.
1922	First rôle in a film – British silent drama *Bentley's Conscience*.
1922, 14 August	First daughter born – Roberte Winifred Alice Loraine.
1923	Bought house "Birchfield", Alton Road, Roehampton, London, SW15.
1924, 17 August	Second daughter born – Beatrice Joan Loraine.
1924, 9 September	To USA to play in *Tiger Cats*. His family joined him a month later.
1925, 23 January	All family back in England.
1925, 3 September	To USA for further acting.
1926, 6 March	Third daughter born – Mary Elisabeth Loraine.
1926, 28 June	Back in England.
1926-27	Little or no work; suffered with depression.
1927, early	Put proposal for film *Epic of the Skies* to the Air Ministry.
1927, 22 July	*Epic of the Skies* rejected by Air Ministry.
1927, 3 August	First night in title rôle in Strindberg's play *The Father*.
1929	By end of year had large overdraft. He and Winifred separated.
1930	To USA and back several times. Film *Birds of Prey* released 18 Nov.
1930.	Financial worries continued.
1933, 23 October	Issued with USA flying licence, giving his age as 52.
1933-34	In USA and Canada. Made three more "talkies" in Hollywood.
1935, January	Flew back to New York.
1935	Sold film rights of *Cyrano* to Robert Korda.
1935, 23 April	After a stay in the Bahamas, sailed on five-day voyage to New York.
1935	Finished last "talkie" in the USA – *Father Brown, Detective*.
1935, 14 October	Landed at Plymouth by ship.
1935, 3 December	Winifred Loraine initiated proceedings for divorce.
1935, 23 December	Admitted to hospital with cancer of the throat. Died of heart attack after operation.
1935, 29 December	Buried in Putney Vale Cemetery, London.

Appendix II: Some Aviation Records, October 1890– September 1910

(adapted from *The Aeroplane*, 24 August 1910)

October 9, 1890. Clement Ader, on a "L'Eole," a bat-like monoplane with a steam engine, flew 164 feet, this being the first machine to leave the ground under practicable power. He made several other machines, one of which, "L'Avion," still exists. Spent 1,000,000 francs, but never flew farther than 300 yards.

December 19, 1903. Orville Wright flew 852 feet on a Wright biplane at Kitty Hawk, North Carolina, USA, this being the first flight on a biplane, and the first with an internal combustion *petrol* engine.

September 26, 1905. Wright flew, on a Wright biplane, for 11.12 miles at Dayton, Ohio, his time being 18 m. 9s. This is the first authentically recorded flight of any considerable duration.

October 4, 1905. Wright flew 20.75 miles in 33m. 17s., exceeding 20 miles for the first time.

September 14, 1906. Brazilian Alberto Santos-Dumont flew for 8 secs., making the first flight in Europe on a petrol-driven machine, a box-biplane with a box tail and which flew tail first. He had made a few short hops on 22 August, but this was his first real flight.

April 5, 1907. Frenchman Louis Blériot made his first flight on his own monoplane. It lasted 6s. He had built seven other machines before making this one successful.

October 15, 1907. Henry Farman, on a Voisin biplane, flew 935 feet.

October 25. 1907. Henry Farman, on a Voisin, flew 2,530 feet. During the flight he made the first recorded turn in the air.

March 29, 1908. Henry Farman and Léon Delagrange, on a Voisin, flew 453 feet, this being the first flight of a pilot with passenger.

April 10. 1908. Delagrange flew 1½ miles, exceeding a mile for the first time in Europe.

June 22, 1908. Delagrange, at Milan, flew 10½ miles, the first long flight in Europe.

July 8, 1908. Delagrange, at Turin, took up Mme. Peltier, the first woman to leave the ground in an aeroplane.

August 8, 1908. Wilbur Wright, making his first appearance in Europe, flew for 1m. 45s. at Hinaudières, France.

September 6, 1908. Wilbur Wright, with Arnold Fordyce as passenger, flew for 1h. 4m. 26s. at Châlons, exceeding the hour with a passenger for the first time.

September 9, 1908. Orville Wright flew for 1h. 2m. 30s. at Fort Meyer, Virginia, exceeding an hour in the air for the first time in America.

September 12, 1908. Lieutenant Selfridge, a passenger with Orville Wright, was killed at Fort Meyer, USA. His was the first death from an aeroplane.

October 30, 1908. Farman flew from Bouy to Reims, 17 miles – the first cross-country flight.

October 31, 1908. Louis Blériot flew from Toury to Artenay, 17.17 miles. Landing twice and starting again, he thus made the first cross-country flight with landings.

December 31, 1908. At Auvours, Wilbur Wright flew 90 miles in 2h. 20m. 23s., winning the Michelin Cup, and exceeding 2 hours for the first time.

January 2, 1909. S.F. Cody, on the Army aeroplane, made the first *observed* flight in England at Farnborough.

March 18, 1909. J.A.D. McCurdy, on the *Silver Dart*, at Baddeck, Nova Scotia, flew 16 miles, completing on this day 1,000 miles flown during the winter over a nine-mile course carefully measured and checked on the ice.

June 12, 1909. At Issy, Blériot, on his Blériot XII, with Santos-Dumont and André Fournier as passengers, made the first flight with three persons in an aeroplane.

July 18, 1909. Paulhan set a height record of 450 feet on a Voisin biplane.

July 20, 1909. Hubert Latham made his first attempt to fly the Channel.

July 25. 1909. Louis Blériot flew the English Channel from Calais to Dover in 37 minutes.

August 7, 1909. Roger Sommer flew for 2h 27m. 15s. on a Farman biplane, beating Wilbur Wright's record made on 31 December 1908.

August 15, 1909. S.F. Cody took up Colonel Capper, the first passenger in Great Britain.

August 22, 1909. Opening of the Great Reims Meeting, the first organised aviation meeting. Nine machines were seen in the air at the same time.

August 25, 1909. Paulhan, on a Voisin, flew for 2h. 43m. 24s., beating Sommer's record, and covered 83 miles.

August 26, 1909. Latham, on an Antoinette, flew 96 miles in 2h. 13m., beating Paulhan's distance, but not his time.

August 27, 1909. Henry Farman, doing 118 miles in 3h. 15m., and exceeding 100 miles for the first time, beat both Latham and Paulhan.

August 29, 1909. Latham beat the height record by exceeding 500 feet, officially, though he actually reached at least 1,200 feet.

September 8, 1909. S.F. Cody flew 40 miles across-country round Aldershot, beating the cross-country record.

September 18, 1909. Orville Wright, at Fort Meyer, flew for 1hr. 35m. 47s. with a passenger.

October 15, 1909. The first aviation meeting in Great Britain opened at Doncaster racecourse.

October 18, 1909. Comte de Lambert, on a Wright machine, flew from Juvisy to Paris, round the Eiffel Tower, and back.

October 30, 1909. Irishman J.T.C. Moore-Brabazon, on a Short biplane with a Green engine, won the *Daily Mail* £1,000 Prize for the first circular mile by a British aviator on an all-British machine in Great Britain.

November 2, 1909. Paulhan flew 96 miles at Brooklands in 2h. 48m., a British record.

November 3, 1909. At Mourmelon, Henry Farman flew 150 miles in 4h. 22m.

November 5, 1909. At Sandown Park, Paulhan, on a Farman biplane, reached a world record height of 977 feet.

December 1, 1909. Latham on an Antoinette at Mourmelon, reached a height of 1,560 feet – the first over 1,000 feet.

December 29, 1909. Léon Delagrange flew 125 miles in 2h. 32m. on a Blériot at Juvisy, exceeding 100 miles and 2½ hours on a monoplane for the first time.

December 31, 1909. Harry Ferguson made the first flight in Ireland on a monoplane of his own construction at Downshire Park, Lisburn.

January 7, 1910. Latham flew over 1,000 metres high at Mourmelon, becoming the first man to reach the "vertical kilometre," or 3,250 feet. He dedicated the record, on reaching the ground, to his friend Delagrange, who had been killed three days earlier.

January 10, 1910. Paulhan. at Los Angeles. California, USA, reached a height officially certified as 4,146 feet.

January 31, 1910. Belgian Charles Van den Born and Ukrainian Efimoff (Mykhailo Yefimov), each on a Farman machine with a passenger, broke world's record for passenger flights, doing 1h. 48m. 50s. and 1h. 48m. 31s.

March 5, 1910. Farman, at Mourmelon, flew for 1h. 2m. 25s. with two passengers on board, exceeding the hour with three people on board, for the first time.

March 21, 1910. Harry Houdini, on a Voisin, made the first flight in Australia, at Diggers' Rest, Melbourne.

April 3, 1910. Lieutenant L.D.L. Gibbs, on a Farman, flew for 1h. 15m. at Mourmelon. The first British aviator to exceed an hour.

April 3, 1910. Emil Dubonnet, on a Tellier monoplane, won the Prix de la Nature by flying 100 kilometres, measured in a straight line, across country for the first time, from Juvisy to Orleans.

April 7, 1910. Daniel Kinet flew, with a passenger, 152 kilometres in 2h. 19m. 4s. on a Farman at Mourmelon. exceeding 2 hours with a passenger for the first time.

April 20, 1910. Roger Sommer, on a machine of his own make, took up three passengers, this being the first time four people had been lifted by an aeroplane.

April 23, 1910. Claude Grahame-White made his first attempt to win the *Daily Mail* £10,000 prize for a flight from London to Manchester. His first stretch carried him to Rugby, 75 miles, thus breaking the World's Cross-country Record. He finally stopped at Lichfield.

May 10, 1910. At the conclusion of the Tours Meeting, Captain Bertram Dickson carried off 18,000 francs in prizes, being the first British aviator to beat the French "cracks".

May 15, 1910. Nicholas Kinet flew for 2h. 51m. with a passenger on a Farman at Mourmelon, for a world's record.

May 21, 1910. Comte Jacques de Lesseps on a Blériot with a Gnôme engine was the second person to fly the English Channel.

May 29, 1910. Glenn Curtiss on a Curtiss biplane won the New York World $10,000 prize by flying from Albany to New York, with one landing, 130 miles in 2h. 32m.

June 2, 1910. The late Hon. C. S. Rolls flew the English Channel from Dover to les Baraques and back, being the first aviator to make the double journey, the first to cross on a biplane, the first to cross from the English side, and the first British aviator to cross.

June 4, 1910. James Radley made the first *public* flight in Scotland.

June 9, 1910. Lieutenant Féquant and Captain Marconnet made the first official military long distance flight, from Mourmelon to Vincennes, 100 miles in 2½ hours, on a Farman.

June 10, 1910. The Hon. Alan Boyle made the first cross-country monoplane flight in Great Britain on an Avis monoplane round Brooklands and Weybridge, Surrey.

June 21, 1910. Armstrong Drexel, on a Blériot, at Beaulieu, put the British height record up to 1,100 feet.

July 5, 1910. Morane and Leblanc, on Blériots, broke all speed records from 5 kilometres in 3m. 14.6.6s. (Morane) up to 100 kilometres in 1h. 19m. 13s. (Leblanc), at the Reims meeting.

July 7, 1910. Belgian Jan Olieslagers, at Reims, on a Blériot, put the long-distance record up to 159 miles in 3h. 39m. 29s.

July 9, 1910. Emile Aubrun flew 100 kilometres with a passenger on a Blériot in 1h. 36m., and 137 kilometres in 2h. 9m. 7s.

July 10, 1910. Olieslagers flew 392 kilometres (about 240 miles) in 5h. 3m. 5s., beating all records for speed, distance. and duration. The official record is Labouchère's on an Antoinette on July 9, as Olieslagers went on after the official closing hour. Labouchère did 340 kilometres in 4h. 37m. Latham put the height record up to 4,540 feet.

July 10, 1910. Walter Brookins reached a world altitude record, 1,902 m/6,180 ft, on a Wright at Atlantic City, USA, but this was not confirmed until 2 August.

July 11, 1910. Armstrong Drexel, at Bournemouth, put the British height record up to 2,490 feet.

July 13, 1910. Morane, also at Bournemouth, raised it to 4,475 feet.

July 16, 1910. Robert Loraine was the first person to land an aeroplane on the Isle of Wight.

July 19, 1910. Armstrong Drexel and Harry Delacombe flew from Bournemouth to Beaulieu on a Blériot two-seater, making the first cross-country passenger flight in Great Britain.

August 1, 1910. Tyck, on a Blériot, at Brussels, reached a height of 5.640 feet, being the first to pass the "vertical mile." *See, however, Brookins on 10 July 1910.*

August 2, 1910. Brookins' world altitude record, 6,180 ft, confirmed – see July 10, 1910.

August 3, 1910. Chavez, a Peruvian, at Blackpool, put the British height record up to 5,750 feet.

August 11, 1910. Captain Dickson, on a Farman, made the first passenger flight in Scotland, carrying 33 stone – 25 stone of humanity and 8 stone of lead.

August 11, 1910. Armstrong Drexel, on a Blériot at Lanark, put the world's height record up to 6,745 feet.

August 13, 1910. James Radley, on a Blériot, flew a measured mile with a strong wind at 76 m.p.h.

August 16, 17, and 18, 1910. John Moisant and his mechanic, Fileux, flew from Paris to Rainham in Kent on a two-seat Blériot, the first pair to cross the Channel. [*Taking-off from Issy, France, at 5.45 a.m., 16 August, they reached Amiens at 7.40 p.m. On 17 August they flew to les Baraques, on the French coast, where fuel was replenished. They set off at approximately 10.50 a.m., and landed at Tilmanstone, Kent, at 11.30 a.m., some 5 miles inland from Walmer. On 18 August, they flew on to Rainham.*]

September 11, 1910. Robert Loraine departed Anglesey at 11.05 a.m., and came down a few yards from the Baily lighthouse on Howth Head, Dublin Bay, Ireland, after a flight of some 60 miles over water.

Olieslagers on the shore at Nice; Rawlinson flies past in his Farman

Moisant and Fileux incoming over Walmer, Kent, 17 August 1910

Appendix III: Aviation-related deaths 1908-1910

Name of Airman	Nationality	Where Killed	Date	Machine
Lieut. T.E. Selfridge	American	Washington	17.9.08	Wright

Thomas Etholen Selfridge fell with Orville Wright, in the first public trial of an aeroplane at Fort Myer.

Eugène Lefebvre	French	Juvisy	7.9.09	Wright

The aeroplane he was testing dropped to the ground from a height of 6 metres (20 ft).

Capt. L.F. Ferber	French	Boulogne	22.9.09	Voisin

He was flying low, and in attempting to turn, one wing tip touched the ground, overturning the machine. Capt. Louis Ferdinand Ferber was pinned to the ground.

Antonio Fernández	Spanish	Nice	6.12.09	Own design

Antonio Fernández Santillana. An aviator from Spain. First flight on machine, which suddenly stopped and dropped to the ground from a considerable height, estimated 1,000 feet.

Léon Delagrange	French	Pau	4.1.10	Blériot

At a height of 40 feet his left wing collapsed, due to having fitted an engine of 40-h.p. in place of the usual 18-h.p. Anzani.

Hubert Le Blon	French	San Sebastian	2.4.10	Blériot

Probably due to the same cause as the above. At height of 150 feet the planes collapsed and he fell into the sea; his death was due to drowning.

Gabriel H-Michelin	French	Lyons	13.5.10	Antoinette

Hauvette-Michelin, flying at dusk at a high speed, collided with a mark-post, which, breaking, fell on his head.

Eugene Speyer	American	San Francisco	17.6.10	*not known*

Killed after a fall of 50 feet.

Thaddäus Robl	German	Stettin	18.6.10	H. Farman

High wind blowing; crowd got dissatisfied at no flying. In descending from a height of about 200 feet was apparently caught in a squall and capsized. He was a former professional cyclist.

Charles Wachter	French	Rheims	4.7.10	Antoinette

Wings doubled up, probably due to the rain having warped some vital part.

Daniel Kinet	Belgian	Ghent	10.7.10	H. Farman

Fell from a height of 100 metres, supposed to be due to sudden stoppage of motor.

Hon. C. S. Rolls	British	Bournemouth	12.7.10	Wright

Bringing up too sharply after a *vol plané*.

Nicolas Kinet	Belgian	Belgium	3.8.10	H. Farman

A stay gave way and the machine was dashed to the ground. Strong wind was blowing. Brother of Daniel.

Ugolino Vivaldi-Pasqua	Italian	Magliano	20.8.10	H. Farman

Motor stopped and machine was smashed; Lt. Vivaldi-Pasqua was killed instantly.

Clément van Maasdyk	Dutch	Arnheim	27.8.10	Antoinette

Motor stopped and he lost control.

Edmond Poillot	French	Chartres	25.9.10	Savary

Machine was seen to suddenly tilt and fall to the earth; probably due to gust of wind.

Georges Chavez	Peruvian	Domodossola	27.9.10	Blériot

Strain after a vol plané. Crash occurred on 23.9.10.

Herr Plochmann	German	Habsheim	28.9.10	Aviatik biplane

Fall from 150 ft. Stalled after a steep take-off and crashed, injuring Plochmann; died that evening in hospital.

Lt. Heinrich Hass (German)	German	Moselle	1.10.10	Wright

Motor stopped at a height of 500 ft.

Capt. L.M. Matsievich   Russian   St. Petersburg   7.10.10   H. Farman
Lev Makarovich Matsievich turned up at too sharp an angle after a *vol plané*.

Capt. L-G. Madiot   French   Douai   23.10.10   Breguet
First solo flight by Louis-Gabriel Madiot. Machine appeared unsteady and suddenly dived to the ground from a height of 100 metres. Probably due to bad steering.

Lieut. D. Mente   German   Magdeburg   25.10.10   Wright
After a *vol plané*, on restarting his engine he seemed to lose control.

Fernando Blanchard   French   Issy-les-Moulineaux   26.10.10   Blériot
He was going great speed, 120 feet up, when he lost control.

Lieut. Saglietti   Italian   Centocelle   27.10.10
At a height of 50 ft. his machine refused to respond to the elevator, he tried to jump clear but fell, and machine crashed on top of him.

Ralph Johnstone   American   Denver   17.11.10   Wright
Unnecessary *vol planés*.

Eng. Cammarota   Italian   Centocelle   3.12.10   Biplane
Adorno Enrico Cammarota. Suddenly capsized and fell; may be due to the motor.

S. Castellani   Italian   Centocelle   3.12.10
Giovanni or Guiseppe. Passenger in the above.

Walter Archer   American   Salida   4.12.10
Believed that there was no such person and that report of "death" was a hoax.

Cecil Grace   British   Lost at sea   22.12.10   Short-Wright
Probably due to inefficient compass.

Signor Picollo   Italian   Sao Paolo   26.12.10
Fell from a height of 100 feet. Killed instantly.

Alexander Laffont   French   Issy-les-M.   28.12.10   Antoinette
Aeroplane "snapped". Unable to regain stability, due to a jammed steering wire.

Mario Pola
Passenger in the above, and owner of the aeroplane.

Lieut. J. de Caumont   French   St. Cyr   30.12.10   Nieuport
Jacques Caumont was flying at a high speed; machine did not answer her helm. Fell 60 feet.

John B. Moisant   American   New Orleans   31.12.10   Blériot
Monoplane dipped its head and dropped from a height of 100 ft. There were several very tricky air currents.

Arch Hoxsey   American   Los Angeles   31.12.10
Unusual currents of air. Machine fell from a height of 300 ft. and turned over twice; aviator managed to retain his seat but was apparently killed by motor falling upon him.

With communications in the Edwardian era somewhat slower than in the present day it was not always easy to confirm whether or not an aviator had been killed in an accident in a foreign country. For example, the Hungarian engineer Aladore Zselyi suffered a serious accident in an aeroplane of his own design at Budapest, Hungary on 1 June 1910. He was reported to have been killed, but *Flight* determined otherwise: 'There having been recently a deal of discussion in aeronautical circles as to whether the Hungarian engineer Zselyi (whose name has been variously given as Zosely and Joseli) was killed last year, Mr. T. O'B. Hubbard, Secretary of the Aeronautical Society, wrote to the Austrian Aero Club to ascertain the facts. The reply is to the effect that although Aladore Zselyi was badly injured on June 1st, he was not killed and is now in perfect health.' (*Flight*, 14 January 1911).

Adapted from *Flight*, 28 January 1911

Appendix IV: Notes on Airmen

BARLTROP, Eric Arthur, born on 11 March 1890 in Dover, was the eldest son of the Rev. Arthur Henry and Mabel Barltrop (née Andrews), of 12 Albany Road, Bedford. Having enlisted as 1363 Sapper Barltrop in the 2nd East Anglian Field Company, East Anglian Divisional Engineers, Royal Engineers, he was commissioned second lieutenant on 16 November 1914, before being attached to the RFC: 'Lt. Eric Arthur Barltrop, B.A. Cantab, R.E., attached R.F.C., was educated at St. John's School, Leatherhead, and at Queen's College, Cambridge, where he took his B.A. degree. On the outbreak of war he enlisted in the Royal Engineers, receiving his commission in the same corps in November, 1914, and being promoted Lieutenant in the following March. In September, 1915, he proceeded to Gallipoli, where he was employed as Brigade Signal Officer, and, on the evacuation of the peninsula, he was sent to Egypt, where he contracted typhoid, and was invalided home in February, 1916. He joined the R.F.C. in October, and, receiving his pilot's certificate on March 28th last, joined his squadron at the front soon after. On April 23rd, during an action in the air, he was shot through the head and killed.' (*The Aeroplane*, 9 May 1917). He is buried in Jeancourt Communal Cemetery Extension, France. (Photo courtesy the Panacea Museum – panaceamuseum.org/news/the-sons-of-octavia}.

♦ ♦ ♦

BENBOW, Edwin Louis was born on 10 December 1895 at Abbotsbury, Dorset and educated 'privately, and at Menton College, France and at Castle House School, Weymouth from 1909-1914. When war was declared he was living in Italy, his father being Director of Botanical Gardens at Ventimiglia.

Gazetted second lieutenant in the RFA Special Reserve on 7 October 1914, he qualified as an RFC Observer on 4 December 1915 and was posted to No. 4 Squadron eleven days later. He qualified as a pilot and was awarded RAeC certificate no. 3109 on 21 June 1916. Appointed as a Flying Officer he joined No. 40 Squadron on 15 July 1916. He would be credited with six combat victories, plus one shared and one "out of control", all achieved on the F.E.8, making him the only F.E.8 pilot to achieve "ace" status (five or more victories). He was awarded the MC on 13 February 1917 for 'conspicuous gallantry in action. He has on several occasions displayed great courage and skill, and has destroyed four enemy machines under difficult conditions.'[358]

Benbow was to survive a duel with Manfred von Richthofen on 23 January 1917. He was in a dogfight with other aircraft when his machine gun jammed, and von Richthofen attacked. Clearing the stoppage, Benbow managed to evade the German and escaped.

They were to meet again in a "dog fight", on 6 March 1917, when it was von Richthofen's turn to survive. The German ace was leading four aircraft into the attack against a Sopwith 1½ Strutter of 43 Squadron, but failed to spot nine of 40 Squadron's aircraft coming up behind. Benbow 'fired a burst at 50 to 20 yards into a machine painted mostly green. He had then zoomed and on looking back saw a machine go down in flames.'[359] As von Richthofen's machine was red and did not go down in flames, Benbow might have seen the Sopwith 1½ Strutter of Lieutenant S.J. Pepler and Captain T.D. Stuart on fire. As to the "green" German, Leutnant Kurt Wolff was noted for flying this colour.

Wounded on 21 March 1917 Benbow was posted to the CFS as an instructor on 2 June 1917 before moving as a flight commander to No. 85 Squadron in May 1918. He was flying S.E.5a no. C1861 on 30 May 1918 when shot down by Hans-Eberhardt Gandert of Jasta 51. Captain C.B.R. Macdonald RAF wrote, no doubt hiding the brutal truth, to the dead man's family: 'He did not suffer any pain, being killed instantly on crashing – the last seen of him, his wings had come off, so there was no hope of saving himself.'[360] He was buried in Duhallow Cemetery, near Ypres.

The Aeroplane reported on 12 June 1918: 'Capt. E. L. Benbow, M.C., attd. R.A.F. (Lt., R.F.A.), who was killed in action on May 30th, was the son of Mr. J. Benbow, of La Mortola, Ventimiglia, Italy. He went to France on Feb. 2nd, 1915, and served with his battery for about 12 months. He afterwards served as observer with the Royal Flying Corps for eight months, then, qualifying as a pilot, did work for which he was decorated with the M.C. by the King at the Investiture in Hyde Park on June 2nd, 1917.'

♦ ♦ ♦

---

[358] *The London Gazette*, 13 Feb 1917, no. 29940.
[359] *Under the Guns of the Red Baron*, p.71.
[360] De Ruvigny's *Roll of Honour, Vol II, Part IV*, p.11.

**BIRCH, William Claud Kennedy**, born on 24 August 1891 at Landour, Mussoorie, India, the only son of Colonel W.J.A. and Dora (née Scott) Birch, was gazetted Second Lieutenant on 4 March 1911.

He had flying lessons at the Grahame-White School, Hendon, and was 'rolling' on 9 October 1912. By 1 November he was making 'good straights', and on the following day was 'rolling and hopping.' At last, on 21 November, he was having 'good practice on No. 7 under Instructor [Marcus] Manton, doing excellent circuits.'[361] Next day, he was 'on No. 5 Grahame-White biplane, doing straights and circuits and figures of eight, flying steadily at 300 feet and landing well.' (*The Aeroplane*, 28 November 1912). 'After having had to wait several days for weather to calm down, at 11.30 Lieut. Birch started second part brevet tests, coming through well on No. 5 biplane.' (*The Aeroplane*, 12 December 1912). He was awarded RAeC certificate no. 375 on 17 December 1912.

He was one of several officers, including George Pretyman, to be posted to the CFS at Upavon, for advanced instruction, and on 15 October 1913 was with several others promoted to Flying Officer in, and to be seconded to, the RFC.[362]

Crossing to France in August 1914 with No. 3 Squadron, he failed to return from a bombing raid on Brussels in early 1915. The Casualty List published on 13 February, however, contained the following correction: 'Officer previously officially reported Missing, now unofficially reported Not Missing: Lieutenant W. C. K. Birch, Royal Flying Corps.' Three weeks later he re-appeared. It transpired that, forced to land with engine trouble in enemy territory in Holland, he 'got away disguised as a ship's fireman',[363] thus becoming the squadron's first escaper. On 31 May 1915, he was among those recommended by Field-Marshal Sir John French 'for gallant and distinguished service in the field.' He was also promoted to Captain (temp.) 'whilst so employed' with effect from 7 June 1915.

Captain (Acting Major) W.C.K. Birch MC, MID*,[364] returned to his regiment, 2nd Battalion (19th Foot) Alexandra, Princess of Wales Own (Yorkshire Regiment), in April 1917. On 5 January 1918 he 'was killed in an accident, when a fire broke out in Hedge

---

[361] Marcus Dyce Manton (1893–1968).
[362] The others were: Lieut. R. G. D. Small; Lieut. M. W. Noel; Lieut. E. R. L. Corballis; Pretyman; and Lieut. G. Adams.
[363] *Three's Company,* p.62, quoting from McCudden's *Five Years in the Royal Flying Corps.*
[364] MC awarded 14 Jan 1916.

Tunnel, near Loos… He could have got out, as he came back to the entrance steps and asked if all were out; was told "No", so went back to save them and so gave his life. He was in command of his regiment at the time. The General commanding his brigade wrote: "A very gallant soldier and will be greatly missed," while his Commanding Officer said: "He had the heart of a lion, and was full of grit."

Another officer wrote: "He was one of the bravest men I ever met."[365]

♦ ♦ ♦

BLACKBURN, Harold was born on 19 January 1879 at Dymock, Gloucestershire. His father, Edwin, a schoolmaster, soon moved to Carcroft, near Doncaster, Yorkshire, where he took up another appointment. Harold, having chosen to be an engineer, is shown in the 1901 Census as 'bicycle maker and repairer'. He moved to London around 1909 and, with Albert Walker, built the Blackburn-Walker biplane, a tailless, three-bay, tandem pusher biplane with a canard elevator and the engine in front of its two occupants. Whether it ever flew is not known.

The 1911 Census lists him, single and aged 32, as an 'aviator', boarding with the Lofting family in Byfleet, Surrey. One of the pioneer aviators, he learnt to fly at the Bristol School, Brooklands, and was awarded RAeC certificate no. 79 on 9 May 1911. It was at Brooklands that he was remembered as the inventor and constructor of the Walton and Edwards "Colossoplane".

He briefly went into the motorcycle manufacturing business, but sold his share of the business. In September 1912, when aircraft constructor Robert Blackburn (born 26 March 1885, and no relation to Harold) moved his flying school from Filey Bay, Yorkshire, to Hendon, Harold was appointed manager and instructor. When the school ceased operations in mid-1913, he became the personal pilot of aeroplane-owner Dr. M.G. Christie.

At the Yorkshire Agricultural Show at Bradford, 22 and 23 July 1914, Harold Blackburn, flying a Blackburn monoplane

---

[365] *De Ruvigny's Roll of Honour*, Vol. II, Part IV, p.13.

(*see photo left*), 'opened the first Air Line Service in Great Britain between cities, flying to a time-table. He did the journey between Leeds and Bradford every half hour from 10 a.m. to 5 p.m...' (*The Aeroplane*, 29 July 1914). (Also flying at the show was Vivian Gaskell Blackburn – no relation to either Harold or Robert!)

Harold was based at Harrogate, Yorkshire, with two flying machines – an Avro and a Blackburn – both of which were taken over by the Government when he joined the RFC on the outbreak of war. These two machines 'had a narrow escape from destruction last week at Harrogate. The night watchman in charge of the tent where the machines were stored suddenly awoke to the fact that the place was on fire. In some extraordinary way he got them out of the tent and saved them undamaged. It is reported that the machines themselves had had petrol poured over them, though fortunately they did not catch fire. The outrage is locally attributed to German waiters at one or other of the big hotels, though it might almost equally have been committed by some personal enemy of the aviator's, who knew that the blame would be put on German agents.' (*The Aeroplane*, 19 August 1914). One learns indirectly that the watchman who so pluckily saved the Avro biplane and Blackburn monoplane belonging to Mr. Harold Blackburn when their tent was set on fire at Harrogate was Mr. Guy Wilton, and that he was rather badly burned in salvaging them. He was at that time a premium pupil with Mr. Blackburn. One learns that he has since joined the Royal Flying Corps, and one hopes that the pluck he showed on that occasion will enable him to distinguish himself on service.' (*The Aeroplane*, 2 September 1914).

Harold went to the CFS at Upavon, Wiltshire, receiving his Certificate 'B' (no. 214) on 19 August 1914, and was gazetted second lieutenant (on probation) in the RFC Special Reserve of Officers as of 29 August 1914. He was confirmed in that rank on 29 September 1914. By 2 October he was flying with Robert Loraine on operations on 3 Squadron.

On 27 January 1915 Harold was made a Flying Officer, and on 24 April 1915 promoted to lieutenant. Rapid promotion followed, being made a flight commander and captain (temp.) on 19 July, and on 1 September to captain (the same day as Robert Loraine).

Early in 1915 he assumed command of 'C' Flight, No. 14 Squadron, which had formed at Shoreham, Sussex, on 3 February. After months of training, the squadron, under Major G.E. Todd, sailed to Egypt in November 1915 in defence of the Suez Canal against Ottoman forces. For his actions, he was awarded the MC on 14 January 1916.

Promoted to Squadron Commander from 5 July 1916 and to be temporary major while so employed, he was given command of No. 22 (Reserve) Squadron, which formed at Aboukir, Egypt, on 24 August 1916.

After further service in England and France, he was serving in the office of the Assistant Quartermaster General when he was promoted to the rank of lieutenant-colonel (temporary) on 17 September 1917. For later work, he was awarded the AFC on 3 June

1919. During the war, he was mentioned in dispatches four times, including a special commendation for his work in the Palestinian campaign.

Continuing in the RAF post-war, he served from 26 February 1920 as a wing commander at No. 10 Group, Coastal Area, Lee-on-Solent. After a spell at the Inland Area Aircraft Depôt, Henlow, in 1923, until September 1924, he became base commander at the Aeroplane & Armament Experimental Establishment at Martlesham Heath, Suffolk, a position he held until November 1928. He was placed on the Retired List on 29 August 1929.

He went to live on the island of Jersey, and was evacuated during the Second World War. Returning there after the war, he died on 29 April 1959. He was twice married.

♦ ♦ ♦

BOARD, Andrew George, born 11 May 1878, was awarded RAeC certificate no. 36 on 29 November 1910, the photograph (left) being taken shortly afterwards (*Flight*, 10 December 1910). Posted back to England on 21 December 1915, he was replaced by Major J.G. Hearson on 22 December 1915, who departed the squadron on 6 May 1916. Awarded RAeC certificate no. 1137, on 11 March 1915, he was later Air Commodore John Glanville Hearson CB, CBE, DSO (5 Aug 1883–9 Jan 1964). Air Commodore Board, CMG, DSO, died on 25 February 1973.

♦ ♦ ♦

BONNALIE, Allan Francis was born in Denver, Colorado, USA, on 29 September 1893. He moved with his parents to San Francisco, California 'where he completed his schooling. During this period, he became interested in the new science of flight, and while in high school became a member of the newly formed Polytechnic High School Aero Club. It consisted of about ten members, and together they built a biplane glider having a Farman-type box tail, undercarriage, ailerons and elevator, but no rudder.'

The Polytechnic High School Aero Club's powered glider. Bonnalie made his first flight from a hill at the Twin Peaks area of San Francisco on 1 November 1911 [photo courtesy www.ahcwyo.org/]

In April 1917, while working for the Gorham Engineering Company, Bonnalie tried to enlist in the Aviation Section, Signal Corps, U.S. Army, but was rejected for being underweight. Later, accepted to the School of Military Aeronautics, at the University of California at Berkeley, he completed the requisite course. On 13 August 1917, with other trainees from New York, he sailed for overseas assignment to Liverpool, England. The group was sent to Oxford University for further training.

Awarded RAeC certificate no.7379 on 23 March 1918, Bonnalie was assigned to 211 Squadron in May. On 13 August, taking off at 2.35 p.m. on a photo reconnaissance mission in D.H.9 no. D1701, he was attacked by six Fokker D.VII's. He and his Observer, Second Lieutenant Thomas Brierley Dodwell, were both unhurt when they crash-landed between Forthem and Lou, south-east of Furnes. For his part in these events Dodwell received the DSO, as per his citation:

'On a recent occasion this officer, when acting as Observer, performed a very gallant and meritorious action. In diving to the assistance of another machine, his own machine commenced to fall out of control. Despite this, he continued to engage three enemy machines that were attacking him, and eventually drove them off, an operation that called for great coolness and skill as the shooting platform was most unsteady. Realising that the machine was out of control owing to the loss of lift in the tail plane, half of this being shot away, he left his cockpit, and, climbing along the wing, lay down along the cowling in front of the pilot, enabling the latter [Bonnalie] to obtain partial control of the machine and head for home. When nearing the ground he climbed back into his cockpit to allow the nose to rise, and the pilot succeeded in safely landing. The presence of mind and cool courage of this officer undoubtedly saved the machine, and deserves the highest praise.' (*The London Gazette*, 2 November 1918, no. 30989).

Both Bonnalie and Dodwell were awarded the U.S. Army Distinguished Service Cross (Dodwell on 8 February 1919).

After the Armistice Bonnalie was attached to the staff of the 2nd Army Air Service, providing a courier service to Koblenz, Germany. In May 1919, he returned to the United States, resigned his commission and resumed civilian life. He spent some eight years at Southern Pacific Railroad in San Francisco. In 1925, he joined the Naval Reserves as a lieutenant, and commanded Reserve Squadrons until the beginning of the Second World War. At the time of Pearl Harbor, he was a lieutenant-commander in the Naval Reserves Production Division, Bureau of Aeronautics, Navy Department, Washington, D.C. He retired in 1953 as a Rear Admiral USNR, and died on 29 January 1983.[366]

Dodwell's war ended on 16 August 1918, three days after his adventures with Bonnalie. Flying with Captain Robert Mainwaring Wynne-Eyton (1886–1959) in DH9 C6348, an anti-aircraft shall burst close to their aircraft, hitting Dodwell's left arm in three places and breaking it near the shoulder. They were then attacked by a German fighter which shot the bottom wing in two, sending the DH9 into a mine-field close to the Dutch border in the waters of the Wielingen, where it sank at 12.30 p.m., two miles from the coast near Breskens. The following statement was issued by the Board of Trade on 6 January 1919:

'The King has been pleased, on the recommendation of the President of the Board of Trade, to award the Silver Medal for Gallantry in Saving Life at Sea to Cornelis van den Heuvel, coxswain of the lifeboat at Cadzand, Holland, and to Jac. Vlisielje, Jac. La Gasse, J. C. Galles, I. Colpa, A. Bos, E. Dyselynck, and B. Daelman.

'On Aug. 16th last [i.e. 1918] a British aeroplane containing two officers was badly damaged by anti-aircraft, guns over Zeebrugge. Van den Heuvel observed that the machine was in trouble and ran and informed a Dutch medical officer in case his services were needed, and this officer telephoned to Oostburg for a motor ambulance.

'In the meantime Van den Heuvel called for volunteers to man the lifeboat, and the other men named above responded to his call.

---

[366] Bonnalie details courtesy of https://oac.cdlib.org/findaid/ark.

'The damaged machine was well within the line of Dutch territorial waters and was still being attacked by two German planes. Van den Heuvel accordingly shouted to the coast battery to open fire and the Germans then hurried away. The British machine was unable to make the beach and was obliged to alight on the minefield off Cadzand, with the upper plane flush with the surface of the water. Notwithstanding the great risk incurred, the lifeboat then proceeded to the rescue of the two occupants, one of whom was found to be badly wounded. The injured officer was gently drawn into the lifeboat, in an almost unconscious state, while another boat, belonging to a patrol steamer, rescued his companion [Wynne-Eyton]. The injured officer was rowed ashore and was then driven to Oostburg, where his arm was amputated the same evening.' (Reported in *The Aeroplane*, 15 January 1919).

It should be said that Cees van den Heuvel dived into the water, swam through the minefield and brought Dodwell back to the lifeboat. Dodwell was taken to the hospital at Oostburg, a few kilometres inland, where his arm was amputated. Repatriated on 15 November 1918 Dodwell relinquished his commission 'on account of ill-health caused by wounds' and was granted the honorary rank of Second Lieutenant. He died in April 1972.

♦ ♦ ♦

BRYAN, Anthony Loftus was born at Saint-Gilles, Brussels on 2 October 1886. He is not to be confused with his father, Loftus Anthony Bryan, who was also in the Army and who would end the 1914-18 war as a gunner lieutenant-colonel. A.L. Bryan was commissioned second lieutenant (on probation), Special Reserve of Officers, on 10 May 1909 in the short-lived (1902–1922) South Irish Horse. He was made lieutenant on 10 May 1914 and captain on 20 October 1915.

Keen on aviation, Anthony went to the Blériot School, Hendon (established September 1910) to learn to fly. On 19 November 1912 'Lieut. A. Loftus Bryan, of Enniscorthy, County Wexford, [Ireland] joined school, had preliminary instruction, and later on L.B.1 for rolling practice.' On 10 December he was doing "straights", and was still doing straights on 20 February 1913, but by 3 March was flying circuits and "figures of 8". On 10 March he 'did a priceless right-hand turn (his first turn) on No. 1 taxi at about 5 ft., and was surprised to learn that height was not considered an ideal one for circuits with 25-h.p.' (*The Aeroplane*, 20 March 1913).

Anthony Loftus Bryan in Slack's Blériot at Hendon, 25 May 1913 (The Aeroplane, 29 May 1913)

Rather than take the test for his flying certificate in England, Anthony went to the Blériot school at Buc, ten miles south-west of Paris, France 'where he passed the three tests for his aviation certificate on May 7th. His average height was close on 1,800 feet and his glides from that height were made with his motor stopped. Mr. Bryan is the first officer of Irish Horse to become an aviator.' (*The Aeroplane*, 22 May 1913). His decision to go to Buc may have been swayed by the fact that his great Irish friend Denys Corbett Wilson, also from Enniscorthy, was also there making some memorable flights, some with Anthony as passenger. A photograph of the Buc aerodrome taken by him on one such flight was published by *The Aeroplane* on 17 July 1913. On 27 May the RAeC approved the ACF's decision to grant Anthony certificate no. 1355.

Later in 1913, the now certificated Anthony was working for Norman Arthur Thompson, who was designing and building flying-boats on the English south coast. Having formed a partnership with Dr Douglas White, a friend who agreed to fund their enterprise, White and Thompson Co. Ltd. could be found at Middleton-on-Sea, Bognor, Sussex.

On 27 January 1914 he attended the fifth CFS course at Upavon, which ran for three months and which he successfully passed. Now considered to be 'a skilful but safe and steady flier' he was appointed to the RFC Reserve on 29 May 1914. Norman Thompson, meanwhile, had designed a twin-engined seaplane, the White & Thompson Seaplane No.1, which was an entry in the *Daily Mail*'s Sea plane Circuit of Britain race, due to have started on 12 August 1914 from Southampton Water with Anthony as its pilot. The war put a stop to the race, but Seaplane No.1 later served in the RNAS with serial no. 883.

Anthony's records show that he was in hospital and on sick leave until 4 August 1914, on which date he was posted to No. 5 Squadron. With effect from 7 August 1914, he was temporarily appointed 'from the Reserve, to be a Flying Officer, and to be seconded [to the RFC]. Dated August 4th, 1914.'[367] Somehow, he went to France on 13 August as a pilot with 3 Squadron. During the retreat from Mons, he was flying a reserve machine back to the squadron when he 'landed uninjured in a back garden.' (*The Aeroplane*, 30 September 1914). As seen, he was able to fly with Robert Loraine on 28 September.

His position in the Army was regularized on 15 October: 'Special Reserve of Officers. Reserve Units. Cavalry. South Irish Horse. Second Lieut. Loftus A. Bryan is seconded for duty with the Royal Flying Corps, Military Wing. Dated August 4th, 1914. Second Lieut. Loftus A. Bryan to be lieutenant, under the provisions of paragraph 103, Regulations for Officers of the Special Reserve. Dated May 10, 1914. [LG 13 Oct 1914]. (*The Army never got the order of his names right – he was A. Loftus Bryan.*)

Again, his personal records show that he was sick and, though made a captain on 4 November 1915, took no further part in the war until posted as Adjutant to No. 39 Squadron on 31 March 1916. No. 39 Squadron was formed at Hounslow on 15 April 1916 for home defence duties.

On 19 December 1916 he was serving on No. 11 Reserve Squadron, but eventually his illness was such that he was granted sick leave to go to Santa Barbara, California, USA, and sailed there on 21 April 1917. He was on full pay until 10 June, when his records state simply: 'Demobilised with effect from 11-6-17 till fit to return to duty. ½ pay from 11-6-17 to 10-9-17.'

At that point his war was finished and he never returned to duty. He seems to have remained in California for a few years, as he married in San Mateo on 24 April 1923, though he died in County Wexford, Ireland on 7 March 1966.

◆ ◆ ◆

CALLAGHAN, Joseph Cruess, one of three brothers to lose their lives in the war, was KIA on 2 July 1918 in Dolphin no. D3671. Of the other brothers, Eugene Owen Cruess Callaghan was KIA on 27 August 1916 in B.E.12 no. 6545, 19 Squadron; and Stanislaus Cruess Callaghan was killed in a flying accident in Canada on 27 June 1917. See *Irish Aces*.

◆ ◆ ◆

---

[367] *The London Gazette*, 18 Aug 1914.

CARR, Reginald Hugh (*seen here at Hendon before the war*), born in Walthamstow, east London on 9 September 1886, was awarded RAeC certificate no. 504 on 2 June 1913 whilst employed at the Grahame-White School, Hendon. He joined the RFC on 8 August 1914 at Farnborough, Service no. 1370. Promoted to sergeant on 9 August, he was sent to Montrose, Scotland, on the same day, where he joined a detachment of No. 6 Squadron commanded by Lieutenant Geoffrey de Havilland. He was soon graded 2nd Class Flyer, and then 1st Class Flyer on 7 September 1914. A whirlwind three weeks later he disembarked in France, all 5' 4½" of him, on 30 September 1914.

He was awarded the Distinguished Conduct Medal on 23 June 1915: "For the conspicuous gallantry and ability with which he has carried out the duties of a pilot." By this time, after only 262 days in the RFC, he had become an officer of the Special Reserve,[368] commissioned second lieutenant in the field on 26 April 1915. Promotion to captain and to major followed, and the AFC was later added to his awards.[369] He retired from the RAF on 19 May 1919, and died in 1968.

◆ ◆ ◆

CHIDLAW-ROBERTS, Robert Leslie, born in Towyn, Merionethshire, on 9 May 1896, went on to greater things as a pilot rather than as an observer. Having enlisted in the Honourable Artillery Company as infantryman recruit no. 2492 on 10 October 1914, he was transferred to the 2nd Reserve Battalion on 12 December 1914, but was commissioned in the Hampshire Regiment on 16 June 1915.

In May 1915, however, he had joined the RFC as an observer. Learning to fly at the Military School at Shoreham, he was awarded RAeC certificate no. 2527 on 23 January 1916. He flew with Nos. 18 and 60 Squadrons before joining No. 40 Squadron on 20 August 1918, having been awarded the MC on 1 February 1918. "Chiddles", as he was known, was credited with ten enemy aircraft shot down by war's end. He was back in the RAF in the Second World War as a pilot officer (Service no. 122393), rising to flight lieutenant and being awarded the AFC on 1 September 1944. He died on 1 June 1989.

---

[368] *The London Gazette*, 23 Jun 1915, no. 29202.
[369] *The London Gazette*, 2 Nov 1918, no. 30989.

**CLEAVER, Frederick Holden.** "Hoppy" was so named 'because of a limp due to some previous campaign.' Born on 11 March 1875, he was a Royal Navy cadet at HMS *Britannia*, Dartford, before being awarded a Merchant Navy First Mate's Certificate on 25 July 1896.

After some time at sea, he forsook the ship for the horse, and served with Robert's Horse and Kitchener's Horse during the Second Boer War in South Africa. In 1914, he obtained a commission to the 20th Hussars, a cavalry unit, and was sent to the Western Front, but was injured after four weeks. Declared unfit for service, he transferred to the RFC, and served with 3 Squadron. He then tried his hand at ballooning, and was awarded the RAeC's Aeronaut Certificate no. 45 on 5 September 1915, returning to France as a balloon operator. Promoted to Lieutenant-Colonel in 1917, he was awarded the DSO in 1917 and made a CBE in 1919.

Colonel H.F. "Hoppy" Cleaver CBE, DSO died on 29 November 1944.

♦ ♦ ♦

CORBETT WILSON, Denys, was born at Imber Court, Thames Ditton, Surrey, England, on 24 September 1882, to William Henry Charles Wilson, a barrister, and Ada Caroline, née Corbett. On their marriage, she wished to be known as Mrs. Corbett Wilson, without a hyphen, and this was the surname taken by young Denys. After Eton (1896-1899), he served until 1902 in the 3rd Battalion, Dorset Regiment during the Boer War in South Africa. Resigning his commission on 4 March 1903, he re-joined the Army a couple of years later as a lieutenant in the Royal Artillery, only to resign his commission once more, in 1909.

Enrolling at the Blériot flying school at Hendon, on 17 September 1911 he 'pancaked while attempting left-hand turn, damaging front part of machine, but not breaking wings.' Then, on 22 September, 'doing straight flights, got tail too high once and propeller vanished suddenly.' He then went to the Blériot School at Pau, France: 'The request of the Aéro Club de France to grant an aviator's certificate to Mr. D. Corbett-Wilson was sanctioned' on 16 January 1912, and he was awarded ACF certificate no. 722.

On the afternoon of 17 April 1912 Denys and fellow Irishman Damer Leslie Allen[370] set off from Hendon intending to fly to Ireland from Holyhead, as Robert had done in 1910.

---

[370] Allen, born Limerick, 30 Jan 1878, was awarded RAeC certificate no. 183 on 20 Feb 1912.

Corbett Wilson's Blériot at Newchurch Farm, Kinnersley, Herefordshire, 18 April 1912

Denys was first away, at 3.32 p.m., followed three minutes later by Allen. They planned to make an overnight stop at Chester racecourse, continuing to Holyhead and across to Ireland when ready. Allen reached the racecourse at 6.43 p.m., but of Corbett Wilson there was no sign. Allen was up early on 18 April, and flew the 85 miles from Chester to Holyhead in under two hours. The waiting crowds watched him fly off in the direction of Ireland, never to be seen again. No trace of him nor of his machine, other than a wheel, was ever found.

On his way to Chester Denys had been blown about by the wind to such an extent that his compass was lost overboard. Not knowing where he was, he decided to land in a large field about fifteen miles from Hereford.

After further misadventures, Denys flew to Goodwick, near Fishguard, on the Pembrokeshire coast, and waited for his French mechanic, Gaston Vial. Finally, having set off at 5.47 a.m. on 22 April 1912, Corbett Wilson successfully crossed St George's Channel to Ireland, though it had been a close call. Running into a fierce squall when some fifteen miles from Ireland, he staggered on until, in a thick mist, he landed in a small field at Crane, near Enniscorthy, County Wexford, Ireland. Unfortunately, running into a stone bank, he broke the propeller and the undercarriage. He had been in the air for a hundred minutes.

Denys Corbett Wilson about to fly to Ireland

He spent some of the summer of 1912 flying in Ireland, not always as planned: 'On Monday last Mr. Corbett-Wilson, who had left Enniscorthy on his way to Kilkenny, via New Ross, lost his way and landed at Fethard… in County Tipperary, so that he is the first aviator in Munster, as well as the first to land in Ireland, and the first to fly across Wales.' (*The Aeroplane*, 16 May 1912). His misfortunes continued on 4 July: 'Mr. Corbett Wilson, arriving from Kilkenny at Powerstown Racecourse to give exhibition flights, flew 30 miles from Jenkinstown in 20 minutes, circled Clonmel at considerable height, but on landing was dropped head first by gust; machine was completely wrecked, chassis, fuselage, and both wings being broken. Mr. Wilson hit front of machine and his goggles cut his face considerably. Happily, except for slight shock he was otherwise unhurt, and was able to leave hospital after his wounds had been attended to.' (*The Aeroplane*, 11 July 1912).

When war broke out, he was visiting his mother at the Villa d'Este on Lake Como, Italy, but immediately returned to England. Arriving in London on 15 August, two days later, at Farnborough, he joined the RFC as an officer of the Special Reserve. Spare pilots such as Denys were employed in ferrying replacement machines from England over to France for the RFC as and when required. For the time being, though, there was a scandalous shortage of suitable aeroplanes, and he was forced to wait to cross to France, in the meantime staying at the Farnborough Queen's Hotel, South Farnborough.

Finally, a Blériot machine was ready to be taken to France, and Denys flew it to the south coast on 16 October 1914. Poor weather – mostly fog – held him up at Dover, but on 19 October, at last able to cross the English Channel, he was directed to 3 Squadron: 'We are a detached flight', he wrote, 'camped in a farm house. I was to have gone out on reconnaissance this afternoon but the Union Jack had to be painted on my wings before they would let me off.'[371]

Denys was soon sent to Paris to collect a new Blériot, as 'the one I brought from England has been condemned as dangerous, they found that the wood was too new and that consequently it warped on getting damp. It got itself into the most queer shapes.'[372]

Six months later, on 10 May 1915, still with No. 3 Squadron, Denys was killed in action. He and his observer, Second Lieutenant Woodiwiss, were flying in the repaired Morane Saulnier, no. 1872 (see Appendix V, page 403), when it received a direct hit from a German shell. The Germans later 'dropped a note to say that Morane No. 1872 had been shot down by A.A. fire over Fournes, and the occupants had been buried near the village.' (*Flying Fury*, p.66).

♦ ♦ ♦

CRIPPS, Sydney Trevor Brander, born in London, England, on 8 March 1899, was appointed from Cadet to Second Lieutenant (on probation) in the RFC with effect from 9 September 1917.[373]

On 28 October 1919 he was given a Permanent Commission in the RAF as a flying officer (RAF Service no. 03199), and was posted to the Middle East on 5 November 1920. On 29 November 1920, F/O Cecil Osborne Rigden (23) took off in D.H.10 E9062, 216 Squadron, from RAF Abu Sueir, Egypt, with Cripps and AC1 Arthur Leonard Goodill (aged 19) on board. They were flying near Heliopolis, Egypt, when, according to the subsequent Court of Enquiry, there was an 'error of judgment on the part of Flying Officer Rigden who, realising when half-way round his turn into wind that he had very little height in which to complete his turn, endeavoured to get round quickly instead of straightening out and circling again.' Rigden and Goodill were killed in the subsequent crash, but Cripps escaped with injuries.

---

[371] Letters from an Early Bird, p.62.
[372] Letters from an Early Bird, p.64.
[373] *The London Gazette*, 18 Sep 1917, no. 30292.

By early 1922 Cripps was with 30 Squadron at Baghdad, Iraq. On 19 December 1922, His Majesty the King was 'graciously pleased to approve' of the award of the DFC to Flying Officer Cripps 'for gallant and distinguished service during active operations in Kurdistan.'[374]

In 1923, he was back in England, at the Experimental Section, RAE, part of Inland Area No. 7 Group, Farnborough. Promotion to flight lieutenant followed on 3 July 1925.[375]

On 5 February 1929, Flight Lieutenant Cripps DFC was placed on the retired list at his own request,[376] and sailed to Canada on the *Aurania* in August 1929. On 14 November 1930, at Detroit, Michigan, he applied for US citizenship, declaring, *inter alia*, that he was 5' 10½" tall and weighed 165 lbs., but there is no record of him becoming a US citizen. He then flew regular passenger trips between St. Hubert (Montreal) and Albany (New York) during the early 1930s.

Joining BOAC he was one of several experienced airline pilots who flew cargoes of food and ammunition to the British forces caught in France in May 1940 by the German invasion. Cripps flew a 4-engined AW *Ensign* airliner, twelve of which had been passed to the control of the Air Ministry at the outbreak of war in 1939. The *Ensigns* were easy prey for the Luftwaffe's fighters and, though two were shot down, Cripps was lucky. His aeroplane was badly shot up over Calais, and he flew across the Channel on three engines. Though another engine cut out over Folkestone, he landed safely at Lympne on two engines and one wheel.

When the time came in June 1940 to evacuate all British and French troops, if possible, from France 'Captain Cripps flew an Ensign to pick up a party from Nantes, only to find the airfield completely deserted, with aircraft burning all over its surface. His second captain jumped out of the aircraft to salvage an abandoned bicycle. Not wishing to return empty, they made for Jersey, and took a hand in the air evacuation from that island which was being staunchly organised by Jersey Airways Ltd. They filled the Ensign with evacuees and brought them over to Exeter.'[377]

In September 1940, twelve complete BOAC crews sailed for Montreal. Their pioneering task would be to fly across the North Atlantic to Britain, each crew flying back a Lockheed Hudson twin-engined aircraft for the RAF. By early November 1940, six Hudsons had been delivered to Gander airfield, Newfoundland. They were to fly back to Britain in loose formation led by a seventh flown by Captain D.C.T. Bennett. Bennett took-off at 22.22 hours GMT, 10 November, followed by the other six aircraft. At 08.50 hours GMT, 11 November, Bennett landed at Aldergrove, Northern Ireland, while Cripps, 'a grey haired

---

[374] *The London Gazette*, 19 Dec 1922.
[375] *The London Gazette*, 3 Jul 1925, no. 33063.
[376] *The London Gazette*, 5 Feb 1929, no. 33463.
[377] *Merchant Airmen*, p.26.

21 of the crew at Gander, November 1940.

Standing, left to right: WR Lyons; DR Gentry; R Adams; CM Tripp; WC Rogers; JA Webber; JD McIntyre; **STB Cripps**; *NG Mullett; AM Loughridge; A Andrew; NE Smith; GR Hutchinson; JW Gray; DCT Bennett.*

Kneeling, left to right: DB Jarvis; HG Meyers; JE Giles; EF Clausewitz; K Garden; WT Mellor.

[Photo: DND, PMR 85-475, from Ocean Bridge, between pp.92-93].

veteran who took his wings in the 1914 war, and on this journey actually passed his 10,000th hour of flying, was circling the airfield.' The two had flown across the Atlantic without visual contact and 'had arrived at their destination within a few seconds of each other.'[378]

Cripps would spend many further hours flying across the Atlantic, at a time when flights of note were continually being made. 'Captain Cripps, the oldest man by 10 years in the Atlantic service, made several such. Just before starting westbound late one Saturday night he bought a copy of a British Sunday newspaper, dated for the following morning. Flying north of a depression he picked up a following wind, and arrived at Montreal at 6.4 a.m.

---

[378] *Merchant Airmen*, p.176.

local time. The newsvendor to whom he handed his British newspaper as a curiosity at 7 o'clock was amazed to find that it bore that same day's date.'[379]

'The best Return Ferry Service time for a direct flight from the United Kingdom to Montreal was 13 hours 30 minutes. The record was set on 10 June 1941 by Captain E.R.B. White… Flying with the wind, Captain S.T.B. Cripps once flew the 3100 miles in the opposite direction in 12 hours 51 minutes.'[380]

In August 1941, two Consolidated Liberator aircraft were scheduled to fly to North America from Scotland. One, a Return Service Ferry Flight, was to carry twenty-two airmen, while the second, with nine persons on board, was to fly two VIPs for the meeting at Placentia Bay, off Newfoundland, between the US President and the British Prime Minister. The first-pilots detailed for these were Captain E.R.B. "Herbie" White and Captain S.T.B. Cripps. At more or less the last minute, the pilots swopped aircraft, with White taking Liberator AM261, and Cripps the other, the VIP flight. White, an experienced veteran of Imperial Airways, took-off from Heathfield, Ayrshire, Scotland, 2 miles north of Ayr on the Scottish west coast, into rain, and crashed into the top of Mullach Buidhe, a large, solid peak on the Isle of Arran.[381] All twenty-two on board were killed.

Prime Minister Churchill, who had already departed aboard HMS *Prince of Wales* for Placentia Bay, had left instructions to his staff on 3 August 1941: 'On or about the 10th [August], an aeroplane, possibly carrying Lord Beaverbrook, will come out to us. This must bring, apart from letters and urgent papers, an assortment of the most important Foreign Office telegrams… Pray put this in train.'[382]

On 14 August 1941 Trevor Cripps landed his Consolidated 32 Liberator, type LB-30A, at Bolling Airfield, Washington, D.C., having arrived 'from an undisclosed port' (Heathfield). Also on board was William Averell Harriman, and the Rt. Hon. Lord Beaverbrook. Harriman was a special envoy to Europe of US President Franklin D. Roosevelt and helped coordinate the Lend-Lease program. He was present at the meeting at Placentia Bay, off Newfoundland, in August 1941, between FDR and Winston Churchill, from which came the Atlantic Charter.

In October 1941, Captain Cripps, flying a British Overseas Airways Corporation B-24 Liberator *en route* from Prestwick, Scotland, to Gander, made the first officially sanctioned landing during a weather emergency. A snowstorm, which prevented the landing at Gander, also closed down airports from New York to Montreal. As fuel was running low it was decided that one of the runways at Torbay could be used even though work on it was not completed. Due to the fact that the airport lacked instrument landing aids at the time, the

---

[379] *Merchant Airmen*, p.185.
[380] *Ocean Bridge*, p.285.
[381] Mullach Buidhe is 2,840 feet (874 metres) high.
[382] *The Grand Alliance*, p.383 – Winston S. Churchill (Penguin Books Ltd, London, 1985).

pilot used local radio station VONF as a homing beacon. The aircraft suffered minor nose wheel damage on landing, but there were no injuries to its five crew and fifteen passengers.[383]

Cripps, who had married Elina Bellini on 28 July 1947, died in Montreal on 19 June 1979.

♦ ♦ ♦

CUTLER, Herbert Dennis was born on 10 July 1887 to Edward and Fanny Cutler in west London. Edward was 'living on own means.'

In January 1912 Herbert was at Eastchurch learning to fly. By 18 February he was 'making good flights' and was 'ready for certificate.' On 24 February in a Short biplane 'Sergeant Cutler, of Territorials, took certificate in fine flight, reaching 300 ft., officially observed by Mr. Frank McClean, Lieut. L'Estrange Malone, R.N., and Mr. J. L. Travers, the instructor. First Territorial to gain certificate at Eastchurch.' His RAeC certificate, no. 189, was awarded on 5 March 1912 and he was one of ten aviators appointed second lieutenant (on probation) in the Special Reserve of the RFC on 27 July 1912.

At some point thereafter, he went to South Africa to fly a Curtiss Model F flying-boat at exhibitions, one of two owned by Gerard Hudson, an engineer at the Koffiefontein diamond mine, some fifty miles from the famous Kimberley mines in South Africa. With the onset of war in August 1914, Hudson offered 'to the authorities for use in the present crisis the two Curtiss hydroplanes, which he recently imported into South Africa… Mr. Hudson's offer is of considerable importance in view of the fact that the Curtiss flying boats are not only the first hydroplane craft introduced into South Africa, but are also the only ones in the sub-continent at the present time.' (*The Aeroplane*, 9 September 1914, quoting a South African newspaper).

This offer came to the ear of the then Commander of the Cape Station, Vice-Admiral H.G. King-Hall RN,[384] who arranged to hire one of the Curtiss hydroplanes, with Cutler as its pilot, 'for £150 per month with the aircraft insured to a value of £2 000.'[385] As of 1 September 1914 Cutler was made an acting flight sub-lieutenant, RNAS, and he and the Curtiss flying-boat were dispatched aboard the auxiliary armed merchant cruiser *Kinfauns Castle* to Niororo Island, eighteen miles north-east of the vast Rufiji delta.

---

[383] www.stjohnsairport.com/about/corporate-information/history.
[384] Admiral Sir Herbert Goodenough King-Hall KCB, CVO, DSO, 15 Mar 1862 – 20 Oct 1936.
[385] In Southern Skies, p.47.

Cutler was given the task of looking for the German light cruiser *Königsberg* (3,814 tons loaded) which had been sent out to sink British merchantmen and was now undergoing repairs to its engines. It was known to be hiding somewhere in the Rufiji river delta, on the coast of German East Africa (today, Tanganyika). The Curtiss was then prepared for its appointed task of locating the *Königsberg*. Though the tropical conditions were not kind to the Curtiss, Cutler had managed to become airborne on 22 November 1914 but, running short of fuel, was forced to alight near another island, from which he was rescued. Then, on 24 November, he found the *Königsberg* twelve miles up-river from the delta. The Royal Navy doubted Cutler's observations on the grounds that their charts showed the depth of water to be too shallow for the German ship at the point indicated.

Before another reconnaissance could be flown, however, it was necessary to replace the Curtiss's leaking hull. As the only other such hull available was that of Hudson's second hydroplane at Durban, it was quickly brought and fitted. Cutler tried again to find the *Königsberg*, but this time failed to return after the Curtiss had suffered engine failure at the mouth of the river and he was captured by German troops.[386] The *Königsberg*, incidentally, was finally sunk by the Royal Navy on 11 July 1915, but not before her guns had been salvaged for use against the British. (This was reminiscent of the removal of six of the eight 4-inch guns of HMS Pegasus, sunk by the *Königsberg* on 20 September 1914.)

Though a prisoner-of-war, Cutler was promoted to flight lieutenant for temporary service with effect from 7 May 1915, and to temporary flight commander with effect from 31 December 1916.[387] He was finally released from captivity on 18 November 1917, on cessation of hostilities in East Africa, and was attached to 8 Squadron, East African Field Force. He left for Britain on the *Hymettus* (4,606 tons) on 9 December 1917, arriving on 30 January 1918.

He was then posted to RAF Station Calshot on 4 April 1918 to re-qualify, and became an instructor on 3 May 1918, before being 'Discharged from the Service in accordance with Demobilization Regulations' on 19 February 1919 and being transferred to the Unemployment List.

He died at the Twyford Abbey Nursing Home, London NW10 on 26 January 1966.

◆ ◆ ◆

---

[386] *In Southern Skies*, p.48. This author acknowledges this volume as the source for much of the Cutler details.
[387] *The London Gazettes,* 14 May 1915, no. 29162; and 1 Mar 1918, no. 30551.

**DARVELL, Francis Edwin**, born in West Ham, London, on 6 June 1890, lived with his father William (born in Ireland), his mother Mary, and his elder sister and brother, Isabella and William, at 34 Elmhurst Road, a stone's throw from West Ham United's football ground.

Enlisting in the RFC on 15 January 1913 as 2nd Class Air Mechanic, Service no. 524, he went to France with No. 2 Squadron on 12 August 1914. Promoted to sergeant (fitter / MT) on 27 September 1915 he put his name forward to become a pilot. Learning to fly at the Military School, Gosport, on a Maurice Farman, he was awarded RAeC certificate no. 2772 on 21 April 1916, and was in time to join No. 40 Squadron before it left for France.

On 9 November 1916 he 'encountered 3 hostile machines over Souchez, 1 of which he appears to have driven down out of control. Observers at the 61st Anti-Aircraft Battery report that the machine fell in a vertical nose dive and appeared to crash.'[388] 'Darvell had lost sight of his victim, which is hardly surprising, since in reloading his Lewis he dropped an empty drum, which whipped back into the propeller, breaking off part of one blade, and then into the tail boom of his machine. With the FE8 weakened structurally, Darvell was forced to land, running into a trench system which caused further damage.'[389]

Four days later, he was injured in a crash on take-off, when F.E.8 no. 6418 crashed north-west of the aerodrome after a wheel came off on a rigging test.[390] He survived the crash, as he did the war, and died in Kent in 1968.

◆ ◆ ◆

DAVIES, Llewellyn Crighton, born in Cardiff on 9 January 1889, was the son of the Editor of the *Cardiff Figaro*. Qualified as a chartered accountant, Llewellyn was practising in Glasgow when he enlisted in the 5th Battalion, Cameronians (The Scottish Rifles) on 4 August 1914. Commissioned second lieutenant on 7 March 1915, and lieutenant on 1 July 1917, his MC for bravery was gazetted on 28 August 1916, whilst serving in France with his regiment. Transferring to the RFC in February 1917, he joined 22 Squadron. Claiming a handful of victories as an observer, he gained his pilot's "wings" in March 1918.

◆ ◆ ◆

---

[388] Royal Flying Corps Communiqués 1915-1916, pp.305-6.
[389] *Sweeping the Skies*, p.19.
[390] Thanks to www.theaerodrome.com/forum/.

DAY, Oliver Leonard, was born on 2 July 1890 at Cowes, Isle of Wight where, in due course, he became an engine turner. At the age of 23 years, 5' 5½" tall and weighing 114 lbs., he enlisted on 10 October 1913 as a direct entrant in the RFC, Service no. 902. He went to France with No. 2 Squadron as a 2AM, in charge of 'B' Flight's workshop lorry.

A Delahaye workshop vehicle, a type used by No. 2 Squadron

Day achieved steady promotion during the war – 1AM on 15 September 1914; Corporal, 1 October 1915 (with 16 Squadron); Sergeant, 1 March 1916 (16 Squadron); Flight Sergeant, 1 July 1916 (40 Squadron); Acting Warrant Officer, 1 April 1917 (48 (Reserve) Squadron), having returned to England on 21 February 1917, where he remained until 9 October 1921.

At the start of the Second World War, he was commissioned as a pilot officer (no. 74751) on probation in the RAF's A&SD Branch. As at 1 March 1942 he was promoted flight lieutenant.

He died in Derbyshire on 10 August 1969.

♦ ♦ ♦

DUNN, Frederick George. "Dusty" Dunn, born on 19 October 1894 at Wylam-on-Tyne, learnt to fly at the Deperdussin School at Hendon in mid-July 1913, before switching to the Blériot School, also at Hendon. He was awarded RAeC certificate no. 728 on 23 January 1914, and became an instructor at Hendon.

Enlisting on 8 August 1914, with Service number 1372, he served, briefly, as a sergeant pilot with a 6 Squadron detachment at Newcastle-on-Tyne (near his home), before transferring to the Reserve Aeroplane Squadron, and being posted to 3 Squadron on 3 October 1914. Commissioned second lieutenant on 27 April 1915, he was promoted captain on 1 December 1915. He was awarded the AFC on 7 November 1918, but was killed in a flying accident on 26 May 1919. He was co-pilot of the prototype Tarrant *Tabor*, RAF serial F1765, on its test flight when pilot error caused it to tip onto its nose. Captain P.T. Rawlings DSC, the other pilot, was killed instantly. Dunn died in hospital on 28 May 1919, having never regained consciousness.

♦ ♦ ♦

FINERAN, George, was born in Newcastle-upon-Tyne on 21 August 1884. On 11 November 1911 he married Jessie Collins, and they had two children, Martha Ena, born 5 April 1912, and Michael George Robert, born 29 September 1913. When war came, leaving his family, he enlisted in the RFC at South Farnborough on 10 October 1914 with Service no. 1764. Posted to 5 Squadron, he went to France on 2 April 1915, and was promoted corporal on 1 June 1915, and to sergeant on 1 January 1916, still on 5 Squadron. Sent for pilot training at the Military School, Ruislip, he was awarded RAeC certificate no. 3746 on 19 October 1916, and was graded 1st Class pilot on 12 December 1916.

Effective from 19 September 1917 he was discharged, 'his services being no longer required having been appointed as a Temporary 2nd Lieut on the General List.' In October 1917, he was made a Flying Officer. He served on 62 Squadron in administration before being obliged to resign his commission 'on account of ill-health' in August 1918, and was granted the honorary rank of Second Lieutenant.[391] He died on 26 June 1942 at the Bolingbroke Hospital, Battersea, London, leaving his estate to his widow, Jessie.

♦ ♦ ♦

FLETCHER, Albert Harry Victor, was born in Durban, South Africa, on 24 May 1893. Taking his RAeC test on a Grahame-White biplane at RNAS Chingford, he was awarded certificate no. 2853 on 10 May 1916. Awarded a pension for his wounds, he died in Durban on 25 June 1948.

♦ ♦ ♦

FOOT, Ernest Leslie. Major Ernest Leslie Foot MC, born 18 May 1895, was serving as a lieutenant in the Ox & Bucks Light Infantry when he was seconded to the RFC. Awarded RAeC certificate no. 2257 on 20 December 1915, he was posted to No. 11 Squadron, and scored three victories.

Having transferred to 60 Squadron, he was shot down in flames on 26 October 1916 in Nieuport 17, no. A.162, by the German pilot Leutnant Hans Imelmann,[392] as noted in RFC Communiqué No. 59: 'An attack made by a patrol of 60 Sqn dispersed a German formation. As a result of the engagement 2 of our Nieuports had forced landings in our lines and a third is missing. The German formation, consisting of 6 machines, attacked and brought down a B.E.2c over Serre. Capt Foot, 60 Sqn, dived at the leader, but was too late to assist the B.E.2c. Capt Foot's Nieuport was considerably shot about, his gun-mounting was

---

[391] *The London Gazettes,* 6 Oct 1917, no. 30325; 6 Aug 1918, no. 30831; 3 Sep 1918, no. 30881.
[392] Hans Imelmann (14 May 1897–23 Jan 1917) was credited with six aerial victories. He is not to be confused with Max Immelmann (21 Sep 1890– 8 Jun 1916), Germany's first "ace" of the war.

put out of action, and he only just succeeded in recrossing the lines. He landed with his machine on fire.'[393]

With 60 Squadron, he scored his fourth and fifth victories, soon afterwards being awarded the MC: 'For conspicuous skill and gallantry. When flying a single-seater scout, he dived on to five hostile machines, which were flying at about 2,500 feet, and drove one to the ground as a wreck. On many other occasions he has shown great determination when fighting enemy machines.'[394]

Following a spell of rest in England, he joined No. 56 Squadron as a Flight Commander on 10 March 1917. On 6 April, however, the night before he was due to return to France, he had a car accident, and was out of front-line service for the rest of the war, though able to serve as an instructor at No. 1 School of Special Flying, Gosport.

After the war he flew for Handley Page on the London-Paris passenger route, but left in April 1923 to become a test pilot for the Bristol company. His luck ran out on 23 June 1923 when he crashed in the only Bristol M.1D monoplane, during the Grosvenor Cup Race, and was killed instantly. 'Leslie Foot was very popular and one of the most competent aerobatic pilots in the country'.[395]

♦ ♦ ♦

FULTON, **John Duncan Bertie**, was born in San Francisco, USA, on 23 July 1876. As a Gentleman Cadet at the RMA, Sandhurst, he was commissioned in the RA on 21 March 1896. Serving throughout the Second Boer War he was awarded both the Queen's and King's Medals with eight clasps, and was twice Mentioned in Dispatches. He was promoted captain on 25 March 1902 (ante-dated to 27 January 1902).

In early 1910 he bought a Grahame-White Blériot-type monoplane from the proceeds of patents for the improvement of field-guns and, in that year, while his battery was stationed at Bulford, Wiltshire, continued to fly and to experiment at his own expense at nearby Lark Hill, Salisbury Plain. He kept his machine in a shed that had been built for the Hon. C.S. Rolls who,

---

[393] Royal Flying Corps Communiqués 1915-1916, pp.295-6.
[394] *The London Gazette*, 14 Nov 1916, no. 29824.
[395] Bristol Aircraft since 1910, p.165.

prior to his death on 12 July 1910, had never used it. He was awarded RAeC certificate no. 27 on 15 November 1910.

On 1 April 1911, with the formation of the Army's Air Battalion, Bertie Fulton was given command of No. 2 (Aeroplane) Company.

During October and November 1911, he travelled to France with Major Frederick (later Sir Frederick) Sykes visiting Reims, and other aerodromes. A direct result of their visit was the organization of squadrons and aerodromes of the RFC. In December 1911, he became the first British officer to secure the Special Flying Certificate of the RAeC, and only the third overall, for which the tests consisted of a 100-mile cross-country flight, a 1,000-foot altitude flight, and a *vol plané*, with engine completely stopped, from 500 feet.

In May 1912, when the Central Flying School was formed, he was appointed to it as Instructor, graded as Squadron Commander. When the Aeronautical Inspection Department, a division of the Military Aeronautics section of the War Office, came into being in December 1913, he was appointed Chief Inspector, and was made a CB in the 1914 New Year's Honours list.[396]

On 31 October 1915 Major Fulton (temporary lieutenant-colonel) was promoted to Assistant Director of Military Aeronautics, retaining his rank. Less than a fortnight later, in his office on the morning of 11 November 1915 feeling unwell, he went to see a doctor, who told him that an immediate operation on his throat was necessary. A second doctor was called in consultation, but neither could prevent Fulton's the death that same evening, at the age of only 39, of one of Britain's most highly-rated airmen.

A moving tribute was paid to him by his friend, Charles Grey, editor of *The Aeroplane*: 'Whether on duty or off Colonel Fulton possessed one of the most winning personalities ever given to man. The gentleness of his manner deceived some people into believing that he was not a strong man, but when they came up against him mentally or physically they found how strong he really was ... One of the best tests of an officer is the way in which he is regarded by his men, and Colonel Fulton's men, whether Gunners, R.F.C. mechanics or A.I.D. inspectors, worshipped him.' (*The Aeroplane*, 17 November 1915). (Charles Grey's obituary ran to two pages.)

♦ ♦ ♦

---

[396] Courtesy of, and from, http://britishaviation-ptp.com/early_aviators_1_50.html.

GARLAND, Ewart James, was born in Toronto, Canada, on 29 January 1897, but his father, on appointment as head of the Australian Dunlop Rubber company, took his family to Melbourne, Australia.

Ewart was a private in the Inns of Court OTC when he was commissioned temporary second lieutenant for duty with the RFC on 29 March 1916. Trained as a pilot at No 2 School of Instruction, Oxford, he was awarded RAeC certificate no. 3672 on 7 July 1916, and was made a flying officer, temporary second lieutenant, in the RFC, General List, as at 26 July.[397] Eight days later he had joined No. 10 Squadron.

On 31 July 1916 his BE2c aeroplane was hit by an anti-aircraft shell when he and his observer, Second Lieutenant F.H. Bickerton, were on an artillery patrol. Bickerton was wounded by a splinter in the shoulder, but Garland escaped unhurt.

On 20 October 1916, Garland crashed his BE2c on landing after a night-flying exercise, but again escaped unhurt. After a short spell of leave he returned to France in March 1917 to find that he had been posted to 16 Squadron.

A few weeks later, having been promoted to flight commander on 27 April 1917 and been given the rank of temporary captain whilst so employed, with effect from 7 April,[398] he was posted back to 10 Squadron as flight commander of 'A' Flight. Mentioned in Despatches on 15 May 1917, he was sent "home" for a rest, and found himself posted to Andover as an instructor.

He returned to France in 1918 with 104 Squadron, crossing to St. Omer on 19 May 1918. Equipped with the DH9 bomber, 104 Squadron joined the VIII Brigade bomber force, forerunner of the Independent Force, on 6 June 1918. 104 spent the rest of the war on long-distance raids into Germany. Such was the opposition, and consequent casualties, on these raids that the squadron had to reform three times before being disbanded in June 1919.

On 3 June 1919, Captain E.J. Garland RAF was awarded the DFC. On 25 June 1919, he was transferred to the Unemployed List.[399] He died at Chichester on 7 March 1985.

◆ ◆ ◆

---

[397] *The London Gazettes*, 29 Mar 1916, & 26 Jul 1916, no. 29682.
[398] *The London Gazette*, 27 Apr 1917, no. 30038.
[399] *The London Gazettes*, 3 Jun 1919, no. 31378; & 1 July 1919, no. 31427.

GOSS, Leonard Sidney. 1391 2AM Goss, who woke the sleeping Robert during the storm in September 1914, was born on 27 March 1893. He was a "motor tester" when he enlisted in the RFC at South Farnborough on 10 August 1914. Two days later he was serving with No. 3 Squadron in France.

He was still serving with 3 Squadron when, on 19 September 1917, he was killed in action. By then he was a corporal observer, having been promoted from 1AM on 1 December 1916. His death was not officially reported until published in a German List by the Red Cross, Geneva, on 29 November 1917.

He was flying with his pilot, Lieutenant Edgar Golding, in a Morane Parasol (Type P), serial no. A234 on a training flight to practise formation flying with another Parasol, no. A6655, with Lieutenants Cuthbert Archibald Sutcliffe and Thomas Humble. They were under strict orders not to cross the lines, but it is likely that the prevailing, strong westerly wind blew them into the clutches of two fighter pilots of the German's Jasta 5. Both aircraft crashed near Caudry. Golding was killed in the crash and Goss died shortly afterwards of his wounds. The others became prisoners of war.[400]

♦ ♦ ♦

GREGORY, Robert, (photo courtesy Nancy Wright) was the son of Sir William Gregory, formerly Member of Parliament for Co. Galway, and Governor of Ceylon, and of Lady Isabella Augusta Gregory, the well-known dramatist and writer on Irish folklore, and sometime friend of the poet W.B. Yeats.[401] Robert, born at Coole Park, County Galway, Ireland, on 20 May 1881, was educated at Harrow, Oxford University and the Slade School of Art. He was a fine athlete and boxer, and was well known as a cricketer (he played for Ireland) and as a fearless rider in the hunting field and in point-to-point races.

On 26 September 1907 he married Lily Margaret Graham-Parry, a fellow student at the Slade, and four years his junior, at St. Mary Magdalene Church, Paddington, London. Best-man was Augustus John. Robert then worked in Paris at the design studio of Jacques Émile Blanche, who declared that his work "had reached the highest level of artistic and intellectual merit." (*The Aeroplane*, 13 February 1918). Robert and Margaret would have three children.

---

[400] Thanks to www.airwar19141918.wordpress.com/tag/3-squadron-rfc/.
[401] Yeats wrote four poems about Gregory between 1918 and 1921, including *An Irish Airman Foresees His Death*.

Robert was commissioned in the 4th Battalion Connaught Rangers in the autumn of 1913, and in January 1916 began his training for the R.F.C. On 12 July 1916, when a Second Lieutenant on probation, he was made a Flying Officer w.e.f. 6 July 1916. Initially he flew coastal patrols off Dover before going to France, and to 40 Squadron, in August 1916.

On 25 September 1916, while escorting a bombing raid by 25 Squadron, he was shot down by anti-aircraft fire. Though his aeroplane was wrecked, Robert walked away unhurt. He was promoted flight commander in January 1917, and squadron commander shortly after. On 9 March 1917, still with 40 Squadron, he and his squadron were ambushed by Manfred von Richthofen and his "Red Circus". Four F.E.8s were shot down. Three of the pilots were taken prisoner while the fourth managed to crash behind his own lines. Every F.E.8 of the rest of the squadron was damaged, 'most of them seriously.'[402]

Robert personally evened the score a little on 30 March 1917 when, on a line patrol in Nieuport Scout A6680, he attacked two Halberstadts which he saw 3,000 feet below flying among the clouds. Diving down from 15,000 feet he attacked, hitting one of them at close range (down to only fifteen yards): 'H.A. turned over and was last seen side-slipping into a cloud near Bailleul.'[403]

On 8 June 1917 Robert, 'the last of those who had flown to France in August 1916, was farewelled.'[404] He was rewarded for his actions on 40 Squadron with the Military Cross, on 18 July 1917, 'for conspicuous gallantry and devotion to duty. On many occasions he has, at various altitudes, attacked and destroyed or driven down hostile machines, and has invariably displayed the highest courage and skill.' Also in July 1917, the French conferred on him the *Croix de Chevalier* of the *Légion d'Honneur* for 'many acts of conspicuous bravery.'

Promotion from Sec. Lt. (temp. Capt.) to temp. Major followed on 31 August 1917, thus making him a Squadron Commander w.e.f. 6 July 1917. In October 1917 he was given command of 66 Squadron in France. The squadron moved to the Italian front in November.

On 23 January 1918 Robert was flying Camel no. B2475 near Monasterio when, at 2,000 feet, the aircraft went into a spin, and dived into the ground with engine full on. No. 762 Driver Frederick Louis Burns wrote a draft memoire about the squadron, in which he said: 'I heard that the C.O. had been inoculated not long before his last flight and that he should not have flown so soon afterwards. The theory was that he had fainted and lost control.'[405]

♦ ♦ ♦

---

[402] *Sweeping the Skies*, p.27.
[403] TNA file AIR 1/1222/204/5/2634/6.
[404] *Sweeping the Skies*, p.34.
[405] www.greatwarforum.org/ quoting from RAF Museum file DC73/104/7.

HAMEL, Gustav Wilhelm was born in Hamburg, Germany on 25 June 1889 to German parents, Gustav Hugo, a doctor, born in Hamburg on 12 December 1861, and Hedwig. Sometime before the 1901 Census Dr. Hamel moved with his family to London, the Census showing them – father, mother and four children – as "Foreign Aliens". On 1 February 1910, Dr. Hamel, now a well-known doctor, became a "Naturalised British Subject",[406] with the 1911 Census showing all the family as naturalised British subjects living at The Hermitage, Portsmouth Road, Kingston-upon-Thames, Surrey.

After Westminster School, young Gustav would become one of the foremost aviators in Britain prior to the war in 1914. Having learnt to fly at Pau in the south of France during the winter of 1910-1911, he returned to the Grahame-White school at Hendon, where he 'borrowed a Blériot … and proceeded to demonstrate his masterly touch.' Flying one of the early Morane-Borel monoplanes, he was awarded RAeC certificate no. 64 on 14 February 1911 (the RAeC incorrectly noting on their index card that he been born in London). He was soon winning races, and was in such demand that much of his time was spent in giving flying demonstrations across the country. He had a bad crash in a truncated Blériot – its wing-tips had been removed – in July 1911 in the Gordon Bennett Race. In that year, too, he would hold the 5 and 10 kilometre World's Records, and was one of the pilots to carry air mail between Hendon and Windsor in September. He would also cross the English Channel four times during 1912.

He survived a nasty accident at Bangor, North Wales, on 12 March 1913 when, over a clump of trees, his aeroplane 'dropped like a stone some 50 or 60 feet. He managed to keep the machine square, switched off, and pancaked straight on to the chassis, which was wiped out without doing much damage to anything else. Mr. Hamel escaped with a few scratches on his legs.' A fortnight later, on 27 March, he had a strange experience when flying from Dover to France. With a favourable wind behind his 70 mph Blériot he expected to make it across in a fast time. The flight began rapidly as expected but, hitting a fog bank, though the engine continued to hum sweetly, his speed fell away to next to nothing as he realised when crawling past fishing boats heading the same way. Clearing the fog, normal service was resumed. He made another crossing on 10 April – his tenth.

---

[406] Dr Hamel, born in Hamburg to Albrecht Wilhelm and Hedwig Hamel, died on 3 May 1922. His widow, Caroline Magdalena Elise Hamel (née Neves), died in London on 13 Feb 1960.

Gustav Wilhelm Hamel standing in front cockpit

When not Channel-hopping, he regularly flew Miss Trehawke-Davies in her two-seater Blériot. On 17 April, with a Mr Dupree as passenger, he flew all the way from Dover to Cologne, Germany, a distance of some 290 miles. *The Aeroplane* wrote on 24 April 1913, not altogether accurately, of young Gustav: 'Mr. Hamel's fine performance on April 17th [1913] has a certain poetic justice about it. Mr. Hamel is an Englishman by birth and education, but he is a Schleswiger by parentage, and the Schleswig provinces are to the Scandinavian race what Alsace and Lorraine are to France, so it is somewhat fitting that a Schleswig Englishman should teach us a lesson as to the possibilities of Teutonic aggression by making a non-stop flight from England to Germany.'

In August 1913, flying over Workington, Cumberland with his mechanic, Monsieur Gondre, they were blown out to sea. So strong was the wind that Hamel had to land on the shore, his Blériot absolutely undamaged.

After Frenchman Pierre Chanteloup had been the first man ever to have looped-the-loop, in September 1913, towards the end of 1913 it became a race to see which British pilot would be first to do it. The honour fell to B.C. Hucks, in France on 16 November, with Hamel succeeding on 26 December 1913. The "upside-down dinner" (see page 189 above) was held for them on 16 January 1914.

Gustav, brilliant aviator though he was, had had his fair share of accidents and mishaps over the past few years but, on Saturday, 23 May 1914, he suffered his greatest and final crash while returning from France with a new aeroplane. Leaving Hardelot at 12.15 pm, he was never seen again.

'On Sunday Commander Samson, R.N., on Short seaplane 140, and Lieut. Brodribb, R.N., on Maurice Farman seaplane No. 72, flew to Dover to assist in looking for Mr. Hamel. No. 72 was wrecked off the pier at Dover, and No. 140 was brought down by engine trouble, and damaged when being handled by an attendant destroyer. (*The Aeroplane*, 28 May 1914).

An extensive search for him was called-off on Tuesday, 26 May, when the Admiralty issued this statement: 'It has been decided to suspend the searching operations by flotillas and aircraft which have been in progress for the last 48 hours for Mr Gustav Hamel.

'In relinquishing this quest the Admiralty desire to place on record their recognition of the services rendered to British aviation by the missing airman. He was without question the foremost exponent in these islands of an art whose military consequence is continually increasing...'

♦ ♦ ♦

HARTREE, **Alan**, was born on 22 December 1887 at Lewisham, Kent. Educated at a school at Hurstleigh, Bishop's Down, in Tunbridge Wells, he was commissioned in the RFA on 9 December 1911, and not long after began flying tuition at the Bristol School, Lark Hill, Salisbury Plain. On 14 May 1912 he was awarded RAeC certificate no. 214, and continued flying at Lark Hill with the RFC contingent, his flying skills being improved at the CFS, Upavon in June and July 1912.

He nevertheless found the time on Friday, 16 August 1912, during the Military Aeroplane Competition, to act as wicket-keeper in an impromptu game of cricket. To 'while away the time M. Védrines went into Amesbury and bought some small cricket stumps and a ball, and, with a Deperdussin skid as bat, defied the world to bowl him out. However, the feat was accomplished by Mr. Harold Perrin, secretary of the Royal Aero Club, and general *factotum pro tem*, to the Judges' Committee. Mr. Cody at point and Lieut. Hartree as wicket-keeper added materially to the joy of the proceedings.'

On 21 December 1912 Second Lieutenant Alan Hartree, Royal Artillery, was appointed to the Reserve, Royal Flying Corps, Military Wing, and with effect from 3 May 1914 was transferred 'from the Reserve, to be a Flying Officer, and to be seconded' to the Royal Flying Corps, Military Wing.[407]

The caption to this photograph reads: 'Aviators at Play: Mme. Védrines batting; M. Védrines bowling; Lieut. Hartree, R.F.A., wicket-keeping; Mr. Cody and Mr. Perrin fielding.' (The Aeroplane, 22 August 1912).

---

[407] *The London Gazette*, 19 May 1914.

With war imminent, Alan's marriage was announced: 'A marriage has been arranged, and will shortly take place, between Second Lieut. Alan Hartree, Royal Flying Corps, fourth son of Mr. and Mrs. Hartree, of Havering, Tunbridge Wells, and Gladys, only daughter of the late Mr. James Henderson and of Mrs. Buchanan Hughes, of Berlin.' (*The Aeroplane*, 8 July 1914).

Although he crossed to France with No. 3 Squadron in August 1914, he appears to have made few headlines in the aerial conflict over the next few weeks, probably having reverted to his "parent" regiment, the Royal Artillery. Ending the war as a captain (temp. major) he was awarded the MC on 3 June 1919.[408] He died on 10 March 1930 at Quetta, Bengal, India, whilst a major in the 24th Indian Mountain Brigade, RA.

♦ ♦ ♦

HAY, John ("Jack"), born at Double Bay, Sydney, New South Wales, Australia, on 22 January 1889, came to England and learnt to fly at the Military School, Gosport. Awarded RAeC certificate no. 3039 on 2 June 1916, he went to France with 40 Squadron in August 1916.

On 23 January 1917, in F.E.8 no. 6388, Hay shot down two German aeroplanes, as reported in RFC Communiqué No. 72: '2nd Lt J Hay, No. 40 Squadron, engaged a hostile machine over La Bassée. The wings were seen to break away from the German machine before it crashed. 2nd Lt Hay then attacked and destroyed the leading machine of a formation of eight. He was then brought down himself and killed.' One of the two victories was gained in the morning, the other on a second flight in the afternoon, when he met his death.

Jack Hay was von Richthofen's seventeenth victory, as the latter reported: 'About 1610 I attacked, together with seven of my planes, enemy squadron, west of Lens. The plane I had singled out caught fire after 150 shots, fired from a distance of 50 metres. The plane fell, burning. Occupant fell out of plane at 500 metres height.'

Hay, with no parachute, no doubt chose a quick death, rather than being burnt in the aircraft. His body, recovered from no man's land under shell fire by two Canadian soldiers, was buried at Aire-sur-la Lys Communal Cemetery, France. One of the Canadians later

---

[408] *The London Gazette*, no. 31373.

wrote 'to Hay's mother in Australia, saying, "I had to bring him in alive or dead; he put up such a magnificent fight."'[409]

Robert, as Jack Hay's commanding officer, wrote on 23 January 1917 to his parents in Australia: 'During a patrol this morning at about 10.15, Lieutenant Hay shot down an enemy biplane, which was seen to crash. In the course of another patrol at about 2.45 p.m. he was seen by two brother officers to shoot down another enemy machine which fell in flames. Later in the same patrol, however, the three officers were attacked by five enemy planes, one of whom shot down Lieutenant Hay, who fell just one side of the line. He was absolutely fearless in his devotion to duty, and his work was uniformly splendid. I have never had a finer officer, and he will be a great loss to the squadron, by whom he was universally beloved.'

Lieutenant St. S. Bell, who shared Lieutenant Hay's quarters, also wrote: 'I witnessed his last great fight – his skill and courage were wonderful. Next day I had the honour of helping carry him to his grave.'

Chaplain D. Burnholm Fraser added, sugaring the bitter pill: 'Though I did not know him personally I have been told by several of the squadron that, apart from his courage and skill, Lieutenant Hay was the best man there. One boy told me they all worshipped him and said: "I don't say that because he is gone, because we often said it while he was with us." He was in no way disfigured by the fall, and there was a full muster of officers and men to show their esteem for him.'[410]

♦ ♦ ♦

HEMMING, Harold, was born in Tooting, London, on 27 March 1894 to Robert, a 'gentleman's hosier' and 'employer', and to Ada Hemming. Educated at Oundle School, he was granted a commission as temporary second lieutenant in the Worcestershire Regiment, and was attached to the RFC as an Observer as of 14 December 1915. In June 1916 he underwent pilot training, and was awarded RAeC certificate no. 3226 on 17 July 1916, qualifying at the Military School, Hounslow on a B.E.2c.

After several months in training squadrons – 31 (Reserve) and 64 (Training) – he joined 103 Squadron on 16 October 1917 and then 109 Squadron on 8 December 1917. On 12 March 1918 he was posted to No. 1 School

---

[409] Quoted in *Sweeping the Skies*, p.24.
[410] Quotes from the *Sydney Morning Herald*, 2 April 1917, in oa.anu.edu.au/obituary/hay-john-jack-1217.

of Navigation and Bombing at Stonehenge, being made a temporary major on 1 July 1918. He was awarded the AFC on 1 January 1919.

In July 1919 he was posted to 274 Squadron at Bircham Newton in north Norfolk flying the large, 4-engined Handley Page V/1500 and was granted a Short Service Commission in the rank of flight lieutenant on 24 October 1919.

In June 1923, having attended a refresher course at the de Havilland Flying School, his flying was assessed as 'extremely good in all respects.' He then entered the 1923 Aerial Derby, held at Croydon on Bank Holiday Monday, 6 August, in DH37 G-EBDO "Sylvia", but was forced to retire from the race on the second lap, landing at Romford, Essex. He would pilot this aircraft on a number of occasions over the forthcoming years. Given a new engine, re-categorised as a DH37A and re-named "Lois" it tragically came to grief on 4 June 1927 during testing of the new engine for the High Power Handicap at Ensbury Park Racecourse, Bournemouth. The aeroplane crashed through the racecourse number board, and the two on board, Hemming and a passenger, 24-year-old Claude St John Plevins, were rushed to hospital. *Flight* (9 June 1927) wrote: 'No bones were apparently broken, but Major Hemming [Managing Director of the Aircraft Operating Company] received injuries to head and face, and it is gathered that there is considerable risk that he may lose the sight of one eye.' This did indeed prove to be the case for Hemming but young Plevins, born on 26 March 1903, died that same day.

Hemming relinquished his RAF commission on 4 June 1931, being 'permitted to retain rank' (flight lieutenant). During the Second World War he was granted a commission in the rank of Wing Commander in class CC of the RAF's Reserve of Air Force Officers, General Duties Branch, as of 1 June 1940. He was then granted an honorary commission on 5 February 1941 as a Wing Commander, at the same time relinquishing his commission in class CC on appointment to his honorary commission in the Royal Air Force Volunteer Reserve.

He married Julia Margaret Owen Jones at Brompton, London, on 10 February 1917. Their daughter, Patricia Joan, born in Salisbury on 2 November 1918, who would serve in the WAAF in the Second World War, died on 15 March 2013. Harold died on 25 May 1956 at St. Bartholomew's Hospital, London.

♦ ♦ ♦

HENDERSON, Kenneth Selby, was born in Longreach, Queensland, Australia on 7 May 1894. Enlisting as Private No. 156 in "C" Squadron, 5th Australian Light Horse Regiment, on 1 October 1914, (attesting on 30 November), he was promoted to lance-corporal on 9 August 1915. He was with his regiment at Gallipoli when he contracted enteritis on 12 September, and then diarrhoea and dysentery, and was taken to St. Patrick's Hospital, Malta, on 16 September 1915 aboard the French hospital ship *Gascon*. On 27 September he sailed on the hospital ship HMT *Koroola* to 3rd West General Hospital, Cardiff, Wales, where he arrived on 5 October.

Discharged on 24 November 1915 to the RFC 'for tuition in aviation at Brooklands', he was granted four weeks leave before attending the flying course at the Military School, Brooklands. He was awarded RAeC certificate no. 2302 on 18 January 1916, and, with effect from 25 November, was gazetted temporary second lieutenant for duty with the RFC.[411]

Finishing his flying training at RFC Beaulieu on 5 May 1916, he was rudely informed that, by taking his discharge in England from the Australian Imperial Force, 'you forfeit all claims to a free passage to Australia, now or at any time hereafter.' No free passage would be needed, for Henderson was killed in action at around 4.30 p.m. on 2 June 1918 near Bailleul when flying S.E.5a no. C1113, No. 1 Squadron (re C1113, see Rigby, page 386.)

◆ ◆ ◆

HEWITT, Vivian Vaughan Davies was born in Grimsby, Lincolnshire on 11 March 1888 to Titus Henry Hewitt, one of an extremely wealthy Lincolnshire brewing family, and Julia (née Morris), who were married in Altrincham, Cheshire in 1886. After Vivian's birth the family moved to Llandrillo yn Rhos and then to Rhyl where William, Vivian's younger brother, was born in 1898. By 1901 they had moved to The Warren at Bodfari, Trefnant, Denbighshire, in North Wales, Julia Hewitt's family home.

After Harrow School Vivian, keen on engineering, was employed for four years (c. 1905-08) by the London & North

---

[411] *The London Gazette*, 29 Jan 1916.

Western Railway Company at their Crewe Railway works, apprenticed to the famous engineer George Wale.

The family's next move was to Windsor Terrace, Hampstead, London NW, where Titus died on 15 December 1910 at the age of 47, leaving a thirty-eight-year-old widow and two sons.

It was whilst living at The Warren, however, that Vivian constructed a large model glider and flew it around the village. After his apprenticeship, he pursued his interest in aeroplanes and in '1909 he rented shed No. 18 at Brooklands and along with two companions went into business servicing and driving racing cars, as well as learning the rudiments of flying.'

His first aeroplane was an Antoinette, a gift from his very wealthy uncle Thomas William Good Hewitt, of Weelsby Old Hall, Great Grimsby, Lincolnshire. Finding the aeroplane rather underpowered and unsatisfactory, however, he 'persuaded his uncle to replace it with a 25 hp Blériot at a cost of £1100.'[412] It may well have been this aeroplane in which he claimed to have been the first person to have flown in North Wales in May 1910.

After the untimely death of his father at the end of 1910, Vivian returned to North Wales, and 'soon moved into a house, Holmfield, 21 West Kinmel Street, Rhyl, where he met a Mrs. Parry who became his housekeeper and who played a great part in his later life.'

In February 1911, he bought a Blériot with a 50 hp Gnôme engine. Needing somewhere to keep it, he acquired a piece of land near Abergele, Conwy and called the place Foryd aerodrome, the address that he gave to the RAeC when later qualifying at Rhyl for his certificate, no. 302, on 1 October 1912. On his land he erected a 'hangar, complete with an extremely well-appointed workshop'. *The Aeroplane* reported on 10 April 1913 that it 'is one of the most adequately equipped work-shops in the country.' In it 'there is a power-driven lathe, a shaper drill, and a grindstone, besides a big equipment of tools. The works do their own nickel-plating, re-magnetise their magnetos, and make their own electric light. Three mechanics are generally employed.'

His hour of glory, though, had come on 26 April 1912 when, the petrol tank of his Blériot filled with Shell motor spirit, he flew across the Irish Sea from Penrhôs to Phoenix Park, Dublin in one hour fifteen minutes, succeeding where Robert Loraine had so nearly succeeded in September 1910. (See also details of Denys Corbett Wilson's crossing to Ireland (page 327)).

From Foryd he 'made many flights, becoming a regular sight in the skies of Rhyl',[413] but on Tuesday, 16 July 1912, 'he flew round Rhyl, Abergele, Prestatyn, Rhuddlan, and St. Asaph... When landing switched off at 500 ft., but, misjudging strength of wind, found that

---

[412] This and previous quote from *Pioneers, Showmen and the RFC*, p.74.
[413] Early Aviation in North Wales, p.24.

Vivian Hewitt in his reconstructed Blériot at Foryd [photo: The Aeroplane]

machine would just hit wire fence at edge of aerodrome… and wheels struck about middle of fence. Fortunately, fence posts were rotten, and lay down flat, so that no damage whatever was done to machine.' (*The Aeroplane*, 25 July 1912).

In early 1913 he was 'getting ready for the coming season. Entirely new wings have been fitted to his Blériot and new wing stays throughout. The warping gear, which was originally of aluminium, has been replaced by steel made in Mr. Hewitt's own work shop, and a number of other stronger fittings have been fitted. Mr. Hewitt has, unfortunately, been unable to work for the last seven weeks owing to jumping off a wall, and, as he puts it, "breaking everything in his foot except the bones."' (*The Aeroplane*, 16 January 1913).

On Thursday, 1 May 1913. 'Foryd, N. Wales. Mr. Vivian Hewitt 1¼ hrs on re-built Blériot over Rhyl at 2,000 ft; then flew to Mostyn, circling iron works, then to Holywell in rain very fast with wind behind. Rough passage near Prestatyn owing to mountains, but landed safely. The wind treacherous at Foryd suddenly getting up to about 40 m.p.h. from dead calm.' (*The Aeroplane*, 8 May 1913).

Vivian intended that his flying exhibitions would bring pleasure to those on the ground, and some entrepreneurs were grateful for the increased business that they brought, as he noted: 'There is an old man in Rhyl who comes to me after every flight with a hen's egg and says, "One of my little hens has presented me with an egg. Will you kindly accept it, Mr. Hewitt?"'

Vivian flew only occasionally in the summer and autumn of 1913, leading to rumours that he had given up flying. A considerable stir was therefore caused in Rhyl and the surrounding district on Wednesday 22 October by his reappearance on his rebuilt Blériot. Flying for forty minutes he found, almost for the first time on record, that the air was quite steady. (*The Aeroplane*, 30 October 1913).

So rare was aviation in North Wales that *The Aeroplane* (27 November 1913) reported: 'Apparently there is no word for "aviator" in Welsh, for recently the local coalman, talking to the landlady of Mr. Vivian Hewitt, at Foryd, asked in Welsh, "Does the man of the wind live here?" On being answered in the affirmative he asked, "When is he going to blow again?"'

He continued to fly occasionally in 1914: 'On Tuesday of last week Mr. Vivian Hewitt flew on his re-built Blériot for about an hour round about Rhyl, and went up the Vale of Clwyd as far as Rhuddlan and back. On Thursday he was up again over Rhyl for 1½ hrs., and also went over to Abergele, about five miles from Rhyl. The next day he was up again for one hour, and had as passenger a small black lamb, this being, no doubt, the first time that a lamb has been carried in an aeroplane.' (*Flight*, Saturday, 4 April 1914).

During the war, with Foryd aerodrome closed, Vivian offered his services to the Royal Naval Air Service. Medically unfit for front-line duties, he was based at Farnborough, where he tested Admiralty aeroplanes. In view of his future involvement with the American Curtiss company, it is to be wondered whether he was employed in testing Curtiss aeroplanes whilst at Farnborough, as six Curtiss JN-3 two-seater tractor biplanes were delivered to the RNAS in March 1915. Also in that year, the Admiralty placed an order with Curtiss for two hundred landplanes and fifty flying-boats, deliveries of which began in the middle of the year.

For reasons that are unclear, but no doubt Curtiss connected, Vivian sailed to the USA on the *Saxonia*, arriving in New York on 25 August 1915 and, having returned to Britain, sailed back to the USA on the *Cameronia* on 17 November 1915, arriving in New York on 7 December 1915. This time he went on 'Inspectional duties.' In the meantime, with effect from 18 November 1915, he was appointed Lieutenant (Temp.) in the RNVR, and was eventually seconded to the Ministry of Munitions. He was again sent to the USA, arriving in New York on 4

(Left): Vivian Hewitt, and Blériot monoplane, at Rhyl, ready to make a crossing of the Irish Sea, April 1912; (right) with black lamb, at Rhyl, April 1914.

Bryn Aber, Cemlyn Bay, Anglesey [photo via www.dailypost.co.uk]

January 1917, his final destination being the Curtiss Aeroplane Company, Buffalo, in New York State. His occupation was given as Engineer – he had helped to develop techniques for the accurate firing of machine guns from moving aircraft – but on a second visit in June 1917 he was an Aeroplane Inspector.

In January 1918, whilst testing a Curtiss biplane, he landed on a ploughed field next to the runway. On impact he was thrown forward, and was concussed when his head hit the instrument panel. Following hospitalization, he was advised that he might be prone to blackouts, and so was forced to end his flying days. Advised to put his skills and knowledge to less dangerous pursuits he was, by March 1918, in Virginia, USA testing eighty-foot-long motor launches (*Modest Millionaire*, William Hywel, 1973).

After his uncle Tom died on 9 May 1930 (born 1857) (his estate was valued at £951,580) Vivian inherited the brewery in Pasture Street and the Palace Theatre (both in Grimsby), over 300 pubs, hotels, parts of Grimsby docks, land, Weelsby Old Hall, and a considerable sum of money. When the brewery became a public limited company in 1934, he sold his interest for £1,250,000, which yielded him an enormous income of some £50,000 a year.

In 1930 he bought Bryn Aber, a house at Cemlyn Bay on the north coast of Anglesey. The story goes that the high wall that surrounds the property was built at his behest to give employment during the Depression but, a passionate amateur ornithologist, he had it built as a windbreak in the hope that wild birds would be attracted to the nearly four acres of grounds, in effect a bird sanctuary.

He was also able to indulge his passion for collecting birds' eggs and bird skins, and it is estimated that, by the time he died, he had gathered some half a million to a million eggs and one hundred thousand skins, having never collected an egg himself nor ever having shot a bird. 'His collecting instincts (already huge) thereafter ran riot,' as he 'assembled rare stamps, gold coins, guns, and objects d'art on a grand scale.' (Clugston & Fuller (2021) *Biosis: Biological Systems*).

With his vast wealth he was able to buy two houses in the Bahama Islands – Tir-Nan-Og, Derby Island, and Mount Vernon, New Providence – and would visit them 'frequently allowing him tax exile status. In the late 1940s he also bought an estate in Co. Cork, Eire that enabled him to import foreign bird skins with few restrictions.'

Dying heirless at Bryn Aber on 26 July 1965, he willed the property to Jack Parry, one of the two sons of his housekeeper. The other son received one of the homes in the Bahamas. Jack's widow, Sarah Olwen Parry, continued to live at Bryn Aber until 2009.

◆ ◆ ◆

HOWARD, Guy Robert, was born on 5 February 1886, at St. Mary at the Walls, Colchester, son of Col. William and Lily Margaret Seymour (née Jackson) Howard of Crowhurst, Sussex. Educated at Haileybury College 1898-1902, he lived at Bexhill-on-Sea, Sussex.

He went to France in August 1914 with the 2nd Battalion Essex Regiment. Present at the retreat from Mons, within a few weeks he had won the DSO: 'Lieutenant Guy Robert Howard, The Essex Regiment (Special Reserve). While in command of a Patrol of the 2nd Battalion, Essex Regiment, on the 24th of September, to the south of Vregny, made a valuable reconnaissance through a thick wood, reaching a point 150 yards from the enemy's trenches.'[414]

He was a captain when he transferred to the RFC. Learning to fly at the Military School, Shoreham, he was awarded RAeC certificate no. 1679 on 28 August 1915. He was CO of 18 Squadron when, on 23 October 1918, he was hit by a flare fired from a Very pistol during a squadron party at Izel-le-Hameau. He died next day at a CCS.

◆ ◆ ◆

---

[414] *The London Gazette*, 9 Nov. 1914, no. 28968. Vregny lies a few kms. north-east of Soissons, across the Aisne.

IRELAND, Harold Mervyn, was born in Toronto, Canada, on 27 February 1889 to an English father and Scottish mother. Awarded USA flying certificate no. Am.464 on 5 April 1916 at the Stinson School, San Antonio, Texas, he joined the RNAS as of 9 May 1916 as a Probationary Flight Sub-lieutenant, and on 1 October 1916 was attached to the flying school at Eastchurch. On 10 January 1917 was posted to Dover. He was made Flight Lieutenant on 1 October 1917, and acting flight commander on 7 March 1918, when posted to No. 11 Squadron RNAS (which became 211 Squadron RAF on 1 April 1918).

Shortly before the end of the war he was awarded the DFC: 'On the 29th of August [1918] this officer was leader of a large formation detailed for a long distance bombing raid on certain enemy docks. A strong and adverse wind was blowing and thick clouds almost obscured the ground, rendering the task of reaching such a distant objective one of great difficulty. Carefully studying the compass and making what he considered due allowance for the wind he led his formation to a point which he judged would be in the vicinity of the objective. A break in the clouds showed that he was correct, and the docks were effectually bombed. During the five months Captain Ireland has been with his present squadron he has led forty-three long distance raids, and the foregoing is only one instance of many in which he has shown judgment, skill and determination of a very exceptional nature.'[415]

At the end of the war, he returned to Canada from Liverpool on 5 November 1918 aboard Canadian Pacific Line's RMS *Melita*. In 1921 he was transferred as a flight lieutenant to Reserve Class 'A', and was excused further training until 30 September 1923. In this year he brought his mother with him from Canada, and settled in Kincardineshire, Scotland as a farmer.

He resumed annual training at the de Havilland Civilian Flying School, in July 1924 (eight days), when it was noted on his record that his 'flying has been of a very high standard, showing at all times great care, and ability much above the average.'[416] Again, after further flying in 1924-25 (15 days), it was noted on his record: 'This officer's flying has been extremely satisfactory. Category 1.'

From 5 August 1925 he was granted an 'extension of service for four years.' He flew a further eight days at the same school in June 1926, when his flying was noted to be 'quite satisfactory.'[417] With effect from 5 August 1927 he was transferred from Class 'A' to Class 'C', and two years later relinquished his commission on completion of service, and was permitted to retain the rank of flight lieutenant. In the Second World War, at the age of 51, he was gazetted acting pilot officer on probation for the duration with effect from 1 February 1941, to serve in the Training Branch of the RAFVR, and 'for service with A.T.C., with higher acting rank of Flt. Lieut.' He died in Toronto in 1972.

---

[415] *The London Gazette*, 2 Nov 1918, no. 30989.
[416] TNA file AIR 76/249/189.
[417] TNA file AIR 76/249/189.

JENKINS, Francis Conway was born on 25 January 1888 to Edmund Ernest, a "hardware agent", and Helen Conway in West Ham, London. He became an "automobile engineer" (according to the 1911 Census, which found him at the Rowley Hotel in Aldeburgh, Suffolk) and was involved in the motor industry from 1905, eventually racing at Brooklands. Turning to aviation there, he became part of Alliott Roe's flying business and, having learnt to fly on Avro machines, was awarded RAeC Certificate No. 74 on 2 May 1911. At this time aeroplanes were highly susceptible to strong gusts of wind and in the space of five weeks Jenkins suffered two serious crashes. The first, with a passenger in an Avro biplane, was 'caught in an eddy and did a spiral dive from about 50 ft. or 60 ft. It speaks well for the machine and the principle of sitting behind the engine, that the passenger got off with a sprained ankle and Jenkins was unhurt… The energy of the Avro School is shown by the fact that the machine was rebuilt and flying again in a week. (*The Aeroplane*, 15 June 1911). The second came when he was entered for the Circuit of Britain Air Race on 22 July 1911. Flying a Blackburn monoplane soon after taking-off he was caught in a sudden and violent gust which threw his aeroplane to the ground. He was saved from certain death when the aeroplane overturned as he had strapped himself in using the special "Birdling" belt.

Brigadier-General Conway CBE (Walter Stoneman 1971)

Undaunted, Conway Jenkins continued to fly and 'made arrangements with Mr. Roe to go on flying the new Avro machines, and he has his eye on the all-British prizes which are at present on offer. The new Avros… promise well, and Mr. Jenkins is very much in earnest in his intention to distinguish himself before long.' (*The Aeroplane*, 14 September 1911).

Soon after the start of the German war he was appointed second lieutenant in the RFC, Special Reserve wef 29 August 1914. Although a qualified pilot he spent the war on the ground in command of various establishments, becoming successively Deputy Assistant Director of Aircraft Equipment, Assistant Director of Aircraft Equipment, Director of Aircraft Acceptance and, finally, on 18 February 1918, Director of Parks and Depots, by which time he had risen to the high rank of brigadier-general. His CBE was gazetted on 7 June 1918.

After the war he was Chairman of Chrysler Motors and Dodge Brothers (Britain) and, being described as Sales Manager, paid a visit to the USA in June 1929. He died on 23 February 1933 after an operation at the Princess Christian Nursing Home, Windsor. He left his effects of nearly £8,000 to his widow, Winifred Vera, whom he had married on 5 October 1912.

◆ ◆ ◆

JAMES, Baron Trevenen ("Baron" was usually shortened to "Bron"), the other officer to be mentioned with Lewis in connection with the development of aerial wireless communication, was born in London on 20 April 1889, the eldest son of Dr. C. A. James MRCS and Annie Lucy James, of The Pollard Elms, Upper Clapton. Educated at Harrow and the University of London, he obtained a commission in the Corps of Royal Engineers: 'The undermentioned Gentlemen Cadets, from the Royal Military Academy, to be Second Lieutenants. Dated 1st October, 1909: ... Baron Trevenen James.'[418]

After a short spell at Gosport, and for nearly two years at Dover (he was based at the Royal Engineers' Brompton Barracks, Chatham in 1911), he began flying lessons at the Grahame-White School, Hendon, on 11 May 1912. He took his flying test on a Howard Wright biplane at Hendon on 1 June 1912, and was awarded RAeC certificate no. 230 three days later: 'Something of a record has just been made at the Grahame-White Aviation School at Hendon. Lieut. B.T. James R.E., one of Mr. Lewis Turner's pupils, obtained his pilot's certificate after having had only three days' practice, that is, mornings and evenings. On the fourth day—last Saturday morning—with a 12 m.p.h. wind blowing, he took the school biplane out and put in the necessary flights for his "ticket" which he obtained in excellent style. Lieut. James, who is at present at Dover, only had a few days' leave in which to qualify and was delayed a good bit by bad weather, so his performance is all the more remarkable. It is his desire to join the Army Air Battalion...' (*Flight*).

He was flying on probation with the RFC at Farnborough in September 1912, before being officially appointed to the RFC on 16 April 1913 as a Flying Officer. It was sometime during this period that, just as he was about to take-off in the two-seater B.E.2, he was asked by a nervous mechanic if he would take him for a trip. The young mechanic 'never

---

[418] *The London Gazette*, 5 Oct 1909, no. 28294.

forgot his first joy-ride in the clattering B.E., and his determination to become a pilot was strengthened from that moment.'[419] 892 AM2 J.T.B. McCudden, who would go on to great things, would also serve with 3 Squadron in France in 1914.

Interestingly, in his book *Fokker Fodder*, author Paul Hare says: 'In March [1912], it [the B.E.2] was fitted with a wireless transmitter fitted by Mr R. Widdington, aerials for which were fitted along the leading edges of the wings. Trials began on 26 March when four flights were made before the apparatus broke down. With the wireless repaired, tests resumed and continued until 11 April'.[420]

In the early summer of 1914, Bron James fitted his aeroplane for wireless signalling (see Lewis, D.S.). He flew over to France in the first week of the War with 4 Squadron, but first spotted for the

James at Hendon, 8 June 1912

French artillery before doing the same for the British. He was appointed Flight Commander and temporary Captain on 28 November 1914. He was later awarded a well-deserved MC: 'His Majesty the King has been graciously pleased to approve of the undermentioned Honours and Rewards for distinguished service in the Field, with effect from June 3rd, 1915, inclusive. Royal Flying Corps… The Military Cross. Lieut. (temp. Capt.) B. T. James, Royal Engineers...'[421]

Three weeks later he was killed in action. On 13 July 1915 his B.E.2c aeroplane was hit by a shell whilst evaluating new equipment on a test flight over enemy lines near Arrêt, between Verlorenhoek and Hooge. Details of his fate were slow to appear: 'As nothing further has been heard about Captain B. T. James, R.E., who was officially reported as missing some weeks ago, it is to be feared that he has been killed, the more so as it is reported by those returned from Flanders that his machine was seen on the ground wrecked and on fire by other pilots.

'An engineer officer of high ability, he devoted himself to the development of wireless telegraphy on aeroplanes as soon as he joined the R.F.C, and to him is largely due the excellent progress made in this department prior to the war, which has resulted in very

---

[419] McCudden VC, p.29.
[420] *Fokker Fodder*, p. 25 – Paul R. Hare (Fonthill Media Ltd, UK, 2012).
[421] *The London Gazette*, 23 June 1915, no. 29202.

good work with far-reaching effects being done by our wireless machines on active service—as officially recorded when Capt. Lewis was most deservedly given a D.S.O...

'Besides being a wireless specialist Capt. James was a sound and reliable pilot, and was, moreover, possessed of a keen sense of humour, as some may remember who know of the incident when he was told off during the manoeuvres of 1913 to take the then Secretary of State for War for a flight at short notice in accordance with that official's earnest desire to be in the air when the King and Queen arrived to visit the camp of the White Army's air scouts...

'The loss of so brilliant a young officer is deeply to be regretted, but his family may find some consolation in the fact that before his death he was able to achieve results in his own special field of activity which have had great influence on the course of aerial warfare.' (*The Aeroplane*, 1 September 1915).

A further announcement appeared on 29 October 1915, as reported in *The Aeroplane*: 'The death of Capt. James was announced in this paper some weeks ago, but this is the first semi-official notification. His age was twenty-six. He was educated at Harrow and Woolwich, and, having obtained his commission in the Royal Engineers in 1909, joined the R.F.C. in 1912. He was mentioned in dispatches in February last, and won the Military Cross in June. A month later he was reported "missing."' (*The Aeroplane*, 3 November 1915). It was not until the casualty lists of 9 November 1915 appeared that Captain James's fate was officially noted under the heading *Previously reported Missing, now reported Killed*. He is commemorated on the Arras Flying Services Memorial, France.

James's former Flight Commander on 4 Squadron, Major G.S. Shephard (see footnote 430), wrote of him: 'It is impossible to speak too highly of his work as an officer, and it is not too much to say that in his line, artillery observation, he was quite the most competent officer in the Flying Corps... We are indebted to him not only for all his flying out here, but also for his work and the experiments he carried out before the War.

'He was so well known for all the work he had done, and it was quite appreciated here that he had been the pioneer in wireless ranging with artillery — that our first successes in this were owing to him. The Army Commander has written about him to Headquarters to that effect.'[422]

(Sadly, James's younger brother, Lieutenant-Colonel Charles Kenneth James DSO & Bar,[423] was killed on 19 May 1918 whilst serving with the 6th Battn. Border Regiment. Born on 19 January 1892 he, too, was 26 when he died. See *de Ruvigny's Roll of Honour* Vol. II, Part IV, p.92, for a lengthy biography and praise of this soldier).

---

[422] Quoted in www.militarian.com/threads/.
[423] Awarded DSO 15 Nov 1916, and Bar 5 Feb 1918. He was also MiD four times.

JONES, Walter George Cottrell. Born on 8 February 1879 at Caersws, North Wales, he had moved to St. Ives, Huntingdonshire, when he joined the Northamptonshire Yeomanry some time before 1899, and served for almost three years of the Second Boer War in South Africa. In 1901, stationed at Bulford Camp, he was listed as a private. On the outbreak of war in 1914 Walter re-joined the Northamptonshire Yeomanry, and fought in France, being promoted to Sergeant some time before late 1916.

Transferred to the RFC, he passed his flying test at the Hall School, Hendon, being awarded RAeC certificate no. 3711 on 21 October 1916. He was appointed to 105 Squadron, Royal Flying Corps as second lieutenant.

♦ ♦ ♦

KEARNEY, Norman Charles, 'was 26 years of age and was the son of the Rev. N. C. Kearney, M.A., of Geelong, Australia, and Wimbledon, and the younger brother of Mr. E. C. Kearney, the inventor of the "Kearney" High Speed Mono Rail System. He was married in December, 1915, to Frances, the youngest daughter of Mr. and Mrs. W. Howes, of Mill Hill Road, Norwich.

'He enlisted in the East Surrey Regiment in February, 1916. He was in the first Battle of the Somme and was wounded at Guillemont on September 3rd, 1916. Later he received a commission in the R.F.C, in which he was regarded as a first-class pilot, and had recently been recommended for the post of pilot-instructor. He leaves a widow and one child of three months.' (*The Aeroplane*, 15 May 1918).

KENT, Ernest. Born on 11 November 1895 at Burnham, Buckinghamshire, Ernest enlisted in the Gloucestershire Regiment, Service no. 10168, on 7 September 1914 before being commissioned in the Essex Regiment's 3rd (Reserve) Battalion at Harwich Fortress. Having been transferred to 2nd Battalion, Essex Regiment, he was in France on 29 February 1916 when struck down by appendicitis, and returned from Dieppe to Dover, England on the hospital ship *Stad Antwerpen* to recover at the Northumberland War Hospital, Gosforth, Newcastle-on-Tyne.

Having requested a transfer to the RFC, he was medically examined on 27 July 1916 as to his fitness to transfer to that corps for pilot training. Passed fit, he was sent for flying training, and was awarded RAeC certificate no. 4340 on 28 February 1917.

♦ ♦ ♦

LETT, Harry Nelson was born on 21 October 1896 at Parkhurst, Isle of Wight, where his father, Evans Lett, was Master of the Isle of Wight Union Workhouse. After education at Churchers College, Petersfield (1905-12) and at University College, Southampton (1912-15), he went up to Queen's College, Oxford, where he 'matriculated but did not go into residence.'

Commissioned second lieutenant in the Duke of Edinburgh's (Wiltshire Regiment), he was promoted lieutenant in the 7th Battalion, Royal Berkshire Regiment and, with effect from 6 October 1916, 'Temp. Sec. Lt. H. N. Lett, R Berks R.,' was 'to be transfd. to Gen. List, Oct. 6th, 1916, with seny. from Aug. 4th, 1916.' Transferred to the RFC he became a qualified Observer before qualifying as a pilot on the DH4 and DH9. He joined 211 Squadron on 2 July 1918.

Awarded the DFC in 1919, the citation read: 'This officer has carried out eighty successful bombing raids and nine photographic reconnaissances, displaying at all times high personal courage and initiative. On 1st November his formation was attacked by about twenty-five enemy machines. Although outnumbered by nearly four to one, the formation destroyed one scout and drove down two others out of control. This fine achievement was largely due to Captain Lett's most able leadership.' (*The London Gazette*, 8 February 1919, no. 31170).

As acting CO of 211 Squadron, it was his sad duty to disband the squadron on 24 June 1919. Leaving the RAF, he joined the Indian Civil Service on 1 November 1921, and served in Burma. He married Gertrude Maria Steidler (1900–1986) in Vienna, Austria, on 17 May 1933. He died in Edinburgh on 21 June 1945.

LEWIS, Donald Swain. the youngest son of Captain Ernest and Maria Lewis, was born at Banstead, Surrey, on 5 April 1886. After education at Uppingham, he passed out of Woolwich and was commissioned second lieutenant in the Royal Engineers on 6 December 1904. He was promoted lieutenant on 23 June 1907. He learnt to fly at the Bristol School at Brooklands in April 1912 under the tuition of Collyns Pizey, going solo on 18 April, 'doing hops and shaping well.' He was awarded RAeC certificate, No. 216, on 14 May 1912.

On 15 November 1912 he was 'selected (on probation) for the Royal Flying Corps' and in 1913 went for further flying at the CFS, Upavon, Wiltshire, going up with Captain Jack Salmond in B.E. no. 416 on 22 January 1913. He was still under instruction in November of that year.

On 4 August 1914, at South Farnborough, he married Margaret Agnes Maude Williams (1881–1942), daughter of a retired Eton schoolmaster. There were to be no children of the marriage.

MiD on 9 December 1914 (Sir John French dispatch of 8 October 1914; gazetted 1 January 1916), he was further rewarded for his outstanding service in the air on 1 January 1915: 'His Majesty the King has been graciously pleased to approve of the appointment of the undermentioned officer to be a Companion of the Distinguished Service Order in recognition of his services with the Expeditionary Force specified below: Lieutenant (temporary Captain) Donald Swain Lewis, Royal Engineers, and Royal Flying Corps. For valuable information repeatedly furnished to the Royal Artillery in regard to the position of the enemy's guns. His direction of our artillery fire, whilst flying, has constantly led to direct hits on the enemy's batteries and the silencing of their guns.'[424]

General "Boom" Trenchard, later the RFC's commander, approved of men such as Donald Swain Lewis: 'Exceptional men like Don Lewis, one of the most gifted radio specialists in the Flying Corps, were only too ready to oblige'.[425] Lewis was also credited with creating the "grid square" map system, which was to revolutionize British wartime cartography. The method up to this point of passing aerial intelligence to those on the ground had been simply to identify 'a target by using terms such as "one hundred yards south of the second 'e' in Zillebeke"'.[426]

---

[424] *The London Gazette*, 12 Apr 1915.
[425] *Trenchard*, p.132. It should be pointed out, without detracting from Lewis' ability, that there would not have been too many radio specialists in the RFC at this time.
[426] *Observers and Navigators*, p.7.

With effect from 2 April 1915 Lewis was made Squadron Commander in the rank of (temp.) major and was appointed to command No. 3 Squadron. Relinquishing command in November 1915, he returned to duties in Great Britain during the winter of 1915-16. On 13 January 1916 His Majesty the King was graciously pleased to approve of the undermentioned Honours and Rewards for Distinguished Service in the Field, with effect from January 1st, 1916, inclusive: ...To be Brevet Majors. Capt. (temp. Major) D. S. Lewis, D.S.O., R.E. and R.F.C. Capt. (temp. Major) G. S. Shephard, R. Fus. and R.F.C.'

The King held an Investiture at Buckingham Palace on Saturday, 15 January, at which Donald Lewis was introduced into the presence of the Sovereign, who invested him with the DSO.

Another promotion soon followed when, with effect from 1 February 1916, he was appointed wing-commander and made a (temp.) lieutenant-colonel whilst so employed.[427] He returned to France that same month to take up command of 2nd Wing, which was then working with the Second Army in the Ypres Salient.

By April 1916 he had, aged thirty, risen in rank to lieutenant-colonel DSO and was CO of the RFC's 2nd Wing (Nos. 1, 5, 6, and 7 Squadrons). On 10 April 1916, he and his observer, Captain Arthur Witherby Gale DSO, 2nd Life Guards,[428] went off together on an artillery reconnaissance patrol in No. 1 Squadron's Morane Parasol number 5132. It was seen to be hit by "Archie" east of Wytschaete at 11.30 a.m. at a height of 6–7,000 feet, and to fall nose first. According to an eye-witness the 'machine was hit by a shell and crippled while patrolling behind the German lines. It was a sight never to be forgotten to see the aviator volplaning homewards. Unfortunately, the strain on the damaged machine was too great, and, while still at a great height [around 4,000 feet], it parted in the middle. The tail part fell in the German lines, and the body came down in "No Man's Land" ... He proved to be Captain Gale, of the 2nd Life Guards. The second body was that of Lieut-Colonel Lewis, squadron commander in the Royal Flying Corps'.[429] Their bodies were recovered, and were buried at Lijssenthoek Military Cemetery. Lewis was the second-highest ranking RFC officer to be killed during the First World War.[430]

Shortly after his death in action, Charles Grey wrote an obituary of him: 'The death of Colonel Lewis is a great blow to the R.F.C, for not only was he beloved by officers and men alike, but even in the R.F.C, where the highest form of bravery is the commonest attribute, he was regarded as exceptionally gallant. Moreover, he was unusually brilliant

---

[427] *The London Gazette*, 10 Feb 1916.
[428] Captain Gale, aged 41, was OC Trench Mortar Batteries, 3rd Division, attached Royal Field Artillery.
[429] From www.greatwarforum.org/.
[430] The most senior RFC officer to die on active service during the First World War was Brigadier-General G.S. Shephard DSO, MC who, on 19 Jan 1918, was flying Nieuport Scout no. B3610 when it crashed at Auchel. Lifted from the wreckage, he died in hospital several hours later.

mentally, for he and the late Capt. Baron Trevenen James, R.E. who was killed some months ago, were between them responsible for the success of the R.F.C. wireless plants, having worked assiduously at this problem long before the war. Both these officers combined skill in the science of wireless telegraphy with skill as pilots and skill in handling men, a most unusual combination of talents and one which makes their loss all the more regrettable.

'I well remember a dear friend of mine, since killed in action, showing me his diary of the fighting round Ypres before Christmas, 1914, and being particularly struck by one entry which, quoting from memory, read thus: "Lewis, R.E., landed for lunch after three hours' spotting with the wireless machine. He flies it by himself and works the wireless at the same time. Went up directly after lunch for another three hours' spell. Heavily Archied all the time. I believe he likes it." He told me then what good work "Lewis, R.E.," was doing and how much everyone admired him. It was for his single-handed wireless work that Col. Lewis got his D.S.O.

'D. S. Lewis was always known in the Corps as "Lewis, R.E.," to distinguish him from "R. E. Lewis," his contemporary in the R.F.C.'s early days.

'Under the new official system of not indicating the date or locality of an officer's death, one does not know at the moment of writing where this gallant officer died, but the German communiqué of April 10th says that "an enemy aeroplane was seen to fall in the village of Loos," so it is possible that this may refer to Colonel Lewis. The dead officer's relatives have, at any rate, the consolation that no one man has done more for the success of his Corps, and that none is more deeply regretted by his brother officers. —C.G.G.' (*The Aeroplane*, 19 April 1916).

◆ ◆ ◆

LOVELAND, Henry William Victor, was born on 23 July 1887 in Guildford, Surrey, the family later moving to 4 Egbert Road, Winchester, Hampshire. He served five years in the Wessex Division Transport, A.S.C., before emigrating to Norwood, Winnipeg, Canada in 1913. He was a photographic manager when he enlisted on 20 January 1916. His unit, the 78th Battalion, Canadian Infantry, Canadian Over-Seas Expeditionary Force, sailed from Halifax, Nova Scotia, on the *Empress of Britain* on 20 May 1916, disembarking at Liverpool, England, ten days later. On 12 August 1916 Lieutenant Loveland was in Southampton, and three days later arrived at Le Havre, France. On 2 January 1917 he was 'attached R.F.C. as Observer on probation.' One week later he went to England to undergo a one-month's course, before returning to France, and a posting to 22 Squadron.

He, too, lies in the Villers Hill British Cemetery, his body having been exhumed from Equancourt Wood.

♦ ♦ ♦

LUBBOCK, Hon. Eric Fox Pitt, born on 16 May 1893, was the son of John Lubbock, Baron Avebury, (born 30 April 1834) and his *second* wife, Alice Augusta Laurentia (daughter of Major-General Augustus Henry Lane Fox-Pitt-Rivers), who were married in 1884. Eric had an elder brother, Harold,[431] born in 1888, a younger brother, Maurice, born in 1900 and also two older sisters, two half-brothers and two half-sisters born to their father and his *first* wife, Ellen Frances (née Hordern, born 1835), who died in 1879.

Though born into the landed gentry and educated at Eton, and then Balliol College, Oxford, the Hon. Eric Fox Pitt Lubbock, enlisted in the MT section of the ASC as a private, Service no. MS/3500, on 5 September 1914. He served with the 69th MT Company ASC, Lahore Division, in Britain and France from September 1914 to February 1915. Commissioned temporary second lieutenant with effect from 27 January 1915, he then served with the 4th Divisional Supply Column from February to August 1915, when he transferred to the RFC.

He was made temporary lieutenant with effect from 1 August 1915 and, finally, temporary captain with effect from 1 July 1916. He was MiD on 1 January 1916.[432]

Having returned to England and obtained his pilot's certificate, he was retained there for a short time on instructional work. In October he went back to France on being appointed Flight Commander of "B" Flight, 45 Squadron (see photograph on page 384). On 11 March 1917, he and his observer, Second Lieutenant John Thompson, set off on a Line Patrol in their two-seater Sopwith 1½-Strutter, A1082, to take photographs of the front line. A short while later they were shot down, and killed, by Leutnant Paul Strähle in his Albatros D.III.

♦ ♦ ♦

---

[431] Lt. The Hon. Harold Fox Pitt Lubbock, Grenadier Guards, born 10 Jun 1888, was killed in France 4 Apr 1918.
[432] His promotions were listed respectively in *The London Gazettes*: 12 Feb 1915, no. 29066; 9 Oct 1915, no. 29321; 29 Jul 1916, no. 29688.

LYWOOD, Oswyn George William Gifford was born in Gosport on 21 August 1895. He began having flying lessons at the Bristol School, Lark Hill, Salisbury Plain, on 1 July 1912. On 15 October 1912 'Mr. Lywood going for brevet tests made two sets of figures of eight, but each time failed to land close enough to mark.' (*The Aeroplane*, 24 October 1912). He seems to have given up his lessons at this point, for on 9 November 1912 was commissioned in the Royal Norfolk Regiment.

Early in 1913 he was in Ireland helping Harry Ferguson with his monoplane, but he was back in England later that year and had further flying lessons, again at the Bristol School, Lark Hill, being awarded RAeC certificate no. 600 on 21 August 1913.

Confirmed as a second lieutenant on 6 June 1913, he was promoted lieutenant (temp.) on 12 December 1914, and during the war was finally promoted major. Remaining in the new RAF, he later achieved the high rank of Air Vice-Marshal CB, CBE. He died on 3 February 1957.

♦ ♦ ♦

MOUTRAY-READ, Anketell was born on 27 October 1884 at Beaumont House, 56 Shurdington Road, Leckhampton, Cheltenham, son of Colonel John Moutray-Read. Destined to serve in the Army, he was educated at Glyngarth School, Cheltenham, and at the United Services College, Westward Ho!. From being a Gentleman Cadet at the Royal Military College, Sandhurst, he was commissioned second lieutenant in the Gloucestershire Regiment on 21 November 1903.[433]

He served with the Regiment's 1st Battalion in India until he joined the 7th Hariana Lancers, with effect from 21 February 1906. Later admitted to the Indian Army and promoted Lieutenant,[434] he was well-known for winning the Services' heavyweight boxing championship in India eight times, and middleweight twice, winning at both weights at the same meeting. He also won the Army and Navy heavyweight championship three times at Aldershot and Plymouth. As one judge remarked: 'Read wins

---

[433] *The London Gazette*, 20 Nov 1903, no. 27618.
[434] *The London Gazettes*, 26 Nov 1907, no. 28083; 24 Dec 1907, no. 28092.

because he never accepts defeat and never knows when he is beaten.'[435] In 1911 he returned to Britain and joined The Northamptonshire Regiment with effect from 7 September 1911.[436]

Learning to fly at the Bristol School at Brooklands, he took his test on Tuesday, 15 October 1912, and was awarded RAeC certificate no. 336 one week later. With effect from 17 April 1913, he was gazetted flying officer, and seconded to the RFC's Military Wing as from that date.

In June 1913 he was thrown from a motor-cycle and was in 'a critical state' (*The Aeroplane*, 26 June 1913). On Sunday, 7 September, again fit for service, he reported for duty with No. 2 Squadron at Montrose, Scotland.

Rejoining the Northamptonshire Regiment and sailing to France on 12/13 August 1914, he was attached to the 9th Lancers then serving on the Aisne. In September 1914 his horse was shot under him and, rolling on him, badly smashed his leg in several places. He was sent to a hospital in Paris for treatment.

His leg mended, he rejoined the Northamptonshires in March 1915, only to be killed on the opening day of the battle of Loos, 25 September 1915. His death was described in the Battalion War Diary: 'Capt. Read had very gallantly gone out to rally a party of about 60 men of different units who were retiring disorganised owing to gas drifting back. The men were led forward again by him and took up a position south of Lone Tree where they maintained themselves for some hours. Capt. Read was mortally wounded during this time.' Tragically, the gas shells had been fired by the British.

Read was awarded a posthumous Victoria Cross on 18 November 1915 for 'most conspicuous bravery during the first attack near Hulluch on the morning of 25th September, 1915.' The citation for his VC stated: 'Although partially gassed, Captain Read went out several times in order to rally parties of different units which were disorganised and retiring. He led them back into the firing line, and, utterly regardless of danger, moved freely about encouraging them under a withering fire. He was mortally wounded while carrying out this gallant work.'

'Captain Read had previously shown conspicuous bravery during digging operations on 29th, 30th and 31st August, 1915, and on the night of the 29th-30th July he carried out of action an Officer, who was mortally wounded, under a hot fire from rifles and grenades.'[437]

The following is further testimony to his bravery and character: 'The relatives of the late Capt. Anketell Moutray-Read have received a letter from the commanding officer of the Northamptonshire Regiment, stating that his name had been noted for the D.S.O. for duties very gallantly performed under heavy fire on August 28th, 29th and 31st, and that for

---

[435] Thanks to www.cheltenhamremembers.org.uk/.
[436] *The London Gazette*, 13 Oct 1911, no. 28541.
[437] *The London Gazette*, 16 Nov 1915, no, 29371.

devotion to duty and bravery on the day of his death his name had been submitted for the Victoria Cross. The CO adds that Captain Moutray-Read was "a splendid man, a most gallant soldier, and was admired and loved by all ranks. His loss is one of those which we shall never be able to replace."' (*The Aeroplane*, 20 October 1915). He is buried at Dud Corner Military Cemetery, France.

◆ ◆ ◆

MULHOLLAND, Denis Osmond, born 6 September 1892 at Donaghadee, Co. Down, Ireland, was a second lieutenant in 4th Battalion, The Connaught Rangers, when awarded RAeC certificate no. 2111 on 24 November 1915.

Remaining in the RAF after the First World War, he was a Wing Commander AFC by 1939, serving on the Administrative Staff of RAF Middle East, Cairo. Promoted to acting group captain he was admitted CBE on 2 June 1943 (King's Birthday Honours). He died in 1949.

◆ ◆ ◆

MUSGRAVE, Herbert (photo courtesy Diane Gravlee) was born on 11 May 1876 in Adelaide, Australia, his father then the Governor of South Australia, Sir Anthony Musgrave (1828–1888). After the death of her husband, Lady Musgrave and her three sons went to England, living at East Grinstead, Sussex. In 1896, after education at Harrow School, Herbert received a commission in the Royal Engineers, and served as a lieutenant for the duration of the Second Boer War in South Africa.

Witnessing the arrival at Dover from France of Louis Blériot on 25 July 1909 Captain Herbert Musgrave RE, appreciating the military significance of the aeroplane, at once went to the War Office to explain the possible dangers that aviation could pose to Britain's security. His suggestion of the formation of a military aviation service, however, came up against men such as Sir William Nicholson, British Chief of General Staff, 1908–1912, who later declared that 'aviation is a useless and expensive fad advocated by a few individuals whose ideas are unworthy of attention.' Needless to say, in such a climate Herbert Musgrave's ideas were rejected.

Undaunted, he continued his campaign for a military aviation service and, when the Royal Flying Corps was formed in May 1912, he was seconded to it from his regiment. He was, at the time, one of only eleven qualified pilots in the RFC. Learning to fly at the Bristol School, Lark Hill, Salisbury Plain, he was awarded RAeC certificate no. 357 on 12 November 1912. He thereafter continued his flying, well into 1913, with the RFC at South Farnborough, both as a passenger and solo.

On 9 July 1913, with effect from 30 April, he was appointed Squadron Commander, with the temporary rank of Major 'whilst so employed', and was put in charge of the RFC's experiments, which included research into ballooning, kiting, wireless telegraphy, photography, meteorology and bomb-dropping. In the autumn of 1914, he was elected an Associate Fellow of the Aeronautical Society.

In April 1914 the Headquarters Flight was formed at Farnborough, and Major Herbert Musgrave was appointed its commander. Two other prominent pilots were Lieutenants D.S. Lewis and B.T. James, who 'never spared themselves in refining the art of wireless telegraphy.'[438] They 'constantly urged development of wireless and carried out many useful and advanced experiments themselves. For example, in June 1914, they flew about ten miles apart for a distance of almost thirty miles communicating with each other all the way.'[439]

When the war came in August, Headquarters Flight was dispersed to bring other squadrons up to establishment. Its wireless section, including Lewis and James, was attached to No. 4 Squadron, which flew to France on 13 August 1914. These two officers would play a major role in the use of wireless telegraphy from the air to the battlefield.

On 8 December 1914, the Wireless Flight became No. IX Squadron, under Musgrave, but with the ever-growing presence of wireless in aeroplanes the squadron was disbanded on 22 March 1915, and Musgrave was transferred to 1st Army HQ.

He married Georgiana Hopkins on 23 April 1915, and their first child, Jeanie Lucinda, was born in 1916. Their second child, Herbert William Dudley, arrived on this earth at East Grinstead on 16 July 1918, six weeks after the death of his father.

Severely wounded on 10 August 1916, Musgrave went home to recover. Returning to France in December 1917 his luck finally ran out on the night of 2 June 1918. Having 'persuaded a battalion commander to let him accompany a patrol, he was killed by a rifle grenade, inside the German lines. He desired no personal advancement, and would have

---

[438] *From Biplane to Spitfire*, pp.44-5.
[439] *The History of 9 Squadron Royal Air Force*, p.5.

thought no other honour so great as to die for his country. Such men, though the records of their lives are buried under a mass of tedious detail, are the engineers of victory.'[440]

♦ ♦ ♦

NEVE, Rupert Ernest, born 15 September 1893, had been awarded RAeC certificate no. 3297 on 2 July 1916. He would be seriously injured on 9 March 1917 when forced to jump from his blazing F.E.8, no. 6399. Ten months later when serving on 40 (T) Squadron at Croydon Sopwith Camel no. B5235 broke up over Purley, Surrey: 'Lt. Rupert Ernest Neve, R.F.C., who was killed in an aeroplane accident near London on Jan. 26th [1918], aged 24, was a twin son of the late A. H. Neve, J.P., and Mrs. Neve, of Maidenhead. Early in the war he enlisted in the Public Schools Battalion of the Royal Fusiliers, and subsequently was gazetted to the Shropshire Light Infantry, but after a short interval transferred to the R.F.C. Last March, after six months' flying in France, he was severely wounded during an aerial fight, but brought his machine safely into the British lines. After a long period in hospital he returned to duty, and acted as instructor at an aerodrome in England. He was recently reported fit for active service.' (*The Aeroplane*, 6 February 1918).

♦ ♦ ♦

O'SULLIVAN, Fergus was born in 1896, the youngest of six children. His father, a brewer's analytical and consulting chemist by profession, was Irish by birth: 'Sec. Lt. F. O'Sullivan, N. Staffs Regt. [6th (T) North Staffordshire Regiment], attached R.F.C, who lost his life, at the age of 20, in an aerial fight on April 23rd, was the youngest son of Mr. and Mrs. James O'Sullivan, of High Bank, Burton-on-Trent. He enlisted in the Motor Machine Gun Service early in 1915, and got his commission in November of that year. As an observer he obtained his "wing" in less than two months.' (*The Aeroplane*, 6 June 1917).

♦ ♦ ♦

---

[440] *History of the War in the Air 1914-1918*, pp.195-6.

**PITCHER, Duncan Le Geyt** was born on 31 August 1877 at Naini Tal hill station, India. The family returned to England, and young Duncan was educated at Sedbergh School in Cumbria. Commissioned on 16 February 1898 into the 24th Regiment (South Wales Borderers), over the next decade he served in India in several regiments. In 1911 he and fellow Indian Army officer Captain C.G. Hoare were sent to England to learn to fly and, having done so, return to India to set up a flying school there. On 26 July 1911 both began lessons at the Bristol School, Lark Hill, on Salisbury Plain, and were awarded RAeC certificates no. 125 (Pitcher) and 126 (Hoare) on 29 August 1911.

In the event, only Hoare went back to India, after a course at the CFS at Upavon. Pitcher, too, was given further instruction there, but was retained at the CFS and on 5 February 1914 was attached to the RFC. He was then attached to 4 Squadron after it had gone to France in August 1914, but was recalled to England on 1 November 1914, for further duties at the CFS. He remained there for the whole of 1915, becoming Commandant, Central Flying School in December 1915. By this time, he was Captain (temporary Lieutenant-Colonel) Duncan le Geyt Pitcher.

He was a Deputy Director at the Directorate of Equipment, becoming Director by 1923. He retired in 1929 as CMG, CBE, DSO, and died on 1 September 1944 at Mount Vernon Hospital, Norwood, London.

♦ ♦ ♦

PORRI, Cyril was born in Grimsby, Lincolnshire, on 11 November 1892 to Louis and Elizabeth Marie (née Lockhart) Porri. His father having founded a news agency on Kent Street, Grimsby, Cyril developed a keen interest in photography. He attended Clee Grammar School in 1906, and then went up to Durham University and to St. John's College, Oxford.[441]

As at 9 September 1914 he was commissioned Temporary Lieutenant in the Grimsby Battalion, The Lincolnshire Regiment – the "Grimsby Chums" – before transferring to the RFC as a Flying Officer (Observer). Becoming an Assistant Equipment Officer in 1916,[442] he was put in command of the RFC School of Photography's training at Farnborough in

---

[441] *The Grimsby Telegraph* First World War Centenary Commemorative Supplement, 29 July 2014.
[442] *The London Gazette*, 20 May 1916.

1917. Ending the war as a flight lieutenant, RAF Service no. 03025, Cyril remained in the RAF.

On 19 July 1920 in St. Omer, France, he married a sixteen-year-old French girl, Jeanne Marie Cannone (born at St. Omer on 23 July 1903).

With effect from 29 November 1921, he was attached to the RAF Middle East Command, Cairo, as a flight lieutenant on Technical Duties (Photos). On 1 January 1929 he was promoted squadron leader, and in due course (4 May 1931) was, once again, appointed to the School of Photography at Farnborough, this time as Chief Instructor. Further promotion came, on 1 January 1936, to wing commander, and in that rank he was appointed Commandant of the School of Photography on 26 March 1936. With that appointment he also became OC RAF Station, Farnborough. He was placed on the Retired List in 1942 but continued on Air Force service until reverting to the Retired List, retaining the rank of group captain, on 30 November 1945.

He died at The Queen Elizabeth Hospital, London SW15 on 23 May 1950.

♦ ♦ ♦

POWELL, Frederick James was born on 13 August 1895 at Patricroft, on the west side of Manchester, Lancashire. By the time of the 1901 Census, he was living with his mother and elder sister at 20 Moor Lane, Crosby, Liverpool. He was a boarder at St. John's Foundation School for the Sons of Poor Clergy of the Church of England, at Leatherhead in Surrey, before joining the Duke of Lancaster's Own Yeomanry, a Territorial unit, in August 1913.

On 21 September 1914 he transferred to the 18th (Service) Battalion (3rd City) Manchester Regiment, as a second lieutenant, and then joined the RFC in November 1914. He was posted to Farnborough for pilot training and was awarded RAeC certificate no. 1130 on 2 March. On completion of further training at Netheravon, Wiltshire, he was appointed a Flying Officer as of 25 May and placed on the General List, having been promoted lieutenant on 2 February 1915,

Training completed, he was posted to "B" Flight, No. 5 Squadron at Abeele, Belgium. Flying the Vickers "Gunbus" he claimed his first aerial victory on 19 September 1915 as per *RFC Communiqué No. 11*: 'Lt Powell (pilot) and 1 AM Shaw (observer), 5 Sqn, in a Vickers with a Lewis gun, when patrolling east of Polygon Wood at 6.0 a.m. and at a height of 9,000 feet saw an L.V.G. at a height of 6,000 feet. The Vickers dived at the

German who also dived firing upwards over his tail. The Vickers followed firing until he had dived so low that it was impossible to follow him further. He was last seen flying very low towards Menin. Immediately afterwards Lt Powell looked round and saw a large machine (German) of unknown type coming up behind him. The machine was a three-seater with two engines, single fuselage, propellers behind main plane, two machine-guns. The machine was very much larger than a F.E.2. Lt Powell turned to engage it when he was about 100 yards away coming straight on and some 30 feet above the Vickers. The German was firing both his machine guns. When he was about 50 feet away 1 AM Shaw emptied a drum into him and he dived straight down just over the tail of the Vickers. One of his engines had stopped and a cloud of smoke was seen coming from the other engine.

'Another machine was seen flying westward along the River Lys. When the Vickers turned towards him this machine went away. While regaining height over Ypres Lt Powell observed an Albatros east of Poelcapelle. The last two drums of the Lewis gun were fired at him at a range of 200 yards. The German replied with his machine-gun but continued to fly eastwards. Having no more ammunition Lt Powell gave up the pursuit.'

Powell and Shaw also featured in *RFC Communiqué 13* for their encounter with an L.V.G. and an Albatros on 3 October and in *Communiqué 14*. This time, in pursuit of an enemy machine, an anti-aircraft shell exploded 'not more than 3 feet to the left of the nacelle hitting 1 AM Shaw in the leg and knocking three holes in the petrol tank just behind the pilot.' With Shaw out of action Powell went up on 4 November with Eric Lubbock as observer and had another go at shooting-down an enemy aeroplane, but ran out of ammunition. The pair had similar misfortune on 8 November when chasing an Aviatik. He gained his second confirmed victory on 19 December.

On 1 January 1916 he was appointed Flight Commander and made temporary captain as at 15 December 1915 and was also MiD on that date. He was awarded the Military Cross on 14 January.

He had one more unconfirmed claim while flying the Gunbus, on 2 January 1916. Now flying his F.E.8, he flew on three separate occasions on 5 February 1916, attacking an enemy aeroplane each time, two Aviatiks and an Albatros. If none of these was a confirmed victory, he had more success on 29 February when he and Second Lieutenant G.W.M. Green[443] as his observer and a 1 Squadron Morane Parasol, no. 5119, flown by Captain R.A. Saunders and Second Lieutenant C.A. Brewster-Joske set on fire an enemy machine over Passchendaele. On 12 March he attacked a single-seater Fokker monoplane and claimed to have hit it. Clouds of smoke were seen coming from the engine.

---

[443] Gilbert Ware Murlis Green would end the war as a fighter pilot credited with eight aerial victories. He was awarded the DSO & Bar, MC & 2 Bars, the French Croix de Guerre and the Serbian Order of the White Eagle, 4th Class (with Swords). Born 24 Jan 1895, he died in Kenya on 26 Aug 1958.

By 12 March, he had three unconfirmed victories, and three more triumphs credited to him.

Powell returned to England in April 1916, and was based at Cambridge, but in May returned to France when posted to No. 40 Squadron as a flight commander. The squadron was the first unit to be equipped with the F.E.8.

In February 1917 he was appointed chief fighting instructor in the RFC's Northern Group, based at York, and from April he commanded No. 43 (Training) Squadron at Ternhill, being appointed squadron commander with the temporary rank of major on 16 May 1917.

He returned to France on 2 August 1917 as commander of No. 41 Squadron. On 2 February 1918, during an offensive patrol over the Douai sector, he was wounded and his engine disabled during a dogfight with Max Kühn of *Jasta 10*. He made a forced landing on a German airfield, and spent the rest of the war as a POW. He was repatriated in December 1918.

He left the RAF on 17 May 1919 but on 12 December 1919 was granted a short service commission in the RAF, with the rank of flight lieutenant, only for this to be cancelled a week later. He was, however, granted a short service commission as a flight lieutenant again on 5 June 1920. After a brief spell in India in 1921-22 with No. 28 Squadron, he was transferred to the RAF Reserve as a "Class A" officer on 5 June 1927, finally relinquishing his commission on 5 June 1931.

On 19 September 1939, soon after the outbreak of the Second World War, he was granted a commission "for the duration of hostilities" as a pilot officer, Service no. 74207, on probation in the Administrative & Special Duties Branch of the RAFVR. He ended the war as an acting wing commander, three time MiD, and on 14 June 1945, in the King's Birthday Honours, was appointed OBE. Later living in Dorset, he died in Cambridge in May 1992.

PRETYMAN, George Frederick, born on 8 September 1891 at Kasani, Simla Hills, India, to Colonel George Tindal and Winifred (née Locke) Pretyman. Pretyman senior was then the Assistant Adjutant-General of Artillery in India and, before his death on 3 August 1917 aged 72, had become Major-General Sir G.T. Pretyman. (see page 44).

Commissioned second lieutenant in the Prince Albert's (Somerset Light Infantry) on 25 March 1911, George junior learnt to fly at the Bristol School, Brooklands, making his first dual flight on 12 August 1912, and his first solo on 3 October. Then came the great day, 18 October 1912: 'Lieut. Pretyman took certificate in great style, landing almost on top of observers, after flying nearly 1,000 ft.' (*The Aeroplane*, 24 October 1912).

Awarded RAeC certificate no. 341 on 22 October 1912, he was posted to the RFC's Central Flying School, at Upavon, Wiltshire, in May 1913 for the third flying course. On 17 July, for example, he went up with Major E.L. Gerrard RMLI in Henry Farman no. 445. Having completed the course in August 1913 to the satisfaction of his superiors, he was made Flying Officer, and was seconded from his regiment to the RFC (Military Wing) with effect from 15 September as per the War Office edict of 15 October 1913.

He then took part in the 1913 military manoeuvres as an observer rather than as a pilot. As the RFC had no trained observers at the time, it is likely that other fellow-officers from his CFS course were also thus employed.[444] One of them, Lieutenant R. G. D. Small, Prince of Wales's Leinster Reg. (R. Canadians), was posted to No. 4 Squadron RFC at Netheravon with George.

When war came in August 1914 George went to France with No. 3 Squadron, having been promoted lieutenant earlier in that month, and was made a Flight Commander and temporary Captain with effect from 8 February, 1915.

A good story is told of George in Major Jack Salmond's biography. Having been to another part of the line Salmond came back to 3 Squadron to find George 'sleeping on a chair in the dining room.'

'"What on earth are you doing here?" the CO asked.'

'"Well – ah – there's a young friend of Hoppy's in my room," Pretyman said.'

'Next morning as Salmond sat alone at breakfast the young friend appeared. She was very pretty, too.'[445]

On 27 March 1915 Lieutenant (temporary Captain) George Frederick Pretyman, Somerset Light Infantry and Royal Flying Corps was appointed DSO: 'For great gallantry, ability, and initiative, on numerous occasions, especially on the 12th instant. The clouds being low he had to fly very low for a considerable period all along the German positions to ascertain their movements, being exposed the whole time to a very heavy fire. On the 13th instant he blew up the centre of a train at Don station, damaged a building outside which a battalion of the enemy were forming up, and drove off a German aeroplane.'[446]

Having survived for nearly a year on active service, George Pretyman was posted to the CFS as an Instructor on 16 July 1915. He was still there in November when he was promoted Squadron Commander 'and to be temporary Major whilst so employed. Dated

---

[444] *Observers and Navigators*, p.4.
[445] *Swifter than Eagles*, p.66.
[446] *The London Gazette*, 27 Mar 1915, no. 29114.

27th October, 1915.' His time at the CFS ended on 28 November, when he was replaced as Instructor by Captain (temporary Major) L.W. B. Rees, RA.[447]

Promoted to (Temp.) Lieutenant-Colonel on 28 December 1916, he was made Staff Officer, 1st Class, vice Major (temp. Lt.-Col.) P. C. Maltby, D.S.O. at the Air Ministry as at 1 May 1918.

Lieutenant-Colonel George Pretyman DSO, OBE married Maureen Kate Heard (1899–1961) at Holy Trinity Church, Brompton, London, on 25 February 1919. She would later achieve success as a murder-mystery writer using the name Maureen Sarsfield.

Remaining in the RAF, George served in the rank of wing commander as OC RAF School, India, before becoming CO of No. 11 Wing, Inland Area, at Grantham, Lincolnshire. By July 1923 he was serving under, once again, Air Commodore E.L. Gerrard CMG, DSO at No. 1 Group, Inland Area.[448]

He died, aged 45, at Alresford, Essex on 4 June 1937, leaving his effects to his younger brother, Wing Commander Edward Radclyffe Pretyman RAF.[449]

◆ ◆ ◆

QUINNELL, John Charles ("Paddy") was born at Tralee, Co. Kerry, Ireland, on 7 January 1891, the son of an Irish newspaper owner. Educated at the Royal School, Dungannon, he joined the *Irish Times* on leaving school. Commissioned in the RA at the start of the war, he transferred to the RFC, and was awarded RAeC certificate no. 1175 on 23 March 1915. Posted to 10 Squadron on 10 June 1915, he went to France with the squadron on 25 July 1915. He served with Numbers 7 and 6 Squadrons, before being wounded on 10 July 1916. Briefly CO of 83 Squadron, he commanded 63 Squadron in Mesopotamia from August 1917 until 21 October 1917 when he returned to England, and was given command of the newly-forming No. 104 Squadron at Andover on 1 January 1918.

He continued to serve in the RAF after the war, becoming Air Commodore CB, DFC (1 Jan 1919), RAF, on 1 July 1935, and served on the training side of the RAF in the Second

---

[447] Lionel Wilmot Brabazon Rees was awarded the VC on 5 Aug 1916. Born 31 Jul 1884, he died on 28 Sep 1955.
[448] A/Cdre Eugene Louis Gerrard CMG, DSO, was one of the first Instructors at the CFS in 1912. Born Dublin 14 Jul 1881, died 7 Feb 1963.
[449] Born Umballa, India 29 Nov 1894, died 1 Nov 1983. RAeC no. 1762 18 Sep 1915.

World War, being MiD on 16 July 1940. Retiring with effect from 11 December 1944, he returned to his great love of yachting and won many races. He died on 3 January 1983.

◆ ◆ ◆

RANSOME, John Edwin was born in London on 1 January 1893, to Arthur, a builder, and Frances Sarah "Fanny" Ransome. At the time of the 1901 Census he was living with his mother, then a school mistress, at Aunsby, Lincolnshire, and was educated at Boston Grammar School (1907–1909).

He enlisted in the Army Service Corps as private no. M2/050084 and went to France on 5 March 1915. He was discharged from the ASC (later Royal) on 12 September 1917 on being commissioned second lieutenant on probation in the RFC. Learning to fly at the London and Provincial School, Stag Lane, Edgware he was awarded RAeC certificate no. 5332 on 15 October 1917. Briefly posted, on 19 October, to 88 Squadron at Harling Road, he was transferred to 104 Squadron at Weyhill, Andover on 1 November.

On Wednesday, 12 December 1917, he was flying B.E.2c no. A1360 in a line-abreast formation at 1,000 feet over Appleshaw, Hampshire, when it was hit in the tail by the aeroplane flown by Lieutenant Edwards. A1360 crashed to earth out of control, killing its pilot. Edwards was unhurt.

At the inquest held by the Coroner, Mr Talbot, at the Town Hall, Andover, Eustace Frank Herbert Adlam, a 17-year old carter from Appleshaw, stated that at 9.20 a.m. on the Wednesday morning he watched four aeroplanes flying abreast. Suddenly it appeared as if one pilot tried to turn to his left, and, in doing so, touched the tail of the other machine. The one that was hit came down on the edge of a wood about 600 yards distant. Running to the spot, Adlam found the machine a total wreck, and the pilot was lying on his right side dead.

Another witness, Second Lieutenant Harrison, said he saw the four machines leave at 9 o'clock, and then flying in formation in line abreast. Deceased was quite experienced, and was just about to graduate as a pilot, having done everything necessary before going to France. All four pilots had about the same experience but, in Harrison's opinion, were too close together. The leader was signalling to the rest, and no doubt Lieutenant Edwards was so keen on watching the leader that, suddenly looking to his machine, he found his nose had swung right round on to the tail of the other machine and struck it before he was able to alter course. Though he lost the propeller of his machine, Lieutenant Edwards was able to descend unharmed.

Captain Bannerman RAMC, from Andover, said that when he arrived near Redenham House, Appleshaw, at 10 o'clock he found the body of the deceased on a stretcher. There were severe injuries to the head and thorax, while the lower jaw and left leg were broken sufficiently to cause death.

The jury's verdict was that the deceased was accidentally killed while flying on duty with his squadron, some of whom wrote to his mother at Oxford House, High Street, Boston. One was his South African-born Flight Commander, Captain Norman Baillie Lovemore, (born 8 April 1895, formerly Trooper 00116 Imperial Light Horse):

'Andover, Hants, 12th Dec, 1917.

'Dear Mrs Ransome, As the Flight Commander of the flight, to which your son belonged, I am writing to express my very sincere and deep sympathy with you in your loss. It is our loss, too, as he was a friend of all of us.

'I am afraid it was one of those accidents, which it was quite impossible for us to foresee or prevent. Every one of us will miss him, and particularly myself, as he was making a fine airman, and was always ready and willing to do his work. Please, once more accept my very deep sympathy. Yours sincerely, N. B. Lovemore.'

Also writing a letter of condolence was Canadian-born Captain Evans Alexander McKay MC, also sugaring the bitter pill: 'He was one of the best pupils I had in the squadron, and very shortly would have graduated as a service pilot. Everybody in the squadron will feel his loss keenly, and all sympathise with you in your bereavement. Any assistance that I can give you in any arrangements you may wish to make will be given freely. Very sincerely yours, Evans A

Captain N.B. Lovemore (left); Captain E.A. McKay MC (right).

McKay, Capt, Andover, 12th December, 1917.'[450]

Ransome's funeral took place with full military honours at St. Thomas' Church, Skirbeck Quarter, Boston, Lincolnshire, with the Reverend W.E. Thomas officiating.

The two 104 Squadron captains were senior members of Robert's Andover Wing. Lovemore would survive the war, with an AFC (3 June 1919), but McKay was forced down on 22 August 1918 and taken POW. Flying DH9 no. D2812, 104 Squadron, with Lieutenant Reginald Alfred Charles Brie (Observer) their aeroplane suffered engine failure just after crossing the lines, and was then attacked and driven down by eight enemy aircraft. Both were taken prisoner.

Having already been awarded the MC (16 August 1917), McKay was awarded the DFC on 21 September 1918: 'This officer led a raid on an important railway station; during this operation, which was most successful, 24 hostile aircraft attacked his formation. In the engagement he displayed fine leadership and skill. Three of the hostile machines were destroyed and one driven down. He is an exceptionally good formation leader, and his determination to reach his objective is only equalled by his coolness and courage when attacked.' McKay was repatriated on 12 December 1918.

♦ ♦ ♦

READ, William Ronald, born on 17 May 1885 into a wealthy family, lost both parents when he was twelve, and was thereafter raised by guardians. After leaving Jesus College, Cambridge, he was commissioned Second Lieutenant in the Hampshire Carabiniers, a yeomanry (cavalry) regiment, on 23 September 1906, before transferring to the 1st (King's) Dragoon Guards, a regular regiment, on 6 March 1907.

Awarded RAeC certificate number 463 on 12 April 1913 at the Bristol Flying School, Lark Hill, Salisbury Plain, he was seconded to the RFC on 28 April 1914. Posted to No. 3 Squadron, he was promoted lieutenant on 14 June 1914.

Recovered from the wound received on 2 November 1914, he was appointed a flight commander on 8 February 1915, with the rank of captain (temporary). He was sent home in December 1915 to command No. 41 Squadron, which was on the point of forming at Gosport. Also at Gosport, however, and without a CO, though it had been forming since 1 March 1916, was No. 45 Squadron. It

---

[450] Information mostly from rosma.co.uk/mw/oba/.

45 Squadron officers, September 1916. Seated, third from left is Captain The Hon. E.F.P. Lubbock (OC "B" Flight); fifth from left is Major W.R. Read (CO, 45 Squadron). [IWM, via The Flying Camels, p.4)

was simple enough, therefore, for Read to be designated as CO of 45, and he took up his appointment on 24 April.

45 Squadron, a fighter-reconnaissance squadron with Sopwith 1½ Strutters, went to France in October 1916.

"Willie" Read, meanwhile, had been MiD (1 January 1916) and awarded the MC (14 January 1916).

Disillusioned by the squadron's heavy losses, and with his superiors' unwillingness to grant fighter support to his outdated 1½ Strutters, Willie requested a transfer back to his regiment. This was granted, and he relinquished command of 45 Squadron on 24 April 1917. In the words of one of his pilots, Second Lieutenant Norman Macmillan, he was 'a very gallant gentleman, whose only fault was loathing of command to slaughter.'[451]

Unhappy with his soldiering, he returned to the RFC, once again tasked with forming a new squadron, this time No. 104 Squadron, at Wyton, Huntingdonshire. The squadron was officially formed on 4 September 1917 with Willie, briefly its first CO, in the acting rank of Major, having been promoted to the substantive rank of Captain on 19 August 1917. Robert would soon come across Willie and his successor as CO of 104 Squadron in less than happy circumstances (see page 206).

In the RAF's post-war awards, Willie Read was awarded the DFC (3 June 1919), and the AFC (1 January 1919) and two Bars (12 July 1920; 1 January 1922). He had various jobs in the post-war RAF, including that of CO of 216 Squadron in Egypt, before finally retiring in the rank of Wing Commander on 17 May 1932, his 47th birthday. He died on 5 March 1972.

◆ ◆ ◆

---

[451] *Into the Blue*, p.47 (1929 edition).

RICKARDS, Gilbert Braithwaite was born on 25 April 1869 to William Henry (merchant) and Sophia at Hulme, Lancashire. He was the fifth of their six children born between 1847 and 1870. Gilbert was educated at Uppingham School, after which he was commissioned second lieutenant in the 4th Battalion, the Worcestershire Regiment, effective on 19 January 1887. He transferred to The Royal Munster Fusiliers as of 10 November 1888, and was made lieutenant on 18 May 1891, but resigned his commission on 9 October 1894.

He returned to the Army soon after the start of the Second Boer War and was given the temporary rank of Captain effective 7 February 1900. He served in South Africa in the 12th Battalion, Imperial Yeomanry, being awarded the Queen's South Africa Medal and five bars. He once again resigned his commission, on 21 August 1901, in which year he married.

At the ripe old age of forty-three, having gone to Brooklands to learn to fly, he was awarded RAeC certificate no. 400 on 21 January 1913. As of 15 March 1913, an Honorary Captain in the Royal Munster Fusiliers, he was appointed second lieutenant (on probation) in the Special Reserve of Officers RFC (Military Wing). In July and August of that year he attended the CFS for further flying. On 9 September he was appointed to the Reserve and was confirmed in his rank in the Special Reserve of Officers. On 5 August 1914 he was made a Flying Officer and a Flight Commander on 11 August 1915 when serving in the Middle East.

Rickards, as did Robert Loraine, struggled to fly well at first and, as Brancker noted, 'eventually negotiated one of the worst landings I have ever seen, and reduced most of a Maurice Farman to matchwood without damage to himself.'[452] It was probably deemed safer to send him off to 30 Squadron at Ismailia in Egypt, where he did well, well enough to be promoted to Captain (Temp.) (1 September 1915) and to merit the award of the MC, gazetted on 29 October 1915, 'for distinguished service in the field in Mesopotamia.'

He returned to England and, on 17 April 1916, was appointed Acting Squadron Commander of 38 Squadron, which had formed at Thetford, Norfolk on 1 April 1916. Then, on 1 May, he was confirmed in the rank of Squadron Commander as a Major (Temp.), and served in No. 5 Wing with its Reserve squadrons.

He had 'the honour of being received by the King' at Windsor Castle on 10 May, when His Majesty conferred him with the Military Cross.

---

[452] *Sir Sefton Brancker*, p.40.

In August 1916 he spent ten days in hospital, which meant the end of his squadron service and, in May and in June 1917, medical boards decided that he was unfit for general service.

It was at this time that the RFC established a training organization in Canada, and on 17 July 1917 Rickards was posted to Canada, serving at the Recruits Depot as its commanding officer until August 1918. He remained on the strength of RAF Canada until 1 March 1919 when posted to Home Establishment. Returning from New York, USA, on the *Olympic*, he arrived at Southampton, England on 8 March 1919. He was twice MiD during the war.

He died at the Queen Alexandra Military Hospital on 14 October 1922.

♦ ♦ ♦

RIGBY, Harry Alexander, born 2 Nov 1896, Melbourne, Australia, was awarded RAeC certificate no. 2651 on 1 April 1916. Commissioned in the RFC on 22 May 1916 and having joined 40 Squadron on 1 August, he left a month later due to illness. Posted to No. 1 Squadron on 2 February 1918, he was promoted to captain shortly thereafter. He scored his first, partial, victory on 13 March 1918, sharing it with eight other pilots, but over the next two months he claimed five more victories on his own, the last on 11 May 1918. Four of his six victories were gained whilst flying S.E.5a no. C1113.

Then, on 17 May, illness once again struck, and his war was over. He was awarded the MC on 21 June 1918: 'For conspicuous gallantry and devotion to duty. He has carried out many low-flying bombing raids, obtaining direct hits on enemy troops, hutments and camps. On one occasion, after attacking a large column of enemy infantry on a road with machine-gun fire, he attacked and shot down in flames a hostile scout. His work has always been carried out with the utmost keenness and determination.'[453]

With many other soldiers, sailors and airmen, most on their way home to various parts of the Commonwealth, or off on some other duty, Rigby sailed from Liverpool on 3 June 1918 on the SS *Scandinavian*, reaching New York on 15 June. Called to arms again in the Second World War, he rose to the rank of wing commander (service no. 250063), and died in Australia on 4 November 1972.

♦ ♦ ♦

---

[453] *The London Gazette*, 21 Jun 1918, no. 30761.

**ROBINS, Arthur Claud**, born on 18 December 1889, had served as a rigger in the RFC (Service no. 102), and was a corporal on No. 3 Squadron when awarded RAeC certificate no. 793 on 21 May 1914. He flew to France in August 1914 as a passenger with Lieutenant G.F. Pretyman, with whom Robert was to fly a number of reconnaissances in 1914. Robert would have served on 3 Squadron at the same time as Robins, who was promoted to Sergeant-Major during the war. Discharged with a disability from the Royal Air Force with effect from 30 April 1920, he spent some time with the de Havilland company in Canada after the war. He died in Swindon, England, in 1957.

♦.   ♦   ♦

ROSS, James Kenneth. On 8 April, the Ross family received the dread telegram stating that their son and brother was missing on 5 April 1917. It was not until 3 June that the Army was able to write to Ross's father with further news: 'The Military Secretary presents his compliments to Mr W.T. Ross, and deeply regrets to inform him that a report has been received from the German Government, through the Geneva Red Cross, which states that Lieutenant J.K. Ross, General List and Royal Flying Corps, 24th Squadron, died on the 9th April, 1917, in the Feldlazarette, at Cambrai.'[454]

Having survived to be taken prisoner, Ross died of his wounds at 10.45 p.m. German time on the evening of 9 April 1917 and was buried in the German Cambrai East Military Cemetery.

Ross was born on 13 October 1897 to William Thomson Ross, a Scot, and to Louisa Jane, a Londoner,[455] the 1901 Census showing that ten members of the Ross family were living at 23 Bishop's Road, Hornsey. James Kenneth was the youngest of them all. Ten years later, the family, now only eight of them, were at 15 Highgate Avenue, Highgate, not far from Bishop's Road. A few years after they had moved to 46 Park Avenue South, Crouch End, London N.

James Ross had just turned eighteen, stood 5' 9" tall and weighed 126 lbs., when, on 12 November 1915, he enlisted in "A" Company, the 2/28th Battalion, London Regiment

---

[454] TNA file WO 339/74996. Feldlazarette – field hospital.
[455] Née Bevan, she was the widow Garland on her marriage on 1 Jan 1889 to William Ross.

(Artists' Rifles), Service no. 5001. He served with them for only 298 days, becoming non-effective on 4 September 1916, the date on which he was appointed temporary second lieutenant (on probation) on the General List, RFC. His commission dated from 5 September.[456]

After training at No. 6 (T) Squadron, he was sent to fill a vacancy in 24 Squadron in France: '19-year-old 2nd Lieutenant James Kenneth Ross of Crouch End, a comfortable middle-class suburb in the north of London, arrived fresh from No. 6 Training Squadron to fill [Captain A.E.] McKay's empty chair. He [Ross] was dead in 20 days.'[457]

No doubt well aware of the likelihood of being killed in action, young Ross made his Will on 13 March 1917, leaving everything, little though it was, to his older sister, Agnes Helen Ross. In a note to his father, thanking him and his mother for all that they had done for him, he said that he didn't want anyone to make a fuss of his death, 'as I shall rest perfectly happy knowing that I tried to do my best.'

♦ ♦ ♦

RUSSELL, Patrick Alfred. 'Sec. Lieut. P. A. Russell, Yeomanry [2nd Battalion Lovat's Scouts], attached R.F.C, killed on April 2nd, was the second son of the late P. B. Russell, and of Mrs. Russell, of Lanton, Kirknewton, Northumberland, and was aged 28. Educated at Edinburgh Academy and Sherborne, he joined the Yeomanry [T.F.] on the outbreak of war, and later proceeded to Gallipoli, where he took part in the Suvla landing and the subsequent evacuation.

He took his pilot's certificate in September, 1916, and proceeded to another front in October, 1916. He was a member of the Duke of Buccleuch and North Northumberland Hunts, and was a prominent rider at the Border Hunt Steeplechase at Kelso.' (*The Aeroplane*, 2 May 1917). He is buried in the Villers Hill British Cemetery, Villers Guislain, Nord, France. See also *de Ruvigny's Roll of Honour*, Vol. III, page 238.

♦ ♦ ♦

---

[456] *The London Gazette*, 14 Sep 1916, no. 29748.
[457] *One in a Thousand*, p.94. Captain Alfred Edwin "Eddie" McKay, a Canadian with 10 victories, had been posted to 23 Squadron. He would be KIA on 28 Dec 1917, still with 23 Squadron.

TANNER, Percy Valentine, born on 14 February 1888 in Rockhampton, Queensland, Australia, gave up his peacetime job of motor engineer and salesman to come to England. Having learnt to fly at the Grahame-White School at Hendon, he was awarded RAeC certificate no. 2654 on 3 April 1916.

Later promoted to captain, he went to 79 Squadron, but was lost on 27 March 1918 in Sopwith F5.1 Dolphin no. C4050. His fate was unknown until after the war, when 'the remnants of a machine, the type and number of which cannot be identified, have been found at a place… about 21 miles South West of Albert. The machine has an unmarked grave near it and on the grave, under a shell case, was found a letter which judging by the contents was addressed to Captain P.V. Tanner 79th Squadron. It has not yet been definitely established that Capt. Tanner is buried in this grave…

'I am to state that whilst the finding of this grave cannot at present be definitely accepted as evidence of the death of Capt. Tanner, yet it is feared that, in view of the fact that no news of him has been received since he was reported missing on 27th March 1918, that it will ultimately prove to be so.'[458]

Little is known of Tanner's final minutes, other than that he took-off at 7 a.m. on 27 March with two others of his squadron – Captain E.B. Cahusac MC in Dolphin C3967, and 2nd Lieutenant D.W. Lees in Dolphin C3798. Attacked by German fighters, Lees was hit by both ground and air fire and was forced to land between Laréville and Albert at 7.45 a.m., while Cahusac was also shot down and taken prisoner. It is possible that they had come up against von Richthofen and Jasta 11 for, later that same day, yet another member of 79 Squadron, American 2nd Lieutenant George Halliwell Harding, was shot down and killed by von Richthofen himself for his 73rd victory.

Captain P.V. Tanner is commemorated on the Arras Flying Services Memorial.

♦ ♦ ♦

---

[458] Letter of 17 Sep 1919 from the Controller of Officers Casualties Dept., London, to the Australian Red Cross Society Wounded and Missing Enquiry Bureau.

TODD, Henry Cuthbert, was born in London on 2 January 1893 to Henry Cuthbert and Laura Todd, Henry senior being a pawnbroker and jeweller.

Henry junior enlisted in the Honourable Artillery Company, and served in France in 1914. As 699 Sergeant Todd, he was seconded to the RFC on 18 March 1916, as 'temp. Sec. Lieut.' Learning to fly on a Maurice Farman biplane at the Military School, Ruislip, he was awarded RAeC certificate no. 2951 on 24 May 1916. On 5 July 1916 he was appointed Flying Officer, and joined 40 Squadron.

22 October 1916 was 'a red-letter day' for the squadron. After the squadron had crashed two enemy Albatros in the morning, Todd 'encountered an LVG two-seater while on offensive patrol in mid-afternoon, forcing it to land.'[459]

On 9 March 1917, a month or so after Robert had left 40 Squadron, a hostile machine was claimed by Todd before his F.E.8 6425 was shot up and he made a forced landing behind the lines. Lieutenant William Morrice in F.E.8 7836 suffered a similar fate.

These losses were one of the reasons for the replacement of the squadron's remaining, outdated F.E.8s with Nieuport 17s. 40 Squadron last flew their F.E.8s on 21 March 1917, with Todd being one of those on escort duty with Nos. 2 and 16 Squadrons.

Henry Todd died in Norwich on 2 January 1969.

♦ ♦ ♦

USBORNE, George Curzon Osbert was born on 23 August 1882 at Arnprior, Ontario, Canada. His family went to live in Honolulu, and George paid them several visits over the years. Educated at Victoria College, British Columbia, he went into the business of automobile manufacturing, before marrying Gertrude Laura Barnes, of Detroit, Michigan, USA, on 10 September 1912.

He enlisted in the Canadian Over-Seas Expeditionary Force's Eaton Machine Gun Battery on 30 January 1915, and was commissioned lieutenant. He went to Reading for flying lessons on 28 December 1915. Seconded to the RFC on 13 January 1916, he was posted to No. 46 Squadron on 25 May 1916. On 14 June 1916 he was made a Flying Officer and joined No. 40 Squadron on 18 August 1916. He stayed on the squadron until 9 March 1917, when, promoted to captain (temp.), he briefly flew with 60 Squadron, returning to England

---

[459] *Sweeping the Skies*, pp. 18-19.

on 31 March 1917. On 23 February 1918 he was promoted to major (temp.) and given command of 112 Squadron on 5 October 1918. He was awarded the AFC on 2 November 1918.

He ceased secondment to the RAF on 7 May 1919, and returned to Canada on 8 September 1919 on the SS *Scandinavian*, docking at Quebec nine days later. Shortly afterwards, he went back to Honolulu, arriving on the SS *Niagara* on 10 October 1919.

♦ ♦ ♦

VALENTINE, James was born on 22 August 1887, 'the only child of the late James Valentine, managing director of the Northern Assurance Company, Moorgate Street, [London], and his mother was, before her marriage, Miss Fanny Roe, a member of an old Norwich family.'

After Dulwich College (1900-03), young James turned to motoring: 'In his early days he was concerned in the motor industry, and was known as one of the most daring and skilful drivers on the road, though he never drove in any of the big races.' In 1910 he took an active part in flying, when he 'acquired a Gnôme engine and joined forces with Mr. R. F. Macfie at Brooklands, the resulting Macfie biplane being an excellent example of its period. On this machine James Valentine and Robert Macfie took their certificate.' Valentine was awarded RAeC certificate no. 47 on 17 January 1911, and Macfie no. 49 a week later.

On 11 September 1911 he was fined £5 and costs by magistrates for driving a motor car at dangerous speed through Newport, Isle of Wight, and was caught speeding again in January 1913, being fined £15 at Croydon 'for driving a motor-car at 39 miles an hour through Morden.' (Another famous aviator, William Rhodes Moorhouse, was also caught speeding on numerous occasions by the over-zealous police and, tragically, would be involved in the death of two people in two separate incidents.)

Valentine then went 'to Paris, where he was taken on as a pilot by the Deperdussin firm', and flew in the 1911 "European Circuit", being 'one of the few pilots, and the only British competitor, to complete the course, which ran from Paris to Reims, Utrecht, Amsterdam, Brussels, Calais, Shoreham, Hendon, and back to Paris.' A few weeks later he finished third in the *Daily Mail* "Circuit of Britain", (Jules Védrines was second). Joining the Bristol company, he flew one of their Coanda monoplanes in the Military Trials on Salisbury Plain in August 1912.

Russian Vickers FB19, with Sopwith 1½ Strutter beyond [Vickers Aircraft since 1908, p.63]

He did little more flying before joining the RFC on the outbreak of war in 1914. Appointed as an Equipment Officer in January 1915, he was posted to the Central British Aviation Depot in Paris, being 'appointed to oversee the acquisition of aircraft materiel by the R.F.C. from the French Aircraft Industry… His success in promoting cordial relations between the parties concerned was rewarded by the French Government' with the Croix de Chevalier de la Légion d'Honneur on 8 November 1915.

In March 1917, following the February Revolution by the Bolsheviks, he was sent on a special mission to train pilots of the Imperial Russian Air Service on British aeroplanes. At first, no British aeroplane was available but, eventually, 'five BE2e and five Vickers FB19s arrived, and training commenced near Moscow.' These aeroplanes were augmented by a few Sopwith 1½ Strutters.

Matters at first were confused. Though British machines were sent to Russian squadrons, the Russian pilots, as yet untrained on the British machines, had to fly other types at the front. Eventually, in June 1917, once familiar with the foreign machines, the Russian pilots distinguished themselves in low level attacks on German positions. (www.greatwarforum.org/).

James Valentine was made a Squadron Commander on 15 June 1917, but shortly afterwards contracted dysentery whilst at the front. Evacuated to Kieff (now Kyiv) at the beginning of July, he died on 7 August 1917 from a heart attack, and was buried in Kieff in the Brats'ke (Brotherly) military cemetery. He is now commemorated on the Archangel Memorial.

For his service, he was made DSO on 4 June 1917. In the same month he was recommended by the Russians for an award. Eventually, on 14 January 1918, five months after his death, King George V gave unrestricted permission for Captain (temporary Major) James Valentine DSO, late Royal Flying Corps, Special Reserve, to wear the Russian Order of St. George (4th Class), awarded for distinguished services rendered during the course of the campaign in Russia.

Probate was granted to his widow, Louisa Eileen (née Knox), whom he had married in 1913.

♦ ♦ ♦

WADHAM, Vivian Hugh Nicholas, was born on 31 December 1891 at Lower Halliford, Teddington. Commissioned in the 5th Battalion, KRRC, he was appointed Flying Officer in the RFC on 5 December 1912. He transferred to 1st Battalion, the Hampshire Regiment on 10 June 1914. He was awarded RAeC certificate no. 243 on 16 July 1912, flying a Farman at the Sopwith School, Brooklands.

The following appeared in the obituary columns on 23 February 1916: 'On January 17th, 1916, killed in action over the German lines in Flanders, Captain Vivian H. N. Wadham, Royal Flying Corps and 1st Batt. the Hampshire Regt., eldest son of Hugh D. and Mabel E. Wadham, of Thamesfield, Shepperton-on-Thames, aged twenty-four.

'Capt. Vivian Hugh Nicholas Wadham was born at Teddington on December 31st, 1891. He joined the Hampshire Regiment from the Special Reserve in June, 1914, and was promoted lieutenant in the following December. In May, 1915, he was gazetted flight commander R.F.C, with temporary rank of captain.

'He was one of the very first officers of the Royal Flying Corps, having been appointed soon after the formation of the Corps. He took his certificate. No. 243, on a Farman, at the Sopwith School at Brooklands on July 16th, 1912, and soon developed into one of the very finest pilots in the British Army.

'He went to France at the outbreak of war with the famous No. 3 Squadron from Netheravon, and after doing much distinguished service he was severely injured in an accident on a Blériot, with Major, now Colonel, Charlton as passenger. After a lengthy period in hospital in England he went out again and was killed as indicated in the brief notice above.

'Besides being a brilliant flier Captain Wadham was a first-class sportsman in every way, and possessed a personal charm which made him beloved by officers and men alike. He was an excellent example of the type of young British officer, who, by his gallantry and sportsmanship, made the old Expeditionary Force a thing apart from all other Armies, and his death will be deeply mourned by all who knew him.' (Quoted in *The Aeroplane*, 1 March 1916).

Wadham was 'A' Flight Commander, 15 Squadron, when he was shot down and killed in B.E.2c no. 2105 on 17 January 1916. His observer, 470 Sergeant Nigel Vincent Piper, was taken prisoner.

♦ ♦ ♦

WALDER, William Thomas, born 13 October 1895, attested for service in the RFC on 18 October 1915 (Service no. 10137) as a 2nd Class AM. He was a 1st Class AM when he was graded as a Qualified Observer on 30 June 1916. He learnt to fly at the Military School, Ruislip and was awarded RAeC certificate no. 3752 on 25 October 1916. Graded a 1st Class Flyer on 22 November 1916, he returned to France on 2 December 1916. He was discharged from 40 Squadron on 9 March 1917 when granted a temporary commission on the General List.

Twice married, his first wife dying in 1921, he died on 5 May 1963 at the Nelson Hospital, Merton, London SW19.

♦ ♦ ♦

WEIL, Louis Marcus Basil, born on 13 October 1898 at Port Elizabeth, Cape Colony, South Africa, was the eldest son of Benjamin "Ben" Weil and Ethel Florence (née Samuel), who were married in the Bayswater Synagogue, London on 12 January 1897. Ethel was twenty-five years younger than her husband who, for some reason, later adopted the middle name Burtie (or Bertie). Benjamin was invited by his younger brother, Julius, who had gone to South Africa in 1876, to take charge of Weil & Co's main forwarding depot at Mafeking, only eight miles from the Transvaal border, Julius having done extremely well as a supplier to the British Army.

With the Second Boer War imminent in 1899, Ben was asked by Lieutenant-Colonel R.S. Baden-Powell's Chief of Staff, Major Lord Edward Cecil, to see about providing the town with supplies, and promises were made that Ben would be paid sometime. It was a gamble for Ben, but he took a chance and, the extensive warehouses of Weil & Co., conveniently located close to Mafeking's railway station in the middle of town, were packed 'to the rafters. Not only with food but medicines, clothing and blankets, tools, rifles, shotguns, powder and ammunition, necessities and luxuries, anything and everything he could lay his hands upon was crammed into store.'[460]

Ben Weil, and (right) seated centre with others of the Town Guard, most of whom carry Lee-Metford rifles (photos: www.awm.gov.au/collection/C49402 & C49467, donated by C. Booth)

---

[460] From Gordon Everson's article *The Man Who Fed Mafeking*.

Just before the Boers laid siege to Mafeking young Louis and his mother left on the last train to Cape Town. Ben, one of the Mafeking Town Guard during the 217-day siege (13 October 1899–17 May 1900), was awarded the Queen's South Africa Medal and the Defence of Mafeking bar (the rarest of all clasps issued during the conflict, his medal selling for £2,645 in 1999).

At some point the Weil family returned to London (where Benjamin was born 24 May 1850; died 8 June 1944). Educated at Clifton College, Bristol, Louis was still two days short of his seventeenth birthday when, on 11 October 1915, he was entered in the RNAS as a probationary flight sub-lieutenant for temporary service. Initially posted to Chingford on 14 October 1915, he went to Redcar on 2 December. There, now 17, he was awarded RAeC certificate no. 2336 on 27 January 1916.

He was then sent to Eastchurch Gunnery School on 26 March 1916. On 23 April he was taken ill when on leave. Having recovered he was sent to RNAS Redcar Flying School as an Assistant Instructor on 9 June. Various reports noted that he was 'too young to command' (30 June 1916); 'Shows great promise as a pilot and as instructor. Very keen. As yet rather young & lacks experience as an officer.' (1 October 1916); 'Should make a good officer.' (1 January 1917).

Back at Redcar he served as an Assistant Instructor. He was involved in a mishap at Scarborough in August 1916 with Avro 504C no. 8600. and was still at Redcar when, on 21 November 1916, he was involved in a taxiing accident to Maurice Farman S.7 Longhorn no. N5037.

On 17 January 1917 he was posted to Dover and was confirmed as Flight Sub-Lieutenant on that same day. It is likely that he went to France shortly thereafter, joining No. 1 (Naval) Squadron. He was killed just after midday on 6 April 1917 flying Sopwith Triplane N5448 when attacked by Hauptmann Paul von Osterroht. Weil's aircraft crashed near Malakoff Station and this is reported as being the first Sopwith Triplane to have been brought down by a German pilot.

(Von Osterroht, with seven victories to his name, would be shot down and killed on 23 April 1917, possibly by the Canadian Flight Sub-Lieutenant J.J. Malone of 3 (N) Squadron in Sopwith Pup N6202 who, too, would be killed in action on 30 April 1917. So it went on.)

On 7 April 1917, a German aviator dropped this message to the RFC: 'Flt Sub Lt Weil RNAS, Jew, shot down in air fight on 6.4.17 lies in Marquion cemetery.' Weil, who was only eighteen years old, now lies in the Sauchy-Estrée Communal Cemetery, Pas-de-Calais, France. His father Ben, saviour of Mafeking, would outlive him for another twenty-four years.

♦ ♦ ♦

 **WEIR**, James George was born on 23 May 1887 at Ardoch Grove, Cambuslang, Lanarkshire, Scotland to James and Mary Weir, and grew-up in the family-owned and run engineering firm Messrs. G. & J. Weir Ltd. at the Holm Foundry, Cathcart, Glasgow. After attending Dollar Academy, he served apprenticeships at the North German Lloyd Works, Bremen, Germany and with his family firm G and J Weir Ltd. from 1903–08. He also went on a science course at Glasgow University and a metallurgical course at Freiburg's School of Mines, Saxony, Germany.

On 24 February 1906 he was commissioned Second Lieutenant in the 3rd (Renfrewshire) Volunteer Battalion, Princess Louise's (Argyll and Sutherland Highlanders) before, on 1 April 1908, transferring to the 3rd Highland Ammunition Column (Howitzer) Brigade, RFA.

Calling himself a marine engineer he went to the Far East in 1909. 1 January 1910 found him in Hong Kong on the SS *Manchuria* on his way via Japan and Honolulu to San Francisco, on the USA's west coast, where he landed on 30 January. He was back in England in time to sail back to the USA on 23 March 1910, now a mechanical engineer and one of thirty passengers aboard the SS *Kaiser Wilhelm II*, reaching New York on 30 March.

Later in that year, 1910, back in England, he learnt to fly at the Blériot School at Hendon. After only five lessons he flew for his "ticket" on 5 November 1910 and was awarded RAeC certificate no. 24 three days later: 'Saturday [5 November] proved another glorious flying day—bright and windless, though a trifle keen. In the morning Mr. Weir, the Blériot pupil—if one who has made such wonderful progress can be termed pupil—flew brilliantly several times, making complete circuits of the ground, at an average height of 30 ft ...

'In the afternoon ... Mr. Weir obtained his R.Ae.C. pilot's certificate as the result of five lessons! He flew the usual test of three flights of 6 mins. each ... but, wherever he flew, the wonderful steadiness of the machine was most marked, and very few people, not knowing that he was a pupil, would have guessed that he had only five times previously been in an aeroplane. A wonderful performance, which proves emphatically the boast of the Blériot firm that flying can be easily taught in six lessons!' (*Flight*, 12 November 1910).

Clearly a man of principle, on 13 April 1911 he struck and knocked down the former fiancé of his sister after he had broken off their engagement. On 27 June 1911 the Courts found Weir guilty of the offence.

On 28 October 1914 he was made Flying Officer in the RFC, and Flight Commander on 24 March 1915. He went to France in May 1915, possibly in a non-flying role, but was back later that year to marry Mora Morton Christie (1896–1979) on 2 December 1915. After further promotion, on 22 June 1916, to Squadron Commander he was made Deputy Assistant Director, War Office (graded as a Staff Captain) (14 December 1916, Assistant Director of Military Aeronautics (21 March 1917) and was specially employed as Director of Aircraft Production on 24 May 1918, on which date he was also made acting Brigadier-General.

Transferring to the Unemployed List on 15 February 1919, he then relinquished his commission in the RAF on appointment to the Territorial Force on 28 September 1920. On 18 May 1923 he was appointed to a Commission in the RAFO, Class 'C' in the rank of Air Commodore.

In 1926 he helped form, and became chairman and managing director of, the Cierva Autogiro Company. He commuted to work daily in an autogiro and Alfred Hitchcock worked the aircraft into the 1935 film *The 39 Steps*. Also in 1935 he became a Director of the Bank of England, and was also deputy director of the family company, G. & J. Weir Ltd.

J.G. Weir CMG, CBE died on 7 November 1973.

♦ ♦ ♦

WHITE, Melville Arthur was born on 28 December 1892 in Picton, New Zealand. He was a Civil Servant in the Post and Telegraph Department in Wellington when he enlisted, and was appointed as a superintending clerk in the rank of staff-sergeant to the Quartermaster-General's branch, New Zealand Expeditionary Force ("NZEF"), as of 5 August 1914. He embarked at Alexandria, Egypt, on 12 April 1915 to join the Mediterranean NZ Expeditionary Force at Gallipoli, but was admitted to Base Hospital, Lemnos, on 18 May, being discharged to duty on 28 May 1915. He returned from Alexandria to No 2 Post, Gallipoli, on 27 August 1915.

Returning to Alexandria on 28 October 1915, he was posted as a staff sergeant-major to NZEF HQ Cairo, and was promoted warrant officer on 28 March 1916 (seniority 1 March 1916). He sailed from Alexandria, Egypt, for England on 10 May 1916 aboard the troopship *Euripides*. On 29 August 1916 he was discharged from the NZEF on taking a commission as second lieutenant (temp.) in the RFC, gazetted 5 September. He 'served with the Expeditionary Force in France and Flanders for 11 days, and was killed in aerial action at St. Quentin 23 April 1917. Buried in Jeancourt Communal Cemetery.' (*de Ruvigny's Roll of Honour*, page 284, Vol. II, Part III).

♦ ♦ ♦

WINFIELD-SMITH, Stephen Christopher was born in Ceylon on 8 March 1892 (or 1893). Educated at Repton School, he was commissioned second lieutenant (on probation) in 3rd Battalion East Surrey Regiment, on 27 July 1910.

After learning to fly at the Bristol School, Brooklands, he was awarded RAeC certificate no. 187 on 27 February 1912. In August 1912 he went on the the first course of flying instruction at the CFS, which ran from 17 August to 5 December 1912.

By October 1913 he was employed as a pilot at the Royal Aircraft Factory, Farnborough: 'The Royal Aircraft Factory pilots, Messrs. de Havilland, Kemp and Winfield-Smith, were all out testing various machines. Among these were the experimental gun-carrying machine, a tractor biplane intended for wireless, and a "B.E. 2" type machine with which wind-gauge experiments were being carried on.' (*The Aeroplane*, 16 October 1913). And: 'It is reported that on Friday last [*19 December*] Colonel J. E. B. Seely, D.S.O., Secretary of State for War, made a flight on a Mark B.E.2 biplane piloted by Mr. Winfield-Smith, one of the professional aviators employed by the Royal Aircraft Factory at Farnborough.' (*The Aeroplane*, 25 December 1913).

At some point, Winfield-Smith also flew the FE2, a machine described by Charles Grey as being inherently unairworthy, though Grey made his comments after it had crashed on 23 February 1914 killing the passenger and badly injuring the pilot.

Winfield-Smith would later deny that he ever said, *à propos* the FE2: 'If ever I get this beast home I shall go to church for a week.' (*The Aeroplane*, 2 April 1914).

When war came in August 1914, Winfield-Smith was with No. 4 Squadron when it flew to France that month. Later transferring to Mesopotamia, he was captured by Ottoman forces following the surrender by Major-General C.V.F. Townshend of the garrison at Kut al-Amara, Iraq, after a siege lasting for one hundred and forty-seven days (3 December 1915 to 29 April 1916). Ottoman forces captured 13,309 men: 277 British officers; 204 Indian officers; 2,592 British soldiers; 6,988 Indian soldiers; 3,248 Indian support staff. On 2 May 1916, 1,306 sick or wounded soldiers were allowed to leave aboard British medical ships, together with 694 nursing and support staff to tend them.[461]

---

[461] https://encyclopedia.1914-1918-online.net/article/kut_al-amara.

After several months, sufficient information had been gleaned as to events at Kut for a list of names to be published, on 19 October 1916. 'Winfield Smith, Flight Comdr. S. C., Capt., E. Surr. R., Spec. Res.' was among those 'recommended by Major-General Townshend for distinguished service during the defence of Kut-al-Amarah.'

Following imprisonment by the Turks, he was repatriated on 7 December 1918. Again, there was a long delay while the awards of further honours were assessed for those who had been at Kut, but Winfield-Smith, who stayed in the RAF as a flight lieutenant, was awarded the DSO on 23 October 1919.

He was promoted to squadron leader on 1 March 1920 (*The London Gazette*, 2 April 1920, no. 31849). On 22 November 1920 he was graded as supernumerary (non-effective-sick), but on 1 August 1921 was in office at the Inland Area Aircraft Depôt at Henlow. Not long afterwards he was 'placed on the retired list on account of ill-health contracted in the Service. 7th Feb. 1923.' (*The London Gazette*, 6 February 1923, no. 32793).

He had become a Freemason in the Old Reptonian Lodge, No. 3725, on 12 October 1920.

With Sydney Cauthery and the company Burovox Ltd., several patents were registered in their names in the late 1920's and early 1930's, relating to such matters as direct call systems; microphones, gramophone pick-ups, diaphragms etc.

He died on 25 August 1971.

Winfield-Smith in March 1912 (The Aeroplane)

Appendix V: Major Eric Lewis Conran

This lengthy biography is intended to illustrate not only the difficulties of a squadron commander during the long war but also to show how, cumulatively, the stress of war itself can affect a person's well-being. There is an obvious and frightening parallel with Robert Loraine's wartime career and poor health.

Eric Lewis Conran was born in Brisbane, Australia, on 22 August 1887. His parents, Henry Lewis Conran (26 December 1861–25 December 1924), an Australian pastoralist and stockbroker, and Mary Louisa (née Molle), were married in Brisbane on 30 September 1886. Moving to England in 1898, the family lived at "Courabelle", Westgate-on-Sea, Kent.

Young Eric 'suffered from lung trouble, which necessitated his leading an open air life. Part of his time was spent in consequence in Switzerland and the Black Forest, and for five years on stations in Australia.' He was subsequently well enough to go hunting in Leicestershire, England and, on 21 May 1909, to be commissioned second lieutenant in 2nd County of London (Westminster Dragoons) Yeomanry.

Turning to aviation, he had his first training flight at the W. H. Ewen School, Hendon on 8 July 1912, when he went 'out for the first time and made wonderful progress.' On 22 October 1912 he was awarded RAeC certificate no. 342.

He was promoted to lieutenant in the Yeomanry, with effect from 12 August 1912. By early December 1912 he was employed at the Blériot School, having 'joined school, intending to go for superior brevet.' In January 1913 he was posted to the CFS at Upavon for the second course of flying instruction, which ran from 17 January 1913 to 17 April 1913. On the course were 'five naval, four R.N.V.R., 15 military and six Territorial and Special Reserve officers, plus 20 naval ratings and 40 military N.C.O.'s and men who joined for a course of ground instruction.' Eric "passed out" second of the group.

Having been made a Flying Officer on 9 May 1913, with effect from 17 April, he joined the newly-formed No. 3 Squadron at Lark Hill on Salisbury Plain. There, his aeroplane was looked after by 892 2AM J.T.B. McCudden, and by 736 2AM D. Abrahams (rigger), both of whom would, occasionally, fly with him in the coming war.

CFS Staff, Upavon, Wiltshire, May 1914. Eric Conran is standing second from the left. Seated third from the left is Captain Godfrey Paine, RN (Commandant), and on his left is Major H.M. Trenchard CB, DSO (Assistant Commandant) [photo Flight, 24 July 1914]

Following a visit to Australia, Conran went back to the CFS, this time as Assistant Instructor on the sixth course, which started on 12 April 1914. He was nearly killed on 1 June 1914 when a South African pupil 'drove an aeroplane into the ground'. The pupil, a member of the South African Union Defence Force, had been under instruction at the aviation school at Kimberley but, when this school closed, the Union Government selected him and five other officers for further flying training. They arrived in England on 15 May 1914 'to be attached to the Royal Flying Corps for training at the Central Flying School.' The only one of the six not to qualify was Marthinus Steyn Williams.

Following the accident, it was six weeks before Conran was able to resume his duties.

No. 3 Squadron had moved to Netheravon on 16 June 1913, where it remained until flying to Amiens, France, and off to war, on 13 August 1914. Conran, having rejoined his squadron, crossed to France in Blériot Parasol no. 616. Along with the rest of his squadron, he flew a number of reconnaissances during the first weeks of the war, performing 'valuable services in saving the Brigade of Guards at Villers Cotterets' and in making 'valuable reports as to the position of the Germans at Chateau Thierry' and was MiD on 8 October 1914 by Sir John French. He had a close shave one day in November 1914 when an enemy bullet severed his oil and fuel pipes, causing his aeroplane to nose-dive some five hundred feet, leaving him 'very badly shaken.'

Appointed flight commander and temporary captain as at 28 November 1914, he was one of the first six RFC airmen ever to be awarded the newly-instituted MC, as per the 1915 New Year's Honours List. There then followed the announcement in *The London Gazette*, on 5 January 1915, transferring his commission to another regiment: '21st (Empress of India's) Lancers. Lieutenant Eric Lewis Conran (flight commander Royal Flying Corps, Military Wing), from the 2nd County of London Yeomanry, Territorial Force, to be second lieutenant, and to be seconded. Dated April 17th, 1913.' Conran would never actually serve with the 21st Lancers, and would resign his commission in the regiment in 1920 on being awarded a permanent commission in the RAF.

In January 1915, he 'had two falls, one due to his propeller being shot away by the enemy anti-aircraft guns'. Then, on 25 March 1915, on a bombing raid with Second Lieutenant Isaac Newton Woodiwiss, Lincolnshire Regiment, as his Observer, their aeroplane, Morane No. 1872, was hit by "Archie". Woodiwiss was unhurt, but Conran was 'badly wounded in back and arm... One shrapnel ball had embedded itself in his right arm and the other had gone in at his side and come out very near his spine.' (*Flying Fury*, p.65). After treatment at Boulogne, he was invalided from there to Dover, England, on the *St. David* on 30 March.

He had recovered sufficiently by June 1915 to be put on light duties at the CFS where, on 1 June, he was graded as Instructor: 'Lt. (temp. Capt.) E. L. Conran, 21st Lancers, from a Flight Commr., and to retain his temp, rank whilst so employed, *vice* Capt. F. F. Waldron, 19th Hussars (June 1st).' (*The London Gazette*, 10 June, 1915).

It was whilst with the CFS that he witnessed the terrible death, on 7 July, of his friend Captain A.H.L. Soames MC. An inquest was held into Soames's death at the Netheravon Military Hospital on 9 July 1915 by Mr. Sylvester, Coroner for Central Wiltshire: 'On Wednesday, Captain Soames, who was in charge of the experiments at the Central Flying School at Upavon, was experimenting with a bomb. It was placed on its nose in a wood near Netheravon Hospital, and was fired by an electric wire, 100 yards long, which was carried through a thick clump of trees. After the bomb had been fired Captain Soames was found on the ground severely injured. A tree near him had been cut through by part of the exploded bomb. The officer's injuries were very severe, but he was still conscious. He died the same night.'

Conran, who was only a short distance away from his friend when he was killed, suffered acutely from shock and was admitted to the Military Hospital, Tidworth. It was not until 18 July 1915 that a Medical Board decided that he had fully recovered.

On 25 June 1915 Conran 'had the honour of being decorated with the Military Cross by the King' at Buckingham Palace.

Returning to the CFS, he suffered another accident when another pupil drove an aeroplane into a ditch on landing.

Graded as squadron commander with the rank of major, he became CO of the Experimental Flight at the CFS from 28 September until 7 December 1915, when his place was taken by Captain G.L. Cruikshank DSO.

Conran's run of bad luck continued when involved in yet another accident. He was sitting in an aeroplane one day in November 1915 when a sudden squall overturned the machine, which landed on top of him. With a broken right leg and left arm, dislocated shoulder and cracked ribs, he was back in hospital until March 1916.

Returning to the CFS, he was appointed Assistant Commandant (graded as wing commander). Clearly, he was not right, for the Commandant, Lieutenant Colonel C.J. Burke, found that, even though he was 'a splendid pilot', he was wanting in his abilities as Assistant Commandant, and on 11 May 1916 asked 'that he be relieved by another officer as soon as possible.' Conran had not helped his case by flying a Maurice Farman with two passengers on 10 May 'to the detriment of the CFS'. (TNA file WO 339/643).

Replaced on 21 May 1916 Conran was given command of No. 29 Squadron at Abeele in France from 2 June 1916. It would prove to be a most unpleasant time for him, culminating in his being brought before a General Court Martial on two charges at Cassel, France, on 14 September 1916.

The first charge, brought under Section 41 of the Army Act, was that he had, between 15 and 31 July 1916 at Abeele, attempted 'to procure the commission by a male person of an act of gross indecency with another male person.' The second charge, under Section 16 of the Army Act, was that he had behaved 'in a scandalous manner unbecoming the character of an officer and a gentleman in that he at Abeele on divers dates between July 1st and August 31st, 1916' sought to induce a junior officer 'to indulge in conduct of an indecent nature.'

The officer in question, and the one who brought the charges, was Second Lieutenant F.B. Sedgwick, who had joined the squadron on 1 July 1916. Initially, Conran thought that he would be an asset to the squadron but, later, found that 'his neglect and want of interest in his work' caused him to change his mind, such that it was necessary for him to take disciplinary steps against Sedgwick.

On 6 July, when two new aeroplanes were ready for collection from St. Omer, Conran drove Sedgwick with him in the squadron car to ferry them back to the squadron. In the event, as only one machine was ready, Conran told Sedgwick to return to Abeele in the car while he flew the aeroplane. On the way back the aeroplane's engine malfunctioned, forcing Conran to make a rough landing in a field, causing painful injury to both legs. Managing to get to Cassel, some 8 or 9 kilometres west of Abeele, he telephoned for the car to come and fetch him. Examined by two doctors, they said that he should go to hospital, but such was his horror of those places that he chose to recover in the care of his squadron.

He would spend the next ten days on his bunk, unable to get much sleep, such was the pain from his latest injuries, but by 20 July he was able to get about on crutches, enough to get to the Squadron Office and lie on a lounge chair. By 25 July, he was sufficiently well to get about in his car, and would take officers, including Sedgwick, with him on outings to various places.

Sedgwick would, however, continue to give Conran cause to complain of his slackness and unreliability. On 3 or 4 August 1916, for example, Sedgwick was Duty Officer for the day, it being the Duty Officer's duty to get up before dawn to study the weather prior to sending up a patrol. On the day in question, however, when he woke up without hearing the sound of aeroplane engines, Conran found that Sedgwick was fast asleep, even though he had been earlier called by the Orderly corporal. Conran gave him a severe reprimand.

Then, on 7 August, Sedgwick was detailed to go on a patrol with a newly-arrived pilot, Lieutenant F.W. Honnet, with orders to remain in close contact with the new man. Later in the day, after Sedgwick had returned alone, with no idea as to the whereabouts of Honnet, it transpired that Sedgwick had gone off in a different direction than the one detailed for his patrol. The squadron then received a telephone call from Honnet to say that he had been forced down by engine trouble, that he was uninjured, but that his aeroplane was smashed-up. When Conran gave Sedgwick another severe reprimand, the latter took it very badly, and sulked. Conran thought that he acted foolishly.

The two officers clashed again on 10 August. Sedgwick, who at the time was the assistant to Lieutenant Pinney in the Squadron Office, was instructed by Conran to stay in Pinney's quarters for the night while Pinney was away. Though Pinney's quarters were only a few steps from the office, Sedgwick said that he would rather go to his own quarters, a hundred yards or so from the office, which Conran thought 'a piece of rather ill-conditioned conduct.'

Sedgwick was in trouble with Conran again, on 25 August 1916. This time, Sedgwick was told to go on a patrol with Second Lieutenant K.K. Turner. Sedgwick was to take-off first and circle round the aerodrome while Turner took-off, but he flew away without bothering to wait for Turner. When Sedgwick returned alone it was concluded that Turner had been lost. Conran was deeply upset at this possibility, as Turner had been a friend of his. Severely reprimanding Sedgwick once more Conran told him that it was possible that he was responsible for Turner's death. In the event, Turner had come down behind enemy lines and been taken prisoner-of-war. He was repatriated on 21 January 1919.

Conran had other concerns about Sedgwick. It was something of a craze at this time for junior officers to play poker and roulette, enough for Conran to stop such activity in his squadron's Mess. Sedgwick simply went off to other squadrons to indulge himself.

Left to right: Lieutenant Frederick William Honett; Second Lieutenant Kenneth Kestell Turner; Captain Selden Herbert Long DSO, MC [photo: courtesy mykmorris98 via ancestry.com]

Conran, suffering from the strain of command exacerbated by his recent injuries, was now subject to fainting fits, which he had never before experienced, and since his last accident had developed a stammer. At the end of August 1916, he was to be sent home for a rest.

Sedgwick, meanwhile, decided that he had had enough of his squadron commander's treatment and brought charges against him. On 4 September 1916, Conran, who was ill in bed, was summoned to the Squadron Office, where a Colonel Ritchie announced, without any preamble, that he was 'under arrest for indecent conduct in your hut' and told Conran to hand over 29 Squadron to Captain S.H. Long MC, one of the Flight Commanders.

After Colonel Ritchie had taken a summary of evidence from Sedgwick and a Lieutenant Lewin (later discarded as a witness), Conran was taken by the Squadron Adjutant, Captain Sydney, to Cassel, where he was handed-over to the 2nd Army's Provost Marshal and locked-up in the Military Police's billet.

Conran's room was furnished with but a table and a chair. As there was no bed, he had to sleep on the floor. He was there for three weeks, during which time he was allowed only one bath. For the first four days he was not allowed out of the room, but thereafter was permitted to leave it for one hour in the company of a lance-corporal. For the last four days, though, he was able to sleep on his bunk bed, which had been brought over from his hut at Abeele.

On 11 September he was introduced to a Captain Macdonald, who was to act as his "friend" at the court-martial. Beginning on 14 September, it lasted for five days and ended with the Court finding Conran guilty and sentencing him to be cashiered.

Brigadier-General Tom Webb-Bowen, commander of II Brigade RFC, concerned meanwhile as to Conran's poor health, sent a doctor to examine him. On the basis of the doctor's report Webb-Bowen said that it was not right that Conran 'should be kept there any longer in his then state of health' and recommended, and it was agreed, that Conran was now to be sent home for a rest.

Once back in England, Conran launched an appeal. As part of his defence, he was examined by the eminent physician, Henry Head, on 16 October 1916, who found that he was 'in a very neurasthenic condition. He stutters in his speaking, his skin is covered with sweat, tapping his knees to obtain the knee-jerk causes a wide-spread general reaction, and his hands and tongue are tremulous.

'I gather that this condition existed at the beginning of September and that it was for such symptoms that he was to have been sent home for medical treatment at the time when he was arrested.

'I do not think that a man in such a state of health could do himself justice before a Court Martial.

'Attention and memory are defective and his manner would certainly make a bad impression. Apart altogether from his present condition I examined into his sexual life and I do not believe he is in any way homo-sexual.' Mr. Head added that he believed Conran to be 'a normal male strongly attracted to women.'

Conran's case went before the Judge Advocate General (JAG) on 5 October 1916, who wrote to the Secretary of State for War on 7 November 1916: 'I have to point out that the Court received and indeed themselves elicited evidence of rumours and gossip in the Squadron commanded by the accused and of impressions and opinions of witnesses as distinct from facts. The only direct evidence of the guilt of the accused was that given by Second Lieutenant Sedgwick which in the circumstances could not be accepted without corroboration. In so far as there was any evidence which can properly be regarded as corroborative evidence shewing or tending to shew the guilt of the accused at all, it was very slight, and the misreception in such a case of evidence of the kind indicated above could not be otherwise than prejudicial to a fair trial.'

The Secretary of State reviewed Conran's case and 'decides that the conviction herein be quashed and in recording this decision adds that he agrees entirely with the views expressed by the JAG as to the irregularity of the proceedings, and the unsatisfactory nature of the evidence adduced by the prosecution.' The Army Council accordingly quashed Conran's conviction.

♦ ♦ ♦

 Francis Balfour Sedgwick, the root cause of Conran's trial, was born on 26 January 1896 at Chesterton, Cambridgeshire, the younger son of Professor Adam and Mrs. L.H. Sedgwick. After education at Sedbergh School, he went to Canada, arriving there on 31 May 1913. Joining the Bank of Montreal in Ottawa, he later transferred to Head Office in Montreal as Private Secretary to the General Manager. Sailing back to England in June 1915, he was commissioned in the 13th Suffolk Regiment.

He went to the School of Aviation at Reading on 16 March 1916 to learn to fly. After short spells at Nos. 2 and 10 (Reserve) Squadrons and at No. 40 Squadron, he was posted to No. 29 Squadron on 30 June 1916. After nine months at the front, he returned to England on 23 March 1917.

Posted back to Canada, he became Assistant Instructor in Aviation at the Deseronto Camp, and later at the Aviation Camp in Texas, USA. Promoted to temporary captain as at 1 September 1917, he returned to England in 1918 but, whilst serving at the 54th Training Depôt Station, Fairlop, Essex, was killed when Sopwith Camel F1417 stalled and crashed on 18 October 1918. A rotten end to a rotten business.

He is buried in the Brookwood Cemetery, Woking, Surrey.

♦ ♦ ♦

Eric Conran left 29 Squadron in September 1916, among whose pilots was a certain Jimmy McCudden. He spent the next three months in England before being posted to German East Africa on recruiting duties from December 1916 to April 1917. Back in England, he was appointed Assistant Commandant of the School of Aerial Gunnery on 24 May 1917, until February 1918, when he commanded No. 4 Training Depôt Station at Ternhill, Shropshire, and then, in August 1918, No. 26 Wing.

On 25 February 1919, he was CO of 38 Wing in Egypt, before, on 18 June, assuming temporary command of H.Q. Training Brigade, later renamed Egyptian Group, at Heliopolis, Egypt, for which His Highness the Sultan of Egypt conferred on him the Order of the Nile, 3rd Class.

On 1 August 1919, he was appointed to a permanent commission in the RAF. On 21 May 1920 he left for England on a long leave but was back at HQ Egyptian Group on 7 September 1920. Four days later he was attached to HQ Palestine Group, Mesopotamia. Returning to England, he was posted to No. 7 Group, Andover, on 13 April 1922.

In 1923 he 'was so unwell with pains in the head that he thought of resigning and returning to Australia on a health trip. The nature of his disease was evidently not suspected, and it was thought that his eyes were the cause of the pains. Spectacles seemed to give some relief.'[462]

The cause of his pain, however, was found to be a brain tumour and, following surgery, he died at 16 Langham Street, London on 6 January 1924 and was buried in Hampstead Cemetery, London.

---

[462] https://trove.nla.gov.au/newspaper/article/57472821.

Bibliography
(Primary and other useful sources)

A Contemptible Little Flying Corps – I. McInnes & J.V. Webb (The London Stamp Exchange Ltd, London, 1991)

Aero, The – (weekly magazine 25 May 1909 – 22 March 1911; monthly April 1911 – May 1913)

Aero Manual 1910, The – compiled by the Staff of "The Motor" (David & Charles (Publishers) Ltd, Newton Abbot, 1972)

Aeroplane, The – Claude Grahame-White and Harry Harper (T.C. & E.C. Jack, London, 1914)

Aeroplane, The – ed. C.G. Grey [weekly magazine issues, June 1911- December 1919]

A History of 24 Squadron Royal Air Force – Captain A.E. Illingworth and Major V.A.H. Robeson MC (The "Aeroplane" & General Publishing Co. Ltd., London, 1920)

Army and Aviation, The. A Pictorial History – Bruce Robertson (Robert Hale Ltd, London, 1981)

A Soldier of the Sky – Captain George F. Campbell (Davis Printing Works, Chicago, 1918)

Aviation in Doncaster 1909-1992 – Geoffrey Oakes (G.H. Oakes, Doncaster, 1995)

Aviation in Scotland – J.D. Gillies and J.L. Wood (Glasgow Branch of the Aeronautical Society, Glasgow, 1966)

Biplane to Monoplane. Aircraft Development 1919-39 – Series Editor: Philip Jarrett (Putnam Aeronautical Books, London, 1997)

Birth of Military Aviation, The. Britain, 1903-1914 – Hugh Driver (The Boydell Press, Woodbridge, 1997)

Bloody April. Slaughter in the skies over Arras, 1917 – Peter Hart (Cassell Military Paperback, Cassell, London, 2006)

Boer War, The – Thomas Pakenham (Weidenfeld and Nicolson, London, 1979; Jonathan Ball Publishers, Bergvlei, South Africa)

Bombing Colours. British bomber camouflages and markings 1914–1937 – Bruce Robertson (Patrick Stephens Ltd, London, 1972)

Born Adventurer. The Life of Frank Bickerton Antarctic Pioneer – Stephen Haddelsey (Sutton Publishing Ltd, Stroud, 2005)

Bournemouth The Aviation Pioneers and Rolls of Rolls-Royce – Charles Rolls Heritage Trust (Charles Rolls Heritage Trust, 2020)

Bristol Aircraft since 1910 – C.H. Barnes (Putnam & Co Ltd, London, 1964 & 1970)

British Aviation. The Great War and Armistice – Harald Penrose (Putnam & Co Ltd, London, 1969)

British Aviation. The Pioneer Years 1903-1914 – Harald Penrose (Putnam & Co Ltd, 1967; Cassell Ltd, London, 1980)

British Flying Boats – Peter London (Sutton Publishing Ltd, Stroud, 2003)

Charlie Rolls – pioneer aviator – Gordon Bruce (Rolls Royce Heritage Trust, Derby, 1990)

Chasing the wind – Kenneth Reid van der Spuy (Books of Africa (Pty.) Ltd, Cape Town, 1966)

'Colonel' Cody and the Flying Cathedral – Garry Jenkins (Simon & Schuster, London, 1999)

Commando. A Boer Journal of the Boer War – Deneys Reitz (Faber & Faber Ltd, London, 1929)

Contact! The Story of the Early Birds – Henry Serrano Villard (Arthur Barker Ltd., London, 1969)

Cross Country – E. Travers (Hothersall & Travers, Sittingbourne, 1989).

Dawn of the Drone, The – Steve Mills (Casemate, Oxford, 2019)

De Havilland Aircraft since 1909 (3rd edition) – A.J. Jackson (Putnam, London, 1987)

Denys Corbett Wilson. Aviation's Forgotten Pioneer – Paul Williams (Pembrokeshire Aviation Group, 1987)

de Ruvigny's Roll of Honour, Vol. I, Parts 1 & 2; Vol. II, Parts 3, 4, 5 – The Naval & Military Press

Distinguished Company – (Sir) John Gielgud (H.E.B. Ltd, London, 1972)

Dorset Flight. The Complete History – Rodney Legg (Dorset Publishing Company, Wincanton, 2001)

Early Aviation at Farnborough. Balloons, Kites and Airships. – Percy B. Walker (Macdonald & Co. (Publishers), London, 1971)

Early Aviation at Farnborough. Vol.II The First Aeroplanes – Percy B. Walker (Macdonald & Co. (Publishers), London, 1974)

Early Aviation in North Wales – Roy Sloan (Gwasg Carreg Gwalch, Llanrwst, 1989)

Echoes from Dawn Skies. Early Aviators: A lost manuscript rediscovered – Frederick Warren Merriam (Air World Books, Barnsley, 2021)

Extraordinary Life and Times of Captain G. W. Mapplebeck D.S.O., The – Peter Mapplebeck (Bustard Productions, Wiltshire, 2015)

Farnborough. The Story of RAE – Reginald Turnill and Arthur Reed (Robert Hale Ltd, London, 1980)

First Flight to Ireland, The – Eddie Little (Reword Publishers, Bramhall, Cheshire, 2003)

First Through the Clouds. The Autobiography of a Box-kite Pioneer – Frederick Warren Merriam (Air World Books, Barnsley, 2018)

Flight, 'Official Organ of the Royal Aero Club of the United Kingdom' – various issues

Flights and Fancies. The true story of an English summer and an aeroplane – George Smart (private, unpublished, in possession of Robert Loraine's family)

Flying Book, The, 1917 Edition. The Aviation World Who's Who Industrial Directory and Vade-Mecum – W.L. Wade (editor) (Longmans, Green and Co., London, 1917)

Flying Camels, The. The History of No 45 Sqn, RAF – Wg Cdr C.G. Jefford MBE, BA, RAF (Ret'd) (CG Jefford, High Wycombe, 1995).

Flying Cowboy, The. Samuel Cody. Britain's First Airman – Peter Reese (The History Press, Stroud, 2008)

Flying Fury. Five Years in the Royal Flying Corps – James T.B. McCudden (Bailey Bros & Swinfen Ltd, Folkestone, 1973)

Flying. The Pioneer Years in Kent – David G. Collyer (North Kent Books, Rochester, 1982)

Flying Units of the RAF – Alan Lake (Airlife Publishing Ltd, Shrewsbury, 1999)

Flying with the Larks. The Early Aviation Pioneers of Lark Hill – Timothy C. Brown (Spellmount, in association with the National Trust, Stroud, 2013)

For Valour. The Air VCs – Chaz Bowyer (Caxton Editions, London, 2002)

From Biplane to Spitfire – Anne Baker (Leo Cooper, Barnsley, 2003)

God Gave Them Wings. British Air Accidents 1786–1914 – Simon Hepworth (Aviation Books Ltd., Merthyr Tydfil, 2022)

Gunners at Larkhill – N.D.G. James (Gresham Books, Henley-on-Thames, 1983)

Half a Life – Major C.S. Jarvis (John Murray, London, 1943)

Handley Page Aircraft since 1907 – C.H. Barnes (Putnam, London, 1976 & 1987)

Historical Records of the Yeomanry and Volunteers of Montgomeryshire, 1803-1908, The – compiled by Lieut.-Col. R. W. Williams Wynn, D.S.O. and Benson Freeman, Esq, R.N.R.

History of 9 Squadron Royal Air Force, The – compiled by Flying Officer T. Mason (no publisher, 1965)

History of British Aviation 1908-1914, Volumes 1 and 2 – R. Dallas Brett (Air Research Publications in association with Kristall Productions, Surbiton, 1988)

History of Early British Aeronautics, The – Brigadier P.W.L. Broke-Smith (Royal Engineers Journal, 1952)

History of the War in the Air 1914-1918, The – Professor Sir Walter Raleigh (Pen & Sword Aviation, Barnsley, 2014)

Howard Pixton. Test Pilot & Pioneer Aviator – Stella Pixton (Pen & Sword Aviation, Barnsley, 2014)

Huntingdon the Aviation Centre - H.M. Buist (Huntingdon Local History Society, 1992)

In Southern Skies. A Pictorial History of Early Aviation in Southern Africa 1816-1940 – John William Illsley (Jonathan Ball Publishers (Pty) Ltd, Johannesburg & Cape Town, 2003)

In the Ranks of the C.I.V. – Erskine Childers (Spellmount Ltd., Staplehurst, 1999)

In the Shadow of the Eagle's Wing – Peter Connon (St Patrick's Press, Penrith, 1982)

Into the Blue – Captain Norman Macmillan MC, AFC (Duckworth, London, 1929); & Wing Commander Norman Macmillan OBE, MC, AFC (Jarrolds Publishers (London) Ltd, London, 1969)

Irish Aces of the RFC and RAF in the First World War – Joe Gleeson (Fonthill Media Limited, 2015)

I Swore I Never Would – Harold French (Martin Secker & Warburg, London, 1970)

La Vie d'un aviateur – Jules Védrines (les éditions des Officines, Paris, 2002)

Letters from a Flying Officer – Rothesay Stuart Wortley (Alan Sutton Publishing Ltd, Gloucester, 1982) [*first published 1928*]

Letters from an Early Bird. The Life & Letters of Denys Corbett Wilson 1882-1915 – Donal MacCarron (Pen & Sword Aviation, Barnsley, 2006)

Life of Robert Loraine, The. The Stage, the Sky, and George Bernard Shaw – Lanayre D. Liggera (University of Delaware Press, USA, 2013)

Magic of a Name, The. The Rolls-Royce Story. The First 40 Years – Peter Pugh (Icon Books Ltd, Duxford, 2000)

McCudden VC – Christopher Cole (William Kimber, London, 1967)

Men Who Gave Us Wings, The. Britain and the Aeroplane 1796–1914 – Peter Reese (Pen and Sword Aviation, Barnsley, 2014)

Merchant Airmen – Anon. (HMSO, London, 1946)

The Millionth Chance – James Leasor (Hamish Hamilton, London, 1957)

Mounted Troops of the British Army 1066-1945, The – Colonel H.C.B. Rogers OBE (Seeley Service & Co. Ltd., New Edition 1967)

Observers and Navigators and other non-pilot aircrew in the RFC, RNAS and RAF – Wing Commander C.G. Jefford MBE (Airlife Publishing Ltd, Shrewsbury, 2001)

Ocean Bridge. The History of RAF Ferry Command – Carl A. Christie with Fred Hatch (Midland Publishing Ltd, Earl Shilton, 1995; University of Toronto Press, Toronto, 1995)

Pioneering Places of British Aviation. The Early Years of Powered Flight in the UK – Bruce Hales-Dutton (Air World, Pen & Sword Books Ltd, Barnsley, 2020)

Pioneer of the Air. The Life and Times of Colonel S.F. Cody – G.A. Broomfield (Gale & Polden Ltd, Aldershot, 1953)[463]

Pioneers, Showmen and the RFC – Guy Warner (Colourpoint Books, Newtownards, 2016)

Plain Soldiering. A History of the Armed Forces on Salisbury Plain – N.D.G. James (The Hobnob Press, Salisbury, 1987)

Power for the Pioneers. The Green & E.N.V. Aero Engines – A.E. Tagg (Crossprint, Newport, Isle of Wight, 1990)

Recollections of an airman – L.A. Strange (Lionel Leventhal Ltd, London 1989; originally published by John Hamilton Ltd, London, 1933)

Reggie. The Life of Air Vice Marshal R.L.G. Marix CBE DSO – John Lea (The Pentland Press Ltd., Bishop Auckland, 1994)

R.F.C. H.Q. 1914-1918 – Maurice Baring (G. Bell & Sons, London, 1920)

Robert Loraine. Actor Soldier Airman – Winifred Loraine (Collins, London, 1938)

Roll of Honour, The. Royal Flying Corps and Royal Air Force for the Great War 1914–18 – H.J. Williamson (The Naval & Military Press Ltd, 1992, Dallington, East Sussex)

Royal Flying Corps Communiqués 1915-1916 – edited by Christopher Cole (Tom Donovan Publishing Ltd, London, 1990)

Royal Flying Corps Communiqués 1917-1918 – edited by Chaz Bowyer (Grub Street, London, 1998)

Royal Flying Corps in France, The. From Bloody April 1917 to Final Victory – Ralph Barker (Constable & Co Ltd, London, 1995)

Royal Flying Corps in France, The. From Mons to the Somme – Ralph Barker (Constable & Co Ltd, London, 1994)

---

[463] This book should be treated with caution, the author having been accused of making several false statements, not least the date of S.F. Cody's first *sustained* flight.

Royal Wiltshire Yeomanry, The, 1907–1967 – Brigadier J.R.I. Platt (Garnstone Press Ltd, London, 1972)

Scottish International Aviation Meeting Lanark, The – Donald Malcolm F.R.A.S., (privately, 1975)

Shorts Aircraft since 1900 – C.H. Barnes (Putnam Aeronautical Books, London, 1967 & 1989)

Sir Sefton Brancker – Norman Macmillan (Heinemann, London, 1935)

Sweeping the Skies. A History of No. 40 Squadron, RFC and RAF, 1916-56 – David Gunby (Aviation Books Ltd., Merthyr Tydfil, 2021)

Swifter than Eagles – John Laffin (William Blackwood & Sons Ltd, London, 1964)

Tartan Airforce. Scotland and a Century of Military Aviation 1907-2007 – Deborah Lake (Birlinn Ltd, Edinburgh, 2007)

They Fought For The Sky – Quentin Reynolds (Cassell & Co Ltd, London, 1958; Pan Books Ltd, London, 1960)

Three's Company. A History of No.3 (Fighter) Squadron RAF [see particularly Chapters 1–5] – Jack T.C. Long (Pen & Sword Military, Barnsley, 2005)

Those Magnificent Men In Their Flying Machines – Don Hale (Ads2life, 2016)

Trenchard – Andrew Boyle (Collins, London, 1962)

Trooper to Dean – Haidee Blackburne (Made by J.W. Arrowsmith Ltd, Bristol, 1955)

Under the Guns of the Red Baron – Norman Franks, Hal Giblin and Nigel McCrery (Grub Street, London, 1995)

Vickers Aircraft since 1908 – C.F. Andrews and E.B. Morgan (Putnam, London, 1988)

War diary – compiled by Winifred Loraine

Wiltshire and the Great War. Training the Empire's Soldiers – T.S. Crawford (DPF Publishing, Reading, 1999; The Crowood Press Ltd, Ramsbury, 2012 [Revised Edition])

Wings over the Island – David L. Williams (Coach House Publications Ltd, Freshwater, Isle of Wight, 1999)

Wings Over Westminster – Harold Balfour (Hutchinson & Co (Publishers) Ltd, London, 1973)

Wings over Wiltshire. An Aeronautical History of Wiltshire – Rod Priddle (ALD Design & Print, 2003)

Wings Over Yorkshire. Pioneer Aviators and their Flying machines. A Pictorial Survey – Ted Dodsworth (Hutton Press Ltd, Cherry Burton, Beverley, 1988)

Wonder Aces of the Air. The Flying Heroes of the Great War – A.J. Smithers (Gordon & Cremonesi, London, 1980)

Words and Music for a Mechanical Man – Oliver Stewart (Faber & Faber Ltd, London, 1967)

Wright Brothers, The – Fred Kelly (Bantam Books Inc., New York, 1983)

Years of Combat – MRAF Lord Douglas of Kirtleside (Collins, London, 1963)

Yorkshire Air Mails. A chronological history of aerophilatelic events with Yorkshire connections… – Richard Beith (Yorkshire Postal History Society, Sheffield, 1983)

Zeppelin in Combat, The. A History of the German Naval Airship Division, 1912-1918 – Douglas H. Robinson (G.T. Foulis & Co. Ltd., London, 1962.

Selected websites:

http://www.apw.airwar1.org.uk/no2sqn3.htm – re 2 Squadron

http://britishaviation-ptp.com/early_aviators_1_50.html – Roger Moss

https://www.flickr.com/photos/alwyn_ladell/30684704780 – Alwyn Ladell

https://www.gracesguide.co.uk/1910_Bournemouth_International_Flying_Week#Persons_Mentioned_in_this_Article

https://www.flightglobal.com/FlightPDFArchive/1910/1910%20-%200519.PDF

http://www.thefirstairraces.net/meetings.php.